SUSANNA DE VRIES is an art historian and lectures at the University of Queensland. Born in London, she studied art history, literature and history at the Sorbonne in Paris and the University of Madrid. She came to Australia in 1975. She has been the recipient of a Churchill Fellowship to study Renaissance art in Italy and has written extensively on art and history both here and overseas. She was made a member of the Order of Australia in 1996 'for services to art and literature'. In 2001 she was awarded a Tyrone Guthrie Fellowship to write in Ireland by the Literature Board of the Australia Council. Her biography of Joice NanKivell Loch, *Blue Ribbons, Bitter Bread: the Life of Joice NanKivell Loch, Australia's Most Decorated Woman*, won the Sligo Non-Fiction prize and was short-listed for the Queensland Premier's Non-Fiction award.

Susanna is the author of the following books, several of which have won awards: *Historic Brisbane and its Early Artists; Historic Sydney: the Founding of Australia; Pioneer Women, Pioneer Land; The Impressionists Revealed; Conrad Martens on the 'Beagle' and in Australia; Ethel Carrick Fox: Travels and Triumphs of a Post-Impressionist; Strength of Spirit: Australian Women 1788–1888; Strength of Purpose: Australian Women of Achievement 1888–1950;* (part-author) *Raising Girls* and *Parenting Girls; Blue Ribbons, Bitter Bread: the Life of Joice NanKivell Loch, Australia's Most Decorated Woman; Great Australian Women: From Federation to Freedom;* and *Great Australian Women: From Pioneering Days to the Present.*

SUSANNA DE VRIES

# Great AUSTRALIAN Women

### from federation to freedom

HarperCollins*Publishers*

**HarperCollins**_Publishers_

First published in Australia in 2001
by HarperCollins_Publishers_ Pty Limited
ABN 36 009 913 517
A member of the HarperCollins_Publishers_ (Australia) Pty Limited Group
www.harpercollins.com.au

**HarperCollins**_Publishers_
25 Ryde Road, Pymble, Sydney, NSW 2073, Australia
31 View Road, Glenfield, Auckland 10, New Zealand
77–85 Fulham Palace Road, London, W6 8JB, United Kingdom
2 Bloor Street East, 20th Floor, Toronto, Ontario M4W 1A8, Canada
10 East 53rd Street, New York NY 10022, USA

National Library of Australia Cataloguing-in-Publication data:

De Vries, Susanna.
    Great Australian women: from Federation to freedom.
    Includes index.
    ISBN 0 7322 6931 8.
    1. Women – Australia – Biography. 2. Feminism – Australia – Biography.
    3. Feminism – Australia – History. 4. Women – Australia – History.
    5. Women – Australia – Social conditions. I. Title.
994.04092

Front cover photograph: Author's Private Collection
Unless otherwise stated, all photographs are from private collections
Cover design by Judi Rowe, HarperCollins Design Studio
Typeset in 11/15 Stempel Garamond by HarperCollins Design Studio

Printed and bound in Australia by Griffin Press on 79gsm Bulky Paperback White

11  10  9  8  7        05  06  07  08

To Marusia McCormick, whose ideas and office organisation have been invaluable; to my literary agent, Selwa Anthony; to Barbara Ker Wilson for editing the manuscript; to Sir William Deane, Governor General of Australia, and to Elvie Munday of the Churchill Memorial Trust for details on the life of Dame Roma Mitchell; to the Hon. Peg Lusink for details on Joan Rosanove; to Prof Sir Frank Calloway, C.M.G., G.B.E., and Deirdre Prussak for help with the chapter on Eileen Joyce; to Alan and Belinda Cox for permission to publish the diary of Martha Cox; to Joyce Welsh for details on Joice Loch and to publishers Hale and Iremonger for permission to use Joice Loch's story as told in my biography *Blue Ribbons – Bitter Bread*. And finally, huge thanks to my husband, Jake de Vries, who as an architect provided valuable insights into the career of Florence Taylor, Australia's first woman architect. Jake compiled the Index and dealt magnificently with the complexities of the computer – without his help this book would not have seen the light of day.

*Susanna de Vries, Brisbane, 2000*

# CONTENTS

# INTRODUCTION

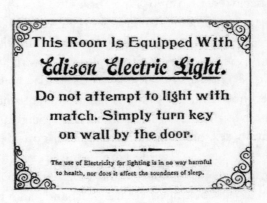

This Room Is Equipped With

**Edison Electric Light.**

Do not attempt to light with
match. Simply turn key
on wall by the door.

The use of Electricity for lighting is in no way harmful
to health, nor does it affect the soundness of sleep.

## *From Federation to Freedom*

In 1901, electric light was so new that users needed printed instructions on how to turn it on and reassurance that it would not cause insomnia or ill-health. Electric stoves, ovens, washing machines, refrigerators and vacuum cleaners would change women's lives *far more* than obtaining the vote. For twenty years after the vote was obtained, there were *no* women MPs in the State or Federal Parliaments at all. However, the invention of these electrical appliances gave women the freedom from endless domestic chores to study or do paid work.

A t Federation, Australia's population numbered 3.7 million, the majority of whom were of Celtic or Anglo-Saxon origin. Language tests (which could be imposed on Orientals and southern Europeans in languages they had never encountered, such as Gaelic), were designed as part of the restrictive 'White Australia' policy to prevent them from entering Australia. The few who did gain entry were usually forbidden to bring their wives. Small wonder that until after World War II the women who achieved greatness (other than Ella Simon and her Aboriginal mother) were of Anglo-Saxon or Celtic stock.

In the Victorian and Federation eras women married young. Henry Handel Richardson's mother married at sixteen, Louisa Lawson at eighteen, Eileen Joyce's mother at fifteen, Edith Cowan at nineteen and Martha Cox at seventeen. Legally a wife's body was deemed the property of her husband. In plain English this meant that church authorities and male doctors told women that their husbands had a God-given right to sex on demand. Many men considered they also had the right to beat a wife who refused them what were euphemistically known as 'conjugal rights'. Before 1925 custody of all children of a marriage belonged to the husband, and this was used against women in cases of legal separation or divorce.

Liberation from restrictive conventions came slowly, but from 1901 onwards, women gradually threw away their corsets and smelling salts, bobbed their hair, raised their hemlines, learned to express their opinions, won the right to vote and enter State and Federal Parliament, and open their own bank accounts. As late as 1960 married women were barred from employment in the ultra-conservative Australian public service.

Working-class women had always worked out of necessity, often as 'sweated labour' in factories or as domestic servants. Opportunities for wider areas of paid work, including the professions, were opened up by the two world wars, as well as the establishment of child care centres.

The first women to graduate in law, medicine and architecture had to struggle for the right to work as professionals. In April 1902, Miss Ada Emily Evans became the first woman to graduate with a law degree in Australia, but under New South Wales law she was not allowed to practise. Plucky Ada Evans went to court to fight for the right to practise, but the struggle wore her out and she was never able to work as a lawyer.

Medical women encountered such discrimination and hostility that Dagmar Berne and Constance Stone (see Chapter 4) had to finish their medical degrees overseas.

Prejudice applied in all spheres. Women artists like Jane Sutherland, Ellis Rowan and Clara Southern, whose lives are documented in my book *Strength of Purpose,* had problems selling what are now regarded as excellent paintings. Authors Ethel Richardson and Stella Franklin, wary of the patronising or savage tones of male reviewers if their gender was known, wrote under masculine names – as Henry Handel Richardson and Miles Franklin. Ella Simon, Joice NanKivell Loch and Louisa Lawson would have jumped at the chance to attend university but lack of money prevented them from doing so. Today they would be urged, 'Don't be shy, please apply' and would receive a loan under the HECS scheme.

Dame Roma Mitchell passed her law finals with top marks, but feared that because she was female, she would never obtain a job in a law office. She was the only woman in her year who managed to do so. Through talent and hard work Dame Roma rose to become Australia's first female QC (pipping the equally talented Joan Rosanove to the post). In the Supreme Court Roma Mitchell, Joan Rosanove and Dr Agnes Bennett encountered the old 'no female lavatories' excuse for refusing work to women. In 1925 barrister Joan Rosanove rented rooms in exclusive Selborne Chambers. Outraged male barristers called a protest meeting and reacted as if a prostitute was being introduced into their midst.

Unfortunately, gaining the right to vote in Federal elections (in 1902, by 29 votes to 6) made little difference to the lives of most women at that time. The majority of wives voted the way their husbands told them to; as a result, few major reforms benefiting women were made. It took another twenty years of female powerlessness until Edith Cowan became Australia's first woman MP. When she took her seat in 1921, one male MP asked the House, amid hoots of laughter, to specify *exactly* how much it had cost to modify the Parliamentary toilets so Mrs Cowan could use them.

But Edith Cowan refused to be silenced. She fought for the poor and disadvantaged, against child prostitution, for women's refuges, pensions for widows and single mothers, and for a woman's right to be properly educated in order to earn her own living. When Edith was fifteen, her father shot and killed her stepmother in a drunken rage and was hanged for murder, causing sensational newspaper headlines. This opened Edith Cowan's eyes to women's lack of power within marriage.

Male prejudice is evident in Australia's failure to give significant women the honours they deserve. In 1996, the *Australian* newspaper invited nominations for twenty outstanding Australians from the past. Caroline Chisholm was the only woman mentioned ... rating one place below a *horse* named Phar Lap.

Fanny Durack fought prejudice to become the first female swimmer in the world to win Olympic gold. Five men but no women were chosen to represent Australia at the 1912 Stockholm Olympics. A fund was opened to cover travel costs for Durack and her chaperone. Not one of the men's swimming associations would contribute. They felt threatened, and no wonder: Fanny broke a *male* Olympic swimming record in Stockholm, a feat which brought her world fame.

Many of the women included in this book belonged to families which were far from affluent. Apart from Louisa Lawson and Ella Simon, who struggled to educate themselves without parental support, these women had at least one parent who valued books and education. In the era before reliable contraception and before the introduction of electricity and labour saving-devices, combining a career, a husband and children was just too hard. Many professional women chose to remain single instead of caring for large families. Often as many as six to twelve children kept most women fully occupied for a large part of their lives. Initially it was *illegal* to give contraceptive advice: those who did so risked a jail sentence. Edith Cowan and Sister Lillie Goodisson dared to speak out about the need for condoms to protect women from sexually transmitted disease. Lillie's husband had died of syphilis (as had Ethel Richardson's father). Syphilis – known as the 'Red Plague' – was the scourge of the Federation era and in the years immediately following World War I, large numbers of men returned from war service in France and Egypt carrying the lethal disease and transmitted it to wives and girlfriends.

The background to most women's lives during this period was one of the constant toil in the home – caring for children, cleaning, washing and cooking on wood-fired stoves. Gas stoves were not introduced into Australia until the 1920s and then only in the cities. Domestic electricity freed women from the intensive labour needed to keep the family home clean. Before its introduction (and before the advent of piped water), most housewives without servants would spend 30–40 hours per week on domestic chores such as boiling water for washing and laundry, ironing with flat irons heated on the fire, sweeping floors and cleaning out grates. Heavy-duty housework, frequent childbirths and child care wore many women out; most looked at least ten years older than women of the same age today. Childbirth was dangerous and painful: mortality was high. Women who survived their childbearing years could expect to reach sixty, but many died in their twenties or thirties giving birth.

Selecting only twenty 'great' women has been difficult. During the period of intense social change between Federation and the arrival of the contraceptive pill in 1962, Australia had large numbers of brave, clever and determined women who struggled to achieve success in various fields. I have included Edith Cowan and Enid Lyons, who pushed through reforms in Parliament, rather than women who campaigned for the vote, and whose efforts have been featured in numerous books. I aimed for a balance between women on the land, in the arts, and pioneers in sport and the professions. Dame Nellie Melba (Armstrong) is undoubtedly a great Australian but her career had been well documented because she paid author Beverley Nicholls to 'ghost' her memoirs. Melba has already been the subject of six biographies, a film and a TV mini-series. Rather than repeat her story, I chose to recount the lives of women who are not nearly as well known, such as the Cinderella story of Eileen Joyce, Australia's first international woman pianist, the truly heroic Dr Agnes Bennett, and the equally heroic Joice NanKivell Loch, Australia's most decorated woman. Joice Loch was awarded a medal by the Greek, Polish, Rumanian and British governments, a museum is being opened in her memory in Greece and she is regarded as a heroine by the thousand or so expatriate Poles and Jews she helped to save from Nazi concentration camps. Coming across her story, I felt much as Thomas Keneally must have when he was presented with the story of Oskar Schindler; however, Joice was a *far* more heroic and admirable character than the scheming Schindler.

Most of the trail-blazing women in this book developed self-confidence through learning to speak in public and express their viewpoints. They fought to achieve financial independence and socially useful occupations, for educational opportunities, for widow's pensions, for reliable birth control and protection from sexually transmitted diseases, for better living conditions for Aborigines and slum dwellers living in urban or rural squalor and for fairer divorce laws for women.

These are the pioneering women of Australia's history that have helped shape Australian society today. All Australians should know their stories.

# CHAPTER ONE

## Sarah Frances 'Fanny' Durack
### *(1889–1956)*
FIRST FEMALE SWIMMER TO WIN OLYMPIC GOLD

## Annette Kellerman
### *(1884–1974)*
THE LONG-DISTANCE SWIMMER
WHO BECAME A HOLLYWOOD STAR

Fanny Durack was the first female swimmer in the world to win Olympic Gold. Her father, Irish-born Tommy Durack, was a popular publican with a fondness for the horses. Fanny inherited both his temper and his muscular physique. Fanny's mother had been a domestic servant before her marriage. Mary's parents had emigrated to Australia to avoid rural Irish poverty and could neither read nor write. Fanny's mother had six children. Whenever she could she helped her husband run the rough, tough Sydney pub he leased from the brewers.

Fanny and her brothers and sisters grew up in an atmosphere of beer, sawdust and the six o'clock swill, when men drank themselves into a stupor as fast as possible before the pub closed. Educational achievements were valued less than survival.

Tommy Durack was a very distant relative of the famous Duracks, who opened up vast areas of land in the Kimberleys and whose exploits are recorded in Mary Durack's epic biography, *Kings in Grass Castles*.

Unlike her more famous relatives, Fanny was not taught ladylike accomplishments. She attended the local State school, where she and other working-class children learned reading, writing and simple sums. Fanny and her girlfriends had no ambitions for a career; they left school at twelve or thirteen to do mundane work which would bring in money. At home Fanny shared a bed with her younger sister in a cramped bedroom above the pub. Fanny was a tomboy and a daredevil. SP betting rings, peroxided prostitutes, two-up schools and fist fights in the pub yard formed the background to her adolescence, enlivened by the sound of the pub's honky-tonk piano. Fanny watched her father act as 'bouncer' and intimidate drunks twice his size: early in life she learned the need to stand up for yourself against aggressors.

In the summer of 1898, when Fanny was nine, the family spent a summer holiday in Newcastle. An adventurous child fascinated by the surf, she ignored her parents' warnings about keeping close to the beach and was knocked down by a large wave. Fanny might have drowned had not a large St Bernard dog seen her struggles, plunged into the surf and rescued her. The dog held the drowning child above the waves until her father could arrive and drag her back onto the sand.

Horrified by the fact that Fanny, his favourite, had nearly drowned, her father insisted she must learn to swim. At that time State schools had no swimming classes or pool facilities. Fanny was taken to

Sydney's only organised bathing establishment for girls and women, run by Mrs Page at Coogee.[1] The swimmers had to wear heavy, knee-length costumes in navy or black wool with short sleeves.

Having paid Fanny's entry fee to the exclusive Coogee Baths, the Duracks lacked the necessary money for swimming lessons. But by watching the other girls and clinging to a rope, strung across the shallow end, Fanny soon taught herself to dog-paddle.[2] As soon as they saw she could stay afloat, her parents allowed her to visit the Domain baths at Woolloomooloo Bay, where part of the harbour was roped off against sharks as a swimming enclosure. A flight of rough, rock-hewn steps led down from the Domain. In one corner females were allowed to swim, sheltered by the overhanging branches of a big Moreton Bay fig tree from the prying eyes of male swimmers. It was thought the men's passions would be aroused by the sight of women in bathing dress.[3]

Fanny's strong arms and powerful shoulders were ideal for swimming and she was totally fearless in the water. At the Domain baths she watched the men swim while the other girls larked around giggling and splashing each other. Fanny soon saw how to adapt her rapid dog-paddle to a breast stroke – then the only style in which women could compete for a championship.

Competition presented problems for girl swimmers in the early days of the 1900s. The ubiquitous and powerful Rose Scott[4] was President of the Ladies' Swimming Association and she frowned upon mixed bathing. Women and girls could only swim in public places in what was known as the 'ladies hour'. The skirts and the weight of female swimming costumes slowed them down in the water. Hampered by constricting costumes, most girls did not take swimming seriously and were happy to frolic around or dog-paddle in the shallows. 'Real' swimming was a sport for men in a male-dominated world that prized 'manly' pursuits and denigrated women's achievements.

At the beach many girls often remained fully clothed, while young men showed off in front of them, performing in the surf or flexing their biceps.

However, soon after Fanny learned to swim, Sydney Council opened a free bathing area which had separate bathing enclosures and changing areas for men and women. Annette Kellerman had not yet struck her blow for women by wearing her revolutionary boy's costume. Fanny and her girlfriends continued to wear bathing dresses made from coarse wool or even flannel, with a high neckline and bloomers or knee-length skirts attached. Men swam naked in all-male sessions in pools; at the beach they wore black wool costumes that covered their chests and torsos.

To earn pocket money for swimming coaching, Fanny persuaded her father to pay her for doing some jobs usually done by her brothers. She helped them hose down the tiled bar of the pub and collect the empty bottles worth money when returned to the brewers.

Fanny's love of the water, her adventurous nature and determination to succeed and her potential as an athlete were recognised by swimming champions Peter Murphy and F.C. Lane, who decided they would coach her. They introduced Fanny to a revolutionary new stroke, the 'trudgen'.[5] This was a mixture of over-arm and breast stroke. Instead of using leg strokes that mimicked the arm movements of the breast stroke, the trudgen used a kick stroke. But it was deemed 'unladylike', no one thought lady swimmers would even attempt it. In 1902 the inaugural New South Wales Ladies' Championships were held at the St George Baths in Cleveland Street, and for the first time the organisers included a race for schoolgirls.

Fanny felt confident enough to enter this inaugural ladies' competition and planned to use her newly acquired trudgen stroke in public. It was her first race and she was nervous. In the general scrum when the starting gun went off, she swallowed a mouthful of water, starting coughing and came last in her heat. That night she cried bitter tears in her pillow but vowed it would never happen again. The next day she forced herself to return to the water and train again, using the trudgen stroke. But it would take another two years before she felt confident enough to enter another public competition. By that time swimming carnivals had become popular in Sydney. When Fanny arrived at the front entrance of Sydney's Lavender Bay Baths, she found it had been closed because the stands were overflowing with people.

However, she was not prepared to let this hindrance prevent her entering the race. Running around the perimeter to the far side of the swimming baths, Fanny persuaded a startled passer-by to give her a leg-up. She scaled the wall, slithered down the other side and made her way through the hordes of spectators to the end of the pool, where the girls were lining up for the race. She explained the situation to the judge, who delayed the start of the race so that Fanny could dash into the changing rooms, tear off her clothes and put on her cumbersome bathing dress.

She ran back, breathless with exertion, and joined the line-up. At the sound of the gun she dived in, swam her trudgen stroke, at which she was now expert, and finished a close second to Dorothy Hill, the leading female swimmer in Australia. A new champion had arrived. At her next swimming carnival Fanny beat all her female rivals and won the New South Wales Hundred Yards Championship.

That win began a long series of successes for Fanny Durack. One of her younger rivals was Wilhelmina ('Mina') Wylie, whose father ran Wylie's Baths at Coogee. Mina was seven years younger than Fanny and had a more retiring nature. A common passion for swimming united them; they trained together and became life-long friends.

By 1911, when Fanny was twenty-one, she and Mina had refined and adapted the trudgen stroke and turned it into an even faster stroke which would later become known all over the world as the 'Australian crawl'.

From the start of her career Fanny defied the prudish conventions which governed female swimming. While most girls only swam during the 'ladies' hours', she braved the sharks and trained in Sydney Harbour, competing against male champions to acquire that competitive edge. Fanny used her own particular adaptation of the trudgen stroke competing against champions like Cecil Healey, Alex Wickham and other male swimming stars of her time. The men treated her in a sisterly fashion and made no special allowances for her. It was a tough school in which to compete, but down-to-earth Fanny Durack had that happy Australian characteristic of 'giving it a go'. She found she flourished in this world of swimming and soon set new records for women's swimming.

But Fanny's training sessions with men aroused the wrath of that powerful member of the New South Wales swimming authorities, Rose Scott, who had extremely firm ideas on how young women should behave in public. (Rose was a strange mixture of prudery and fiery feminism, as related in the story of Louisa Lawson.) Rose Scott saw sexual danger in mixed bathing and on several occasions publicly denounced girls for swimming in the presence of males. Scott prudishly complained that 'any girl … exposing herself at public swimming carnivals was liable to have her modesty (i.e. her marriage prospects) hopelessly blighted'. Scott's reactionary opinions were backed up by the Catholic Archbishop Kelly, who told the press that mixed bathing was offensive and promiscuous and could undermine the fabric of society. The Archbishop denounced in the Sydney papers

> the indelicacies of the so-called up-to-date woman, who moves like a man and has no proper sense of decency … mixed bathing in pools and on the beach is destructive of that modesty which is one of the pillars of Australian society.

Fortunately for Fanny, the Mayor of Randwick, Maxwell Cooper, defied the Archbishop. The Mayor declared that swimming was a coming sport; furthermore, the beauty of the female form had appealed to the world's great painters and sculptors and should not shock Australians.

Although from a Catholic background, Fanny ignored the grim warnings of both Rose Scott and the Archbishop. To her, marriage seemed light years away. All she dreamed of was swimming for Australia in the Olympics. She wanted to follow in the footsteps of the male athletes with whom she trained in Sydney Harbour – although at this time, entering the Olympics seemed a highly unlikely ambition for any young woman, however talented.

In 1894, Baron Pierre de Coubertin, who was responsible for reviving the ancient Greek formula of the Olympic Games, was voted President of the World Olympic Federation. The Baron, like many other swimming authorities down the ages (including those who penalised Australian champion Dawn Fraser), was a reactionary. He stuck to the formula of the Greeks, who had never allowed women, on pain of death, to compete in or even to watch the Olympics. The Baron drew the line at putting women to death for watching, but he detested the idea of seeing them competing and perspiring in public, and forbade women to take part.

Baron de Coubertin saw 'his' revival of the Olympic Games as a masculine celebration of virile sports. Every athlete had to be an amateur, scorning all monetary reward: otherwise they would be termed professional and unable to compete. For years he refused to listen to protests that women (and blacks, as he called them) should be allowed to compete. His first revival of the Games took place in 1896, at Athens with exclusively male Caucasian athletes competing.

By 1904, at the St Louis Olympics, the American Committee insisted that eight female archers should be allowed to compete, provided they wore long skirts and blouses with long sleeves and high necks. The lady archers proved a star attraction: they behaved demurely and managed not to offend anyone. Women were seen as lending grace and interest to the spectacle.

The 1908 Olympics were held in London. 'Lady' athletes were now allowed to participate in gymnastic displays as well as figure-skating and tennis. They had to be sedate, graceful and chaperoned at all times. Their participation and the interest they aroused among spectators were important in allowing women to participate in spectator sports.

But competitive swimming for women was still not accepted. Australia's first female champion, Annette Kellerman, born in Marrickville, Sydney, in 1884, was never allowed to compete in the Olympics. She had originally learned to swim because it was thought the exercise would strengthen her leg muscles, wasted by a disease which may have been infantile paralysis. She went on to become a champion swimmer years before Fanny Durack.

Annette's father was a German musician who spent long periods out of work. Annette felt she *had* to make money to support her mother and sisters, and became a professional long-distance swimmer. Funded by various newspapers, she broke all previous long-distance records by swimming down the River Thames and along the Danube. In 1907, accompanied by her German-born father, Annette attempted a long-distance swim in America wearing a less constricting boy's costume, a one-piece design in black wool which covered the entire body and had short legs. It lacked the constricting sleeves and bloomers of women's bathing dresses. She was arrested for 'indecent exposure' on a Boston beach.

Kellerman had no money to pay a lawyer, but she defended herself in court by protesting that attempting to break swimming records in a regulation women's costume equipped with sleeves and heavy bloomers was 'like swimming in a ball gown'. The judge proved understanding and dismissed the case.

Overnight, Annette Kellerman became a sensation. She had struck a blow for women in every sport, and one that would change the future of women's swimming.[6] She had made history.

Annette's photograph was splashed across the newspapers worldwide. Spotted by a Hollywood producer, she became a star of silent movies such as the very popular *Neptune's Daughter* (1914) and *Daughter of the Gods* (1919). In one film the courageous Annette had to dive into a tank full of alligators. She succeeded in coming out alive but this daring feat gave her nightmares for many years but, by now, she was adored by millions of fans in America and Europe.

Her movie career ended with the advent of talking films. She then went into vaudeville and became a music hall star, singing in five languages. She returned to Australia, then lived for a time in Britain, where she wrote a children's book, *Fairy Tales of the South Seas,* for her Australian nieces.[7] Annette and her American husband, James Sullivan, lived in California. When widowed, she retired to Australia and settled in Queensland.

Annette died on the Gold Coast in 1975. In accordance with her wishes, her ashes were scattered close to the Great Barrier Reef. 'Neptune's daughter' had returned to the sea.

Annette Kellerman's courageous stand against ridiculous rules for women swimmers would be an encouragement for young Fanny Durack in her endeavours to obtain better treatment from domineering sports officials.

In 1912, five years after Kellerman had appeared in public in her boy's one-piece swimming costume, the organisers of the Stockholm Olympic Games decided, against de Coubertin's express wishes but with approval from the International Olympic Committee, to include two swimming races and a diving contest for women. Baron de Coubertin was horrified but was outvoted by the rest of the Committee. This historic decision finally opened the way for women swimmers from Europe and America to compete against each other.

Ten thousand miles away in Australia, young Fanny was breaking records against other women, but to compete overseas she had to struggle against the prejudice of committee members of the New South Wales Ladies' Amateur Swimming Association, including the formidable Rose Scott. The Association strictly forbade female members to swim in competitions or swimming carnivals where men were present either as spectators or competitors. (Scott and her supporters feared men might catch a titillating glimpse of female thighs and ankles and become sexually aroused.[8])

By today's standards, Fanny's competition swimming costumes were modesty personified, made from coarse (and sometimes scratchy) black wool with cap sleeves, a round neckline and short legs, a little like Annette Kellerman's long-distance swimming costume. No one could accuse Fanny of immorality when wearing such a costume. But Rose Scott and her supporters were determined to enforce the rules.

There was a head-on collision. Fanny and *her* supporters realised something had to be done to change public opinion: they wrote letters to members of the Association demanding a change in the rules. A public debate ensued in swimming clubs around Australia. Challenged, the New South Wales Ladies' Amateur Swimming Association reluctantly reversed its ruling against mixed competitions.

This landmark decision meant that Fanny Durack, and eventually her friend Mina Wylie, could be the first Australian women swimmers to represent their country at the Olympics. But although in theory women swimmers could compete, no money was provided to pay their fares and expenses.

Male officials organising Australia's team of swimmers to compete in the 1912 Olympics in Sweden agreed with the ultra-conservative members of the Ladies' Swimming Association that women should not compete. But the men had totally different reasons for their stance. They wanted all the available funding in order to get to the Olympics themselves. They felt threatened by the idea of women competing and raised all the old objections that 'nice' girls swam only for pleasure, not to compete: competition swimming was and should remain an exclusively male sport.

When the names of the five men chosen to represent Australia at the Stockholm Olympics were announced, a furore erupted. Fanny Durack and Mina Wylie had been excluded. Not one single official sporting body would put up money to pay for them to go to Sweden.

Women from all over Australia deluged Australia's Olympic officials with letters of protest. Women's organisations and swimming clubs organised petitions and rallies. Fanny's lack of sponsorship and chances of success were hotly debated in the newspapers. But there was still not enough money to pay her fare and her chances of competing seemed slim indeed.

Then, totally unexpectedly, Fanny had a stroke of luck. Her cause was championed by a family friend, Margaret McIntosh, the Irish-born wife of Hugh McIntosh, a former pub owner who was now a major sporting and theatrical entrepreneur. Hugh McIntosh had excellent 'political' connections and his wife used them to open a public fund to help Fanny to travel to the Olympics and to pay the expenses of her sister to accompany her as chaperone. (Provision of a chaperone was insisted on by the Olympic Committee; at this period 'nice girls' did not travel alone.)

The popular press championed Fanny's cause and she became famous Australia-wide. Thousands of warm-hearted, generous Australians (including customers at Tommy Durack's pub) passed around the hat to send Fanny to the Olympics. Cheques and money orders poured in to newspaper offices from all over the country.[9] Only the men's swimming associations refused to make any contribution whatsoever to Fanny's costs.[10]

The New South Wales Ladies' Swimming Association made a last-ditch stand and queried the costs of sending a woman to compete in only one event, but it was hopelessly outvoted, and so Fanny was officially allowed to represent her country with their reluctant blessing. But even after such an outcry in the press, no official help was given to Fanny. It was ordinary Australians who raised the money to send Fanny, and her sister, to Stockholm as Australia's first female Olympic swimmer.

To Fanny the fact that she was actually off to the Olympics seemed like a dream. She and her sister boarded the gleaming ocean-going liner at Circular Quay in a fever of excitement. As they leaned over the rail coloured paper streamers were thrown to the ship by well-wishers: a local brass band serenaded Fanny as the ship slowly moved from her moorings and steamed away through the Heads.

This was Fanny's first visit abroad, her passport to adventure, fame and self-discovery. She enjoyed every moment of the voyage while training hard in the ship's pool every day. When the Durack girls arrived in the port of London they transferred to another ship bound for Sweden.

Totally unexpectedly, three weeks after Fanny had sailed from Sydney, the Australian Olympic Committee suddenly changed their minds and allowed Mina Wylie, who was only fifteen, to follow Fanny to Stockholm. Mina's father was to act as official coach to the two inexperienced girls who formed Australia's Olympic Ladies' Swimming Team.

Fanny and Mina met up in Stockholm. They had been provided with uniforms – green swimming caps, green woollen swimming costumes with short sleeves and legs and long green cloaks to cover their legs and bodies. The Olympics took place in a seawater pool on Stockholm Harbour. The world male swimming record for the 100 yards then stood at 1 minute 26 seconds: Fanny and Mina were determined to break it. With the eyes of the Australian press upon them they were both scared, knowing they had to do battle for Australia against the world's best female swimmers.

Fanny and Mina found the water in Stockholm Harbour far colder than that in Sydney. They were dismayed when they were only permitted to train for half a mile a day in the Olympic Pool.[11] They requested permission to enter the relay race, each girl volunteering to swim two laps instead of the standard one lap. Fanny began to develop a hatred for organisers when their request was brusquely refused.

In Stockholm the two Australians found themselves competing against girls with rich indulgent parents who had trained in luxurious heated pools and spent their lives being driven around by chauffeurs. Yet all that swank and swagger counted for nothing when the starter's pistol went off.

Fanny Durack, the battling publican's daughter, broke the Olympic male swimming record on that eventful day in July 1912, and it made her world-famous. In her first heat she recorded a time of 1 minute 20.2 seconds, winning against the more experienced British champion, Daisy Curwen. For the finals Fanny and Mina lined up against a German and two other English champions, Daisy Curwen having withdrawn through indisposition.

The atmosphere was tense with excitement. An Australian reporter at the scene recorded:

All competitors present got away to a good start. Miss Durack at once went to the front. At fifty yards, she was leading by three yards from the English and German girls, who were neck and neck with Mina in the rear. Durack swam into the side of the pool, recovered and using a beautiful Australian crawl won by four yards in the excellent time of 1 minute 22.2 seconds.[12]

At twenty-three, Fanny had won the world's first Olympic Gold presented to a woman swimmer. The press acclaimed her as the world's greatest woman swimmer. Mina came in second, passing the English and German girls at the 80-yard mark and winning a silver medal. Fanny chose a long white dress and a flower-trimmed hat to accept her medal from King Gustav of Sweden and the press was allowed to take photos of her in her Olympic regulation swimming costume.

There was national hysteria in Australia when it was announced that the first gold and silver Olympic medals for women's swimming had both been won by Australians. Fanny had clipped four seconds off the previous world record held by a man. By modern standards the girls' world records were slow, but in 1912 they were something to boast about.

Six days after Fanny had won her gold medal, at the request of Olympic officials she gave a solo exhibition of the Australian crawl and set another world record of 4 minutes 43.6 seconds for 300 yards. Australia's Gold and Silver Girls were then invited to tour Europe and give swimming exhibitions. In the process, Fanny once more broke her own record for the 100 yards. The two girls, still accompanied by Fanny's sister as chaperone and with Mina's father as their trainer, returned home to more brass bands and speeches and still more exhibition swims.

Her time overseas had changed Fanny. She had now seen how other people lived. Although not well educated, she was quick and intelligent. She realised that Australia was antiquated and narrow-minded in its ultra-conservative views: one of the few modern nations to have an irrational fear of mixed bathing. Fanny spoke out against the practice of segregated bathing both in public and private. Her frankness won her powerful enemies who feared 'contamination for the Australian way of life from overseas'. Fanny was told in no uncertain terms by her critics that things went on overseas that 'very properly should not be allowed in Australia'.[13]

Such was the level of public interest in Fanny Durack that additional women's events in swimming were scheduled for the next

Olympics, to be held in 1916. Newspapers boasted how Fanny would win even more medals. But before Fanny and Mina could exploit their remarkable talents in the next Olympics, World War I broke out.

'The lamps are going out all over Europe', proclaimed Britain's Foreign Minister, Sir Edward Grey. He was right.

The war against Germany and her allies meant Fanny and Mina gave up all hope of more travel and international stardom for the duration of a war that shook Western Europe to its foundations.

But in those war years 1915 to 1918, Fanny broke twelve world records over distances varying from 100 yards to 1 mile, swimming in Sydney pools. Mina partnered her, pacing her friend closely.

When the Germans surrendered and the war finally ended, the next Olympic Games were planned at Antwerp in 1920. Once again Fanny and Mina hoped to challenge the women swimmers of the world and bring back gold to Australia.

The Americans were quick to respond to the challenge. This caused some surprise in swimming circles; up to that time the Americans had produced no major female swimming stars of their own.

In 1918 Fanny and Mina, the two super-girls of Australian swimming, were dispatched to America with an Australian manager to swim for their country. Things did not go as planned with this tour. Through some curious oversight, the officials of the Australian Swimming Union had failed to complete the necessary entry papers and the Australian girls suffered the mortification of being banned from entering competitions which they knew they could easily have won.

Another point raised against them was the fact that while Fanny and Mina were unpaid and had amateur swimming status, Mina's father, as their manager and trainer, was paid for his time and effort. The critics implied that he was acting in a professional capacity. The Americans, eager to get rid of foreign competition which threatened their own swimmers, claimed that if the Australian girls were associated with a professional, their amateur status was forfeited and they could not compete. So Fanny and Mina were forced to return home to Australia without even getting their costumes wet. Fiery Fanny neither forgave nor forgot.

On 12 August the following year, another pre-Olympic contest was arranged between Australian and American women swimmers in

Chicago. On that occasion the Australian girls triumphed with ease. Fanny won the 440 yards freestyle and Mina took the 100 yards breast-stroke championship. Back home their success was announced over the radio and in newspaper headlines. Australia celebrated and everybody awaited the next championships with confidence.

The American organisers were furious: every possible help had been lavished on their women's team, who were now using a new type of crawl. Fanny was fascinated by this American crawl with its faster leg beat and wanted to have an opportunity to practise it in private – she hoped to be able to use this stroke in their second contest in New York. But the American organisers gave her no opportunity. For five days Fanny and Mina were forced to attend a series of swimming galas and boring official dinners, and were driven long distances to make exhibition swims at various clubs. When they protested to the American race organisers that they were being asked to perform in public too often, when all they wanted was time to practise for their Olympic events, no one would listen.

The second American-Australian contest took place on 17 August 1919 in New York. Once again the race organisers found many reasons why Fanny and Mina's practice time in the pool had to be curtailed. Fanny began to scent a plot. She was worried and slept badly. Worn out by travelling and confrontation, she did not swim her best and failed to win.

The results reached Australia by cable.[14] Readers learned that their very own 'unbeatable' Fanny Durack had only managed third place in the 100 yards. The Americans were jubilant. They boasted that their girls had established superiority over the Australian Olympic stars. American swimming officials decided to capitalise on the mood of national jubilation by announcing a third swimming contest, to take place at a special meeting scheduled in Philadelphia for 30 August 1919.

By now Fanny and Mina were thoroughly unhappy with the organisation of their visit. At Philadelphia they still were not allowed sufficient time to train in the Olympic-size pool. The administrators who controlled Philadelphia's sporting events were powerful, wealthy business men intent on their own glorification through sport. They were totally uninterested in the complaints of two 'difficult' young women from the other side of the world. Mina was still in her teens, unsure of herself and a more pliant character than Fanny, who loathed pompous officials and decided it was high time to teach the hostile American organisers a lesson in fair play.

As soon as the Australian swimmers arrived at the pool, Fanny coolly announced that as an amateur she would not be taking orders from anyone. She declared that she had not been given time to train properly for the race.

'I'm not going to swim,' she said firmly.

A furious American organiser towered over her. 'Listen, sweetheart', he shouted, 'You get right out there and swim ... or pay your *own* expenses to get home'.

Fanny glared at him. She had already formulated a plan to make the organiser look foolish, but wisely did not say a word. The stadium was crowded with excited spectators and press. A lesser woman would have been daunted ... but not Fanny.

At the start of the race Fanny removed her green cloak, threw it down and stood demurely on the blocks with the other competitors, awaiting the starting gun. Just before the gun went off, Fanny dived into the pool, took off in a whirl of threshing arms and legs, reached the steps halfway down the pool and climbed out.

Flash bulbs flared and cameras clicked as angry race officials surrounded the Australian girl in her green costume, her long hair streaming around her. Fanny kept cool. She waited till the hubbub died away and said laconically, 'Well, I got in there and swam, didn't I? What more do you want? Now I'm going home to Australia.'

Fanny won her battle. The rest of her tour was cancelled by furious officials. A defiant Fanny was shipped back to Australia entirely at the expense of the American Swimming Federation.

On her return the Australian press insisted Fanny was still the greatest swimmer in the world. Had she not broken over twelve records? The American press picked up the story and retaliated that she was not. Everyone in swimming knew the real test would come at the next Olympics, to be held the following year in Antwerp.

Fanny was determined to show her superiority over the American girls. She trained almost non-stop, swimming miles every day in Sydney Harbour as well as her marathon running sessions and physical training in the gym. She had always had a typical Australian laconic sense of humour. She laughed and joked with the press who came to interview her and watch her training sessions telling them that by now she had swum the equivalent of the entire circumference of the earth.

Australians were convinced she would succeed. But only a week before her boat was due to sail for Europe, Fanny developed severe pain in her left side. She was rushed to hospital. The surgeon who operated found that her appendix had burst. Fanny developed post-operative complications. With her resistance lowered, she caught pneumonia, followed by typhoid fever. It was the end of her dreams of further Olympic glory.

To add to her misery, an American swimmer at the Antwerp Olympics, Ethelda Bleibtrey, won the Women's 100 and 300 yards races, beating Fanny's previous world records.

At thirty-one, Fanny realised that she could not hope to maintain her form for another four years until the 1924 Paris Olympics. Sorrowfully she retired from competitive swimming.

Shortly after she reached her decision, she accepted a proposal of marriage from a family friend, Bernard Martin Gately, a horse trainer. They were married at St Mary's Cathedral in Sydney. Crowds lined the route to cheer Fanny. The marriage was a happy one, although Gately was not a very successful horse trainer – so in addition to his activities as a trainer, Fanny and her husband ran a pub together. In her spare time Fanny still swam for pleasure and devoted herself to coaching deprived and gifted children in championship swimming. Her sorrow was that she and Bernard never had children.

Bernard Gately died in 1942, and as a way of conquering her grief, Fanny threw herself into organising her favourite sport. Ironically, she became one of the sporting administrators she had once fought so vigorously. She was appointed a life member of the New South Wales Women's Amateur Swimming Association.

Pubs were the only thing Fanny knew apart from swimming. So, like Dawn Fraser, that equally famous and controversial Olympic swimmer, she became sole licensee of the Newmarket Hotel, Elizabeth Street, in the centre of Sydney.

In 1955 it was announced that the following year, Fanny Durack would attend the Melbourne Olympics as an official guest and a race official in the swimming events. But Fanny was taken into hospital for an operation where it was revealed she had cancer. There was no further treatment the doctors could give her. She accepted that her days were numbered with her customary spirit, and continued her daily swims and her coaching sessions with small children. Brave and determined as ever, Fanny announced she would attend the Melbourne Olympic Games even if she had to hire an ambulance to take her there.

She never got the chance. Fanny Durack, game to the last, died during the night of 20 March 1956. Her funeral took place at St Michael's in Stanmore, Sydney. Champions from every era of Australian swimming attended along with the public who had loved and admired Fanny Durack. She was buried at Waverley Cemetery.

Nearly twenty years later, Fanny's old enemies, the American Swimming Association, archived her swimming triumphs for posterity in the International Swimming Hall of Fame at Fort Lauderdale, Florida, and placed a photograph of her on display beside one of Annette Kellerman.

Fanny and Annette represent the archetypal Aussie battler, embodying virtues that Australians hold dear: a strong sense of fair play, courage, determination, a laconic sense of humour and the ability to make the best of life. Every woman in sport today should be proud of these outstanding women.

# CHAPTER TWO

## Louisa Lawson
### *(1848–1920)*

## Mary Gilmore
### *(1865–1962)*

### POETS AND JOURNALISTS WHO CHAMPIONED
### THE RIGHTS OF WOMEN AND THE DISADVANTAGED

Louisa Lawson and Mary Gilmore had a great deal in common: they both tried to improve the lot of women, the poor and the disadvantaged. They both experienced unsatisfactory marriages. Yet what started out as friendship between an older writer and a younger one (Mary was seventeen years younger than Louisa) turned into mutual loathing and a bitter feud. As Louisa Lawson's star waned, that of Mary Gilmore ascended. Louisa Lawson went to a pauper's grave, unmourned and friendless: four decades later Mary Gilmore, having achieved literary fame, would be mourned by hundreds and given a State funeral.

Louisa was born into rural poverty. Her father, Henry Albury, attempted various occupations without success before running a shanty pub. Her mother, Harriet Albury, English-born daughter of a Methodist minister, was embittered by her husband's financial failures. She insisted on removing Louisa from school at thirteen, even though the young girl always had her head in a book and dreamed of becoming a teacher. Louisa would always yearn after the literary glory she never achieved.

Both women had tough bush childhoods which formed their characters. Mary Ann Cameron was born in a slab hut near Goulburn belonging to her maternal grandfather. Her first years were spent surrounded by gum trees and wattles; she would love the land with a passion all her life. She came from a long line of clever, talented Orangemen and Scottish crofters. Her father eventually became a building contractor and travelled all over outback New South Wales and Southern Queensland in search of work.[1] Sitting beside him on the horse-drawn wagon, or on the front of his saddle as he rode, at the age of five, Mary learned at first-hand about the hardships endured by settlers, drovers and teamsters and their ruthlessness towards the Aborigines, with whom she sometimes played. (Her father became a 'blood brother' of the Waradgery tribe). During her childhood, Mary absorbed a store of experiences which would surface decades later in her book *Old Days, Old Ways,* in which she wrote about rural povety, families whose children lived on damper and treacle and the odd roast possum leg, and the hardships of the bush.

Unlike Louisa Albury's poverty-stricken family where no one valued education, Mary Cameron's father encouraged her to read and to become a pupil-teacher in a tiny bush school at Cootamundra, run by one of her uncles. By the age of twelve, she was fluent in ancient Greek and Latin.

Louisa Albury, also highly intelligent, did not study Greek but was taught at school to appreciate and write poetry. She too wanted to become a pupil-teacher, but instead she had to leave school at thirteen. Although her father was practically illiterate, he had a tremendous gift for storytelling which both Louisa and her eldest son would inherit.

Louisa shared Mary's sympathy for the poor and disadvantaged: like Mary, she had lived among them. Louisa was the eldest daughter in a family of nine surviving children. While Mary's mother encouraged her daughter to read and study, Harriet Albury bitterly resented her eldest daughter's love of learning and her passion for poetry. She burned her daughter's first poems as well as some of her favourite books. Louisa never forgave her. Her mother also deplored what she regarded as Louisa's radical ideas, and forced her to look after her younger siblings and do housework.

Louisa's father, basically a kind man, had a weakness for alcohol. Like Mary Cameron's father he became a small builder but failed dismally. After his only horse broke its neck pulling an overloaded cart across a creek, Henry Albury consoled himself with drink. Too poor to buy another horse, he stopped working altogether. There was no dole or unemployment benefit, and Louisa and her siblings were reduced to begging or fossicking the local mullock heaps for specks of gold, until finally her father opened a shanty pub.

Surrounded by insecurity, stress and poverty, Louisa and her mother argued constantly. Domestic service in the city would have presented one avenue of escape for Louisa, but her mother refused to let her seek work in the city. Louisa bitterly resented her life of drudgery; marriage to anyone at all was the only way left to escape from her nagging mother.

Henry Albury's general store and pub catered for rough, rowdy goldminers. To attract customers, her father encouraged Louisa, who had a fine voice, to sing in the bar. The miners enjoyed Louisa's singing and suggested that they should pass round the hat to collect money so that she could have her voice trained. But Louisa's mother prevented her daughter from taking this opportunity to make something of her life.

## Louisa's Loveless Marriage to a Man with a Lust for Gold

Louisa's spirit was unquenchable: she dreamed of becoming a writer and being involved in the world of books. Her father's drinking bouts and her mother's nagging prompted her to seek escape by making a hasty marriage to a man obsessed by the idea of finding gold. At eighteen, Louisa was a relatively unsophisticated but attractive bush girl. After yet another row with her mother, Louisa was sitting crying in the bush when she was consoled by a sturdy, bearded gold prospector named Neils Larsen.[2] Larsen, born in Norway, was a sailor who had jumped ship in order to join the gold rush in Australia.

Neils was not Louisa's first suitor. Decades later, she would dedicate some beautiful poems on love and loss to a man she did not marry, for reasons which remain unclear. All we do know is that on 7 July 1866, tall, statuesque, auburn-haired Louisa walked to the Wesleyan church in Mudgee to marry a man almost twice her age whom she scarcely knew. Neils Larsen was kind-hearted and generous, but if his temper was roused and he had been drinking, he could become physically violent, something Louisa failed to realise when she accepted his proposal. Neils Larsen's lack of education was in sharp contrast to Louisa's hopes for a career of her own. She married in haste and repented at leisure – although lack of money would ensure she enjoyed little leisure for the rest of her life.

Accounts differ as to how Neils Larsen became 'Peter Lawson'. Either at their wedding or at her eldest son's christening, the officiating minister 'Australianised' his name.

Louisa joined her husband in his tent on the diggings. In spite of months of backbreaking labour he failed to find gold. Soon Louisa, to her dismay, found she was pregnant. They had no income, no savings, no furniture and not enough money to pay for a doctor to deliver her baby.

Legend has it that Louisa's first son, the future poet Henry Lawson, was born in a tent on the Grenfell goldfields. The birth was difficult. Louisa had post-natal complications known then as 'milk fever', which made breast-feeding extremely painful.[3] Bringing up a baby in a tent in the muddy goldfields, having to cart all drinking and washing water by hand from the nearest creek and boil it, and having little money for food proved stressful and exhausting for Louisa.

The Lawsons and their baby son moved from goldfield to goldfield living in various squalid, fly-ridden, cockroach-infested slab huts and shanties, blazing hot in summer, and cold in winter, when the wind blew in gusts through the gaps between the roughly cut slabs. Meanwhile, Peter Lawson's constant search for gold yielded virtually nothing.

When Louisa fell pregnant once more Peter Lawson finally listened to his wife's pleas and became a selector, buying a small block of land on a low-interest mortgage. Lacking any capital, the Lawsons had no choice but to take whatever land was allotted to them, however harsh. Wealthy squatters had usually tied up all the best land and the waterholes. Louisa exchanged life in a tent for life in what was virtually a shack, surrounded by rural squalor and poverty on forty acres at Eurunderee, near Mudgee (then known as New Pipeclay). Louisa's husband chose this area because it was part of the goldfields; he hoped some small pocket of undiscovered gold might remain on this scarred land, pitted with trenches from previous mining. Most of the trees had been cut down to build pit props and shafts. Their little wooden house had a dirt floor, and no piped water or sanitation. Louisa cooked over a wood stove which provided heating in winter. Their furniture was made from packing crates; their diet consisted of bread and dripping, treacle and salt beef.

Louisa, like all women of this period, which viewed women's role as bearing child after child, lacked access to reliable contraceptive advice. All she had were old wives' remedies which failed. Under these extremely squalid living conditions she soon bore her husband two more sons.

Her third pregnancy and birth proved difficult and dangerous. For months after her child was born she could not sleep at night, dozing off for only short periods, and had no desire to eat. Almost anorexic, trying unsuccessfully to breastfeed, the normally hard-working Louisa would sit motionless for hours on end, crying to herself and rocking backwards and forwards while baby Peter howled and Charlie and Henry fended for themselves. This period of mute inactivity exasperated her husband. At that time no one knew anything about the dangerous and distressing hormonal disturbance we now call post-natal depression. There were no anti-depressant drugs to treat Louisa's condition. Some women who suffered from it would fill their pockets with stones and jump into the dam, but Louisa resisted the temptation to commit suicide. Still devout and religious, she found comfort in prayer. As her sons grew older and were less work, she recovered – but throughout her life bouts of depressive illness would re-occur when she was under extreme stress, and her post-natal depressions coloured her view of sex and child-rearing.

She was now able to take over the running of the property again and drive their horses into town to buy provisions. Horses held no fear for her: on one occasion she halted and subdued a team of bolting horses, an incident Henry Lawson would later recount in a short story.

Peter Lawson spent a great deal of time away from home, chasing his dream of finding gold, which for him was a true gambling addiction. It finally became obvious that the proceeds from farming their small selection were as negligible as those from his gold-prospecting, and Peter decided to work with Louisa's father as an unskilled 'humpy' builder. Lacking any transport he had to walk to distant building sites and camp there overnight. This meant that most of the farm work was thrown onto Louisa's shoulders.

When he did return home, Peter worked hard on digging the unyielding soil of their selection and over the course of a year constructed a large dam. To earn more money Louisa took in sewing in addition to looking after the children, cleaning the house, cooking the meals and doing the washing. She also milked the cows night and morning, sold milk and butter, helped to harvest hay and fattened the calves, bottle-feeding those that were sickly. The strain of hard physical work and the constant money worries took their toll in blinding headaches and renewed attacks of depression.[4] Her only escape lay in writing poetry and reading favourite poems aloud from her old schoolbooks.

Louisa did not want any more children until they could afford to rear them. At that time a husband 'owned' his wife's body; she could not by law deny him 'conjugal rights'. The only form of contraception available to Louisa was *coitus interruptus*.[5] She was soon pregnant once again, following physical violence when she sought to resist her husband. In later life she would describe married bedrooms as 'chambers of horror'. The same sad drama was played out all over the bush between women reluctant to bear children and their husbands: at this time many bush women bore six to sixteen children, many of whom died young.

After another difficult pregnancy, Louisa gave birth to twins, Gertrude and Annette. The Lawson babies became the marvel of the district, the first twins to be born in Eurunderee. Annette was fair, plump and placid; Gertrude dark, bad-tempered and grizzly. Louisa adored Annette and called her 'a golden child'.

One day in January 1878, while Peter was away from home, Annette ran a high fever. Louisa harnessed the horses and drove her fretful baby to the hospital at Mudgee where she had given birth to the twins. Sick with terror, she waited in the passage outside the ward until the nurses told her there was nothing more they could do. Annette, her 'golden child' was dead. Another depression followed; once more Louisa could neither sleep nor eat. It was feared that she might die. Her mother was summoned and reluctantly arrived to care for the three boys and little Gertrude. The only advice Louisa received was provided by her unsympathetic mother, who told her it was high time she 'pulled herself together'.

Louisa turned to writing poems to relieve her misery. She sat at the rickety table and wrote a moving poem, 'My Nettie', dedicated to the memory of Annette. It was later published in the Mudgee *Independent*. Other poems followed, including 'Mary! Pity Women', describing a mother's desperate journey on foot with a sick baby to a doctor, in which the baby dies en route. These were followed by other verses about lonely, depressed bushwomen, based on her own experiences.

Louisa had a talent for writing poetry but she was a working-class woman who had been denied education: she would never have the time or leisure to develop her talent to its full extent. In spite of their back-breaking years of toil and drudgery, Peter and Louisa Lawson never managed to achieve even a modicum of financial security. It was a fate from which Louisa attempted to escape in vain.

When Henry was eight, Louisa realised he was exceptionally talented and sensitive, a child apart. She was desperate that somehow Henry should receive the education she had been denied and a chance to escape rural poverty. The nearest bush school was over five kilometres away; Henry was a sickly child and she feared he could not manage the walk. Louisa campaigned fiercely for a school to be built in their own area, but as she was 'only a woman' she was not allowed to enter the public meeting, although *she* had organised it. She was told that the subject of a school could only be discussed by men, and was forced to stand outside the hall and attempt to hear her own arguments poorly presented to the meeting by her husband. This experience taught Louisa a lesson about women's lack of power that she would never forget.

Eventually the campaign she had originated did succeed and a tiny bush school opened at Eurunderee. Henry was one of the first pupils, but at the age of nine he suffered an unknown fever which left him near death, and caused him to lose a great deal of schooling. By the time he turned fourteen he had suffered major hearing loss. A diffident and withdrawn boy, he aimed to become a writer. Louisa encouraged him and gave him what little extra schooling she could.

Her second child, Charlie, had severe personality problems and a terrible temper. His aggression and bad behaviour at school caused his father to beat him so severely that he nearly killed his son – whereupon Charles ran away to live with his maternal grandmother. He turned into a teenage hoodlum in trouble with the law. Young Peter was a gentle, musical boy, somewhat withdrawn. Gertrude's black moods and explosive temper were perhaps inherited from Louisa's mother.

Now thirty, Louisa was desperate to avoid having more children. The arguments and violent episodes when she refused to have sexual relations with her husband continued. Years later she would write with deep feeling about women subjected to domestic violence and advise them to gain some form of financial independence through paid work.[6]

Peter Lawson, equally desperate to escape the hard life of a small farmer, still frequently left home to search for gold. Years later, Henry Lawson's stories would describe incidents based on his mother's exploits when she was left to run the selection alone. In one story a woman single-handedly extinguishes a bushfire and saves her wooden home. In another the wife tries to prevent their dam bursting. Henry described how the bush wife stood 'for hours in the drenching downpour' and dug an overflow gutter to save the dam, hurting her back. It was all in vain: the next morning the dam was broken. The wife thought how her husband would feel when he came home and saw the result of years of work swept away overnight, the ruin of their hopes, and she broke down and cried. In other stories, Henry describes how a woman left to cope alone 'fought' crows and eagles that wanted to carry away her chicks by aiming a broomstick at the birds and screaming to frighten them off. On another occasion the woman in his story protects her children from a mad bull by shooting him through a crack in their slab hut. The bush wife then skins the bull and sells the hide to a dealer. Henry Lawson described how his mother 'fought pleuro-pneumonia – dosed and bled the few remaining cattle and wept again when the two best cows she had reared from birth died'.

The problems between Louisa and her husband worsened and badly affected young Henry, who was old enough to feel the resentment between them. Henry was fascinated by the ethos of 'mateship' in the bush and usually sided with his father, although it was his mother who encouraged his literary talents. Louisa was convinced that Henry would become a writer of great power and originality. (In later life, embittered against Louisa after he had left his own wife and children and become an alcoholic, Henry would refuse to acknowledge her influence in his writing.[7])

Louisa and her husband parted company after her husband took on a building contract in the Blue Mountains, together with a partner. Although the farm still did not pay, Louisa was not yet prepared to walk away from it after all the backbreaking work they had put into their 'selection'. The children now needed less supervision: she felt she had the time and energy to earn extra money. One of the few opportunities of employment open to women without much education was offered through the rural post offices. Louisa became a country postmistress and ran a small general store. Discrimination against women in the workplace meant that she had to obtain the licence to run the post office in her husband's name rather than her own. Now she found herself working double time. She still had domestic duties, responsibility for her children, Gertrude and Peter, farm chores, a vegetable garden to maintain and all the accounts to pay.

After a couple of years of this drudgery, to Louisa's dismay she found that in spite of all her additional work, she and her children were still living in poverty. Then a long drought set in. Their selection gradually turned into a dustbowl. Reduced to skin and bone, their cattle stood around the homestead lowing pitifully. Lacking money to pay for agistment, there was nothing Louisa could do to save the poor beasts. She had to watch the calves she had raised to maturity die a painful death.

It was the end of her dream of independence. Her husband, with whom she kept in contact, viewed her intending departure from the property with relief and promised financial support if she and the children sold up and moved to the city. They could not sell out. In 1882 Louisa, now thirty-five, walked off the selection empty-handed and moved herself and the children – Henry, Peter and Gertrude – together with their few sticks of furniture to Sydney, renting a house close to Circular Quay. She had nothing to lose and a specific goal: to make life easier for her children than it had been for her.

## Life in the Rocks, Sydney

Louisa has left us no descriptions of the Rocks and Circular Quay but Mary Cameron, arriving there about the same time to take up a teaching post, described the Quay as: 'full of masts as a pincushion is of pins. The sky was pierced to heaven with masts'.

In the days when Mary and Louisa made their separate ways to Sydney from the bush the Rocks area was a slum, a far cry from the up-market tourist area of today. In their day sewers overflowed into the gutters, rats abounded, prostitutes lingered on street corners and pale-faced women worked over their sewing machines as 'sweated labour' to feed fatherless children.

Louisa knew all about rural poverty: she now experienced at first-hand the grinding hopelessness of the inner-city poor. Both Louisa and the sensitive, talented Henry, who shared his mother's left-wing views, were distressed by the numerous derelicts and alcoholics they saw. In those days there was no supporting mother's benefit. Her husband only sent maintenance money sporadically. Louisa made and remade their clothes, and they lived on bread and dripping, bread and jam and black tea.

Henry was not cut out for office work. He was hopeless at bookkeeping and other administrative duties. Writing for a living was insecure and poorly paid, so out of the question. Finally he took on work as a coach painter, and, urged on by Louisa, attended night classes to obtain his matriculation. But his workmates teased him about his deafness and he failed his matriculation examination. His frustrating deafness made Henry even more shy and reserved than he was already.[8] After work he took to drinking alone in dockside pubs and hotels.

The indefatigable Louisa decided to try to make money by running a lodging house. Once again they packed up their few possessions and moved to a larger house in Enmore Road, Marrickville, where she rented out rooms. Peter Lawson's financial contributions became less and less frequent, and Louisa considered taking legal action against him.[9] But lawyers were expensive; instead she began to take in washing and sewing as well as lodgers. To spare her children pain, she kept up a pretence of being separated from her husband by misfortune. But in truth the marriage was over.[10]

In 1887, Louisa was so worried by Henry's drinking bouts and subsequent fits of depression that she used money she managed to scrape together from her lodging house to buy a share in a small left-wing monthly news-sheet, *The Republican*. It was owned by William Keating, one of Henry's left-wing radical friends. Louisa hoped to train Henry to become the magazine's editor.

Just as Mary Cameron (later Gilmore) would throw her energies left over from teaching into writing for the newspapers, so Louisa now threw herself heart and soul into publishing *The Republican*, as though to make up for all the lost, lonely and embittered years that lay behind her. Determined that women should have a voice in an all-male world, she and Henry together wrote and edited the struggling political news-sheet under the pseudonym 'Archie Lawson'.

Louisa was a quick learner. She soon realised that while *The Republican* was too radical to pay its way, the 'hole in the market' was for a paper designed for women. She saw clearly that with hard work such a newspaper could make a profit and inspire other women to escape unhappy marriages and seek financial independence. She approached potential advertisers and sold some space: soon she was in business – Australia's first female publisher. Symbolically, she called her newspaper *The Dawn*. The cover featured a young woman blowing her own trumpet.[11]

On 15 May 1888, Louisa produced the first issue of this historic paper designed specifically for women and staffed by women. She was both publisher and editor. Henry was now often away working with his father. Using the ground floor of 138 Phillip Street as a combined office and printery, she worked long hours. Once Louisa took over the printery, she replaced the male staff with women, who she felt would work harder and appreciate their jobs.[12]

Bearing in mind the difficulties women encountered in business, she used a fictitious name as editor, calling herself 'Dora Falconer'. This lasted until January 1891, when she felt confident enough to use her own name.

When Henry returned from working with his father in the Blue Mountains, he helped to produce *The Dawn*. After a hard day's work Louisa would go out to dinner with her female staff, leaving Henry to turn the handle of the press with a faraway look in his eyes as he composed poetry in his head.[13]

Louisa was creative and hardworking. But it now became apparent that like many creative people, she suffered from manic depressive illness. She alternated bouts of furious creativity with deep depression. She would work half the night to bring out her paper, and the following day, once it was mailed out to subscribers or on the news-stands, she would collapse with exhaustion, wondering if it had all been worthwhile. Depression would set in. Her daughter Gertrude tried to help her mother. She described how in these black periods Louisa would withdraw 'into herself' and refuse to speak or eat.

Louisa employed several experienced female typesetters on the paper. She campaigned tirelessly for women's rights at a time when they had very few. Most married women still surrendered any property or money they earned or inherited to their husbands (as the British Married Womens Property Act of 1875 was slow to take effect). Women could be divorced for lapses in fidelity (considered totally normal in a man) and children of the marriage were considered the property of the father if the mother defied society and requested a legal separation or divorce.

On New Year's Eve, 1888, shortly after she had started the paper, Peter Lawson, still working in the Blue Mountains, died. In his will he left his wife £1103, a considerable sum of money for that time. But to obtain her bequest, Louisa had to bring legal proceedings against her husband's business partner, which drained her funds and was stressful.

After she received the money, she improved her printing plant and moved to larger premises in Jamieson Street. She proved to be a shrewd businesswoman as well as a skilful editor. By the following year she was employing ten women working in shifts, including editors, printers, binders and unskilled hands. She also took in outside work on contract to keep her presses running constantly.[14] There was even a messenger girl rather than the usual messenger boy.

Women were delighted to see subjects that interested them in print; from its first issue *The Dawn, A Journal for Australian Women* was a success. The subscription price was three shillings per annum and it was also sold on news-stands. The magazine highlighted the achievements of women and their struggles to enter the workforce. Louisa had enough business sense to realise that a purely political journal would not survive. She wrote or commissioned feature articles on household management, cookery, fashion, gardening and farm work and included some literary criticism. Poetry was also featured (some written by Louisa) and short stories by both Louisa and Henry Lawson.

*The Dawn* was designed as a publication that women would keep for future reference, so Louisa insisted it was printed on high-quality paper.[15] Subscriptions were received from readers as far away as Longreach, Hobart and Darwin, from the Librarian of Sydney University and from wealthy women like English-born Margaret Scarlett (who became Mrs Quong Tart, wife of the famous Chinese businessman and philanthropist), and from women physicians like Dr Dagmar Berne and Dr Ida Carlson.[16]

In *The Dawn*'s first year of publication a series of feature articles dealt with Sydney's destitute children, inequities facing women under marriage and property laws, the need for life insurance to protect families and the importance to women of the Divorce Extension Bill.

There were grave problems when Louisa's female employees sought admittance to the powerful all-male New South Wales Typographers' Union, which had previously refused to accept women as members. Men sacked by Louisa instigated a boycott, through the Trades and Labour Council, of all printing establishments employing women. They intended to punish her. In a clumsy attempt to force her to replace women with men, male Union members picketed and harassed Louisa's female staff as they arrived and departed from the printing works. The Union even appealed to the paper's advertisers to boycott her paper.

Louisa fought back like a lioness. One Trade Union official who visited the premises received similar treatment to the old bush remedy she had meted out to tramps who harassed her on her selection. The Union man, who was wearing a smart pair of white flannel trousers, refused to leave the printery; he kept telling her how the Union could close her down. Undaunted, she threatened to pour over him the contents of the sludge bucket, containing ink washed down from the printing presses. The union official realised he had met his match and departed.

In the October 1889 issue of *The Dawn* Louisa wrote a powerful leading article demolishing the arguments used to exclude women from Unions. She thought deeply about the problems facing working women and was one of the first to advocate provision of childcare facilities for overworked mothers of large families. Slowly she won her battle for survival in a man's world.

Articles in her magazine helped to raise money for Ragged Schools, designed expressly for poor children, for whom she organised collections of cast-off clothing. She became actively involved with campaigning for a refurbished tomb for Henry Kendall, her favourite poet, canvassing subscriptions from politicians such as Henry Parkes and from Lady Carrington, the Governor's wife. She raised enough money to buy an additional plot on which to build a much grander monument, but this was never used. What would now be termed 'the blue rinse set' took up Henry Kendall's cause as their own and Louisa was sidelined from their committee. This experience taught her a sharp lesson about colonial society and its class-ridden structure. She decided that never again would she work with middle-class 'do-gooders', but would run her own organisations. Louisa's strength lay in the fact she appealed to women of *all* backgrounds. No one could accuse her of being 'a rich do-gooder in a posh hat' (as working-class women dubbed some upper-crust suffrage committees who advised them how to run their lives).

In May 1889, Louisa launched her campaign for votes for all women, rich and poor. She was not in favour of Australian women chaining themselves to railings, slashing paintings, destroying property or throwing themselves under racehorses, as Mrs Pankhurst's suffragettes in Britain had done. Instead, Louisa hoped Australian women would achieve their goal by peaceful means. She used her magazine to pioneer the Australian Suffragist movement. Australian suffragists like Rose Scott ruthlessly tried to eclipse her influence by founding their own upper-middle class movement. However, Louisa Lawson, from a more humble background, was truly the 'founding mother' of the Votes for Women campaign in New South Wales, while Vida Goldstein was Louisa's equivalent in Victoria.

'Who ordained that men should make the laws which both men and women must obey?' became Louisa's rallying cry for women seeking the vote. That same year Louisa announced the formation of the Dawn Club, an organisation for women concerned with social reform. Quong Tart's English-born wife, a founder subscriber to *The Dawn*, [17] persuaded her wealthy husband of the rightness of the women's cause. Quong Tart kept his Pitt Street tearooms open in the evenings for the Dawn Club's monthly meetings.

Most of the members of the Dawn Club had been denied the right to a similar education to their brothers' and were always expected to defer to the opinions of men. Louisa found them timid and lacking in the self-confidence or experience to speak well in public. She realised that public speaking was important – she, too, needed tuition. She persuaded the debating club of the Sydney Mechanics' School of Arts to admit her as a member and encouraged other women to join so that they could gain the necessary experience.

Louisa also supported the entry of women into the professions and to become prison warders, factory inspectors and magistrates. Her campaign for prison reform was designed to protect women against rape in gaol: she wrote articles demanding that female prisoners be guarded by women warders rather than by men, something now taken for granted. She wrote about domestic violence:

> Women seem to bear the brunt of society's burdens – especially in marriage ... But it is not only in the poorer classes that women have been driven by unkindness, ill-usage or cruelty, to ask why the love which seemed so strong a security before marriage so often becomes hate when the bond is tied ... Men become demoralised by the absolute rights over women which, after marriage, law, custom and opinion give to them ... Women must learn that if they do not claim personal respect neither can their sisters. Women's habitual self-effacement leads to all manner of weakness. An [abused] woman will tell lies to shield her

husband – or perhaps her own pride if she is bruised or injured ... she will swear it was not her husband but purely the result of an accident. If he squanders the money, she works harder to replace it. If he drinks she hides the fact and shelters him with lies. The result is that in time she does not own her own body or mind.[17]

Through the Dawn Club and her influential editorials Louisa helped to change public opinion towards enfranchising women and giving them more independence. She believed deeply that women must support and help each other and was in advance of her time in pleading for refuges for homeless or battered women to be established in Sydney. She asked:

> Is there any place in our town in which a homeless woman could shelter? And have we taken pains to have its location and purpose so well advertised that no one could fail to know of it?[18]

Politicians did not wish to devote funds to such a cause. They ignored Louisa and her newspaper. But all through 1890 and 1891 Louisa steadfastly continued to hammer away for refuges for battered women, describing how:

> We could quickly fill the largest building in Sydney with women and children who now, in order to receive food and shelter ... are bearing blows, insults, servitude and degradation.

Women were overjoyed to find a magazine that expressed their concerns and *The Dawn*'s circulation increased. By now Louisa realised she had the necessary 'gut instinct' for publishing possessed by most media barons. To increase circulation she gave away thousands of sample copies to prospective advertisers, to keep up the ratio of advertising to editorial. She was an excellent editor and along with political articles continued to include items which the *Australian Women's Weekly* would later use effectively – recipes, fashion, health and childcare. She herself wrote over 200 of the journal's leading articles.[19]

During the economic depression of 1891–95, Louisa urged women to seek office employment in the then male-dominated fields of shorthand and typing. She campaigned fiercely for improved factory conditions and encouraged tailoresses and seamstresses to form a Union to improve their working conditions and hours. These unfortunate women either did piecework at home or were used as 'sweated labour' by factory bosses. Often there were no proper eating or toilet facilities in their workplaces.

In October 1896 Louisa wrote an article urging women to learn to ride bicycles. She defied some members of the clergy, who thundered against the indecency of women wearing long socks and knickerbockers known as 'bloomers', which many of the clergy considered both indecent and immoral because they revealed women's ankles in public. Louisa, who had spent years in the bush with only a horse and cart, realised that the bicycle was a far easier means of transport and would give working-class women, as well as female doctors, nurses and teachers, mobility. Bicycles were cheap to maintain and did not require feeds of corn or hay or stables. The bicycle would give women more control over their own lives.

*The Dawn*, Vol 4, No. 3, dated 1 July 1891, contains an article in Louisa's distinctive style suggesting that to cut the amount of housework for women:

> Greater simplicity of life, dress, food and surroundings would at once mitigate, if not abolish, the evil … Our forefathers ate too much and drank too much (especially the latter).

She attempted to free women from the cult of consumerism, to simplify their lives and to conserve their health through natural remedies and self-sufficiency. This makes her seems startlingly modern for her time, but her paper contained no hint of New Age vegetarianism, mantra chanting or crystal gazing.

*The Dawn* aimed to free women from the tyranny of fashion rather than lure them into buying ready-made clothes to make factory owners rich. There were articles on how to make simple but tasteful clothes and how to renovate dresses or hats. The paper occasionally supplied readers with paper patterns – until a rise in postage rendered this impractical.

Louisa used her imagination and drive to pioneer many of the publishing gimmicks routinely used by magazine publishers today to increase circulation. She turned *The Dawn* into a household journal by including articles for children.

Because poverty and an embittered mother had denied Louisa a formal education, she was keen that other working-class women should be able to take advantage of the newly won right to higher education for females. *The Dawn* raised funds to pay for residential accommodation for young women at the new Women's College of Sydney University. In 1892 she instituted a scheme for subsidised courses of study in technical colleges for her readers. Provided the women brought in twenty new subscribers to the magazine, Louisa's publishing company would pay their fees.[20] The women could select from fifteen subjects ranging from arts and crafts to philosophy. Louisa's originality was amazing.

She championed a new view of marriage as well as paid employment for women inside or outside the home. She wanted the divorce laws liberalised so that they were fairer to women.

## Louisa Lawson meets Mary Cameron

In 1894, Louisa published Henry Lawson's first book, *Short Stories in Prose and Verse*. The book failed to make money in Australia's restricted market, but its publication helped Henry to obtain a two-book contract with the publishing company of Angus and Robertson. A couple of years earlier, Henry Lawson had been encouraged to continue writing verse when, through his mother, he met a young schoolteacher and aspiring poet named Mary Cameron.

Mary and her mother, Mrs Mary Ann Cameron, were lodging in a Sydney boarding house in Sydney's Bligh Street, in the city centre. Like Louisa, Mrs Cameron had left her husband, Mary's father, because she'd had more than enough of the hardships of bush life.[21]

Mary Ann Cameron was working on Sydney's *Daily Telegraph* as one of Australia's first female journalists, writing fairly conventional accounts of social events under the pen-name 'Busy Bee'. Her tall and fairly prim daughter, Mary, had taught at Silverton, near Broken Hill. At a time when most young women were married by the time they turned twenty, Mary foresaw herself as a spinster, left 'on the shelf' ... although some of her poems show that she was longing to have a husband and a child. Mary described herself as 'a gawky country girl dressed in a home-made frock'. Her photograph shows a pleasant-faced girl with softly curling hair which she kept unfashionably short, wearing a prim high-necked blouse.

At the time Mary was introduced to Louisa Lawson by her mother, she had arrived in the city looking for a teaching job in a state school and was sharing her mother's room. The two mothers without husbands and with a great deal in common became friends, as did their children.

Mary, following in her mother's footsteps, had already written a few articles for the Wagga papers (illegally and under a pen-name because teachers in the State system who wrote for the press could be dismissed.) For a brief period while her mother returned to the bush to wind up her affairs, Mary moved into the Lawsons' tiny spare room as a paying guest. Initially Louisa, worried about Henry's lack of drive, saw Mary as the making of him and encouraged their friendship.

This is how Mary described Louisa's dark-eyed son when she first met him:

> Henry [Lawson] was in the sappy twig stage ... The face was weak, the chin underdeveloped, the look effeminate.[22]

Henry was scarcely good husband material at this point, but he was interested in Mary.

Henry and Mary, thrown together in the small house while Louisa was away for long hours at work, discovered that as aspiring poets they had a great deal in common – although Henry was a year younger than strong-minded Mary and far more immature.

They became good friends. Henry had a poem accepted by the *Bulletin*, known as that time as 'the bushman's friend', and was paid ten shillings for it. Louisa was outraged that they paid her son so little but Mary was impressed. She longed to be published by the *Bulletin*. Arm in arm the two poets, an unlikely couple in many ways, took long walks around the Rocks area where they saw babies abandoned in doorways, drunken men, and prostitutes lurking in alleyways swarming with rats.[23] These images of poverty shocked Mary deeply.

Louisa started to become alarmed. Much as she liked Mary Ann Cameron and had to admit that Mary (who seemed about to become a teacher at Neutral Bay Primary School), with her strong character and principles, might well be the making of her weak, vacillating but talented son, Louisa realised from her own experience that marriage meant children. At that time, when married female teachers had to stop working, Mary would not be able to continue as the bread-winner. If they married, what would Henry and Mary – and their children –

live on? Louisa remembered her own poverty-stricken bread-and-dripping days surrounded by grizzling toddlers and crying babies. She had not made all those sacrifices to see Henry and Mary repeat the story of her own marriage.

Louisa concocted a plan that would nip any incipient romance in the bud. The goldfields of Western Australia were luring young men in search of gold. Paying their fares, she would send Henry there together with his younger brother, Peter – a slight fellow without ambition – to fulfil their father's dream of finding gold. That should solve the problem: doubtless clever Miss Cameron would find someone closer to her own age if Henry were not there.

Approaching absence intensified the situation between Henry Lawson and Mary Cameron. In her later years Mary would claim that Henry Lawson had begged her to elope, telling her that all three of them would go to Western Australia, far away from his mother's domination.

This proposal (often doubted) could well have been made to avert a long parting. However, an ambitious young schoolteacher like Mary, accustomed to seeing wives of poor men scrubbing, cleaning, baking, digging gardens, concocting toys for children out of scraps and being continually exhausted, and aware that an impoverished Louisa had given birth to Henry in a tent, was not going to put herself into the same position.

It would seem more likely that at the dockside, Mary and Henry kissed and said fond goodbyes. Perhaps they promised faithfully to write to each other, but Mary may well have been relieved that a situation which could have got out of hand would now be resolved by a long parting. Mary's mother was still away and Mary continued to board at Louisa's untidy home. In later years, Mary claimed that she did write often to Henry Lawson in Western Australia, but never received an answer. Perhaps the letters *were* of an amorous nature. However, Mary, her pride deeply wounded from receiving no replies from Henry, stopped writing. She was accepted by Neutral Bay Primary School, threw herself into her new teaching post and started attending meetings of a utopian socialist group who met at MacNamara's bookshop, where they were addressed by the charismatic socialist, William Lane.

Much later, Mary Gilmore would claim that Louisa Lawson intercepted and destroyed all letters to her from Henry, which was why their relationship came to nothing, and that young Gertrude Lawson knew that her mother had done this but was too scared to say so in front of Mary.[24]

Certainly Mary did turn against Louisa – but if she was not physically attracted to Henry Lawson, considering him 'callow and immature' (ironically enough confirming Louisa's opinion of her son), would she have been writing him love letters? Of course, Mary may well have described Henry as immature in a fit of pique because she thought he had not responded to her letters.

By the time she met Henry again, he was back from Western Australia, having failed to find gold. By now he had taken up with flighty, insecure eighteen-year-old Bertha Bredt, daughter of one of his mother's feminist friends. Bertha, whose German father had died leaving her mother badly off, resented the authority of her stepfather, William McNamara (the Socialist bookshop owner), and the fact that her mother had had another baby. Mrs McNamara, busy with her radical Labor work and a new baby, had no time for Bertha, who was looking for a way of escape from the McNamara household. Henry, now a published poet, seemed to provide the answer. Bertha slept with him, though it is doubtful if she loved him but, believing she was pregnant, they married.

By now Mary was spending a great deal of her free time at McNamara's Bookshop, where William Lane's socialist group were planning to found a commune in South America. At the bookshop she saw Henry Lawson from time to time, and they resumed their earlier easy friendship ... although Mary maintained her unforgiving attitude towards his mother. In this way, she learned about his engagement to Bertha Bredt and did not appear upset by it.

In May 1891, young Mary Cameron was transferred to Stanmore Public School. Tall and upright in her usual high-necked white blouses and long skirts, Mary was by now deeply involved in supporting the miners' and shearers' strikes and helping William Lane raise the money to send members of his New Australia left-wing movement, inspired by left-wing principles, to start an idealistic Utopian settlement in Cosme, Paraguay. She was attracted to a special member of the group, a tall, muscular bushman called Dave Stevenson, who was a cousin of the famous writer Robert Louis Stevenson. Like many handsome men, Dave flirted with many women, but Mary thought they had a special understanding. He was going on the first group to South America with William Lane. She had made up her mind to sail with the second group and take over running a school in the commune once a schoolhouse had been built.

We have no way of knowing whether Henry, feeling trapped by McNamara, who was anxious to get rid of the cost of supporting his step-daughter, wanted to escape from marriage with the emotionally unstable and immature Bertha. Did he make a last-ditch appeal to Mary Cameron, the woman who could possibly have saved him from alcoholism and guided his literary talent? If he did he would not have been successful: by now she had set her heart on Cosme and Dave Stevenson.

On 31 October, Mary resigned from her teaching post and sailed from Circular Quay on the *Ruapehu*, bound for Paraguay. The party arrived at the Cosme settlement in January 1896.

Back in Sydney, Henry did the decent thing and married Bertha, who exerted pressure on him by claiming she was pregnant. He lived a hand-to-mouth existence writing poems and short stories and turned increasingly to drink.

Out in the wilds at Cosme in the jungles of Paraguay, far from the nearest village, Mary Cameron lived in a grass hut which she shared with lizards, toads and tarantulas and taught the dozen or so children of her fellow pioneers. She had been disappointed on arrival by whispers among the women that Dave Stevenson had had a passionate affair with the only unmarried girl in the settlement, a young nurse called Clara Jones, who had very quickly married someone else and was now rumoured to be grieving for the devil-may-care Dave. Cosme was a tight-knit community; like many communes it was riven by dissensions and jealousies. Unmarried girls were in short supply, and Mary's feelings for Dave waned.

The commune lived on a monotonous diet of home-grown vegetables, gluey grain and monkey stew. Mary, busy with her teaching, wrote a few short stories about life in Paraguay but longed to marry and have a child. She wrote to her mother but received no answer. She also wrote to Henry, telling him about the commune. Months later she learned that her father had died over ten months ago of kidney failure, all alone, while her ambitious mother was pursuing her career in the city. Mary felt bitter remorse that she had lost contact with her father after her mother had left him.

By this time Mary was seeing a great deal of another handsome young bachelor, Will Gilmore. With her literary and journalistic ambitions, Mary made a strange choice of husband; it is most unlikely that had she remained in Sydney she would have married anyone like uneducated Will Gilmore. He was a burly shearer from a down-at-heel property in Victoria, who possessed all the charm of the Irish and a kind heart. He had left school at twelve, had no use for books and poetry, but was regarded as a good, steady man, well suited for pioneering the tropical mosquito-ridden jungle that surrounded Cosme.

They got to know each other when Will was injured while saving some of Mary's pupils in an accident, and she was asked to read him to sleep. Mary demurely dressed as always, read an excerpt from one of Dickens' novels. A little later she wrote a poem showing her sexual attraction to Will after he had kissed her for the first time:

'He kissed me twice today, He took me in his arms, O God! The flesh of light! I cannot sleep, I will not sleep, I shall not sleep tonight.'

Will and Mary married on 29 May 1897 and for a time were blissfully happy, even though life at Cosme was primitive in the extreme and group morale so low that forty of the colonists departed.

Mary's first and only child, William Dysart Cameron Gilmore, was born at Villa Rica, the nearest town to isolated Cosme with a trained midwife. Mary went there alone: there was not enough money to pay the train fare for both Will and herself. She was horrified to find that the hospital was riddled with fleas and flies, and the 'expert midwife' turned out to be drunk.

She returned to Cosme with her baby son to find the defections and expulsions within the commune continuing. Life eventually became so difficult at Cosme that the penniless Gilmores left the commune in November 1899 and moved to Villa Rica. During this period Mary, a devoted young mother, was still very much in love with her husband. Then Will went further south, to Rio Gallegos in southern Patagonia, where he obtained a labouring job on a ranch. It was a hard and isolated period for Mary, who helped to support her adored baby son by giving English lessons. She wrote to her mother but received no reply, and she also wrote to Henry Lawson, telling him of the failure of her hopes and dreams for the community and of the birth of her son.

In September 1899, Mary Ann Cameron, Mary's mother, died after a brief illness, but it was weeks before the news reached South America. Mary, by now quite disillusioned by William Lane's experiment, wrote to her husband on 25 February 1900 saying that she now realised that 'Communism is a failure – not attainable – and enforced Communism is *worse* than none.'

It was time to go home. The Gilmores returned to Sydney via Liverpool and London, where they found a letter from Henry Lawson awaiting them – he and Bertha and their two children were living in London. Mary and Will stayed with Henry and Bertha in their cramped apartment; Mary observed that their children, Jim and little Bertha, seemed sad and cowed. Henry was elated that Blackwood's of Edinburgh were to publish a volume of his short stories and delighted to share the news with Mary, a fellow writer. For her part, Mary took a violent dislike to Bertha. It appears that, unwilling to marry Henry herself because he did not physically attract her, she nevertheless resented Bertha for having done so. It raises the question: did Mary want Henry Lawson for herself because Will Gilmore was proving intellectually her inferior – or did she want some of Henry Lawson's soaring literary reputation to rub off on her so that she too could enter the literary life which had such a powerful appeal for her?

The Lawsons' marriage was now in deep trouble. Bertha accused Henry of drinking the money she needed for the children. She also claimed that he had hit her when he was drunk, though Mary could see no bruises. Jim and little Bertha Lawson were moody and difficult. It appeared that Bertha had had some kind of nervous collapse and been admitted to a lunatic asylum for a month after threatening to harm her own children.

Henry turned to Mary in his time of trouble, asking her if she and Will would take Bertha and their children back to Australia, as he did not feel his unstable wife should travel alone. He planned to leave on another ship as soon as his next book had gone to the printer.

Mary hesitated then agreed, believing this plan was in the best interests of the children. They travelled steerage, the cheapest class.

Bertha was often hostile to Mary, blaming her for the break-up of her marriage. She flirted openly with one of the officers and neglected her children, who attached themselves to Mary. After the ship's propeller was damaged in mid-ocean they had to turn back and head for Bombay; they were held up for so long that Henry joined them there. He was glad to see that Mary and Will seemed content with each other (after the horrors of Cosme the Gilmores seemed to be happy enough during this period), but he wept when he discussed his own marriage. He now saw Mary as an ally, someone who would not judge him. He confided in Mary that he feared Bertha's mental condition was so unstable he could not face old age with her. He showed Mary a crumpled letter from a pregnant young woman called Hannah, whom he had fallen in love with while in Melbourne. He hoped he could start a new life with her. With Bertha's history of mental illness he believed he would get custody of their children.

However, when their ship reached Melbourne Henry learned that Hannah, tired of waiting for him, had formed another relationship, and their baby had died as a result of a backyard abortion. He started drinking heavily.

Back in Australia, three years after leaving Cosme, with only ten shillings in their pockets, life did not look so rosy for the Gilmores. It wasn't long before their differences became apparent. Mary yearned to enter the world of journalism which had meant so much to her mother, and to publish books and poems like Henry Lawson. But Will's only experience was on the land, so this was where they must live.

Very unwillingly, but feeling it her duty as a married woman, she accompanied her husband to the bush at Strathdownie, near Casterton, in Victoria. Will's ageing and frail parents had an isolated rundown property there which Will, a dutiful son, proceeded to run for them.

Mary felt lonely and isolated at Casterton, yearning for the literary world of Sydney that she had hoped to join one day. She and Will moved out of his parents' tiny home to a cottage eaten by white ants which Mary named 'Hilltop'. It was from Hilltop that she observed the poverty-stricken rural world that she would describe so well in her poems and in her narrative writing. Will was often away working as a labourer on other properties. Mary was devoted to her son, little Billy, but felt lonely and isolated in the bush. The resulting mood of depression made her irritable with Will on his return and recriminations ensued. She submitted a few poems to the *Bulletin* and began a correspondence with A.G. Stephens, literary editor of the famous Red Page, which pulled her through a bad patch.

But life was hard as a bush wife without help. Mary complained to A.G. Stephens that by the time she had washed and baked, ironed and scrubbed, swept, cleaned and dusted, cooked three meals a day, darned and stitched and made Billy's clothes by hand, 'there was not much time left for writing'. During this time, however, she was building up a store of bush lore which would be her literary capital for years to come. Her depression lifted after being given the hope that the *Bulletin* would publish some of her poems.

That week of 1 October 1903, when the *Bulletin* published an *entire page* of her poems, would change Mary's life. She always maintained that what made her as a writer and a poet was Stephens' lengthy critiques of her poetry, which made her strive to do better and better. (Mary's first collection of poems, *Marri'd and other verses,* written in Cosme and Casterton, was finally published in book form two years later in 1910.)

In 1908 she was delighted when the editor of the *Australian Worker* magazine invited her to write a special page for women: she would do this for the next twenty years. Henry Lawson was also writing occasional pieces for the same paper. He and Bertha were now living in Manly. Henry was drinking heavily and had attempted suicide.

Finally Will's father died, his widow went to stay with her daughter, the property was leased and Mary and her husband were free to leave Casterton. Billy was nearly thirteen and Mary was longing to live in Sydney and be part of the literary life. It was decided as a temporary measure (a measure that would last for the rest of Will's life) that Mary would go and live in Sydney with Billy while Will would go to Queensland with his brother and investigate what the possibilities were of obtaining farming land there. Their separation would be reasonably amicable. Will Gilmore, in view of all the support Mary had provided at Cosme and at Casterton, agreed to give her a monthly income from the property he took up in Queensland.

From then onwards, Mary and her husband saw each other only for brief periods. He faithfully paid her monthly maintenance, unlike

Louisa's husband Neil Lawson – who provoked Louisa continually over his refusal to pay maintenance for his children. Although Will Gilmore could not share his wife's literary and reformist interests, he was a steady, hard-working man who provided her with a small income.

A few years previously Louisa had financed Henry's publication of *When the World was Wide and Other Verses* and his most famous collection of poems, *While the Billy Boils*. Henry's marriage to Bertha was now over except in name; he was seldom at home, spending nights in his favourite pubs or drunk in some gutter. Bertha was eventually admitted to a mental hospital once more, which seemed to aggravate Henry's alcoholism, possibly through guilt. He was then put in prison for failing to pay maintenance to Bertha. A public subscription was raised for the release of Henry Lawson, who now wrote that he was 'weary, very weary of the faces in the street'.

Billy Gilmore, Mary's teenage son, was beginning to show the same alcoholic tendency as Henry Lawson (a fact Mary tried to cover up all her life). Mary still blamed Louisa for her broken romance – but by now she must have realised what a gruesome fate would have awaited her as the wife of Henry Lawson. After 1907 Henry was jailed several times for failing to pay maintenance for his children. He also spent several periods in a mental hospital, but at the same time his fame as the alcoholic but brilliant poet of the bush was growing fast. Although Mary enjoyed boasting in her old age that she and Henry Lawson had been romantically involved, it seems that the romantic involvement had been more from Henry's side, and that Mary had seen herself as a caretaker of Henry's remarkable talent. She resented Bertha's neglect in nurturing it. Mary chose to ignore the fact that it was *Louisa* who had been the major formative influence on Henry Lawson's unique style.

As Louisa Lawson declined in health and descended into poverty once more, Mary Gilmore went from strength to strength, her features becoming craggier, her reputation increasing, and her readers loving her more and more.

Mary composed short poems which went straight to the heart of her readers. 'The Passionate Heart' (1918) reflects her horror of the slaughter of young men in the trenches of France, alongside lyrical poems such as 'Never Admit the Pain', 'Gallipoli' and 'The Flight of the Swans'. Another of her books, *The Tilted Cart* (a pioneering name for a covered waggon) appeared in 1925, when she was in her mid-sixties. In *The Wild Swan* (1930) Mary expressed her anguish over the destruction of the land by white farmers as well as the loss of Aboriginal folklore, and she took up the same themes in *Under the Wilgas* (1932). In what has become an Australian classic book, *Old Days, Old Ways* (1934), Mary wrote down accounts of pioneers, with special emphasis on the life of pioneer women. The book was a great success and the following year Angus and Robertson published a second volume, *More Recollections.*

'Fear not the years, They have gifts to bring,' wrote Mary triumphantly – and for her they did. Mary's weekly page for women in the *Australian Worker* brought her into contact with many working men's wives with sad tales to tell. She printed their heart-rending letters and wrote back to the women, who were deeply grateful to her. They came to trust Mary Gilmore as their friend. The *Australian Worker* magazine saw the printed correspondence as a useful political tool for their cause.

When Billy Gilmore was old enough to live and work with his father he set off for Queensland. This left Mary living alone in a series of Sydney boarding houses. She suffered periods of loneliness and depression, which may have been responsible for her claims that she was responsible for Henry Lawson's genius. It was now that Mary publicly claimed Henry *had* loved her and asked her to elope with him to Western Australia.[23]

After Henry's premature death in 1922, Mary, understandably upset by the whole affair, made more claims about his love for her. She started saying that were it not for her, Henry's poetic genius would *never* have flowered at all. These exaggerated claims may have been prompted by her hatred of Louisa and Bertha Lawson as well as her wish to increase her own standing in the literary world. She insisted on spending a night in the room in which Henry Lawson had died, and suffered psychologically as a result. Henry had died in poverty, but Mary was determined he would not go to a pauper's grave. She declared she would go to Canberra to tell the Prime Minister, Billy Hughes, that Australia's greatest poet was dead. In the end money was provided for a State funeral and Henry's coffin, covered by the Australian flag, was buried with due pomp and ceremony. Mary was one of the many people who raised contributions for a statue in his memory in Sydney's Domain.

Mary Gilmore became even better known after she wrote *Hound of the Road* and *The Rue Tree* (signifying the Holy Cross of Calvary) which made her a great favourite with Catholic readers. By now she was established as an important literary figure: the dream she had nurtured all these years. On occasions she wrote very average verses, but in her best poems she shows a truly lyrical gift. She had a way of writing in simple language which went straight to the heart. Aborigines, the Australian landscape, its wildlife and the people of the bush evoked the best in her and she wrote about them with sincerity, simplicity and strength. *Tunes of Memory* contains the memorable line: 'The world begins anew in every child.' *The Tilted Cart* contains poems filled with childhood memories and images of the bush. 'Botany Bay', her compassionate verses about an old convict, would have ensured her immortality, had she written nothing else:

> I was the conscript sent to hell
> To make the desert the living well
> I split the rock, I felled the tree,
> The nation was – because of me.

Mary's guilt about having lost touch with her father may have meant that she greatly exaggerated his importance as a bush historian and an expert on Aboriginal lore. Certainly the way that she described his role on George Grey's expedition is grossly exaggerated. But by now no one questioned a word she said. She had become the grand old woman of Australian literature while poor Louisa Lawson was dead and forgotten.

## Honours and fame for Mary Gilmore

The Great Depression of the 1930s was a terrible period for so many readers of the *Australian Worker* but for Mary Gilmore it was a successful time. She was now a literary icon, to whom who younger writers applied for advice.

In 1934 her most famous book, *Old Days, Old Ways* was published. Three years later she was awarded a DBE (Dame of the British Empire) in recognition of her literary achievements and her community activities. She cherished this hard-won recognition which had come late in life.

In World War II, during the tense months of 1942 after the fall of Singapore, when the Japanese forces advanced ever closer to Australia, her stirring poem 'No Foe Shall Gather Our Harvest' made her a symbol of Australian defiance of Japanese power. By this time most of Australia's fighting men were overseas, and this poem had a huge effect in boosting morale on the home front. Perched high in a tiny apartment in the heart of King's Cross – in those days Sydney's Bohemia, she continued to write and encourage other writers and gather tales of pioneering days, looked after by a succession of housekeepers.

Mary outlived her husband and son, who both died in 1945. Both were affected by the alcohol which had destroyed Henry Lawson. The shock caused Mary to fall ill, but her brain remained clear and her spirit undaunted. At eighty-one she maintained her firm belief in social justice and continued her crusade against power and privilege. Her column titled *Arrows* still appeared each week in the *Tribune*.

She had been born in the days of sailing ships, when the *Cutty Sark* and other clippers berthed at Circular Quay surrounded by wool drays and teamsters in cabbage leaf hats. By the time she was old and frail, commercial aeroplanes were circling the world. In 1954, when she was eighty-eight, she wrote a poem called 'The Lesser Grail', which simply but powerfully expressed her belief that:

> Age changes no one's heart, the field is wider, that is all Childhood is
> never lost, concealed, it answers every call.

By now, Mary Gilmore had become a living legend, while Louisa Lawson was forgotten. Over 600 people attended Mary's ninety-first birthday party, which was organised by the Committee for founding the first Chair of Australian Literature. The sum of five hundred pounds was collected for this project which Mary had long advocated.

She was one of the founder-members of Sydney's Lyceum Club for women; a founder and Vice-President of the Fellowship of Australian Writers and a life-member of the Royal Society for the Prevention of Cruelty to Animals. As a public figure, streets, buildings and old people's homes were named after Dame Mary Gilmore. Journalists, scholars and politicians as well as aspiring writers sought her advice.

Her image was perpetuated in portraits by Joshua Smith and Mary McNiven, but the most outstanding one was painted for her ninetieth birthday by William Dobell, and Mary donated it to the Art Gallery of New South Wales. Regarded initially by some critics as a 'caricature' but loved by Mary herself, this portrait has become one of the Art Gallery's best-loved paintings.

## Disaster for Louisa once *The Dawn* was silenced

Louisa Lawson had worked just as hard as Mary Gilmore to improve social conditions for women. She urged parents to educate their daughters so that they could earn a living in case of bereavement, financial disaster, marital separation or divorce. She was a staunch advocate of women gaining the vote, although Rose Scott and her clique of upper-class ladies refused to give Louisa credit for this, and for all her years of support for women's suffrage in *The Dawn* magazine.

Louisa was also way in advance of her time in advocating the setting up of government hostels or refuges for alcoholic women or women wishing to leave prostitution; she assured her readers that these women were 'more sinned against than sinning'. She also suggested that idealistic young women offering themselves as missionaries overseas should first turn their attention to improving the terrible conditions suffered by Aborigines.

Louisa Lawson published the final issue of *The Dawn* when she was fifty-seven. As her biographer Brian Matthews has observed: 'What finally silenced *The Dawn* in 1905 was not the perceived or actual failure of its idealistic visions – although the women's movement was beginning to lose some momentum – but a collapse within Louisa herself.'[24]

The reasons for Louisa's collapse were many. Henry's alcoholism and periods in jail and her lack of money to help him were major components. Louisa had constantly campaigned against the evils of drink – now she realised that her adored son, whose brilliance she had fostered from childhood, was destroying himself through drink. Slowly, before her eyes, the drama of Henry Lawson's alcoholism unfolded: after wild nights in pubs and drinking clubs, tearful promises never to touch a drop again were followed by a few days of abstinence, black moods, withdrawal symptoms, then more wild nights followed by sleeping it off on a park bench or in the gutter. Louisa feared, quite rightly, that alcohol was turning the writing of her brilliant child into maudlin sentimentality and the rehashing of old themes.

Her son Charlie was no more comfort to her than Henry. Occasionally he returned to the family home, especially when he was in trouble with the police. He spent many nights in gaol or in the gutter. Although no formal diagnosis was ever made, Charlie Lawson was probably schizophrenic. He could on occasions be tender and thoughtful towards his mother but on bad days he would sit for hours in his room at her house, arranging and rearranging his collection of knives, vowing vengeance on those he felt were plotting against him. Several times he threatened to turn his mother out onto the street. [35]

Louisa's third son, Peter, also suffered psychiatric problems. She had always hoped he would become a musician, but with a wife and children to support he was forced to accept odd jobs as a piano tuner rather than as a performer.

Apart from severe family problems, Louisa had been driven to the limits of her endurance by the pirating of her invention of an improved mailbag fastener, a buckling device she had realised was necessary during her time as postmistress at Eurunderie. Louisa had patented her invention in New South Wales and sold her fasteners in quantity to the New South Wales Post Office, intending that future sales should provide a retirement income when she gave up publishing. But a male rival copied her invention and destroyed Louisa's market. To protect her patent she became involved in a costly and stressful legal battle. She was awarded a small amount of compensation, reduced on appeal to a very meagre sum. Louisa felt the justice system had failed her. The stress of this case caused her blinding migraines.

Her second stroke of bad luck came in 1900 when she was thrown from a tram as she was boarding it, much hindered by her long, clinging skirt. She suffered a fractured knee and spinal injuries[36] and was bedridden for almost a year. Once again there was scant compensation. Her daughter Gertrude took over running the magazine[37] but everyone wanted to deal with Louisa rather than her deputy. Advertisers fell away in droves. When Louisa returned to work, her old fire, inventiveness and vitality seemed to have ebbed away.

In spite of these disasters, Louisa's desire for women's emancipation was as strong as ever. She joined the council of the Women's Progressive Association and continued to campaign for the appointment of women to public office and the right to advance in professions from which they were virtually barred.

Louisa Lawson's long fight was finally over when she closed down *The Dawn* because of her bouts of ill health and depression.

## Louisa Lawson: the final years

Louisa kept herself busy in her retirement and wrote articles and short stories on a freelance basis for other publications. She also wrote a series of poems about the grief and pain of love; it was now that she indicated that she had loved another man before she met her husband. Some of the poems, published in a volume titled *The Lonely Crossing*, are haunting in their intensity.

> We will part now, you and I,
> With a frozen smile and a faint good-bye ...
> For we each could save it, but neither will,
> As we stoop to injure and strike to kill.

Louisa Lawson's life was one of unremitting struggle and family disaster. If she had had the educational advantages and the stable income from a separated husband that Mary Gilmore enjoyed, would she also have become venerated as a poet and writer? As it is, her reputation has been growing steadily since her death.

Towards the end of her life Louisa created a garden and decorated her final home, a small stone cottage in Renwick Street, Marrickville. In her retirement she spent a great deal of time with her grandchildren and enjoyed writing *Dert and Do*, a novel based on the amusing doings of two lovable children.[25]

Over the next decade she faced increasing loneliness and impoverishment. Although she had been reasonably successful as a publisher and managed to save money, she lost much of it in the 1892 crash of the Australian Joint Stock Bank. She still suffered badly from migraines, aggravated by her fall from the tram. Her daily routine was often disturbed by harrowing visits from the volatile and sometimes violent Charlie. There was no pension to support her and her precious savings were dwindling rapidly. She still managed to sell a few poems and short stories to newspapers, but she was paid a pittance. As a result of her financial problems and family sorrows, her old 'abstracted fits' of depression and lack of concentration returned, accompanied by a reluctance to eat properly. Louisa was further distressed when the local Council placed an embargo on her property at Marrickville, preventing her from selling her land, which she had also acquired an investment for her old age.

Her son Peter lived from hand to mouth, going off to the country to take piano tuning jobs. He had by now become a relatively harmless religious maniac, but like Charlie he suffered from a sense of injustice and a persecution complex. Eventually Peter was admitted by his wife to Gladesville Hospital suffering from 'melancholia and delusions'. His admission statement noted that the cause was 'heredity and worry'. He was discharged three months later as his condition had improved, but when his mother fell ill there could be no room for her in his already overcrowded household.

Gertrude had married, but after her husband was killed at Gallipoli she had to raise and educate her two sons on very little money. She lived far away from Louisa and could be of little assistance to her mother in her approaching senility. Henry Lawson was now a frail, legendary, pathetic figure, well known on the streets of Sydney.[26] He died of a cerebral haemorrhage two years after Louisa.

Louisa attempted to keep track of Henry's whereabouts from 1896 onwards. The last half-dozen entries in her private papers are lists of Henry's visits to gaol or his periods in mental and other hospitals. She notes that in February 1910 he was found drunk 'in the gutter'.[27] Louisa still had her 'good' days, but on her 'bad' ones she exhibited classic signs of depressive illness coupled with the onset of senile dementia. As her health deteriorated, she stopped cooking, ate only at irregular intervals, and did not clean the house or take baths. She let her beloved garden go to rack and ruin and became very forgetful. On one occasion she totally failed to recognise her own grandchildren.[28] At other times, she would be found wandering in the street, unclear about her own identity or where she wanted to go.

At the end of her life, Louisa Lawson who had tried so hard to care for her wayward children, had no one to care for her. At 4 pm one hot, humid afternoon in early January 1920, the resident doctor at Gladesville Hospital for the Insane recorded the admission of Louisa Lawson by her son Peter and his wife Elizabeth, who had too many problems of their own to be able to care for her.

In the days before psychiatric drugs became available to control symptoms of madness and mania, mental asylums were terrible places, staffed by poorly trained nurses, positively Dickensian in their cruel treatment of patients. Little money was spent by politicians on State mental hospitals. The wards reeked of unwashed bodies, urine and faeces.[29] Surrounded by raving, screaming, incontinent patients, some of whom had to be forcibly tied to chairs to restrain them, Louisa lived out the final eight months of her life. Like most patients with dementia, she was more often than not unaware of her surroundings or how she had come to spend the end of her life in such a place. In her lucid moments she cried bitter tears and begged to return to her home.

Louisa Lawson died in Gladesville Mental Hospital in August 1920. It was a tragic end for a truly inspiring woman who had worked so hard to improve the lot of other women. She was given what was in effect a pauper's funeral and is buried in the Anglican section of Rookwood cemetery. No statue or monument – other than a block of Housing Commission flats in North Bondi named after her – exists to commemorate Louisa Lawson, who, when the vote was granted to Australian women in 1902, was publicly acclaimed as the originator of the suffrage campaign.

Mary Gilmore died on 3 December 1962, the historic anniversary when the Eureka Uprising is commemorated. Unlike poor Louisa, she was granted the honour of a State funeral at St Stephen's Church, Macquarie Street. In accordance with her wishes, her ashes were buried in her husband's grave at Cloncurry, Queensland. This seems a fitting gesture, for he had faithfully supported her during the hard years while she established her place in Australian literature.

# CHAPTER THREE

## Martha Caldwell Cox
*(1854–1947)*
PIONEER OF THE 'NEVER-NEVER'

Martha Cox represents all those pioneer women who went out with their husbands into wild country and managed to survive drought, bushfire, loneliness, deprivation, and childbirth without medical aid. They all helped to make Australia what it is today. Martha was intelligent and diligent but had little schooling: her memoirs are no literary masterpiece but are entertaining and written in a distinctively Australian voice.[1]

Martha deserves to be as well-known as Jeannie Gunn, author of *We of the Never Never*.[2] Jeannie, a Melbourne 'lady schoolteacher', horrified her family and friends by marrying Aeneas Gunn, part-owner and manager of The Elsey, a vast cattle property hundreds of miles south of Katherine, in the Northern Territory. Jeannie described Elsey homestead as 'mostly verandahs and promises' but those rooms that were finished were 'neat and well-cared for'. Jeannie, who had no children, was provided with a cook and Aboriginal women as domestic helpers; she had ample free time to keep a lively and entertaining journal.

Martha Cox, on the other hand, was a working-class battler with five children. Jeannie Gunn spent only eighteen months in the 'Never-Never'; following her husband's tragic death she returned to Melbourne. After Martha's husband died she battled on and ran his three properties successfully, staying in the 'Never-Never' until she was in her seventies. In addition to caring for her family, Martha drew water, cooked, cleaned, and broke in horses. When necessary she acted as camp cook for shearers and tank sinkers. She helped her husband to clear land, grub out stumps and build fences.

Selectors' wives rarely wrote about their experiences.[3] Squatters' wives, on the other hand, were fond of writing journals, some of which have become part of the canon of early Australian literature. They went to the bush with pianos, silver cutlery and porcelain dinner services. Martha Caldwell was the daughter of two penniless Irish migrants, Annie and Matthew Caldwell, who leased a small mixed farm in the Adelaide Hills. Martha had no silver or porcelain and certainly no piano. Taught by her elder brothers to handle a gun, Martha was also a fearless horsewoman.

She wrote her memoirs in her old age when finally she had the time to sit down and take up her pen. The journals of most squatters' wives complain about the servant problem, the flies and a monotonous diet of mutton and damper. Martha does not mention these. Instead she writes with authority about the price of sheep and wool, how to mend a fence, how to hand-rear a lamb. Her love of dogs and horses shines through her memoirs, which reveal without a trace of self-pity the grim realities of life on a small selection.

I was first shown Martha's memoirs when I was a guest on a historic property in New South Wales named Livingstone Gully owned by Belinda and Alan Cox. Alan is the son of the nephew of Martha's husband, David Cox. Martha Cox's memoirs are significant historically, written from the selectors' point of view at a time when selectors and squatters were at loggerheads.

Martha's two elder brothers were William and John, and she had four younger sisters – Olive, Sophia, Agnes and Priscilla, the youngest of whom was born a few months after their father's death in 1834. Martha felt a special responsibility for her youngest sister.

In 1860–61 the New South Wales Government passed two Selection Acts which made it easier for those lacking capital to purchase land on easy terms. When Martha was ten, her widowed mother sold off their stock, packed a covered horse-drawn wagon with food, water and bedding and set off from the Adelaide Hills to Southern New South Wales. They took eight weeks to reach the Murray River. Whenever the going was rough, Martha and her sisters walked in front of the wagon to ease the load on the horses. Stones cut their feet until they bled, bramble bushes tore at their pinafores and bare arms. Each night the girls and their mother slept on mattresses inside the covered wagon while the boys took turns to keep watch against bushrangers. They lived on salted meat and game, tinned fish, potatoes, jam and flour, washed down with billy tea.

Annie Caldwell took up a 'selection'[3] of 230 acres at The Billabong, 9.5 km from the present-day town of Holbrook (then known as Germanton) in her son's name: in the 1860s women were regarded as chattels of men and were not permitted to own land.

The family worked together to build a slab hut large enough to act as a dormitory for their mother and the eldest girls; the rest of the family continued to sleep in the covered wagon. The hut with its dirt floor also served as a dining room and as the kitchen when it was too wet to cook outside. The children and their mother cleared 10 acres of trees and undergrowth in order to get in a crop of wheat. There was a demand for home-made cheese at Albury, so Annie Caldwell and her daughters worked hard milking and making butter and cheese to bring in additional income.

Lack of money and a huge workload meant that Martha's schooling was minimal. At first there was no school; eventually one opened at Fern Hill, some miles away, but the schoolmaster turned out to be an alcoholic. Martha wrote in her memoirs:

> Our schoolroom was in the rear of the [shanty hotel] premises and our schoolmaster often found his way round to the bar. [In his absence] the more studious among us read our books, or worked on our sums. We worked on slates, but had to copy our figure work into an exercise book and take it home each night to show our parents some evidence of our progress. It was five miles to school, and I rode there side-saddle every day on Cocky, my bay pony, on a man's saddle.

(It was regarded as 'improper' for females to ride astride at that time or to wear trousers.) As soon as Martha was fourteen she left school to help her mother.

Five years later, at the age of nineteen, Martha met a young selector, David Cox, one of five brothers. David was the son of Joseph Cox and his second wife, Mary (née Maloney), who owned a fine property named Livingstone Gully, also in New South Wales.[4] Martha's memoirs are very discreet over the details of her courtship but it is clear that the young couple were very much in love. David Cox was tall, muscular and fair-skinned.

His father Joseph had been born at Cashel in County Tipperary. David Cox was born at Brungle, near Tumut, in 1839. Although Joseph's first wife, who had died on the ship coming to Australia, had been anglican, Mary was a Catholic and David had been brought up a Catholic. Martha's family were devout Catholics, also from Ireland, so her mother raised no objection when David asked permission to marry Martha, knowing he also came from a hard-working, highly respected pioneering family.[5] David was not the eldest son, so he would no have inherited Livingstone Gully. Since there was not enough land to support all five sons, Richard Cox bought out his younger brothers' interests, which meant David had the capital to buy stock and set up his own property but not to buy vast tracts of land. So he became what was known as a 'selector' – selecting uncleared acreage bought at a low rate of interest from the New South Wales goverment.

Martha relates that:

> David had already selected two adjoining blocks on Ingram's run, near Book-Book, before I married him. He had built a temporary home for me out of wooden slabs with a dirt floor and I went there to start housekeeping on my own. We had hopes of extending our holding but the squatter on the big station wanted rid of us. He selected [took a lease on] the land around us where the water came from and so 'peacocked' us out. We stuck it for twelve months with our stock dying from lack of water and then decided all we could do was to sell out at the cheap price the squatter up at big station offered us and look elsewhere for a better farming proposition.

Wealthy squatters with capital were determined to lock up the land and squeeze out poorer selectors. They adopted devious tactics to block off selectors' access to water, and got them off the land by 'dummying' or 'peacocking'.[6] The squatters could also force selectors off 'pre-emptive' leased land by these measures.

After the disappointment of losing land on which they had worked so hard, Martha and David took up another selection, this time on a pre-emptive lease, which in return for a deposit gave them the right to buy the land once it was subdivided. This time David was more cautious; he did *not* build a home on the land – instead, he and Martha slept in their wagon. But after six months of backbreaking work cutting down trees and grubbing out stumps, the Lands Department notified David that he must select another block: 'their' land had been gazetted as an agistment block for cattle on the move. David would get his money back eventually, but he and Martha would have to start all over again the backbreaking toil of clearing the land on another block.

Martha was convinced that a wealthy squatter had bribed the Lands Department to get them removed on a pretext. She wrote bitterly:

> Those rich squatters always find the means to beat working people like us in the end. David was disgusted by the whole affair. He was forced to forfeit our cleared block and it took twelve months before our

money was refunded. So back we were, in the covered wagon and on the road again searching for a property. But now I was with child so went home to my mother on The Billabong, to wait the turn of circumstance and my first child.

Martha's first son, Joe, was born at The Billabong, with her mother acting as midwife.

Grubbing out stumps to clear land by the sweat of your brow and then losing the land for the second time was soul-destroying. The Coxes decided to take up their third selection in partnership with someone who had capital and political influence, so that the squatters could not throw them off 'their' land again. David chose as his partner his brother-in-law James Gormly, a shrewd businessman with good contacts and a seat on the local council (eventually he would become Mayor of Wagga). On the tacit understanding that he would look after their interests with the Lands Department, Gormly put up the capital for a large block of land adjoining the Cox's selection. For their part, David and Martha Cox agreed to supervise Gormly's stock as well as their own.

They 'selected' two ten-acre blocks known to have water between Cobar and Bourke, then uncharted wilderness in the Western district of New South Wales, lacking any road or rail connections. The land was known as Corongo Peak, in the Condobolin district, which suffered from harsh winters and searingly hot summers. There were no schools or medical facilities. Martha, accustomed to having her mother and siblings around her, now found herself several days' horseback ride from the nearest white woman and even further from a doctor. She wrote:

> We decided I should stay out at Wollongough Station, two days ride away, while Dave would go to our new land at Corongo Peak, get a water tank made and a hut built, which would take time. Wollongough was owned by a distant relation of my husband, named King.
>
> Our journey to Wollongough Station took a week. Dave drove a team of twelve horses in the wagon, while I drove the lighter vehicle, which was big enough to seat six people. So there I was driving the tilted wagonette with young Joe on my lap. I had loved driving horses since childhood. One horse was good but Jess, a jibbing chestnut mare, gave me a lot of trouble whenever we came to a hill. Dave always drove

ahead so that I would be able to follow his tracks. Sometimes he would have to ride back and deal with Jess when I failed to get her to budge. She played up badly, seeming to know that I was handicapped by having young Joe on my lap. We picked up supplies of meat and fresh milk at stations as we journeyed along. When we reached Wollongough Station, Dave departed for Corongo Peak in the wagonette leaving the wagon and team with me at the station.

Mr and Mrs King were kind and considerate; but my thoughts were always in the west with Dave busy making a home for us in isolation.

Then came a terrible drought. Every green blade of herbage was gradually burnt off. Six months passed without a drop of rain. Cattle and sheep gathered round the homestead, the sheep bleating piteously as the tanks were low and the heat was insufferable. Mr King and some men set off on the droving track with the sheep in search of grass. Mrs King, who was new to the bush and its hardships, went home to her parents in Victoria to await the breaking of the drought. Only Mrs Daly, the housekeeper, and I were left to battle through as best we might.

The days grew hotter and hotter. The ground was cracked and dry as ashes. There was not a green blade to be seen as far as the horizon and the nights were stifling. Strange as it may seem in such dry conditions, at twilight mosquitoes attacked us in myriads from their haunt in the saltbush and we had no mixtures to spray rooms against then. A plague of fleas made things still worse. The little wretches would swarm onto my legs and attack me when I had to collect the eggs from the hens in a shed some distance from the homestead. If only we had had a decent supply of water things would not have been so bad, but by now the station-tank was dry. Only by digging down two or three feet in the bed of the tank were we able to get a bucket of thick sludgy water which had to be boiled and clarified before we could use it.

Kangaroo rats, or paddy melons, arrived in droves looking for water. Little Joe, who was just able to toddle, used to have great sport among the poor creatures. But the kangaroo rats were no sport for us women as they threatened to foul our limited water supply. Mrs Daly and I got hammers and put in stakes and covered the whole tank with wire netting.

Only the arrival of 'Red Jack' the mailman, tired by his long and blistering journey through drought-stricken country, relieved the monotony. His bulging saddle bags were crammed with letters. He would stay and rest a few hours, and get refreshment for himself and a feed for his jaded horse. He brought letters occasionally from Dave and the Kings but his visits were few and far between. I learned that Dave had to cart water from Kildary Station, over 20 miles away, and there was no sign of rain. A tank was being sunk by Dave and men he had engaged. They were making the first tank on Gormly's lease and then building a temporary slab hut for us.

The drought continued. There was no water to spare for Martha's vegetable patch so the plants withered and died and they found it impossible to buy dried vegetables. Martha perseveres with her story of heroic endurance.

Mrs Daly and I were often left without meat as the sixteen-year-old delivery lad seemed to forget our delivery day, or jibbed at a fifteen-mile trip in the heat. Then we had to fall back on tea and damper with a little dripping to help it down. Mrs Daly was good at 'beggars on the coals', as she called the thin dampers that she baked. If we only had had a drop of real, fresh pure water to make a decent cup of tea. At first we managed to get along without serious ailments but I fretted over little Joe, on our limited and monotonous diet.

At long last the rain came, the King family came back, and with them the stock, with more bought to replace losses. The yellow-baked land became green again in a surprisingly short space of time, the tanks were full once more. Dave wrote to say that he had made things ship-shape at The Peak, as we called it, and was returning for me in a week or two. I began to put things together for the big journey.

Eventually Dave returned, bringing 600 merino ewes he had bought at Forbes. He and Martha then started out on their six-week journey by horse-drawn wagon to Corongo Peak.

Dave drove the wagon with the team and I drove the tilted wagonette. Two old shepherds we had engaged brought the sheep and a few cows for fresh milk. Unfortunately the ewes began lambing much earlier than we had expected, giving us much trouble. I often had two or three sickly lambs to care for behind me in the wagonette.

When we reached the Lachlan River, we found it swollen from the recent rain and we traversed the old narrow bridge with great difficulty.

We both had to unload our goods from the wagon and take our stuff across in a boat. Dave hitched the wagonette behind the wagon, I rode ahead and led one horse across the stream. The water rose well over the deck of the wagon by mid-stream. Somehow we landed high and dry without damage or loss of any of our provisions.

The stages [distance between places of rest on the journey] were far drier now, and at stations we had to pay a shilling a bucket for water for the thirsty horses which meant paying ten shillings a drink for the team [a great deal of money at that time]. But it hurt me to see horses suffer. On several occasions Dave took them in the darkness five or six miles, and gave the poor animals a real blow-out with no one the wiser.

A shower fell about 20 miles from Cobar, filling little hollows and giving the sheep a drink. I will never forget the bleating of those poor famished animals when they smelt the water. At Cobar we struck a friendly settler who allowed Dave to water the sheep at his new tank, a hundred at a time. From there on we had free water and plentiful grass all the way. After six weary weeks, we and our belongings arrived at our future home. With a tank full of water and plenty of grass for our stock, it looked as if good luck had greeted us at last.

The next morning I went out for my first look at Corongo Peak. As far as the eye could scan the plain stretched away to the skyline. A world of mulga, wilga, box, but not a sign of a stringy bark, which would have been helpful for our building operations. Our cabin being still incomplete, we slept in the covered wagon. But as it was impossible to keep the cockroaches away, we took meals in the open air.

Our dining table consisted of a sheet of box bark, sap side up, supported upon four stakes driven into the ground. Our tablecloth was a length of unbleached calico, and cooking utensils included a camp oven, frying pan, a few pots and sundries, a couple of kerosene tin boilers, one for cooking purposes, and the other for boiling the clothes in on washing day.

Under primitive conditions, Martha cooked for shearers and tank sinkers, and carried out household tasks and farm work without any of the household aids and appliances we take for granted today such as hot and cold running water, electricity and refrigeration, or a local shop. Martha made her own butter, cheese, jam and soap. By spending every penny they earned on developing their property, she and David would finally achieve what her mother had never known: a proper homestead with a kitchen and real furniture instead of packing cases to serve as tables and chairs.

Keeping clothes clean in hot dusty conditions was difficult, as Martha describes:

> A couple of iron tubs, a lump of common soap, and unlimited elbow grease completed our laundry equipment when a set of old-fashioned flat irons were added.
>
> Each night we sat at our camp fire where the outback firewood glowed brightly. If we wished to read, we could retire to the covered wagon which served as our bedroom till the cabin was ready for us. Illumination was supplied by a tin slush-lamp. The tin was half filled with dirt and then rendered mutton fat was run in till it was full. A wick was inserted consisting of a thin greased stick wrapped in one of my old cotton stockings, which had been well greased also.
>
> We were too far from civilisation to indulge in the luxury of kerosene lamps. When your nearest neighbour is nearly 30 miles away it is difficult to replace a broken lamp glass or replenish the stock of kerosene. Many people wonder how women, many of whom had enjoyed every domestic comfort before coming to Australia, could endure such a hard and isolated life in the bush where there was no possible escape from nervous strain and constant backbreaking work.
>
> All our food was of the simplest kind and not always overflowing in quantity; the work was strenuous, and, to a woman, often unusual, to say the least. But for the sake of husband and childen and the fulfilment of their shared plans, most selectors' wives tackled the job with sleeves rolled up, and a smile on their face, although hard work and harsh conditions turned many young women to skin and bone or sent them blind from the sandy blight.

Gypsum in the drinking water, (a hydrous calcium sulphate which acts as a clarifying agent) kept it clear. Martha continues:

> It was decided to sink two more tanks on Gormly's land and one on our own lease. Five men were employed. In due course the tanks were made ready for the downpour, which we expected from day to day.
>
> Alas! The winter slipped by. Six months passed, and still no rain. The summer heat returned, each day hotter than the last. The sky remained

cloudless. Day by day the water went lower in the tank. The sides and beds of the new tanks gaped with cracks. Our flock of sheep was now over a thousand, if rain did not come soon it meant ruin for there was no chance of shifting the poor sheep. Every green thing disappeared and only the dry grass seed, which the sheep licked up, stood between them and starvation. We had no thermometer to test the heat, but the temperature must have ranged from 100–120 [Fahrenheit or 37–48° Centigrade] degrees for weeks together. It was the Wollongough drought over again – but worse. I used to pity Dave and the men building a bark-roofed shearing shed in all that glare. We lived off meat and damper, our vegetables had long since withered and died. I was now feeling the strain a good deal. My nerves were getting jumpy and my gums started to bleed. I could not sleep at night with thoughts of our poor sheep, and what might happen to them, whirling through my brain.[7]

It was terribly hot outside, and I was just about to step out of the door of our hut when I saw the head of a large black snake at the doorstep. I stood stock still, stiff with fear. Three minutes or more passed while the ugly brute kept darting its tongue and staring at me. I stood near the table, trembling and praying I would find something to hit it with.

Eventually the snake moved its head round as if it were about to crawl away; then swerved round again, and crawled behind one of our three legged stools along the back wall. Quick as a flash I slipped out, secured a stick and came back and killed the wriggling brute. I sank down on a stool quite exhausted after I had nearly battered the creature's head off. As luck would have it, Dave chanced to come in for the tape measure just after, and gave me a nip of brandy which revived me.

So great was the heat that magpies fluttered down in front of the hut. They would hop timidly to the door, and then, one after another enter and betake themselves under the table to escape the rays of the sun, which had already killed numbers of smaller birds. In a short time, finding no opposition, birds came in greater numbers, and though I might be moving round they remained unafraid. When I went out to scrape a dish, I would tap the plate with a knife or fork. Down those poor birds would come, hopping around, and greedily picking up the scraps of food. I grew very fond of them. The poor birds seemed grateful for food and shelter. They would perch on the roof of the hut in the late afternoons and sing for us. I had never heard magpies carol like them; they sounded like silver flutes.

The rays of the scalding sun would almost fry a steak in the open glare. A hot wind blew most days. Eventually Gormly arrived in his little buggy with a team led by 'Red Rover', a lively mare. He wanted to inspect the tanks that were under construction at different places on the property, and he asked me to pilot him through the trackless bush to them in his buggy. Gormly was a splendid driver, but I must confess that I sometimes felt scared at the pace he drove through the bush.

'Hang on to my arm, Mrs Cox, if you're afraid of being shaken out of the buggy,' he would say after a particularly rough jerk.

I managed to guide him to the tanks. When we arrived, he told me that I was better in the bush than most men, which was certainly a compliment coming from Gormly, who was never known to praise anyone.

Gormly came across two men with horses and drays about four miles down who had cut through our fence and 'pinched' a night's feed. Gormly flew into a rage accusing them of bushranging the grass. The men laughed and asked when did Gormley last see grass there? There was an angry exchange of words.

Gormly, a huge hot-tempered man, threatened to thrash the drovers should they touch his water tanks. Martha's love for horses made her defy Gormly. She told the men to give the exhausted and gasping animals a good drink and that she would take responsibility for her actions, adding: 'I don't suppose we ever missed that drop of water.' She describes two diversions in her hard outback life:

One day an Afghan peddler with his cart arrived. How I longed for the pretty ribbons and laces he offered, but each of us needed a pair of stout laced boots and a new pair of scissors was essential for me as I had lost mine. I made all our clothes and when they wore out, remade them for my child. In those days there was no money to spare for anything that was not considered essential.

Our next visitor was unexpected. A teamster called at a pub at Tindary Station, near Cobar, went on a drinking spree, and in a bout of 'the horrors' walked off into the bush without food or water, drunk and not knowing what he was doing. The shanty keeper reported the matter to Tindary. A station hand and a black tracker sent out to locate him found a pocket knife and a length of string under a gum tree. In the meantime the poor wretch had arrived at our place, his tongue too swollen to speak. He pointed to his mouth and groaned. His eyes were rolling and he kept darting a look behind and around, as though he feared violence. 'The horrors' were still on him.

Fortunately I had seen this before so I gave him weak tea in spoonfuls, then soup in the same way. Little by little I got a bit of nourishment into him, and in time he was able to tell us his story.

He had found himself hopelessly bushed, sat under a tree and saw devils coming after him. In terror he tried to cut his throat, with his blunt tobacco knife, but was only able to make a scratch, as we could see. Then he tried to choke himself with a bit of string, but couldn't manage it. He then must have become unconscious for he could not remember how he reached the track to our place.

Martha nursed the unfortunate man and when he was well enough to be moved, Dave harnessed the horses and Martha held their heads while Dave lifted him into the wagon. It was not an easy manoeuvre:

As one horse reared in panic, Dave shouted to the teamster to take me away as I would be killed. But I hung on; I knew our horses were not vicious, only frightened. Dave set off for the bush inn at Tindary. When he returned that night he smiled and handed me a bottle of port wine, 'A present from our late guest,' he said with a smile.

It was roughly seventy miles to Bourke, our nearest business centre. It took Dave over a week to go there and back. In the drought it was impossible to buy preserved vegetables which we relied on with our water supply so short. When my husband was away at Bourke I had to manage the whole place entirely on my own. Our old shepherd camped in a hut not far away, but he was away with his sheep all day. I became used to roughing it in time but I was always very pleased to see Dave's wagon heave in sight again.

The drought continued and the sheep had nothing to eat but dried trefoil seed. Things were becoming desperate. Dave talked about killing sheep and boiling down their carcasses for their fat to make tallow and sheepskins before our water gave out and forced us to abandon the place, losing everything for which we had worked so hard.

Night after night we talked the matter over. Day after day the sky remained cloudless. That sun burnt the very souls out of us and tried our courage to the limit. It seemed as if the earth would never receive a downpour of rain again. We found piles of dead sheep each morning. There was no railway communication from Dubbo to Bourke then so it was impossible to shift the sheep.

Our sheep were good merinos and had been expensive to buy. It seemed terrible to slaughter the poor things and I had raised some as bottle-fed lambs. But water in the tank was shrinking day after day. What was to be done? The heat sometimes soared as high as 120 degrees. Our shepherd had lost a number of sheep the day before, and Dave had ridden off that morning to search for them. The sky was clear and the sun was roasting. I was washing clothes in a kerosene tin and young Joe was playing close by the door of our hut. Towards noon clouds began to gather in the sky, but I took no notice of them – we had had clouds like that before. By now I had lost hope that the drought would ever break and jumped in fright at the sudden roar of a thunder-clap. The sky was as black as ink. Again the lighting flashed in jagged streaks across the sky, followed by crashes of thunder. I ran outside and brought my child into the hut. A raging wind had sprung up and a red fog of dust made it impossible to see anything. The wind was so strong I was scared lest our tiny hut would keel over. The wind shipped a sheet of bark from the roof, then another and another. The rain came down in streams. I never saw or heard anything like it. I was terrified, and little Joe was crying in my arms. I felt like crying myself when I thought of my husband out in the midst of it all.

The torrents of rain continued. Sheet after sheet of bark was torn from the roof and whirled away. Water from the tank overflowed into a gully and entered the hut and I feared my child would drown. All I could do to save him was stand upon an old stretcher bed holding little Joe in my arms.

An hour later, McGoobery, one of the tank sinkers who had run down from his tent a mile away rushed into the hut. Only one sheet of bark still remained on the roof. He stood on the table and hung on to the sheet till the wind slowed.

All I remember was McGoobery shouting above the wind, 'It's a mercy that little Joe and you are alive!'

In an hour the wind dropped, the rain ceased, and the sky was blue again. My terror passed. I felt overjoyed, knowing that the drought had broken so we did not have to kill the sheep or leave our land.

About 5 o'clock that afternoon poor old Dave turned up on foot, drenched to the skin, but wearing a smile that I had not seen on his face for over twelve months. McGoobery and he would shift all the provisions up to the shearing shed and would stay there till the hut had been fixed. I was not bothered because drought had delayed our plans to build a proper house and so, in spite of the cockroaches, we were still sleeping in the covered wagon, and only used the slab hut for cooking, eating and washing.

The water was knee deep, so Dave had to carry me and Joe to the wagon where we found our bedding dry as a bone, thanks to that good tarpaulin tilt that covered the wagon.

By next day the waters had retired. We were filled with happiness and felt like Noah and his family after they came out of the Ark. What astonished us was finding frogs in thousands. I shall never forget the noise of their croaking. I could never have believed so many could have suddenly sprung up from nowhere, like a plague of mice. On the morning before you could not have found a single frog, and now they covered the ground, little and big, young and old. Little Joe had the fun of his life catching them and seeing them hop around. In a short time we had three tanks full of water and plenty of grass.

However our remaining sheep got 'the scours' [persistent diarrhoea] from the sudden change in diet to rich young grass.

Learning of the rain, James Gormly despatched 2000 sheep out in charge of his eldest son, who landed them in fair condition on their block. He then went back leaving Dave in charge. Gormley had not stocked up before the drought. Had that rain not come when it did, we would have lost all our sheep.

Dave, relieved of worry, set to work to build a comfortable house for us. That rain had made all the difference, giving us some guarantee of permanent occupation. Dave worked with a will, and before very long we had a comfortable habitation which proved a blessing, especially to me, after the roughing I had experienced sleeping in that wagon, where clouds of red dust settled on everything as soon as I cleaned up.

In October our shearing started. We had three shearers. I had to cook for all hands and I remember how fussy those shearers were over their tucker. Shearing is very trying work, bending so long over greasy, smelly sheep puts men off their appetite, and they need something tasty to tempt them to eat.

We had no butcher, baker or storekeeper so I was hard put 'to make a do of it'. But the men seemed to like my bread and brownies. Our great drawback was lack of vegetables because our tank water was too precious to use on a vegetable garden. All I could do was to give our shearers some preserved vegetables which Dave bought at Bourke and which came originally from Adelaide. I used to pour boiling water on those preserved vegetables and heat them up in the pots; they were not a bad substitute for the real thing. [This is the second mention of the fact that they were not eating fresh vegetables.] Dave was a splendid shearer and I was always up at the shed helping the men out when shearing started. Dave shore a ewe first and told the men that that was the way he wanted his sheep shorn.

'Pink 'em, but don't cut 'em,' he would say. The fleece was light and naturally a bit broken after such a season, but it was merino and fetched 9½d a pound, which was reckoned a good price at that time. But the clip took a long time to reach the market and it was another three months before I could finally send our wool cheque to the bank.

Jim Gormly came out to us again. I must say he now changed his tune and showed a deal of consideration for me in many ways. As well as cooking for the shearers, I had been doing the cooking for the tank sinkers but Gormly soon put an end to that, saying that the men should cook for themselves and that I was doing 'far too much altogether'. He warned that I would break down. [Martha must have been showing signs of illness.]

One day our old shepherd reported he had lost twenty sheep. The shepherd was eating his breakfast next day in the lean-to along with the rest of us, when Gormly swore at him. The old shepherd answered back that he had done his best to look after them and could not help it. Gormly began to shout at him. Jumping up in a rage, he stormed over to the man, grabbed him by the neck and told the shepherd to hold his clapper [tongue] or he would leave him in such a state he would only be fit for the hospital.

Next day the old shepherd asked Dave for his money. David tried to make the old man see reason but nothing would dissuade that shepherd, who was terrified of Gormly and his threats and insisted on departing. So Dave and Gormly had to take over the task of shepherding for a whole month. I laughed to myself, knowing that Gormly's temper had ensured he would have to work hard for a change. It took a month to obtain the services of another shepherd as our part of the outback was considered 'the back end of the world' in those days.

White shepherds used to buy the sexual favours of black women by giving them, their fathers or husbands, tobacco and tea. The Aboriginal men, who often had several wives, did not object to pimping for their wives if enough incentive was provided.[8] The white shepherds often infected these full Aboriginal or part-Aboriginal women with venereal disease and then they returned them to their tribe who did not nurse them, but abandoned them to their fate, a practice that sickened Martha, who brought food to sick and abandoned Aboriginal women on several occasions.

At this juncture Martha was also worried about little Joe.

I couldn't think what was ailing our child. He lost his appetite. His skin was dull and flaking and his face as pale as putty. His legs became puffy and sore, and his teeth were in a bad state, bleeding at the gums. I had never seen anything like it, and all the usual medicines that we used in the bush did him no good. I was far too worried about Joe to think of myself.

Joe was showing the classic symptoms of scurvy, caused by lack of vitamin C, normally derived from vegetables and citrus fruits. Martha was too busy worrying about her husband and child to notice her own declining health. Her usual optimistic, energetic personality changed and she became weepy and irritable. At that time little was known about scurvy in the bush (although mariners had been aware of its danger for a long time).[9] Eventually Joe's leg became infected and Dave took him and Martha to the nearest doctor, in Bourke, which meant a drive of more than two days. Martha recalls:

We stayed at Sprowl's Hotel. After the loneliness and isolation at Corongo Peak, Bourke seemed like a big city to me. Mrs Sprowl had gone to Sydney on a trip, so Miss Pierce was housekeeping for her while she was away. She was the first woman I had seen for two and a half years. I cried with relief to talk to a woman again after so long on my own. However that doctor was a real fraud and gave me little satisfaction. He said that Joe had evidently injured his leg in some way and advised me to take him home and keep him in bed with his leg bandaged.

On the way home we stayed a night at Davidson's Station. Mrs Davidson immediately noticed Joe's poor condition. She asked what the doctor had said so I told her. She said that the doctor was very wrong, that my poor child had scurvy. She told me that David should go on home, and I should stay there with Joe while she did what was necessary to cure him, and that it was our child's diet that needed attention. She gave him plenty of vegetables, both cooked and raw, which surprised me as normally doctors said raw foods were too hard for children to digest.[10]

Martha herself was also suffering from the onset of scurvy but neither she nor the doctor recognised the early warning signs, which included bleeding gums, fatigue and irritability. Little Joe sickened long before she did; young children have less resistance and show pronounced symptoms of the disease much sooner than adults.

The Davidsons could afford to keep a Chinese gardener on their station who managed to grow them fresh vegetables. Martha records:

In a week Joe was much better, and ere long, Dave came back and took us home. Mrs Davidson filled up the back of the trap with vegetables to keep Joe going for quite a time. It was a blessing to see little Joe running round bright and happy again after such a long spell of sickness. Joe's bout of scurvy made me understand just what the poor sailors used to suffer on long voyages in sailing ships.

Some months had passed since our return from Bourke, when one day, a handsome gentlemanly-looking man rode up to the house inquiring if this was Mr Dave Cox's place. When I answered it was, he politely asked if I was Mrs Cox and introduced himself as Mr McDonald, a friend of Miss Pierce, whose acquaintance I had made some months ago out at Bourke. Mr McDonald had ridden over from Tindary Station where he had seen Miss Pierce, who was employed to teach the children [this echoes Martha's own schooldays with an alcohol addicted teacher] but finding the company too rough, she had asked Mr McDonald to call and convey her kind regards and say that she would very much like to spend a week or two with me. The poor lass was wretched where she was. I said that I should be glad to see her and that Dave would take a spare horse and bring her back. Mr McDonald thanked me, and rode off.

Eventually Miss Pierce arrived exhausted by the long journey. We were as happy as could be together. Miss Pierce was a lovely young woman, thoughtful and capable, without a bit of nonsense about her. Although born in the city she adapted to outback life very well and I became like a different woman by reason of her company while she said she felt like a bird liberated from a cage after working for horrible people as a governess. She only came for 'a week or two', but it was six months before we parted.

Not surprisingly, Martha, who has not had the chance to speak to another women for nearly two years and had survived illness and drought, burst into tears of joy at the thought of having a woman friend. She continued:

Mr McDonald came again for a visit, stayed to dinner, and had a long chat with Miss Pierce that afternoon before riding away. He told us he was managing a station out between Davidson's property and Bourke, about twenty miles from that place. He seemed to be in the girl's thoughts, for she often spoke of him. Then a month after his visit, she 'let the cat out of the bag' and admitted they were engaged to be married.

Their marriage took place at Davidson's station. I was her matron of honour and Dave gave her away. The clergyman had to come all the way from Bourke to marry them. The Davidsons made a grand affair of the wedding, and champagne flowed freely at the feast that followed. I felt the parting from my friend deeply, like losing one of my own family. When they drove off in their fine buggy, drawn by a spanking pair of horses, I faced the lonely Corongo Peak with a heart as heavy as lead and Joe felt her absence greatly too. She had been teaching him all the time she had been with us, and he had become attached to her.

Now Martha was pregnant again. She records:

> My second child, Mary Ann, was born at Bourke in 1879.
>
> Returning again to The Peak with my daughter, I faced the old lonely life once more and was beginning to feel the long strain of isolation and hardship on my health. I suffered severe headaches and pains in arms and legs and often could not sleep. I tried to battle against weakness and fatigue, but at length it threatened to get the best of me, and Dave began to feel anxious.

Martha's headaches and joint pains from lack of vitamins indicated the slow onset of scurvy. It would all be part of her disease that she slept badly. It is possible that she was suffering symptoms of clinical depression in which energy decreases. Physical illness and a harsh life had now changed her totally from the optimistic, tomboyish girl with flowing dark hair who set out jauntily for a pioneering life at Corongo Peak. Yet her loyalty to Dave, who accepted her as his partner in this enterprise, makes her loath to let him down and leave. She continues bravely:

> Good rains fortunately put a little fresh life into me. The tanks filled, the grass grew with its usual quickness, and the flocks soon regained condition. Gormly arrived and the two men held a conference as to the best course to pursue. I was sleeping even worse and the pains were worse and my hair started to come away in handfuls. They could see that my health was breaking under the strain, and both were agreed that they would never be able to sell out to better advantage. They felt that if they missed this chance they might not get another like it for a couple of years more and so they decided to get out while the going was good. And I was inwardly glad to think I might soon be able to say good-bye to Corongo Peak.
>
> As soon as Gormly got back to Wagga he set things moving with the agents, who got into touch with a man named Attenborough who had come from Melbourne to Wagga in search of grazing land. After a full inspection of the two blocks, tanks, sheep, etc., Mr Attenborough decided to buy us out, lock, stock and barrel, as they say, and the sale was completed. Gormly and Dave were well satisfied with the price obtained.

What would Dave and Martha Cox do now? Martha goes on:

Meanwhile my mother, now in her fifties, and my brothers had sold the property at The Billabong, and had gone cattle-raising in Queensland.

Dave and I made up our minds to try our luck in Queensland too. We had been kept informed of my family's experience there while we were at Corongo Peak and they wrote that it was useless to think of taking sheep up there as the dingoes proved too serious a problem. David proposed that we go up to Queensland and see what the country was like. If my mother and brothers could make good money farming cattle in Queensland, there was no reason why we should not do the same.

I asked about the blacks. David assured me that the blacks were all right if you treated them with a little consideration. He added, 'They haven't wiped your folks out, have they? Some settlers start off by pumping lead into the poor devils, and only then wonder why their cattle were speared and folks got killed.'

So we packed our household effects into that old tarpaulin covered Yankee wagon and headed off.

Our way lay west at first to Wilcannia on the Darling River, then slowly over sandhill country north till we crossed the border in the north-west corner of New South Wales. We had a team of twelve good horses. We halted after a long trek and camped out in the wilds of Queensland. There was plenty of coarse feed with cotton-bush and saltbush which the horses seemed to fancy. Having rested a few days, we pushed along through the strange bush, steering for my brothers' property[11] where at length we arrived, delighted to end such a tiring journey.

It was a joy for me to be with my dear folks once again. We rested there for a week or so. Life seemed to begin all over again with my mother and my brothers around me. We talked over old days when I'd been a happy girl full of life and spirit and eager to have a farm of my own. I knew that many brave women had gone out into the wilderness with their men, resolved to overcome all hardships, worked themselves to the bone and ruined their health. I hadn't thought it would happen to me.

Dave and my brothers had long talks over our prospects in Queensland. They had been cattle-raising there for some time, and were able to give my husband good advice. We had a fair amount of cash in hand, and it was now only necessary to find good land and obtain stock to put on it. By now I was feeling stronger.

My brothers had two good Aboriginal servants, who they had named Jimmy and Judy. We became very friendly with the pair of them. When at length Dave had made a tour of inspection of the country and had secured two ten-mile pastoral leases, and we were about to make a start for our new home, my brothers offered to let us take Jimmy and Judy with us as interpreters, should any blacks appear, as well as being able to assist with the work on the place. Judy was a fine help in the house, and I was glad to see that she was eager to come away with us. Jimmy turned out to be a very good stockman.

It took us a good many miles of travel to reach our new home after leaving my brother's place. We settled about 90 miles from Charleville. Dave located a freshwater spring in a rocky basin a foot or two in depth in a knoll which afforded sufficient water for domestic use and for the horses. The spring seemed permanent and clear. We called one block 'Chester', and the other 'Woodbine'.

We were now in the wilds of Queensland with some twenty square miles of rough country at our disposal. We had no roof to shelter us and no furniture beyond the few things we had been able to stow away in the wagon. We had been so long on our journey from Corongo Peak that our rations were running low when we reached our leases. It was not a very cheerful prospect for me, being so far away from civilisation and camping once more in the heat of the wagon until we could build another hut and with no vegetable garden until I could make one. So there we were back to damper, salt beef and dripping.

David was worried about the future. But I told him we had roughed it before and supposed we could rough it again. He was concerned that it wasn't much of a place to bring me to and I hadn't been in good health for some time – perhaps the right thing would be to take me back to my mother's and leave me there for twelve months and give the game a try-out by himself?

I felt guilty about letting him down with my share of the work. All I wished for was a little more strength to carry me along. I tired easily and was just not the same woman who went out to Corongo Peak so full of enthusiasm. All that work and worry had taken it out of me.

Dave had to go to Charleville for supplies to carry us along. He greased the trap and got things ready for the Charleville trip on Wednesday morning, taking Jimmy in case he ran across some blacks.

We were told there were some pretty wild tribes in the Queensland bush and it would take him a week to get back.

I must confess that my heart trembled within me when I saw the wagon disappear from sight in the grey-green of the bush. David's words with regard to the possibility of encountering hostile blacks on his journey came back to my mind. If there might be danger in that direction what about me, left in the wilderness with poor elderly helpless Judy? I had not spoken to Dave of my own fear, lest it upset his plans and I didn't wish to make things harder for him.

In spite of her weakened state, Martha's courage and determination shine through. She must have been constantly aware that medical help was over a hundred miles away and it would take at least a week by covered wagon to reach a doctor.

We were there to rough it, Dave had said, and it would not do for me to cave in right at the start of a new adventure. So I choked back my fears, as best I could, and tried not to think of the pain in my knees and elbows. I turned my attention to the camp, trying to make things more ship-shape with good old Judy's help.

That night Judy roasted a snake she had caught for supper. She begged me to eat a bit of the flesh, which, truth to tell, was as white as cooked eel. Needless to say, I declined Judy's tempting offer.

The night closed on us and I was dead tired. Life must go on I told myself. I lifted my sleepy children up into the wagon and, climbing in myself, was soon asleep. Fortunately that night passed without incident.

I awoke at dawn the next morning to see Judy lighting the fire with dry bark and sticks. I watched her through a hole in the canvas. Gazing across the bush towards a clearing, she saw a large party of blacks armed with spears approaching. Dropping her bundle of sticks she uttered a cry, and running quickly to the tail of the wagon, screamed to me to come quickly. I looked where she was pointing and saw black forms moving forward in the timber. I felt weak in the limbs. I did not know what to do and thought only of my sleeping children, who were just beginning to stir. What if the blacks should murder them and me, loot the wagon and take Judy away with them? David would never find us then. But I knew this was not time to faint or think of possible horrors to come.

Determined to protect the children, I leaped down from the wagon. Knowing that the blacks dread guns, I seized a longish smooth stick lying at the fire, and wrapping the greater part of it round with one of Dave's old coats, I leaned it against a wheel of the waggon and returned to comfort the little ones.

On came the blacks, fully fifty of them, brandishing their spears and nullahs, and uttering wild yells. My heart almost ceased to beat. They came nearer and their yells frightened little Joe, who began to cry. I felt that we were doomed and started to pray. The mercy of God was upon us, for the next moment Judy thrust her head in at the back and cried, 'No be afraid Martha. That fella black people belong my tribe. They woan hurt you Martha. I go yabber longa them blackfella, tellem you good fella longa me.'

Up they swept while Judy went out to meet them. While she talked to them they calmed down and dropped their weapons. I asked Judy to tell them to go away. Seeing them doubtful I called Judy back to the wagon and gave her Dave's tobacco to give them and to ask them again to go away.

How their eyes sparkled when they saw the tobacco. Judy broke the thin sticks in two and gave each of them a piece. Picking up their weapons, they made off into the bush and disappeared from sight. Judy informed me that her tribe were on their way to Pittagaroo for their annual corroboree. I had heard of hostile tribes along Cooper's Creek (which was no great distance away), and had originally believed they must be from there. The shock made me vomit and I was head-achey for the rest of the day. What a mercy it was that we had brought Judy along.

Meanwhile, Dave had left Jimmy to guard their camp while he completed his journey to Charleville. On his return, he found that Jimmy had been menaced by another very hostile group of Aborigines. Dave threatened them with his gun and they ran away – much to Jimmy's relief. He was more afraid of his fellow Aborigines than he was of David.

After her husband's return, Martha continues her story:

During the next month my health broke down completely. My weak condition reacted upon my baby. As we were over one hundred miles from medical aid, there was nothing for it but to give in. David drove me and the little ones back to my brothers' place, leaving Jimmy and Judy in charge of our things.

Martha's brothers later brought back to their property the faithful Judy and Jimmy, together with the wagon and goods the Cox's had had to leave behind. Martha describes how when she reached her brothers' place she:

> ... had to take to bed for a fortnight. My mother cared for and weaned the baby. Soon we were able to start for Melbourne, taking my younger sister, Priscilla, with us to help us through.

David chose the longer route to Melbourne rather than Sydney, as they could follow the Darling and other rivers and be assured of water. The route to Sydney meant transversing large tracts of land between the rivers and the Great dividing Range. Martha's 'nerves' were symptomatic of her illness. Her physical symptoms included joint pains, weakness and fainting, and she was suffering from skin flaking away on face and hands, tender gums and hair loss. In the last stages of scurvy sufferers bleed from hair follicles and develop large black bruises beneath the skin from the tiniest knock. Her menstrual periods may well have stopped. At this time, fertile women gave birth on average every two years but Martha's cycle of birth was probably interrupted by deprivation of vitamins C and B. Just as she gives us no details of her childbirth experiences, so she does not dwell on her painful symptoms. But it is evident she was seriously ill and even she acknowledged 'there was nothing for it but to give in'. The journey to Melbourne was 800 miles in searing heat, travelling in a double-seated buggy.[12] This is how she describes it:

> ... there I was, a sick woman with a young child as well as a freshly weaned baby to feed and without a drop of milk most of the time.
>
> It is a marvel that I did not lose my baby. I had none of those special nourishing preparations for infants, no soothing syrups out there in the land of the Never-Never in the middle of nowhere. I fed the baby on sops [bread and water], arrowroot or cornflour, mixed with milk, whenever we could get it, which was seldom.
>
> On that nightmare journey little Joe, Priscilla, David, myself and the baby slept beneath the buggy at night, or beside the camp fire if a cold snap came. It was risky for a woman. Drovers or bushrangers

passed by while we were sleeping. Some unfortunate women had their husbands held to ransom with a gun while the men had their way with their wives and daughters so I stayed quiet as a mouse while the drovers passed by.

Several times, when the sun was at its highest, I nearly fainted from weakness in that awful heat on the road. Dave and Priscilla had to lay me down under a cotton bush to rest and revive before I could go on.

At last we struck a coach at a wayside inn just before we reached Wilcannia. Dave put us aboard and left the buggy and horses at the inn.

At Wilcannia I had to rest for a week before I could continue. Then on we went by coach to Hay, where we met with great kindness and consideration at the hands of the landlord of our hotel, who gave us a letter of introduction to a hotel keeper in Melbourne.

We left a week later, crossing the Murray River at Echuca, where we took a train for Melbourne and I lost no time in consulting Dr Fitzgerald, one of the leading doctors. I felt very ill and weak the morning David took me to see him. I was disappointed to find that doctor gruff in manner. He told me that my system was completely run down with the hardships I had been through and the lack of nourishing food, especially green vegetables and pure water and insisted it would take some time to recover my health.

'If you take your wife back into the wilds again you'll soon have to bury her there,' Dr Fitzgerald warned my husband. The doctor prescribed medicine and gave strict instructions that I was not to travel for some time.

So I remained in Melbourne with Priscilla and the children and David went back to get the buggy, intending to travel across country to join us at my sister Olivia's place near The Ten Mile later.

At the end of a month, my health having somewhat improved we left Melbourne on Cobb and Co's coach bound for Albury and from there to my sister Olivia's home at Germanton [Holbrook].

I was overjoyed at returning to civilisation once more. Coronga Peak had been bad enough but the wilds of Queensland and that terrible journey had almost finished me. My husband was feeling the strain and was also far from well but managed to pull through. He had brought the buggy and our few possessions safely from out Wilcannia way and it was a great joy to me that we were all united once more.

The old Cox homestead was at Livingstone Gully, near Wagga. David and his sister, the late Mrs James Gormly, had been born at Tumut but the rest of the children (from Mr. Cox senior's second marriage) first saw the light of day at the old homestead at Livingstone Gully.

David's mother was well advanced in years and in failing health. Dave had been anxious about her condition for some time. So, after staying a while at my sister's place, Dave drove us down to the old family homestead at Livingstone Gully. That good old lady [Martha's mother-in-law] was looking very feeble, but was delighted to see her son again after such a long absence. We were not privileged to have her long, however, for she grew weaker each day, and soon she passed away.

By now I was sufficiently recovered to take up my domestic chores once more. Dave cast his eyes around for a piece of suitable country available for selection and found one on Murraguldrie Creek, a few miles from Humula. Dave's brother, Laurence, owned a property on Kyeamba, nine or ten miles away and had married my sister, Agnes, and so things fitted in nicely from a family point of view.

In 1880 we made a start on a property we named 'Woodburn' where David took up 640 acres. Later we got 320 acres in addition. We also bought an adjoining farm of 150 acres soon afterwards, and these, with pre-leases, gave us over 3000 acres of country. Rough and hilly it was, to a great extent, and heavily timbered, but the flats were suitable for cultivation, and, best of all, we had no worries about water so there was no tank-sinking to pay for. The rainfall ranged from 20 to 25 inches per annum, and we felt that, now, at long last, we might be able to build a permanent home. Our previous undertakings had been more like gambling experiments but now we would make ourselves a real home at last.

As usual, great trees had to be grubbed and burnt off, or hauled away out of the road before we secured a clearing for our home following ringbarking and constant suckering off the big trees. The biggest cost, (after our new and commodious house was built, the home I had dreamed of owning for so long) was our fencing. This ran into a lot of money for wire. Outback we practically did no fencing at all, but here, owing to closer settlement on smaller areas it was compulsory, or there would have been constant boxing [mixing of stock] and trespassing. Some of the hill country was extremely rough, but it suited the sheep, being high and dry and sheltered, more or less, in the cold weather. As far as the living and general conditions were concerned we were better off than before, and I was gradually growing stronger again.

'Plenty of green vegetables and the best spring water you can get,' the Melbourne doctor had impressed upon me. Now, at long last, I would have both. David fenced in a good vegetable patch with three wires and a top rail, and I soon had it under cultivation. What a change to see green cabbages and lettuce and other vegetables, not forgetting good potatoes, flourishing in plenty. Those vegetables and that spring water just about saved my life, and enabled me to live long past the allotted span – I passed my 84th milepeg[13] of life in April last (1937).

David stocked up with a thousand merino ewes. The lambing ran to eighty per cent and the flock settled down and was doing well. However, when mustering came, David was surprised and disappointed to find only 500 lambs. We had branded with an earmark, Dave hated the idea of fire branding, although it was really necessary. However things went better with the next lambing, and we had no further worry in the matter of loss of stock.

My third child, Frederick (Andrew Frederick), was born in 1882, Louis (David Louis) in 1885, and Margaret Clare was born in Wagga in 1890. Our Joseph was now a big strapping lad of 16 years, well able to help his father about the place. The seasons were fairly good, an improvement on what we had experienced. The lambing was mostly good and our flocks increased until we received quite a tidy cheque in wool proceeds every year and the nearer railway communications helped us considerably.

Wagga was a fine business town within easy reach of us, even before the coming of the motor car. There was no slipping away then from a farm to get a supply of goods before breakfast and being back by noon. It took us a whole day with a buggy over shocking roads. In wet spells one would often see loaded wagons covered with tarpaulins, waiting at camps for a week for the road to dry and harden enough for them to reach Wagga.

We made all our own candles, soaps, jams and preserves and raised our own poultry and eggs, our milk and butter. We killed our own beef and mutton, so there was little to buy as regards food supplies, and, as for vegetables, we always had more than we needed. I made all our bread. Apart from shoes which I found I could not make, there was little to buy in the matter of household requirements, while there was mostly something to realise upon for a bit of cash. Industrious people were able to 'make a do of it', and save money on their properties, especially when the seasons were good. There was always plenty of work, but we bush folks who had pluck and wished to get on didn't care a button about the backbreaking toil. We were hard at work early and late. Now we and the children had our health and strength back, we even found time to make a bit of simple social fun and recreation with the neighbours. I loved our home and our free bush life and little thought it would ever change.

The first of our misfortunes was the death of my youngest sister Priscilla. Only the year before[14] she had married Mr Meredith and gone to live at Albury.

Our dear mother had been brought down from Queensland by my brother, as she was advancing in years, and wished to be amongst us all in the Riverina. She stayed first with one married daughter and then another, but she spent most of her time with Agnes. Mother passed away at the residence of my sister, Agnes (Mrs Laurence Cox) at Tea-tree Creek, Kyeamba. She had been a good, devoted mother to us all. Mother's birthday was on May 24, the date of Queen Victoria's birthday, and she would have been 70 years of age had she lived a month longer. She was buried in Wagga cemetery.

And now I come to the part of my story which is hardest of all to tell, the death of my beloved husband. Fifty-nine years of age seems early for such a strong, and apparently robust life as his to terminate. It was a cruel blow to which I found it hard to reconcile myself; we had been partners in life and all our undertakings. Dave died in September, the spring of the year. He was away on 'Kookoona', the property we had recently purchased and he had temporarily moved there during the lambing season. Fully 90 per cent of the lambs lived, the best we had so far had. Dave had taken our sons Joe and Louis up to help him with the work and written to tell me that 'I will go into Wagga on Saturday morning and buy a pony for Clare. Tell her I am bringing the pony home for her.' Clare [their youngest daughter] was nine years of age. She was a good rider, and the thought of the promised pony filled her with joy.

But on that very Saturday, David suffered a fatal paralytic stroke and was taken into a private hospital in Wagga. My old friend, James

Gormly, informed me by telegram and sent his son to Currawarna with a vehicle to bring me into town.

I sat by his hospital bed for two days before my husband was able to recognise me. He was unable to speak (nor was he ever to utter a single word to me, one side of his body being completely paralysed). I did not leave his beside for any length of time. On the ninth day he passed peacefully away. On September 25, 1898, my husband was laid to rest in the Wagga cemetery.

Now I was all alone facing the problems of life on the land with five children, three boys and two girls.

Joseph was now 25 years of age, Mary Ann 21, Frederick 17, Louis 14, and Clare 9. All of them were devoted to me and eager to do their best, so that although sorely stricken I had my children to console me and help me to struggle on. The management of the property was left in the hands of three executors until Clare should reach the age of 21, when everything was to revert to me to manage as I thought best. In the meantime I was to live wherever I liked, and educate the children as I wished to. It all seemed unreal. I was carried along as though in the grip of a terrible dream. It seemed so hard that after planning more intense farming operations at Kookoona and a move there David should be so suddenly and so unexpectedly stricken.

There was no time to sit and grieve. I *had* to be strong for all of us. The whole of the estate was to be under the general direction of the three executors of my husband's will for the time being but I had to do much of the running of the properties. Clare was being educated by an excellent governess. She would reach her majority in a little over 12 years and when she turned 21 I would have a free hand to make my own decision as to the disposal or retention of any portion of the estate. I was able to exercise a certain personal authority in conjunction with the executors, and certainly stood up for my own judgement where I thought it was to the advantage of the properties.

I was sad to leave the home we had built. But it was now vital we took up residence on 'Kookoona,' our Currawarna farm, so that with the hard work of us all, we could build it up. My sons worked splendidly. No doubt they felt that it was up to them to show their mettle now that their father was gone, and so much depended upon their efforts. Now and again I found time to slip up to the Woodburn property to see how things were going along there and visit the old homestead and my garden, now much neglected. When I found it necessary to complain of defects in the management I did not hesitate to speak my mind to the executors.

In the spring of 1904 good rains followed winter and there was a lush growth of grass everywhere in September and October, promising ample feed for the summer. The country looked a picture and stock was rolling fat but the grass ripened and dried under the fierce summer heat. Christmas was so hot we could eat little of our Christmas meal. The standing harvest crops were a source of worry. What if a spark should ignite a fire? What about my much loved home in case of bushfire? I tried to drive such thoughts from my mind, but each day brought greater heat and glare.

The last day of 1904 with its New Year's Eve associations was an awful day of heat and scorching wind. James Angel, one of our neighbours at Woodburn, had driven down to Wagga in the morning to attend to some business. The heat was almost insufferable. The thermometer registered 112 degrees at 2 pm, but the wind sweeping up from the north-west to the south-east made matters more trying. Mr Angel, with his sharp eyes, was one of the first to notice smoke in the north west. He knew what that meant with so much dry grass a foot in height. Mr Angel put his horses into the buggy and started back for Humula at a fast pace. He had 42 miles to cover, but his thoughts were not merely for his own safety, but also for the safety of his neighbours. He yelled out a warning to each and all as he raced by, telling them of the onrushing fire. It was dark when he reached home and sent warning messages to other land holders in the neighbourhood.

At midnight, as New Year arrived, so did the bushfire. The dryness of the country and the excessive growth of withered grass fed one of the most disastrous fires ever known in the State of New South Wales. A terrific gale fanned the flames and the fire travelled at a speed of 15 miles per hour in spite of the efforts of men to save their homes and sheds.

I and the rest of the family were at our Kookoona property, near Currawana, when the fire broke out. Fortunately it did not cross our side of the river, but we knew the Woodburn property must be right in the course of the onrushing flames. I felt my heart sink at this next dire misfortune. What of the poor cattle and horses up there? They would all perish. An old acquaintance was keeping a friendly eye on the property, said he would do what he could but little could be done by one man against a galloping fire. Our neighbours would be worked to death trying to save their own stock and homestead. The fate of our family homestead and the stock was too dreadful to think about.

It was the worst fire ever experienced throughout the State of New South Wales. Many declared that the intensity of the fire was not only due to the gale behind the flames, but to the phosphorus distributed by the rabbit poisoning that had been carried on for years. Even in broad daylight, when matches were struck, they burned with a white flame. We were afraid for both properties.

Woodburn adjoined Mr James Angel's property. Joe raced off on horseback to see what could be done to retrieve any stock that might have escaped and soon discovered what ravages the fire had wrought. Our neighbour had done his best to safeguard our horses and cattle by rounding them up into the stockyard, thinking, as the ground was fairly bare around the yard, that the flames would not approach it. But he could do nothing for our unfortunate sheep. The fire roared up as a rolling wave of flame. Red hot fragments of bark and timber were born by the wind through scorching air, across roads and over streams, setting up fresh lines of fire which advanced on that disastrous New Year's Day, 1905.

Joe found not one stick of our home at Woodburn left. Flames had made a clean sweep of the place. Here and there the iron frame of a bedstead, or the remains of a sewing machine, arose above the ashes. Not a woolshed or outhouse remained, all our farm machinery destroyed, all our fences gone. For me there was a double blow. All the labour, all the cost of raising up a comfortable home after years of patient waiting had been wasted. Like hundreds of others in a similar plight, we were not insured. Tragically some of our neighbours were burned to death while others narrowly escaped with their lives by rushing to ponds and creeks, and submerging themselves while the flames swept over them, often crouching in the water beside kangaroos and other bush creatures.

One corner of our paddock was blackened and the fence I had helped build, nothing but a row of stumps. In piles, five or six deep, lay 1400 charred bodies of a flock of prime fat wethers [castrated rams] for which I had recently refused 15/- per head in cash. Those poor panic-stricken animals had clambered over each other desperate to escape the flames. (At the shearing a few months earlier, the tally had been 3600). Now only 1600 wethers, less than half our stock, remained. Fortunately the cattle and horses in the stockyard escaped, though a few of the young cattle died after we got them back. Those sheep that had survived were now faced with starvation, as not one blade of grass was left to graze upon. Joe got in touch with me and told me that he would have to take the sheep away to grass as soon as he could as they would soon become too weak to travel. I discussed terms with a neighbouring grass-owner for agistment, as we had as much stock at Currawarna as the place would carry.

Joe went round and notified the neighbours of his intention to take our sheep away and asked them what he should do about 'boxed' sheep [Sheep mixed with those from other properties.] Not one raised the slightest objection. 'Take 'em away, Joe, quick as you can, and get them to grass; we can easily whack up [settle up] afterwards,' they said.

I was now faced with the onerous task of reconstruction at Woodburn and a heavy outlay of money as sheds and fences had to be replaced. My bankers proved most kind and considerate. So the hard job was tackled, and in the course of time most of the damage was repaired and I could pay off the debt. I had been through rough experiences but that fire was quite the worst I had known.

It took time to put things back in the flourishing state they had been in before the fire. Twelve years passed by. Martha resumes:

At last my youngest daughter, Clare, was of age, and no longer needed the executors who acted as her guardians. Now the total responsibility of managing both properties was on my shoulders. The seasons were fairly good, I had learned a great deal about farm management, enjoyed the help and companionship of my children after my husband's death but, of course, in the natural order of things they all married with only my eldest son, Joseph, remaining single.

I had completed life's allotted span of three score years and ten ... My children were making their own way in life. They had been so good and so devoted that I resolved to provide for them before the time of the final parting came. Before making my final decision I consulted with my banker who approved of the plan and gave me sound advice in all important particulars. I called the children to a family conference, and told them what I proposed to do. It certainly afforded me pleasure and ease of mind.

My next step was to dispose of the Woodburn property with all the stock it carried. In the final disposition of my estate, Kookoona went to Frederick and Louis, while to each of the other children was apportioned cash in equal shares. I managed to arrange everything and it was good to feel myself free from business cares at last.

Martha went to live in Wagga Wagga with her eldest son Joseph in a comfortable home in Wollundry Avenue. She was 93 when she died, outliving her eldest son by three years. The death certificate gives the cause as 'arteriosclerosis' leading to a fatal heart attack. She was buried on 10 March 1947, in the Cox family tomb at the Roman Catholic Cemetery, Wagga Wagga, beside her husband and children.

I have read at least a hundred journals of pioneer women but Martha Caldwell Cox's account of her life is certainly one of the most remarkable. Her fortitude, resourcefulness and endurance through natural disasters are distinctly Australian attributes. These memoirs are her true memorial.

# CHAPTER FOUR

## Dr Dagmar Berne
*(1865–1900)*
*and*
## Dr Constance Stone
*(1856–1902)*
### FEMALE PIONEERS IN MEDICINE

Today around half the students in Australian medical schools are female: many of them receive the highest marks as well as student prizes and awards. How ironic then that Australia's first women doctors were despised by their male colleagues for their lack of intellect and had to struggle to obtain hospital residencies and registration once they had qualified. But once women finally *did* manage to register as doctors, many had *outstanding* careers in medicine, working calmly under stress to save the lives of thousands, in peacetime and during wartime.

It is sad to discover that among this bright and dedicated group of pioneer women doctors how few received the honours accrued by their male peers. While Dagmar Berne is commemorated by the Dagmar Berne Medal, which is awarded to the top female medical student at the University of Sydney, neither Dr Constance Stone nor Dr Lucy Gullett have an award or a statue in their memory. These remarkable women doctors were the driving forces that founded the first all-women hospitals in Melbourne and Sydney, designed expressly for women who could not afford medical treatment.

The history of European medicine shows that male prejudice against female doctors is, relatively speaking, a modern phenomenon. *Diseases of Women*, one of the earliest texts on gynaecology and obstetrics pre-dated the Italian Renaissance. It was written before Gutenburg's printing press was invented by a *female* academic named Trotula, who taught medicine at Salerno University in the eleventh century. Trotula's text was written for nuns and abbesses as they acted as midwives and obstetricians.[1] As the rich began to demand physicians who specialised in delivering babies, men took this up as a profession. From the fourteenth century obstetrics and gynaecology passed under the control of male physicians and 'barber' surgeons who lined their hoods with fur and set up colleges and professional associations to regulate just who could deliver babies and charge for their services.[2] They insisted women had to pass an examination run by six male surgeons and six male midwives or *accoucheurs* to deliver any baby, rich or poor and soon it became the accepted wisdom that *men* were in charge of healing women's bodies and delivering their babies.

In 1874, Dr Henry Maudsley, writing in the London publication *Reproductive Medicine* argued that women should not be allowed to enter the profession of medicine. He declared that their skulls were smaller than those of men, therefore they lacked the necessary brain power to study and could become sterile if they attempted something so difficult. Maudsley (in his day a well-known doctor with an interest in psychiatry) also claimed that if women were allowed to practise medicine, their menstrual cycle would make them 'irrational' during their monthly periods. He described how women were *far* too delicate to deal with the drunks, prostitutes and raving tertiary syphilitics, who filled the outpatients departments of major cities.

The influx of men into gynaecology was difficult for women in the prudish nineteenth and early twentieth centuries as many women experienced embarrassment discussing any medical complaint that occurred 'below the waistline'.[3] At the time of Federation modesty demanded that women's legs and ankles had to be kept covered. Amelia 'Bloomer' bloomers for women cyclists were considered an outrage. The Victorians even swathed the legs on pianos out of modesty. Therefore problems of an 'intimate nature' such as vaginal discharge from thrush or cystitis referred as 'uterine catarrh' could not be discussed with a male doctor. Vaginal and pelvic examinations were a source of deep embarrassment for both doctor *and* patient. Modesty dictated that women remained fully dressed while the gynaecologist poked and prodded away under the long skirts, unable to see anything at all. One result was the large number of women who died of untreated cancers before women were admitted to medical practice and could examine them.

To understand the struggles of Australian female pioneers of medicine it is necessary to know something about the woman doctors who encouraged them to seek medical registration at a time when this was hard for a woman. Dr Elizabeth Blackwell (1821–1910), whose family emigrated from Britain to New York, when she was sixteen, was the first woman in the world to register as a doctor. She described how 'the whole idea of winning a doctor's degree assumed the aspect of a great moral struggle and the fight possessed immense attraction for me'. Elizabeth Blackwell founded the New York Infirmary for Women and Children to treat poor and disadvantaged women and to train women doctors before returning to England to help other women in their fight to qualify in medicine. One of the girls she talked to at a public lecture was Elizabeth Garrett (Garrett Anderson after marriage), bored by an idle life at home. Dr Blackwell's example changed her life.

In 1870 Dr Elizabeth Garrett Anderson (1836–1917) became the second woman in the world to register as a doctor but was refused entry to a British medical school due to her gender. She had the necessary funds to qualify as a doctor in Paris. Having struggled herself she was very sympathetic to the difficulties placed in the path of Australia's first women medical students like Dagmar Berne and Constance Stone.[3]

Dr Garrett only gained the right to practise medicine in England through legal advice that a loophole in the constitution of the Society of London Apothecaries (who used the word 'person' rather than 'man' in their admission regulations) could admit her as a doctor. The Society found they could not legally prove that Dr Elizabeth Garrett was not a 'person' so was forced to admit her as a practising doctor. In 1874, Dr Garrett and Dr Sophia Jex-Blake founded the London School of Medicine for Women. Remembering her own experiences of male prejudice, Dr Garrett gave pioneer women medical students suffering prejudice, like Dagmar Berne, jobs in the first London women's hospital at a time when such training positions, essential to secure medical registration, were denied to women in Australia.[4] Constance Stone would also seek Dr Garrett's help when she qualified in medicine and surgery but could not obtain registration in Australia

Male doctors defended their monopoly on healing by insisting that childbirth (then conducted without anaesthesia) was so gruesome that women would faint if they had to watch children being born – a strange statement, considering that women had to *undergo* childbirth. The Vice-Chancellors and Deans of Sydney and Melbourne University Medical Schools were totally opposed to women practising medicine of any kind. They said so, *very* loudly.

In the early 1880s, women were admitted to Arts and other courses at Sydney and Melbourne Universities, but ultra-conservative professors in the Faculty of Medicine still refused to admit females. By 1884, Sydney University's Medical School caved in and admitted women from other disciplines to its courses. In 1887, Melbourne University's Medical School received applications from seven young women studying for Arts degrees.[5] Next women's right to study medicine was put to a vote and carried by a majority of ten. The Vice-Chancellor voted against admitting any female students to the medical school, claiming that male students as well as medical staff would be embarrassed if women dissected naked bodies in front of men and that 'decent young women' would be embarrassed at lectures dealing with 'intimate parts of the human body'.

The Dean of Sydney University's Medical School, Professor Thomas Anderson Stuart, argued that women should not become doctors. Women, he claimed, were physically and mentally unsuited to the physically and mentally demanding life that medicine entailed. Facing pressure from more enlightened colleagues, the Dean was forced to admit that Sydney's Faculty of Medicine had one excellent female medical student, a Miss Dagmar Berne, who had been studying medicine for two years and whose 'presence had neither inconvenienced nor embarrassed male students or teaching staff'.[6]

Professor Anderson Stuart was out of date in his thinking. Surgery and on occasions childbirth had been harrowing before the introduction of chloroform in the 1840s for doctors and patients but childbirth changed dramatically after the invention of anaesthetics and the introduction of more sanitary conditions in operating theatres. Before anaesthetics were used, patients were primed with laudanum (opium) or alcohol, strapped down on the table and subjected to the surgeon's knife or bone saw, their screams muffled by a gag or leather strap on which they were told to bite hard. Conditions were insanitary – sawdust was used to catch blood and the bandages covering amputated organs and changed only once a week. Operating theatres and hospital wards reeked of putrid flesh, urine and excrement, and bed linen was rarely changed. The use of carbolic as a disinfectant, coupled with Semmelweiss's discovery in Vienna that infection was reduced if doctors and medical students washed their hands before examining wounds and pregnant women, would change the entire practice of medicine.[7]

From 1891 onwards, a handful of determined and dedicated women managed to get themselves admitted to medical schools in Melbourne and Sydney,[8] and eventually, decades later, admitted to study medicine in other Australian states. (The Medical School of the University of

Western Australia was only founded in 1957 and most other Australian medical schools in the 1960s.)[9]

Australia's first female medical students were initially awarded good marks by male professors. But gradually it became apparent that however hard they worked, they would not be allowed to qualify. At Sydney University, Professor Anderson Stuart consistently failed *all* women medical students in their final year, however good their previous marks had been, effectively preventing all women from graduating in medicine for years. Only in 1893, when the professor went on leave overseas, was the first woman allowed to graduate. For years Sydney University Medical School applied a hidden quota system for female medical students (as did many British medical schools) although this was always denied.

Lack of finance or any scholarships for women ensured they gave up and entered a different course. Some, like Constance Stone and Dagmar Berne, had to travel overseas to gain a degree, which would admit them to practising medicine. Even then many teaching hospitals flatly refused to accept female graduates and effectively banned them from the wards where the most valuable experience was gained.

Dr Kate Campbell would become one of Australia's most respected pioneer paediatricians and save the lives of hundreds of Australian babies. Her efforts would be honoured by the award of DBE (Dame of the British Empire) but when she was newly qualified, she faced enormous prejudice against women in medicine. Dr Campbell described the prejudice:

> At the end of our course there was fierce competition for residentships. The Alfred Hospital *refused* to take any girls at all, even the brightest. Always the same excuse, if any of us women protested: 'We haven't any toilet arrangements!' the administrators would say. Women were admitted to the Melbourne Hospital but somehow 'accidentally' given all the dirty work ... Only men were assigned to work for 'leading lights' in medicine ... There was no social life ... At night, you might have a confinement, get to bed for half an hour and an hour later be called out again.[10]

In order to get a job, women like Constance Stone ran their own all-women hospitals. Many pioneer women doctors never married, or, if they did, often decided against having children because their work was so demanding. Those who could afford the time for raising children usually had mothers, aunts or unmarried sisters who took their place in the family – or else they simply gave up medicine.

All doctors before World War I worked eighteen to twenty-hour shifts, day in, day out. All hospital residents, male and female, were paid a pittance and regarded as being lucky to be there at all as the only entry into medicine lay through getting good references from their consultants. Female residents were paid even less than their male counterparts although women doctors worked hour for hour with their male colleagues and were 'on call' virtually round the clock.

## Dagmar Berne

Dagmar Berne was the first woman to study medicine in Australia. Today, the Dagmar Berne prize is presented each year to the female medical graduate obtaining the highest marks in final year, from money donated by Dagmar's mother after her premature death. Few of those to whom it is awarded know the sad story which lies behind this coveted medal.[11]

The short life of Dagmar Berne held the promise of a brilliant career, but was blighted by male prejudice, ultimately responsible for her death. A photograph taken when she was a medical student reveals Dagmar as blonde and typically Scandinavian in feature, with an open face and candid eyes. She had an equally attractive, caring personality and was universally liked by her fellow students at Sydney University.

Dagmar's Danish-born father had emigrated to New South Wales and died when she was young while attempting to save a drowning man from the Bega River. Her mother married again; her second husband, a pastoralist, died when Dagmar was in her teens. Her mother then took her eight children (Dagmar was the eldest daughter) to Sydney, where she insisted that her girls as well as her boys should attend private school. Dagmar was sent to the exclusive Springfield Ladies' College in Potts Point. Here marriage and motherhood were considered of prime importance and the curriculum specialised in dancing, deportment, conversational French, needlework and other handicrafts. To Dagmar, who was studious by nature and fascinated by science, the social ambitions of most of the girls, who dreamed of debutante balls, wedding dresses and wealthy husbands, were entirely foreign. She spent only two terms at the College before letting her mother know that she thought the fees were too high for the 'little amount of real learning that I am getting'. She begged to be allowed to study chemistry with a private tutor, so that she could enter Sydney University, which had just opened its doors to women.

At seventeen, Dagmar left school and studied science privately. The following year, convinced that she had failed her university entrance exam, she was so despondent that she decided to set up a private girls' school in Sydney's Tempe, aided by her sister Florence, who was only sixteen. Dagmar hoped the school would bring in some funds as well as provide education for her other sisters. Dagmar interviewed parents of potential pupils, found premises, bought desks and schoolbooks. A few days before the school opened she was astounded to receive a telegram from the Registrar of Sydney University, congratulating her on passing their entrance exam. So it was left to her younger sister, Florence, to open the school. There were six pupils, including two of their younger sisters.

Dagmar Berne arrived at Sydney University in 1885 and studied Arts for a year before she was allowed to switch to medicine. The staff of the University's Medical School were deeply divided over admitting women students. Some were in favour, but the Vice-Chancellor, Sir Henry N. McLaurin, as well as the Dean of the Medical School, Professor Thomas Anderson Stuart, both bitterly opposed the decision to admit women into medicine.

Prof. Anderson Stuart was so bigoted that he stated in public: 'I think that the proper place for a woman is in the home; the proper function for a woman is to be a man's wife, and for women to be the mothers of future generations.'[12] He had nothing against Dagmar personally. He and her other teachers found her a model student, intelligent and hard working. Fellow students described her as quiet and reserved; men admired her courage for attempting the medical course. As the eldest girl in her large family, Dagmar had many duties at home so she mixed little in university activities.

While Prof. Anderson Stuart outwardly accepted women in his medical course, inwardly he was smarting that the university authorities had forced him to accept Australia's first woman medical student. He was determined that no woman would qualify as long as *he* was in charge. Dagmar optimistically believed that, having at long last been admitted to the university Medical School, she was now on an equal footing with the male students.

At the end of her first year in medicine, Dagmar obtained Honours in Botany, Chemistry, Zoology and Anatomy, which indicated that if she continued with the same grades she would have a good medical career.

In her second year of medicine, Dagmar attended Professor Stuart's lectures. He never told her that he planned she would fail examinations he marked but this was his hidden agenda. After her outstanding success in first year exams, Dagmar was never allowed to pass another examination at Sydney University. Following exhausting weeks of study, she would seek out the examination results on the notice board. She saw men who had received far lower marks in the first year examinations achieve a pass, but somehow her name was never on the pass list. She would tell her mother in despair: 'Mama, I've failed again. I know I work hard enough, but sometimes I think it's just because they don't *want* to pass me.'

After four years of hard and intensive study at Sydney University, Dagmar finally realised that male prejudice was too strong and she would never be allowed to qualify in medicine.

In 1888, Dagmar met Britain's Dr Elizabeth Garrett Anderson, who was on a lecture tour of Australia. Dagmar explained the difficulties of her position to Dr Anderson. She told Dagmar that she had suffered from *exactly* the same prejudice in England – and won by finishing her exams abroad. She encouraged Dagmar, telling her that the battle had been won in Britain and advised her to confront the authorities who ran Sydney's Medical School in order to clarify her position and her prospects.[13] If qualifying seemed impossible she should come to London and work in Dr Anderson's all-women hospital.

Fired by Dr Garrett Anderson's support, Dagmar and her mother did confront the Vice-Chancellor. He flatly refused to help Dagmar and made it quite clear that so long as he was Vice-Chancellor *no woman would graduate in medicine.*

Dagmar now clearly realised that as long as leading authorities in the Medical School were against women qualifying she would *never* pass. The authorities reckoned she would soon become so depressed and ashamed by her continuing failure that she would abandon the course.

Sailing ten thousand miles to London seemed her only option if she wished to continue studying medicine. Dagmar was encouraged to finish her studies in London by the fact that Dr Garrett Anderson had offered her a training residency in her hospital. Dagmar's determination was strengthened by the fact that her sister Florence had had enough of running a school and also wanted to study medicine.

Mrs Berne was very supportive to the idea and agreed Dagmar and Florence should go to London. Both girls had been left a legacy and could afford to live there, provided they chose inexpensive lodgings and allowed themselves few luxuries.

Dagmar, who had a kind forgiving nature, even went to farewell the man who had failed her, Professor Thomas Anderson Stuart. After the interview, she told her family that he had been positively avuncular and begged her to give up the idea of practising medicine. 'You're far too *nice* a girl to do medicine,' he had said, patting her on the head and dismissing her. But Dagmar, undaunted, replied quietly but firmly that she was *determined* to qualify as a doctor.

Mrs Berne was unhappy at the suggestion that her daughters should transfer their entire capital to London. She advised them to take only a portion and leave the balance in Sydney, where it would earn a much better rate of interest. Both girls readily agreed.

Dagmar's years at Sydney University gained her matriculation to London University's Medical School. Florence had to sit the first year entrance exam, which she passed. The girls found cheap lodgings and lived modestly, working steadily towards their goals. In 1889 Dagmar entered the Royal Free Hospital; two years later she passed the Society of Apothecaries' exams in anatomy and physiology with flying colours. But years of poor diet, damp accommodation in a London basement and foggy, chilly winters took their toll on a girl accustomed to Sydney's warmer climate. Dagmar suffered recurring bouts of pleurisy and pneumonia; on one occasion she rose from her sickbed to sit an exam, which she passed. But her health was seriously weakened. She knew that once she had gained clinical experience she must return to the milder winters of Sydney.

In her last year of training, Dagmar received a letter from her mother informing her that their Sydney bank had failed in the financial downturn that characterised Australia in the 1890s. The girls' capital was lost, along with the rest of the Berne family money. Her brother Frederick had to leave school and was looking for work; her younger sister Eugenie was helping support the family by teaching. By this time the money the two sisters had brought to England had nearly run out. This news signalled the end of all their hopes. Florence realised that Dagmar was so near to completing her course that loss of income to support her was a tragedy. There were no government grants, no scholarships available for women to study medicine.

'There's not enough money to carry us through', Dagmar declared.

All night long, her sister's phrase haunted Florence. She realised she had teaching experience, which Dagmar did not.

The next day, without telling her sister, Florence went to an employment agency and found herself a resident job as a governess. She arranged with the bank to transfer her remaining money to Dagmar's account. Florence countered Dagmar's ensuing protests by saying that they could not let their mother down. There was only enough money for one of them to qualify as a doctor. It had to be Dagmar, who was now able to continue studying in spite of her weight loss and a persistent cough.

Dagmar finally qualified as a doctor in 1893 and went to work at the North Eastern Fever Hospital in Tottenham, just outside London, as a resident. After two years there she returned to Sydney.

On 9 January 1895, Dr Dagmar Berne registered her Diplomas from the Royal College of Physicians and Surgeons of Edinburgh, the Faculty of Physicians and Surgeons of Glasgow and the Society of Apothecaries, London, with the Registrar of the Medical Board of New South Wales. She was only the second Australian woman to register with the New South Wales Medical Board, the first being Dr Constance Stone who also had to go overseas to get her degree.

Dagmar Berne set up a practice in rooms in Macquarie Street, the most fashionable area for doctors. She worked hard to help support her mother. Her sister Eugenie, who was teaching, came to live with her. Eugenie was worried by Dagmar's pallor and her racking cough and persuaded her sister to undergo the appropriate clinical tests, which showed that she had tuberculosis.

Family friends, the Morrisseys, who owned Yarrabundie Station at Trundle, in New South Wales, suggested Dagmar should move out there to work, hoping the dry climate might halt her illness. Dagmar stayed with the Morrisseys, from whose home she continued to practise. She saw practising medicine as a vocation and would often refuse to accept fees from those she considered needy or destitute.

According to one of her patients, Mrs Long:

> Dr Berne was very frail and sick and was sometimes so weak she could hardly shake a bottle of medicine. She was still very pretty with a neat slim figure. As a doctor she was very conscientious and capable and everyone in Trundle loved and respected her, for she was so kind and took such a great interest in all her patients, especially the children. She was always very concerned in the treatment of mothers following childbirth, insisting they have plenty of rest ... before they began their ordinary domestic work again. She was probably far in advance of her time as far as this was concerned. She believed that far more women doctors were needed as women understood these things far more than any male doctor could.[14]

Dagmar Berne knew she had not long to live, but she was happy in the career she had sacrificed her own health to undertake. She did not return home in her last days but worked unselfishly right to the last, caring for her patients.

She died at midnight on 22nd August 1900, a martyr to male prejudice against women qualifying in medicine.[15]

Although baptised an Anglican, Dagmar worked tirelessly for patients of all denominations. Catholic patients and friends in Trundle presented their local Catholic Church with a pair of altar vases in her memory. Dagmar's coffin was returned to her grieving family in Sydney and she was buried in Sydney's Waverley Cemetery. The Dagmar Berne Medal ensures that her name lives on among women medical students.

## Dr Constance Stone

The first woman to be registered as a medical practitioner in Australia was Dr Constance Stone (married name Jones). Ironically this woman, who never sought publicity for her work but heroically toiled away to save the lives of others, had initially been turned down as a student by the Medical School of the University of Melbourne due to her gender because they thought she would not be strong enough to cope with medical work.

Constance was born in Hobart in 1856, the eldest child of an English mother and Welsh father, who earned a modest income as an organ builder. Constance's mother had been a governess before her marriage. Books were greatly valued in their household and Constance and her sisters were educated at home by their mother. Like so many of the Welsh, the family were keen chapel-goers and had a strong sense of the Protestant work ethic. Constance was given books but no luxuries as the Stones saved their money for their children's schooling and university, believing strongly in the power of education to transform lives. In later life, Constance Stone described her parents as 'broadminded, especially for those days. They allowed us to make up our own minds as to what we wanted to do.' One of her sisters followed her into medicine, while her brother William became a well-known engineer.

Like Dagmar Berne and other middle-class girls around the pre-Federation and Federation era, Constance Stone started her career as an untrained primary teacher, running a small family school until she was twenty-eight. But anatomy was her passion; she dreamed of becoming a doctor. By now women were admitted to all faculties of Melbourne University except medicine. Undaunted by a stiff rejection letter when she applied to the Medical Faculty at Melbourne, strong-minded Constance Stone would not take 'no' for an answer. She wrote to the Dean of the Women's Medical College in Philadelphia, an institution inspired by the example of Dr Elizabeth Blackwell. Constance enclosed copies of her teaching qualifications, asking if the Women's College would admit her. She was overjoyed when they agreed and sailed to America to study. Constance did not have the money to return to Australia so would not see her family again for many years.

In 1885 she graduated with an MD from Philadelphia's Faculty of Medicine. But at that time Philadelphia could only provide a three-year medical course. The Australian medical authorities, horrified at the thought of a woman doctor in their midst, informed Constance Stone she would need British qualifications in order to gain registration in Australia – which did not have reciprocity with America at that time.

While sitting her American finals, Constance was also enrolled at Trinity College in the University of Toronto. In 1888, the year of Australia's centennial celebrations, she was awarded first-class honours in medicine and surgery from Toronto University.

The remarkable Dr Stone was now in her early thirties. She sailed for London with two aims. First, to obtain a higher degree and her British qualifications, and second, to work with the famous Dr Elizabeth Garrett Anderson, who had by now been joined by Dr Mary Scharlieb, an outstanding surgeon. Their 'new' Women's Hospital (later the Elizabeth Garrett Anderson Hospital) was entirely staffed by women and, of course, admitted only women patients. It was considered a Mecca for women doctors all over Britain. At this unique hospital Dr Stone gained valuable insight not only into the practice of medicine but also into hospital administration. She made up her mind that one day she would found a similar hospital in Melbourne.

In 1889, Constance Stone gained her British qualifications by sitting the examination of the British Society of Apothecaries, still the only English body at that time which would grant a medical qualification to a woman (due to the 'person' rather than 'man' clause under which Dr Garrett Anderson had registered as a clinical practitioner).

The following year, Dr Stone became the first woman to be registered with an Australian Medical Board and was placed on the register in Victoria.[16] She was now one of Australia's best-qualified doctors. Fortified with this knowledge, she rented rooms in Melbourne's Collins Street, and hung up her brass plate. But it proved hard to attract paying patients, even though she charged only a minimal fee. Mainly she saw women and children. Australian working-class men felt threatened by the notion of women examining their bodies.

Constance Stone was in single-handed practice; she had to be on duty every night as well as every weekend. No male doctor would do a swap and accept clinical responsibility for her patients in return for covering for her, as men in private practice did.

However in the surgery Dr Stone's pleasant yet highly professional manner and her feminine appearance overcame much of the initial distrust felt by patients, both female and male. She was dismayed to find that so many poor families were unable to afford even the smallest fee: through contacts in the church she set up a free dispensary and clinic known as the Collingwood Free Medical Mission. At that time Collingwood was a slum area. Large numbers of people attended her clinical sessions as free patients, the only medical service available to them.

In 1893, Constance Stone was joined by her younger sister, Clara, one of the seven pioneer women who demanded the right to attend lectures at the Melbourne University Medical School, basing their demand on the fact that the rest of the University was open to them. Clara Stone became the second woman to qualify from Melbourne's Medical School. She and her sister, two remarkable women, now treated working-class women in Melbourne and its surrounding suburbs. Since they found it impossible to carry a medical bag on a bicycle, they did their rounds by horse and buggy. As so much of their work was for free medical missions, unpaid, they lacked the money to employ a full-time groom. Both sisters became expert at handling horses. Moreover, Melbourne could be dangerous; they were advised to take pistols with them during night calls in the slums.

Through her medical missionary work in slum areas for the City Mission, Constance Stone met and married the Rev. David Egryn Jones, who shared her sense of purpose. He was the Minister of St David's Welsh Church in Latrobe Street. (Dr Clara remained single for the rest of her life, believing, like so many pioneers of medicine, that it was too difficult to combine medicine and family duties.) Both the sisters ran clinics from the hall of St David's Church. They saw, without payment in their clinics, sixty women in a single day, three days a week, helped by female volunteers.

Inspired by the work of Dr Elizabeth Garrett Anderson in Britain, the Stone sisters and other newly qualified women who found it difficult to gain hospital residences decided to set up the first Australian women's hospital. They aimed to treat working-class women free of charge and to abolish the ordeal of ward rounds, where women who could not afford fees had no option but to endure examinations by physicians and their medical students, who often treated working-class women in a patronising manner. Women doctors saw how these women suffered in childbirth and sought to improve conditions for them.

Many churchmen had a patronising attitude to women, seeing childbirth in pain as the punishment meted out to Eve for feeding

Adam the apple. Male doctors who were influenced by Biblical attitudes accepted pain as part of women's lot in life. They and their pastors quoted God's words to Eve in the Book of Genesis: 'I will greatly multiply thy sorrow and thy conception: *in pain* shalt thou conceive and bring forth children'.

To combat this defeatist approach to pain and to give working-class and other women a chance of good treatment, in 1896 Melbourne's Queen Victoria Hospital was founded by twelve medically qualified women, on the instigation of Dr Constance Stone. She had seen Dr Garrett Anderson's hospital in London and wished to duplicate this dedicated approach to women's health in Australia. Now in Melbourne for the first time Australian working-class women (many too poor to pay to visit the doctor) were treated free of charge or for a tiny fee by women doctors, and if they needed it provided with contraceptive advice. This was revolutionary since in America, Margaret Sanger's pioneering family planning clinics had been raided by the police, prams and babies scattered in disarray and women attending the clinics taken to the police station.

Dr Constance Stone invited eleven other women who shared her vision for women's health services to cooperate in setting up the Women's Hospital. It was to be entirely staffed by the voluntary labour of women doctors and be known as the Queen Victoria Hospital for Women and Children. The group used Dr Constance's home as their base in order to raise funds for the new free hospital; from there they also established the Victorian Medical Women's Society. Before the establishment of free hospitals for women in Sydney and Melbourne, many male doctors flatly refused to treat poorer members of the community or the destitute and homeless unless a fee was paid in advance. There was, of course, no state or commonwealth medical insurance.

A committee, headed by Women's Suffrage leader Annette Bear-Crawford, was appointed to run the new women's hospital and to secure permanent premises with inpatient facilities. A 'Shilling Fund' was organised by their treasurer, Annette Bear-Crawford, who spoke about the hospital at Suffrage' meetings. Women throughout the state of Victoria donated a shilling to help set up the hospital.

In July 1899, the Queen Victoria Hospital for Women and Children was officially opened. Besides Clara Stone who was in charge, other dedicated doctors such as Lilian Alexander, Edith Barrett, Constance Ellis, Mary de Garis and Janet and Jean Greig formed the teaching staff.

Dr Helen Sexton, a close friend and supporter of Clara Stone, specialised in family planning (a euphemism for birth control) and in treating sexually transmitted diseases, including syphilis, something 'nice' women were not supposed to speak about, let alone treat. This fatal disease was rampant in Melbourne and Sydney around the time of Federation and women with it were treated like criminals rather than making attempts to contact the men who had infected them. Dr Sexton felt that it required a special clinic to treat women who had been infected by their husbands or boyfriends. Later Dr Sexton's work in Melbourne providing contraceptives to married women would be taken up in community clinics in Sydney by the courageous Sister Lillie Goodisson (q.v.).

Grim sanitary conditions in housing for the poor resulted in epidemics of typhus and typhoid and a resulting overload of patients in the Queen Victoria Hospital. Smallpox was another problem that doctors had to face when dealing with working class patients. The fault lay in bad housing for the poor, which had either appalling sanitary conditions or no sanitation at all. The Governments of the day thought it cheaper to send in rat inspectors, provided with a pack of small dogs to hunt the rats, rather than allocate funds to vaccinate the children of the poor. It was only through pressure applied by women doctors that many humanitarian measures in preventative medicine were forced through around the time of Federation and later that century.

All the women doctors worked extremely hard to establish the Queen Victoria Hospital, which was responsible for saving the lives of countless women and children. Dr Constance Stone, the woman who had the vision and the energy to set up the hospital, did not live long enough to see the full success of her all-women's hospital. Worn out by an enormous clinical and administrative workload and by working long hours, she contracted tuberculosis from one of her women patients, suffered a prolonged and high fever and died. This remarkable woman was still in her early forties. She had saved countless lives by her unstinting dedication to her patients at the expense of her own life.

# CHAPTER FIVE

## Dr Agnes Bennett
*(1872–1960)*

## Joice NanKivell Loch
*(1887–1982)*

### DISTINGUISHED WOMEN WITH MULTIPLE AWARDS
### FOR HUMANITARIAN WORK

## Dr Agnes Bennett: Order of the British Empire, Order of St Sava and the Royal Red Cross of Serbia

Agnes Bennett was born in Sydney. Her father was a doctor who had migrated from England with his American-born wife. Agnes' much-loved mother died in childbirth when her daughter was only five. Her father worked very hard at his medical practice and Agnes and her brothers were brought up by a housekeeper. When Agnes was ten, her father married again, choosing an Australian, a widow with her own children to rear, from a rather different social background to his own. Agnes, upset at seeing this woman replacing her own mother in her father's affections, was moody and rebellious. Perhaps if her stepmother had handled the situation better, things might have been different but conflict ensued and her stepmother turned against the highly intelligent but strong-willed little girl.

Agnes loved her father very much but he was rarely home until late. However during the time they did spend together he encouraged her to believe that she could go to university when she was old enough, like her brothers.

Tragically for Agnes, her father had a fatal heart attack when she was only fifteen. By this time her stepmother actively disliked her clever but argumentative stepdaughter and made her life a misery. Agnes's only support at home was Bob, the brother closest in age to her. In later life Agnes reckoned that being an orphan disliked by her stepmother had the effect of making her more self-reliant than most girls of her own age.

Her father's will had left the necessary money for Agnes to continue attending the Sydney Girl's High School. In Agnes's class were two future authors, Ethel Turner and Louise Mack. Like them, Agnes loved study and books. Agnes topped the class in several subjects, including science. At that time young women had very limited choices: the only degree courses open to women at Sydney University were arts subjects. Agnes enrolled in the Arts Faculty, although she longed to do medicine like her eldest brother.

After years of conflict with her nagging stepmother, Agnes delighted in the freedom that university offered. In her second year she was able to switch from arts to science subjects, including geology, in which she was the only woman in her year. She was tall, athletic and sun-bronzed in summer and attractive to men. She enjoyed sport and became a university tennis champion. In second year she fell in love with a fellow student and her love was reciprocated. They planned to marry once they had finished university. It was a terrible shock when her fiancé, a strong swimmer, drowned in a freak accident. A sand bar collapsed beneath him and he was sucked down by a rip.

Agnes was desolated.[1] This was the third death of someone close to her and she was not yet twenty. She channelled her grief into her studies: perhaps the experience of grief and loss made her wary of loving again, for she never married.

In 1894 Agnes became the first woman at Sydney University to gain a science degree and was awarded first-class honours.

But her dreams of a scientific career were soon shattered. All her letters replying to job advertisements remained unanswered: it seemed that male employers did not want a woman, even one with a first-class degree. Somehow or other she had to earn money so that she could escape from her stepmother's constant nagging and become independent.

The only paid jobs for middle-class women in the 1890s were as teachers, governesses or nurses. Agnes answered an advertisement for a governess and went to the outback of New South Wales to work on a remote property. Then she read in a newspaper that because British female medical graduates had experienced similar problems obtaining the right to use the dissecting rooms at Edinburgh University, a Scottish doctor, Elsie Inglis, had founded Edinburgh's Medical College for Women. Agnes made up her mind to travel to Edinburgh, study at this college and follow in her father's footsteps. Her stepmother told her she was ridiculous, and that she should marry one of the men in the local tennis club. She flatly refused to provide any financial help for Agnes to study medicine, although there was enough money in Dr Bennett's estate to have done so.

So Agnes borrowed the necessary money for board and tuition by enlisting the sympathy of her late father's bank manager. He trusted her and loaned her money which she agreed to pay back with compound interest once she had qualified as a doctor. Agnes departed on a ship bound for Britain; as the liner pulled away from Circular Quay and the paper streamers thrown down by the passengers snapped, Agnes realised she was embarking on a new life.

In London, her father's birthplace, Agnes stayed at the Lyceum Club in Piccadilly, a home away from home for professional women and women in the arts. She explored the city, delighted to be seeing places she had only read about. Then she took the night train north to Edinburgh.

It was autumn. She found Edinburgh Castle and the stone buildings of 'Auld Reekie' fascinating and revelled in their historic associations. Then winter came and with it snow and sleet. Accustomed to the sub-tropical climate of Sydney, Agnes soon pronounced Edinburgh the 'coldest grimmest, grimiest place I've ever seen'.

She rented a damp, cheap basement apartment in an old stone tenement near the medical school, caught bronchitis and was unable to study for several weeks. Dr Elsie Inglis, worried that such a promising student as Agnes had not attended lectures for some weeks, came to visit her and insisted that Agnes should take better care of herself. Dr Inglis took a liking to the young Australian and began to invite her out on Sundays to high tea at the Inglis family home.

Elsie Inglis, a pioneer responsible for giving jobs to many young women in medicine, became Agnes Bennett's role model, her inspiration and mentor. Agnes studied very hard, passed her exams with flying colours and received excellent letters of reference from her lecturers. She dreamed of becoming a surgeon at the Edinburgh Infirmary, a hospital where many great discoveries in medicine had been made.

To her dismay she discovered the same prejudice she had encountered when she applied for scientific posts. The men who sat on hospital appointments committees turned her down and accepted men with much poorer exam results than hers as trainee surgeons.

In spite of Agnes Bennett's first-class degrees in medicine and surgery, the only institution that would employ her was Larbet's Mental Hospital. This was a grim stone pile miles from Edinburgh and civilisation. In the era before the development of psychiatric drugs and anti-depressants, seriously ill patients were treated with a strange mish-mash of dubious remedies, such as cold-water treatments, restraining chairs and strait-jackets, or else kept in padded cells. She worked at Larbet as a house officer for fifteen months to get her medical registration. Agnes now realised that medicine was just as restrictive and anti-female as science or geology. The powerful and very conservative male doctors who ran the teaching hospitals would never allow her to specialise in surgery. She would never be a surgeon. It had all been in vain.

She decided the only thing to do was sail home again, hoping that, in a new country like Australia, the situation for women in medicine would be easier. Back in Sydney, Dr Bennett applied for various hospital appointments but no one bothered to reply.

Refusing to be beaten, she had her name and degrees engraved on a brass plate, rented a room in Macquarie Street, engaged a secretary and went into private practice. But as she had few contacts who would send patients to a mere woman, she had very few patients. Eventually she realised she did not have the money to pay the rent for her expensive consulting room. Moreover, the repayments on her bank loan were due. There was nothing else to do. She had no option but to close her practice, sub-let her premises to a male doctor, and take another job that no one else wanted, at a mental hospital in New South Wales. Here, the 'difficult' patients were treated very harshly by the nursing staff. Dr Bennett wanted to do her best for the patients, which put her in conflict with the male Superintendent. At this juncture a friend of her father's came to her rescue: he wrote from New Zealand offering her a position as Registrar in a maternity hospital in Wellington. Agnes accepted and spent several satisfying years in New Zealand delivering babies.

In 1915, the year after World War I broke out, Agnes turned forty-two. By now almost every able-bodied man had gone away to war and each day the newspapers printed fresh horror stories of young Australians and New Zealanders fighting in the terrible trench warfare of France. Agnes' two brothers were in France and she badly wanted to help in the war effort, but her offer to enlist was refused. She was told that neither the New Zealand or the Australian Army wanted women doctors. 'Stay home and knit for the war effort!' the Army recruiting office advised.

Knitting was not on Dr Bennett's agenda. Undaunted, she offered her services to a French Red Cross hospital where an old friend from university days, Dr Helen Sexton, was working. Dr Sexton put in a good word for her and Agnes Bennett was offered a job as a surgeon. She booked her passage on the next boat sailing for Europe.

When Dr Bennett's ship arrived in Port Said, she looked over the rail and saw stretchers bearing wounded soldiers in what looked like

Australian and New Zealand uniforms being carried down the gangplanks of some ships flying the Australian flag. Port Said was in chaos. Men wounded at Gallipoli lay around on stretchers on the dockside, many crying out in pain. There was only one Army doctor to help the thousands of wounded men, many of whom seemed on the point of death.

Agnes asked a medical orderly where they had come from and was told, 'Er. Galy-poly ... some funny name like that. They're Anzacs wounded in the Dardanelles poor sods.'

Dr Bennett was a volunteer and did not have to answer to anyone for her actions. All she saw were wounded men in pain who desperately needed her operating skills. She went below to her cabin, packed her bags, then marched down the gangplank and buttonholed the first high-ranking officer in British uniform she could find.

'You need me,' she said. 'I'm a surgeon.' His jaw dropped but she was right: they needed every surgeon they could find.

Using a storage shed as an emergency operating theatre, Agnes operated throughout the night, helped by a young medical orderly. There was no anaesthetic so she gave shots of morphine until that ran out, then had to operate without any pain relief. The patients had to be restrained by medical orderlies. Their cries of pain made her feel sick but she saved hundreds of lives.

By ten o'clock next day she had signed all the necessary papers and become the first woman doctor commissioned into the British Army. The Army top brass had previously refused to accept women doctors into the armed forces, because they thought them incapable of shouldering the responsibilities and duties involved.

Issued with British Army uniform complete with leather Sam Browne belt and army boots, Acting Captain Agnes Bennett, R.A.M.C., accompanied a trainload of wounded in a train bound for Cairo. As a member of the Royal Army Medical Corps, she had temporary accreditation to the staff of the British Army Hospital in Cairo.[2]

At last she had found her true *métier* – surgery. In Cairo she proved herself a brilliant surgeon as well as an excellent administrator. At the British Military Hospital she found overcrowded wards, long operating lists and stretchers of wounded lining the corridors. Typhoid and dysentery were common. Beds were scarce until she and two male doctors commandeered an Army lorry, drove to some abandoned tourist steamers on the Nile, ripped out the bunks and returned in triumph.

Agnes was overjoyed to hear that Bob, her favourite brother, was now in Alexandria. At this point she had spent nearly six months in an operating theatre or on the wards with little free time. She boarded a train to Alexandria and spent an entire day with him.

By now most Gallipoli survivors were on their way back to Britain. The workload was easing. It was time to move on. Dr Bennett caught the train from Cairo to Port Said and boarded the next ship bound for London. She arrived just in time for the night raids by German Zeppelins.

She was assigned on a temporary basis to the R.A.M.C.'s Millbank Hospital. Then a chance reunion with Dr Elsie Inglis changed the course of Agnes Bennett's life once more.

The redoubtable Dr Inglis had also been rejected by the British Army for war service. But Elsie Inglis refused to take no for an answer. She formed the Scottish Women's Field Hospitals, which she funded from the proceeds of a lecture tour in America. Now she was in London buying equipment for several tented field hospitals to go to France, complete with operating theatres and mobile ambulances which would be driven by women.

She told Agnes Bennett that a female senior surgeon and administrator was urgently needed to run a new unit which would be leaving for Ostrovo, in Serbia, as soon as the French units were away. In Serbia, Serbian and French forces were fighting as Britain's allies against a combined enemy force of Austrian, German and Bulgarian troops. Would Acting Captain Bennett (recently gazetted for an Order of the British Empire for her heroic rescue work at Port Said) take command? Of course she would.

Agnes Bennett went off to Edinburgh where she assumed control of the employment of ward orderlies and cooks as well as shipping arrangements for all the personnel and medical and camping equipment. At Ostrovo medical orderlies were to be provided mainly by the Serbs. Foreseeing language problems, she engaged a bunch of high-spirited 'gels' from wealthy Scottish and English families keen to get away from home on war service and arranged for them to receive training in first-aid as volunteer ambulance drivers, along with the other women who had volunteered as cooks and ward orderlies.[2]

It was a huge task to organise the shipment of people, equipment and all the medical supplies for the field hospital from Edinburgh to the northern Greek port of Salonika, as the British Army called Thessaloniki – a city of cobbled streets and ancient churches built in the days when the city was second in importance to Constantinople, capital of the Byzantine Empire. Thessaloniki was a clanging, teeming city of metalworkers, throbbing with life.

From 1916 onwards Dr Bennett had total control of a medical unit on the Serbian front. In addition, Dr Bennett (her temporary British Army commission now ended) was in charge of setting up a base outside Thessaloniki on which they could fall back if attacked by the enemy. Accordingly, the Scottish Women's Base Hospital in the Balkans was set up on waste ground connected by a dirt track to Thessaloniki. The nearest village was Charilaos. No one else wanted the land because it was the preserve of thieves and murderers. (Today it lies close to the busy Thessaloniki airport.)

Once the Charilaos hospital was running, she left behind enough personnel to cope with special cases which would be evacuated from Ostrovo. Then, from an office near the Thessaloniki docks, she set about organising the transport of seventy large tents and hundreds of crates of medical equipment and tinned food to the front line near Monastir (today's Bitola) in Serbia – a huge task rendered more difficult by language difficulties, potential theft of the supplies and the usual privations of war.

The Balkan War had begun with the assassination of Grand Duke Ferdinand, a relative of the Austrian Emperor, at Sarajevo. This had acted as a powder keg for the rest of Europe. By now food was scarce and very poor in quality. The French had already established two tented hospitals in the area, but one had been sacked and looted by Bulgarian troops and all the personnel killed.

Just as Dr Bennett arrived at Ostrovo Field Hospital, the Serbs, brave guerrilla fighters disastrously short of guns and ammunition, began to retreat before an attack by the well-trained troops of the Austro-Hungarian Empire. Serbian casualties were enormous. Dr Bennett and her fellow doctors were appalled by the enormous number of wounded men who died in the lorry-ambulances that carried them from the front line over pot-holed roads to the Scottish Women's Field Hospital.

During World War I, nearly 2000 courageous Australian women doctors and nurses travelled to Britain at their own expense, having been refused entry to the medical forces of the Australian Army due to their gender. At great risk to themselves, Dr Bennett and her assistant, Dr Elsie Dalyell, (a Sydney-born pathologist who had been a junior at the Sydney Girls' High School when Agnes Bennett was a prefect) moved their small operating unit close to the front lines. This had the effect of saving more lives but meant Dr Bennett and Dr Dalyell were operating under the most primitive conditions, often without running water.

The Ostrovo field hospital commanded by Dr Bennett consisted of a row of huge tents and a long low shed, formerly a barn, divided into two compartments. This housed the operating theatre and emergency X-ray room. Wounded Serbian soldiers, often screaming in pain, arrived in the lorry-ambulances driven by girls who were no longer bored debutantes but heroines. They drove over dirt tracks and roads pockmarked by shell holes and bomb craters to the Scottish Women's Field Hospital where patients lay on straw palliasses or stretchers on the ground in the hospital tents. Other tents acted as camp kitchens. Food was often in short supply once the tins brought from Scotland ran out. Lack of food and medicines coupled with savage rats, so bold that they gnawed patients' wounds and ran across their faces, made the work of the medical orderlies all the harder.

In the midst of this horror the women doctors were surprised to find such dramatically beautiful views of Lake Ostrovo and across the valley. 'The mountains are twenty miles away but in this clear air it seems more like five miles. The line of dazzling snow on the peaks against a clear blue sky is the most wonderful sight I have yet seen'[3] – so Dr Elsie Dalyell described the view from Ostrovo.

Agnes Bennett was eventually joined by another woman doctor from Australia. British-born Dr Lilian Cooper had travelled to Serbia from Brisbane. She too had faced stiff opposition from male doctors to become the Queensland capital's first female doctor. She arrived at Ostrovo with her long-term companion, Jean Bedford, a teacher turned ambulance driver. They were both exceptionally brave. Jean Bedford soon took command of the ambulance runs, which were frequently strafed from the air by German fighter planes. In addition, German aircraft regularly bombed the area.

Heavy bombardment and the stream of ambulances which arrived each night from the front lines with more wounded patients meant that none of the doctors got much sleep. On urgent cases they operated by candlelight far into the night: it was vital that shrapnel should be removed immediately from festering wounds. In summer the heat was blistering; in winter the cold was so biting in the unheated and draughty tents that staff and patients became frost-bitten. Doctors and nurses alike were forced to wear heavy greatcoats taken from dead soldiers or battered old fur coats over their uniforms. Dr Bennett wore an ancient sheepskin coat over her winter uniform and sported a distinctive Australian bushman's hat. All three doctors wore woollen mittens rather than rubber gloves when they operated.

Danger was all around them. No one knew when the Germans and Austrians might attack or bands of Bulgarian guerrilla fighters arrive by stealth in the night and shoot the lot of them; this had happened in several other field hospitals. The Australian women doctors were greatly admired by the Serbs and the French for their coolness under fire, their laconic sense of humour and their acceptance of horrific working conditions.

Summer brought dense clouds of malarial mosquitoes: they did not have enough mosquito netting to combat them and anti-insect sprays had not yet been invented. As a result malaria decimated staff *and* patients. Those staff members who died were replaced.

One of the replacement cooks was the Australian writer Miles Franklin, (her real name was Stella Franklin and she had been born at Talbingo, near Tumut in New South Wales). After the publication of her ironic autobiographical novel *My Brilliant Career*, she went to work in America but returned to Britain at the outbreak of war. She enjoyed using assumed names and enrolled as a ward orderly at Ostrovo under the highly improbable name 'Franky Doodle'. Miles Franklin soon applied to switch from ward orderly to camp cook, hoping to write a novel about her war experiences. But the Australian writer contracted malaria, and was shipped back to Britain as a casualty. Back in London, she wrote a few chapters of her proposed book about her time in the Balkans but was unable to get the projected novel published, a fate that would dog many of her manuscripts. In fact, Miles Franklin is probably best known today for the leading literary prize she bequeathed to Australians, rather than for her published work, other than *My Brilliant Career*.

By the time Miles Franklin was evacuated from the Ostrovo field hospital the seventy khaki tents were leaking like sieves onto the patients' stretchers. It was impossible to obtain new ones. In summer the tented wards were filled with fleas and flies as well as mosquitoes. Many patients arrived from the trenches crawling with lice and had to be deloused by orderlies before the doctors could operate on them.

Dr Bennett, known as 'The Chief' by her Serbian medical orderlies, who spoke little English and with whom she had to communicate in schoolgirl French, was greatly admired for her surgical skills and her fairness as a commander.

Life was not easy in a field hospital. Digging camp latrines was a repetitive and highly unpopular chore. Eventually the water supply ran out. A new well from a neighbouring village turned out to be polluted and typhoid and dysentery broke out. The disease of trench foot among soldiers who had lived for months in open shell holes or trenches as the rain fell or the snow melted around them and water soaked through their boots was appalling. The men's toes swelled, blackened and if untreated they fell off.

The Crown Prince of Serbia visited the Ostrovo Field Hospital on several occasions, deeply grateful to the courageous women doctors who risked their lives operating on Serbian soldiers. He awarded Dr Bennett, Dr Dalyell and Dr Cooper the highest Serbian medals 'for valour' – the Order of St Sava and the Royal Red Cross of Serbia.

Shortly after one of his visits, the booming of big guns warned that the Germans and Bulgarians were advancing rapidly. To avoid wholesale slaughter, plans were made to retreat to the Field Hospital at Charilaos, on the outskirts of Salonika. At this stage Dr Bennett had been feeling ill for some time but refused to admit it. As Commander of the field hospital she attended a farewell dinner with the Serbian and French commanders, and returned to the Field Hospital to find that although the Bulgarian troops had halted their advance, low-flying German planes had bombed the tented wards. Orderlies and patients had been severely wounded. The operating theatre set up in an old barn was blazing and had to be hosed down to extinguish the flames. Dr Bennett was exhausted but joined in to help douse the flames and save the precious equipment. Adrenalin kept her going but once the danger had passed she went to her tent, feeling faint and nauseated. Catching sight of her pale face in a small mirror on her wash-stand, she saw a lined and elderly woman looking back at her, like a total stranger. Then she blacked out and collapsed.

The next day they struck camp and loaded everything onto lorries to take to Salonika. The Serbian orderlies lined up to kiss the hand of their beloved 'Chief'. Dr Bennett was feeling so weak she could scarcely stand, but she managed to speak a few words of farewell to each of them. Although burning with fever she was determined to leave 'her' field hospital on her feet rather than be carried out on a stretcher. Her Serbian driver and some of the orderlies had tears in their eyes as they saw her being driven away down the bumpy dirt road. Once the car was out of sight, Dr Bennett collapsed completely, her teeth chattering with fever, feeling alternately boiling hot or freezing cold. It was obvious she had a very severe case of malaria. Would she survive the journey?

At Salonika she vainly made the attempt to get out of the car and walk. She was too ill to protest when burly orderlies lifted her onto a stretcher and put her aboard a lorry bound for the Scottish Women's Hospital at Charilaos, which she had set up over a year ago. There she made a good recovery, but was told that she had had a lucky escape. At Charilaos she learned that the Serb orderlies who had stayed on at the Ostrovo Field Hospital had been massacred by the advancing Bulgarians.

Like Agnes Bennett, Dr Elsie Dalyell got away safely, joined the British Royal Army Medical Corps and worked in Salonika. From there she went to a teaching hospital in Vienna, where she published a number of papers in medical journals and was widely respected in her profession. After the war, however, she had huge difficulty finding a job suited to her qualifications when she returned to Sydney.

Finally Agnes Bennett was thought to be well enough to be shipped back from Thessaloniki to Sydney on a troop carrier. While she recuperated at her sister-in-law's home, bouts of malarial fever returned from time to time. She wept to learn that Bob, her favourite brother, whom she had last seen in Alexandria, had been killed at Passchendaele, in France. It made her all the more determined not to give up her wartime service.

As soon as she was well enough, Agnes Bennett volunteered for active service once again. She returned to Britain as medical officer on a troop-ship, in charge of a regiment of soldiers, and had a narrow escape when the convoy was torpedoed. Then she went back to Scotland to work at the Glasgow Infirmary, now flooded with casualties. Normally the hospital had a staff of fifteen to twenty doctors. Now Dr Bennett and one other doctor had to cope only assisted by a couple of third-year medical students. Dr Bennett's administrative workload, as well as her operating list, was enormous. Along with war casualties she operated on women workers from the local munition factories, several of whom had arms and legs blown off in accidents.

'I had to do the major operations myself without the assistance of an anaesthetist,' Dr Bennett wrote. 'There was no option but to let third-year medical students give the anaesthetics.'

In 1919, after the war was over, Agnes Bennett returned to Sydney. In spite of her proven dedication and courage, her Serbian and British medals and her years of operating experience, because she was a woman she *still* failed to get a post in a Sydney hospital.

The New Zealand maternity hospital where she had worked wanted her back, so she stayed there until her retirement. Then she returned to Sydney, her birthplace, where she lived quietly in a small house on the North Shore until her death in 1960, by which time her heroism was all but forgotten.

### Joyce NanKivell Loch: Order of St Sava, Order of the Redeemer, Order of the Phoenix, the Polish Cross of Virtue, the Polish Cross of Merit, Member of the Order of the British Empire and other medals

Like Agnes Bennett, Queensland-born Joyce Loch, journalist, author and aid worker, was a member of the Lyceum Club. She too was honoured with the Serbian Order of St Sava, awarded for her work on malaria prevention carried out at the American Farm School near Thessaloniki, where she worked in what became known as the Greek 'refugee crisis', that followed the massacre of Greeks at Smyrna.

The influx of a million and a half Greek refugees who had lived outside Greece for generations took place in 1922, after some 200 000 Greeks had been murdered by the Turks at Smyrna. As a result of this

Turkish 'ethnic cleansing', Greek men, women and children, including hundreds of thousands of widows and orphans, fled from Turkey and Asia Minor and arrived as homeless refugees in Greece, one of the world's poorest countries.

The amazing life of Joice NanKivell Loch is told in my biography, *Blue Ribbons, Bitter Bread: The Life of Joice NanKivell Loch, Australia's Most Decorated Woman*.[4] It is impossible to tell her full story in a single chapter.

Joice NanKivell Loch was as outspoken, compassionate and dedicated as Agnes Bennett. Both women wanted to become doctors but lacking funds for university fees and without a sympathetic bank manager to give her a loan, Joice became an author and journalist instead. Later she worked as a volunteer medical orderly with worldwide Quaker Famine Relief, although she never became a Quaker herself.

Joice NanKivell was born in 1887 at Farnham, a huge cane plantation owned by Fanning NanKivell, in which her grandfather, Thomas NanKivell, was a partner. Her father managed the plantation, and his brothers managed other plantations nearby. As her mother went into labour at the height of a cyclone, without a doctor or midwife, Joice was brought into the world by Daisy, an indentured Pacific Islander. Daisy, kidnapped from her island home by 'blackbirders', had been brought to Queensland as an indentured labourer and became Joice's adored nursemaid. Joice and her brother, Geoff, had a favourite playmate called Tinker, a part-Aboriginal boy who had been abandoned by his mother. Both the NanKivell children were witnesses to Tinker's death in a terrible accident when he was taken by a crocodile during a duck shoot. Joice's early contact with Daisy and Tinker nurtured her deep and enduring concern for the homeless and displaced.

When the Queensland Government insisted that the 'Kanaka' indentured labour system must cease, the NanKivells' heavily mortgaged plantations became unproductive and virtually valueless. In searing heat, amid mosquitoes, scrub ticks and disease-bearing rats, Joice's father, his brothers and their white overseers attempted in vain to cut the cane themselves but were infected by rat bites and several men died of leptospirosis.

Joice's mother, Edith, struggled to run the huge homestead with dwindling funds and staff. The NanKivells' menu changed from beef and imported French wines to kangaroo stew and parrot pie. In desperation they had to sell off their furniture and even Joice's much-loved Shetland pony.

Joice's parents now discovered to their horror that the sugar plantations owned by Fanning NanKivell and Company had been heavily mortgaged by Thomas NanKivell. Foreclosing, the bank took everything in settlement of outstanding mortgages – Joice's parents were ruined. Her grandfather, Thomas NanKivell, survived as he had put his assets in his wife's name; by doing so he sacrificed the future of his children and grandchildren. Joice and her parents had to walk off the property with nothing but a few books and clothes.

Joice's father accepted a job as 'manager' of a sheep property near Morwell in Gippsland, working for a miserly uncle. Joice's mother was horrified to find that the manager's house was nothing but a dirt-floored hut, lined with newspapers. Their new residence was crawling with mice and snakes, and lacked running water or any form of sanitation.

Joice had to grow up fast. She worked hard, baking, cleaning, tending lambs and calves, and cooking for seasonal workers such as shearers and fencers. She realised that her dreams of becoming a doctor would never came true – there was no money to pay university fees.

During the bank crash of the 1890s the Gippsland property fell into debt and had to be sold. Joice's father bought a heavily mortgaged rundown farm at Myaree. Here Joice and her family experienced the tragic consequences of severe drought and bushfires in which Joice's pony burned to death. Once again the NanKivells failed to make any money.

As things went from bad to worse Joice's father took refuge in alcohol and her once genteel mother, worn out by house and farmyard chores, suffered periods of depressive illness. Joice and her younger brother, Geoff, worked as farmhands and stockmen and never forgave their grandfather for the effect the bankruptcy of Farnham in Queensland had on her parents.

Joice's Uncle Harry, a general practitioner, came to spend a holiday with the NanKivells. During his stay at Myaree Uncle Harry was called in for an emergency operation: since the nearest hospital was over a hundred miles away, he had to operate on a little girl on the NanKivells' dining-room table. Joice assisted him during the operation, her first experience in medical procedure. Encouraged by her uncle, she started to read his old medical books and learned about anatomy and basic medicine. As a result she became proficient at stitching up wounded animals and they saved on fees for veterinarian services, an expenditure the NanKivells could ill afford.

Joice attempted to make money by writing a children's book, *The Cobweb Ladder*. But with the outbreak of World War I in 1914, paper rationing meant the book's publication was delayed. When it was eventually published, it found few readers as everybody was preoccupied with the war.

Joice's brother Geoff (like Agnes Bennett's brother) was killed in action in France. Joice's father was so distraught by the loss of his son and heir that he decided to sell their farm. This decision meant Joice was now free to leave the land and the drudgery of farmwork and cooking for shearers and escape to Melbourne. Geoff's death and the struggle of the past years had seriously affected her mother's health and almost broken her spirit.

Joice wrote a second book in memory of her brother, *The Solitary Pedestrian*. As a published author, at a time when male journalists were away fighting in France, she obtained a part-time job reviewing books in Melbourne's *Sun-Herald*. She also worked as secretary to the Professor of Classics at Melbourne University, a 'learning experience' as she called it. Her deepening knowledge of classical Greek history and literature gave her a yearning to visit Greece.

Joice NanKivell was introduced to Sydney Loch, a tall, distinguished hero of Gallipoli, after she reviewed a book he wrote about the Dardanelles campaign. The two become good friends and it was not long before they fell in love. In 1918, just as the war ended, they married. Their marriage angered Joice's father, who believed writing was a useless occupation, but it pleased Joice's mother, who wanted her daughter to leave Australia and find a new life in the wider world. She gave Joice a farewell gift of a small Australian flag, which Joice promised to keep always on her desk.

The newlyweds sailed to London, where they planned to work as freelance authors and journalists. They were both working as Fleet Street journalists when Sydney met an old schoolfriend, who had been recruited as an undercover agent in Dublin by British Military Intelligence, under the name of Major X. Coincidentally, Joice and

Sydney were planning to go to Dublin, as they had been commissioned by their publisher to write a book about the 'troubles' there.

In Dublin, the Lochs were befriended by the Irish literati, who supported the rebel Sinn Fein in its demand for home rule in Ireland. At that time Dublin was swarming with armed thugs, nicknamed the 'Black and Tans', recruited by the British.

Bombs were planted in public places by Michael Collins and his followers in Sinn Fein and the fledgling IRA. Joice narrowly escaped death when a bomb was thrown in her direction, killing several babies and young mothers. Meanwhile, the Black and Tans were conducting house-to-house searches for gelignite and guns stored in secret IRA 'safe houses'.

The Lochs had rented a dingy furnished apartment in the house of a widow, Mrs Slaney, unaware of her strong IRA connections. They were horrified when the Black and Tans raided the widow's house and found guns under her bed and gelignite among her pot plants. Forbidden to arrest a woman, they arrested Sydney Loch instead. Suspected of treason, for which he could have been hanged, Sydney was imprisoned in Dublin Castle, headquarters of the British forces in Ireland. Joice successfully pleaded for her husband's release, but Michael Collins' men were now convinced that he was a British spy.

On 'Black Sunday', undercover British agents were shot in their beds by Michael Collins' gunmen – but their friend, Major X, managed to escape. The situation became so dangerous that when their room was once again searched by Sinn Fein, Joice and Sydney contemplated leaving Ireland immediately. However, they decided to stay on at Mrs Slaney's and finish their book about the Troubles, *Ireland in Travail*, which they hoped would be fair and reflect the viewpoints of both sides.

They finally left Ireland after being warned by Major X and other friends that Sinn Fein had put a price on their heads unjustly believing that Sydney was a British spy. In London, just before *Ireland in Travail* was published, they heard on BBC radio that Michael Collins had been assassinated. It was time to leave Britain. But where should they go?

A friend suggested eastern Poland, where Quaker Famine Relief was providing free train fares, board and lodging to volunteer aid workers. The Lochs decided that Poland would provide excellent material for another book. Their British publishers, John Murray, encouraged them to go there, hoping that from Poland they would be able to travel into Russia and obtain an eyewitness view of the activities of Lenin and his Bolsheviks for inclusion in the new book.

At Quaker headquarters they were interviewed by stern, dour Miss Ruth Fry, who expressed the opinion that the Lochs would not 'mix well' with Quakers. However, so many aid workers had died in Poland that replacements were urgently needed. Eastern Poland had been devastated by Lenin's troops: pursuing their 'scorched earth' policy, they had burned Polish and Ukrainian villages to the ground, slaughtering the inhabitants or sending them to work-camps in Siberia. Those refugees who survived were now returning to find their homes burned to the ground, their cattle gone and their fields turned into wasteland. These refugees, as well as Quaker volunteers who had come to help, were dying of malnutrition and typhoid. All they had to eat was bitter bread made from roasted acorns and tins of sardines sent out by Quaker relief trains from London. Each night bands of starving children beat on the door of the old railway carriage Joice used as her office and sleeping accommodation. She wondered how the Quakers could so fervently believe in a God that allowed such misery. In a desperate attempt to raise money for Polish famine relief, Joice tried to interest the British press in articles she had written on famine in Poland – in vain. Most Fleet Street editors preferred to publish articles about Lenin's triumphs in Russia.

In the midst of so much misery and hunger Joice became pregnant. Sadly, three month into the pregnancy she collapsed from malnourishment and overwork and lost the baby. At the time of the miscarriage Sydney was away, organising teams of horses to plough the refugees' land. To ease her pain the Quakers provided tickets for her and Sydney to visit Moscow, which sparked Joice to write an ironic novel set in contemporary Russia, *The Fourteen Thumbs of St Peter.*

On their return to Poland Sydney's horse teams continued to plough the land and to distribute seed corn to the villagers to ensure their survival. Slowly things improved. President Pilsudksi's fledgling Polish Republic got back on its feet and the need for assistance from the Quaker volunteers became less acute. In gratitude for their contribution to the restoration of eastern Poland, both the Lochs were decorated by the Prime Minister of Poland.

On a visit to Quaker Headquarters in Warsaw Joice heard about the horrors of the massacre of Greeks at Smyrna and the need for trained medical orderlies to help the million and a half Greek refugees, victims of the Turks' 'ethnic cleansing'. These Greek refugees had inhabited Turkey and Asia Minor for centuries. Joice remembered her time in the Classics Department at Melbourne University and her desire to visit Greece. When the call came for volunteers, both Joice and Sydney raised her hands, as did their friend Nancy Lauder Brunton, an American heiress turned humanitarian.

Nancy departed for Thessaloniki while Joice finished her work in the Polish medical centre. Sydney still had several months of work to do in Poland, setting up an orphanage and farm school for Polish children.

On a warm evening in May 1923, Joice climbed down from the train that had brought her to Thessaloniki onto a crowded platform, all her worldly possessions contained in a single suitcase. All around were dazed Greek refugees, carrying their few possessions bundled up in sheets and pillowcases. Many had lived in Turkey for generations, and spoke only Turkish.

The next day Joice travelled by horse-drawn cab to the huge refugee camp in the grounds of the American Farm School, not far from Thessaloniki. On the way she passed by the old Scottish Women's Hospital, established by Agnes Bennett, now being used as a camp for the thousands upon thousands of refugees who were pouring into Thessaloniki from Asia Minor.

At the Farm School, Joice and Nancy Lauder Brunton worked side by side, giving inoculations against typhoid, feeding the starving and tending the sick and dying. In addition Joice wrote articles about her experiences for the British and Australian press. A few months later, Sydney arrived from Poland. The Lochs worked tirelessly for the refugees, who were gradually rehoused in villages of tiny concrete-block cottages, built by the cash-strapped Greek Government.

On a camping holiday by the sea Joice and Sydney visited one of the new refugee villages. Pirgos (today called Ouranoupolis) was named after the huge fourteenth-century Byzantine tower which dominated the skyline. The villagers lacked medicines of any kind and were facing starvation because the olive saplings and vine cuttings provided by the Government had died in the fierce summer heat. The Lochs brought seeds and medicines to the villagers the next time they visited. At the request of the Mayor of Pirgos, Sydney shot a wild boar which was devouring the villager's few chickens.

In gratitude, the Mayor offered the Lochs the old Byzantine tower by the sea for a peppercorn rent. Joice and Sydney were estacic: they had been planning to look for a place to settle down, now that the worst of the Greek crisis was over. Villagers helped them clean out the donkey manure that had accumulated on the ground floor. After electricity had been installed in two rooms, the Lochs moved in, planning to become full-time writers.

Fate thought otherwise. Knowing that Joice had a well-stocked medicine chest, poverty-stricken villagers, who lacked even an aspirin or a bandage, began to come to the tower, seeking her assistance for their sick children, their aged parents and themselves. Bent over her typewriter, hard at work, Joice used to mutter a few exasperated words, but would always go out to help those in need.

One day Joice visited a sick old man, living with his daughter and her husband. The old man, a former rug weaver, was dying of malnutrition (most of the family's meagre income went towards feeding the bread-winner). Joice, horrified by their poverty, asked the village carpenter to build a loom and commissioned the old man's daughter (who was also a rug weaver) to weave and sell her a rug. Soon it became clear that many rug weavers were living in the village. They were all desperate to earn extra money, so Joice ordered more looms and purchased wool and dyes. So the Pirgos Women's Rug Weaving Cooperative was born.

Joice started to design the rugs herself as she felt that Byzantine rather than Turkish motifs had to be used in their design.[5] She learned from the village midwife-cum-witch the secret of dyeing wool, using local plants. During the years that followed, Joice sold many hand-woven 'Pirgos Rugs' to friends in Britain, Australia and America. (Pirgos Rugs are no longer woven but now command high prices from Greek collectors.)

In 1939, as Hitler threatened to invade Poland, the village celebrated a wedding. The bride was a beautiful young woman whom Joice had saved from death some sixteen years previously. The young men performed the threshing dance in memory of Greeks slaughtered by the Turks. The Lochs were guests of honour, and everyone rejoiced that the days of acorn bread and famine were over and the olive harvest safely gathered.

Their joy was short-lived. That night the Lochs heard on the BBC that Hitler had invaded Poland and Britain had declared war on Germany. They believed Greece would remain neutral: Greek friends assured them that Hitler had no intention of invading Greece.

Once again the Lochs offered their services to Quaker Refugee Aid to Poland. Sydney was appointed Head of Friends Relief Mission in Bucharest to look after thousands of Polish men who had fled from the Germans and the Russians to neutral Rumania. Joice was made responsible for aid to Polish and Jewish women and children who had also fled there.

They said sad goodbyes to friends in the village and to holy men from the monasteries of Athos, as well as Quaker and Farm School colleagues. Joice packed her battered typewriter, her medical books and the miniature Australian flag her mother had given her before she left Australia. Once more they headed into danger.

Joice and Sydney took the overnight train to Bucharest, a city of huge contradictions: lush restaurants and cafes, elegant boutiques and fashionable woman ... and emaciated women and children begging in the streets outside the city centre. Male Polish refugees were being interned by Rumania's King Carol, who was anxious to curry favour with Hitler. Many escaped on skis and fled across Europe to join the Free Polish Army in Britain. Joice tried to raise money for exit visas for the women and children without success.

That Christmas, the Polish women and children sang carols and gave Joice small dolls they had made themselves. Jewish refugees, caring for thousands of orphans who had lost their parents in the concentration camps, thanked her for providing them with clothes sent from Britain. Joice was overworked and badly needed an assistant, preferably someone middle-aged, caring and sensible. Instead, Father Ambrosius, the Polish priest to the internment camps, recommended Countess Lushya, who turned out to be young and beautiful.

At twenty-two the charismatic Countess Lushya was the sole survivor of a family of Polish aristocrats. She had no typing skills but possessed a quick mind, a flair for organisation and aristocratic friends in Rumania. She told Joice that she could persuade these friends to open their homes for benefit concerts in aid of the Polish refugees. Lushya was hired and within a few weeks had taken over the fund-raising.

Lushya recruited a group of Rumanian princesses, resplendent in Chanel and Dior clothes and ropes of pearls to raise funds for exit visas for Polish refugees. Benefit luncheons with French champagne and Russian caviar were held to raise money for the Polish women refugees and their children, whose escape Joice was planning. The British Foreign Office had meanwhile agreed to fund the escape of the remaining male prisoners, who included some members of the Polish Government in exile.

Sydney and Joice each received a medal from King Carol, whom Joice described as having 'the saddest eyes' she had ever seen. The King, whose late mother was British, was under huge pressure from Hitler as well as his own Cabinet ministers and the pro-Nazi Rumanian Iron Guard. His position was further aggravated by the Russians, who were planning to invade on the western front of his oil-rich country.

The Iron Guard began to round up high-profile Jews and hung them from meat hooks. Suddenly German officers appeared in Bucharest and the British and French flags outside the Lochs' hotel were replaced by the red-and-black Swastika. Joice and Sydney were caught in the crossfire of street fighting but managed to escape. In the meantime the Russians invaded oil-rich Bukovina.

By now Rumania's royal palace was under siege by the jack-booted Iron Guard and King Carol was forced to abdicate. He departed into exile, taking with him his Jewish mistress, Magda Lupescu. It was rumoured that he had also shipped out much of the country's gold bullion.

The Lochs knew they *must* get the Polish refugees and the Jewish orphans in their care out of Rumania immediately. Sydney departed aboard a chartered river steamer with his group of male Polish refugees on forged visas. Joice was desperate to get her group of refugee women and children out before the Nazis sent them to concentration camps. Fortunately, the day before the German Army entered Bucharest in full force, money was provided by a wealthy Jewish couple who pleaded with Joice to smuggle their young daughter and orphaned nieces out of the country to an aunt in Haifa. Joice agreed to take the children to Israel, as long as their forged passports were sufficiently convincing.

The large-scale escape she planned was code-named 'Operation Pied Piper'. The cover for the exodus of hundreds of women and children was a Quaker Mission day excursion to Constanza, a beach resort on the Black Sea. On arrival in Constanza they did *not* go to the beach; instead, they boarded a ferry that took them to Constantinople and freedom.

Their escape was fraught with danger. At one stage the ferry was ordered to turn back by the Iron Guard. Lushya and Joice feared they would all be arrested and taken to a concentration camp. But all the Iron Guard wanted were the crates of Rumanian gold being shipped out aboard the ferry, destined for King Carol, now safely exiled in Portugal.

The full story of the dangers and tensions of Operation Pied Piper and Joice's heroic spy mission to Budapest on behalf of British Intelligence is related in my book, *Blue Ribbons, Bitter Bread: The Life of Joice NanKivell Loch, Australia's Most Decorated Woman*. From Constanzan, Joice took her party of refugees to British-run Palestine via Constantinople (Istanbul) and Cyprus. Their ship was bombed and shelled by German planes, but, miraculously, the vessel did not sink. The Lochs brought almost 2000 refugees from Bucharest to Cyprus in to separate parties and then took them to Palestine.

In the final years of World War II, the Lochs cared for thousands more Polish orphans whose parents had been murdered in Stalin's gulags. The Polish children were released after Britain started to give aid to Communist Russia. Joice wrote a report to Quaker Refugee Aid in London begging for funds to feed them. She described how 'their shaven heads appeared too large for their emaciated bodies, their eyes burning with fever and starvation, their feet chafed by Army boots far too big for them.' She fought for 'her' orphans to receive clothing, food, accommodation and a special school – for which she was awarded another medal by the Polish Government in exile. (Twenty years later in London, I met a Polish woman who had survived childhood due to Joice Loch and her 'Camp of a Thousand Orphans'.)

After World War II ended, the Lochs returned to northern Greece to find their tower home and the village of Pirgos (now renamed Ouranoupolis) ravaged by the Andartes, the Greek Communist rebels. Joice succeeded in raising funds to rebuild the village and re-opened Pirgos Rugs, which once again saved the village from starvation and saw her awarded another Greek medal.

Tragically, in 1955 Sydney Loch died at the age of sixty-six. Joice lived on in widowhood for another twenty-seven years. Joice continued to care for the people of Ouranoupolis. She brought exhibitions of Pirgos Rugs to Australia and wrote several more books, including the bestselling children's book *Tales of Christophilos*, which raised enough money to bring a continuous supply of unpolluted water to Ouranoupolis.

At the age of 95 Joice Loch died in her tower home, mourned by hundreds of monks and Greek villagers, by Australian, British and American diplomats and the governor of Macedonia. A Greek Orthodox Bishop, who is also an Oxford don, gave her funeral oration and named her as *'one of the most significant women of the twentieth century.'* She is buried beside her beloved husband in the cemetry of Ouranoupolis.

Joice Loch's rescue of thousands of refugees from Nazi death camps and her work with Polish and Greek refugees was recognised by Greek, Polish, Rumanian and British governments. She was recommended for a British decoration, the MBE, by Lord Eccles and then Australian Ambassador to Greece, Hugh Gilchrist.

A Joice Loch Room housing her manuscripts, rugs and photographs in the Byzantine Museum in Ouranopolis will eventually be opened in Joice's old home, the 'tower by the sea'. 'The Lady in the Tower' as the locals called her, is especially revered by Greeks, who were justifiably annoyed that some Australian bureaucrats had treated shabbily valuable Loch artefacts entrusted to their care. A statue, a Joice Loch clinic or a medical scholarship commemorating an outstanding woman in whom humanitarian ideals were joined to medical skills, literary talent, bravery and the capacity to inspire love in the thousands of refugees whose lives she helped restore, might make amends.

Agnes Bennett and Joice NanKivell Loch were both awarded medals by foreign authorities. Joice Loch was awarded more medals than any other Australian woman: two more than the redoubtable war heroine Nancy Wake.[6] These remarkable women should have bronze plaques in the walk of fame around Circular Quay, as well as roads, shopping centres or clinics named after them in our State capitals. Joice Loch *has* been honoured by a museum, but it is in northern Greece. The fact they have been ignored in Australia raises the question: why have we failed to recognise some of our most heroic women who have been honoured overseas for their outstanding achievements?

# CHAPTER SIX

University of Western Australia Department of Music.

## Eileen Joyce
### *(1908–1991)*
THE GIRL FROM BOULDER WHO BECAME THE WORLD'S
MOST LOVED CLASSICAL PIANIST

On the platform of New York's Carnegie Hall, Eileen Joyce played her favourite piano concerto, the Rachmaninov No. 2, to a huge audience. Her shapely shoulders and arms gleamed pale as alabaster against the black silk organza of her evening gown with its plunging neckline. Her reddish-gold hair provided a striking colour note in contrast to the sober plumage of the orchestra. Caught up in the joy of performing, she played the lyrical yearning melodies of Rachmaninov with passion, panache and elegance. For Eileen Joyce, music was a union between the brain, the soul and the hands.

Once the last chords of the concerto died away, her audience burst into a frenzy of applause. Dozens of red and white roses were thrown onto the stage. An hour later, wrapped in a fur coat, Miss Joyce left Carnegie Hall and autographed a few programs as eager fans threatened to engulf her. Guards kept them back as she walked to a waiting limousine. Fame, applause and constant praise were the spurs that drove her to continue performing: by this time, the self-style 'barefoot miner's daughter' from Boulder, Western Australia was a very wealthy woman indeed.

Musical genius (defined by the Oxford Dictionary as 'natural aptitude') is not chosen by its possessor: many virtuosos lead frenetic and often solitary existences travelling around the world, in and out of different hotels, adored by their public but rarely enjoying harmonious relations with their husbands and children. Genius is a jealous god and demands sacrifice, especially from women endowed with it. Perhaps Eileen Joyce needed the applause, the fame and prestige as compensation for her deprived childhood spent in dusty shanty towns in outback Australia. 'I had to fight for everything,' she explained to journalists, 'my artistic rise came through toil, illness and suffering.'

Eileen Joyce was a twentieth-century Cinderella. She married Prince Charming, acquired an elegant Mayfair apartment in London, a beautiful country house, a wardrobe of gowns designed by leading couturiers. Yet, underneath her beauty and her wealth, Eileen could never forget her teenage insecurities of her looks and background. As compensation for them, she always sought to be the centre of attention. As though to reassure herself she had good-looks and money, she commissioned no less than *nine* portraits by different artists.[1]

She dreaded the thought of ageing, and always claimed that her birth had not been registered because she was born in a tent in northern Tasmania 'in 1912'. She also claimed that her parents had led a gypsy-like life as itinerant fruit pickers. Wearing bearded or hand-embroidered silk or satin gowns designed by Norman Hartnell, dressmaker to the Queen of England, Eileen would say that as a child she wore ragged dresses and ran barefoot through the bush with Twink, her pet kangaroo, at her heels. It was a charming and romantic fairytale that Eileen never tired of telling. If journalists asked probing questions and asked for names or dates, she would deflect their interest with questions of her own – if they persisted, she became defensive and claimed a slip of memory, or else she terminated the interview.

The truth was just as strange as the legend Eileen embroidered about her barefoot days as Raggedy Eileen with a pet kangaroo on a leash. She *was* a miner's daughter, but there the truth ended. She *did* have a birth certificate, but did not want anyone to see it and learn her real age. In very old age, cosmetic surgery, skilful hairdressing and her lively personality made Eileen appear decades younger.

It has been difficult to piece together the story of Eileen Joyce's childhood because she laid false trails and told stories which contradicted each other. It would appear that when Eileen was born, her father was working in the silver-lead mines of Zeehan, an isolated area north-west of Hobart. Convinced that a birth certificate must exist, I contacted the Registrar of Births, Marriages and Deaths for Tasmania, who arranged for a search to be made. If it could be found, he agreed to send me a copy. He added that Zeehan, Eileen's birthplace, was by no means the idyllic bush setting she claimed – and as it appears in the 1951 British film *Wherever She Goes*. Zeehan had no orchards in which her parents could have worked; at the beginning of the last century it was a landscape of disused pit heads and mullock heaps.

When the copy of Eileen Joyce's birth certificate arrived from Tasmania, it revealed that she was born on 1 January 1908 (she claimed her birthdate as 21 November 1912.) Hence she was four and three-quarter years older than the date shown in all the reference books. Numerous stars of film, stage and the performing arts routinely lop a few years off their age for the sake of their careers. But *why* did Eileen Joyce give herself an entirely different birth date? This was the first of many paradoxes and unanswered questions I encountered about this enigmatic, complex and insecure genius of the piano.

The remote silver mining community of Zeehan, at one time Tasmania's third largest town, lies 291 kilometres north-west of Hobart. Joe Joyce, Eileen's father, was illiterate and had emigrated from Southern Ireland without a penny in his pocket. (For some unknown reason he is called 'Will' Joyce in the film *Wherever She Goes*. Joe was thirty-one when Eileen, his first child, was born. He had married Eileen's mother, Alice Gertrude (née May) when she was only fifteen, a decade younger than himself. Neither of them could read or write; they were hard-working, unpretentious people, though Eileen's mother told her that the Joyces were related to the great Irish writer James Joyce. Eileen's mop of reddish-brown hair, her blue eyes and freckled nose were distinctly Irish, but she was led to believe that her love of music and strong rhythms stemmed from the Spanish descent claimed by her slim, dark-haired mother.

By the time Eileen had learned to walk, Zeehan's profitable deposits of silver were running out. Like most of the miners' families, the Joices lived in a wooden shack, lacking sanitary facilities and electricity. There were no medical services or rubbish collections provided. Instead of the beautiful bushland Eileen conjured up in later years, they were surrounded by mullock heaps, abandoned pit heads, and bush huts infested by flies and cockroaches. Most of the huge Tasmanian trees had been chopped down to build pit props. When the mining company laid off Joe Joyce, there were no unemployment benefits: for a pair of illiterate migrants who now had children to feed, this spelled ruin. Eileen told journalists that her father had 'a passion for finding gold.' Convinced that he could find gold in booming Western Australia, where his brother had emigrated, Eileen's father left Eileen, her mother and her infant brother, John, in the family shack at Zeehan and went off to Kununoppin in Western Australia, to work a claim with a fellow gold miner, convinced – like so many others – that he would strike it rich.

With no money coming in life was hard for Alice Joyce as she waited for her husband to send for them to join him.[2] Later, Eileen would claim that her father's brother sent money to pay their fares to Kununoppin, telling them that Joe Joyce had found gold on his claim.

Believing their years of deprivation were over, Alice packed up their few possessions and took the children on a ship from Burnie (sometimes Eileen said Hobart) to Melbourne and then on a different ship to Adelaide. By the time they reached Perth their money had run out and they were forced to hitch a ride on a carrier's covered waggon over the next 600 kilometres to Kununoppin.

Describing this journey to her biographer, English author Lady Claire Hoskins Abrahall, Eileen claimed that they slept under the stars and in farm sheds, but made no mention of Twink, her pet kangaroo.[2] In *Prelude* (a book written for children), Lady Abrahall somewhat improbably has Twink, wearing a collar and lead, accompanying Eileen all the way. However, in her introduction, the author admits that 'Eileen Joyce had lapses of memory', so she had to invent some of the story. Another of the author's inventions was an imaginary character, a writer called Daniel (in *Wherever She Goes* he appears as an artist) who gives Eileen a mouth organ.

Lady Abrahall's book described how when finally they arrived at arid, dusty Kununoppin, Eileen's mother was horrified to find that the seam of gold had proved disappointing. Joe Joyce and his perpetually optimistic partner had not struck it rich: on the contrary, Joe had now run out of money.[3] At Kununoppin each miner worked his own claim, usually with a partner who helped him lower the bucket on a windlass to haul up rocks and take them to the crushing machine to see if they contained gold. Alice and the three children had to live in Joe's cockroach-infested tent, lacking water or latrines, while he toiled at his claim from dawn to dusk. Traditionally miners lacking cash lived off damper and any rabbits they managed to shoot. Each night the miners drank, gambled and brawled over their claims – fist fights would erupt all round.

Eileen hated Kununoppin. According to Lady Abrahall, Eileen attended a small bush school run by a stern, gaunt teacher, Miss Blenheim. The little girl had a long walk through the bush to reach school. She went bare-footed, as she had outgrown her only pair of shoes and her parents could not afford new ones. She claimed she had nothing to wear other than a ragged dress which she had found in a garbage bin. Eileen hated Miss Blenheim, who caned her for some trifling misdemeanour, and became an unwilling and difficult pupil.[4]

Joe Joyce finally decided that he could not subject his family to such a hazardous and primitive life. Much to Alice's relief, he found a job working for wages with a gold mining company in Boulder, where his brother ran one of the town's twenty-six pubs. The area between Boulder and Kalgoorlie was so rich in gold it was known as The Golden Mile.[5]

Like Kununoppin, Boulder was flat, arid and dusty, without a blade of grass. All the trees had been cut down to build pit props and the tall towers housing the wheels that operated the mine machinery. Faded sepia photographs show Boulder as a shanty town with row upon row of miners' tiny weatherboard cottages. Hastily constructed by the mining company, these shacks lacked running water or sanitation and were built so close together that if a drunken miner walloped his wife, the noise would reverberate through the hessian-lined walls of the next-door cottage. Miners who had made their fortunes and the mine managers lived in brick houses in Kalgoorlie, not in Boulder. An able-bodied man working on the Golden Mile for wages could earn a good living wielding a pick, or gathering wood for pit props or to fuel the mining machinery. Poverty-stricken Italian and Irish migrants flocked to Boulder. So did French and Japanese prostitutes, lured by the prospect of earning good money in the many brothels operating from tumbledown wooden shacks along the Golden Mile. Eileen saw it all too closely to blot out the memories.

Remote Boulder was an unsanitary dust-bowl, scorching hot in summer and freezing cold in winter. The clatter of the mining machinery, the long conveyor belts rattling overhead, the clouds of dust that settled everywhere: these formed the backdrop to Eileen's formative years. Men were intent on making quick money or else drowning their sorrow at *not* making it. Life was rough and tough: brothels, alcoholism, gambling and wife-bashing were rampant.

Doubtless, Eileen did not care to reveal the gritty realities of life in a dirt-floored wooden shack lacking running water or indoor sanitation, surrounded by hordes of flies, fleas, cockroaches and rotting rubbish. Lady Abrahall relates how the Joyce family ate simple meals at a table made from an old crate and owned little more than a few truckle beds. Neighbours lent them wooden chairs. Eileen and Alice carried buckets of water from the standpipe at the end of their street, water that had been piped in 300 miles by the mining company. They heated water for washing or laundry on a wood-fired stove. Boulder's red dust had to be beaten out of clothes with a stick before they could be washed. Even so, garments which had been white became pink-red, and they soon learned to wear coloured clothes.

Joe worked very hard and made money, so that his family would be financially secure.

In spite of her family's relative affluence in later years, the story of that barefoot raggedy child earning pennies for playing a mouth organ was firmly entrenched in Eileen Joyce's mind and she kept repeating it. (In later years, however, among trusted friends, she would sometimes laugh about the 'wilder excesses of journalists' and admit that the stories about her childhood 'had gone too far'.) Eileen's younger sister, born at Boulder a few years after the Joyces settled there, claimed that the family was never destitute and homeless or forced to beg for food as Eileen had told journalists.[6] There was always enough food on their table, although initially their home was far from luxurious.[7]

Eileen's cousin, John Joyce of Kalgoorlie, relates that while Alice was having her second daughter, Eileen stayed with him and his parents in their cottage in Vivian Street, Boulder. Mr Joyce insisted that as far as he knew, Eileen's father was never out of work: he saw no reason why Eileen would ever have had to beg for money to feed starving siblings as she sometimes claimed.[8] Local historian Miss Rika Eriksson grew up in Boulder with Eileen and she states that Eileen's father owned a butcher's shop during Eileen's childhood.

Boulder was working-class and proud of it but some people wanted a better life for their children. Joe wanted his children to attend school and paid the few pence a week charged by the nuns at St Joseph's Primary School. Eileen walked to school, not barefoot as she claimed but wearing white socks and sandals and a clean cotton frock made by her mother. On her way to school, she would have seen semi-naked prostitutes lounging outside their shacks – something else she carefully omitted from the edited tales of her childhood.

During her journey from Tasmania to the west, Eileen claimed she heard a piano for the first time in her life and it had made a great impression on her. Now she was eager to take the piano lessons offered as an optional extra at St Joseph's.

As part of her own legend, Eileen maintained that in order to find the money for the sixpenny lessons, she played tunes on her mouth organ to the miners, who showered her with pennies.[9] She said her father was furious and forbade her to do this again.

Sister Augustine, the piano teacher at St Joseph's, recognised Eileen Joyce's talent, and she was then given free music lessons. She was also encouraged by Sister Ita and Sister Vincent. She used to practise from 4 am to 8 am on the battered old honkey-tonk piano in her uncle's hotel, and described how she would 'transfer tunes she had learned to play on her mouth organ' onto the chipped keys. Eventually, when her uncle moved his old piano into her parents' cottage, it was properly tuned.[10] What Eileen omitted from her legend was that once her extraordinary talent was recognised, she was allowed to practise on a far better piano in Nicholson's music store at Boulder, free of charge.[11]

Eileen's character was one of huge contradictions: she could be confiding and warm or very secretive. She could be tight with money or extremely generous, according to her mood. In mid-life she could be warm and outgoing with friends but guarded, secretive, even prickly, with strangers, with whom her mood could swing from a larrikin sense of humour to the *froideur* of a theatrical *grande dame* and she could be extremely difficult when things did not suit her. To her friends she was loyal and loving, someone very special indeed. Only when she finally became world-famous did Eileen feel secure enough to reveal some aspects of the truth about her childhood. In a taped interview with Felix Hayman, producer of the ABC's morning music program, Eileen told him that her father eventually had made money and invested it and revealed that in later life she had fallen out with members of her family over what they regarded as 'inaccuracies' in her press interviews. During the final years of Eileen's life, Eileens's sister said that Eileen 'outgrew' her family in Boulder, that they felt slighted by her and that she and Eileen had *never* been close.[12]

Eileen never revealed the full truth about her childhood to either of her husbands, to friends or to her biographer, Lady Abrahall, who was a keen patron of music and drama.

When Eileen turned ten she was entered for a music exam set by Trinity College, Dublin. Sister Augustine had wanted her to sit for the

Primary Grade but Eileen insisted on going for the more difficult Intermediate Grade. She performed so well that the visiting examiner gave her the highest pass marks possible. He told Sister Augustine and the Mother Superior at St Joseph's that Eileen should be sent as a boarder to the much larger Loreto Convent in the Perth suburb of Claremont, some 600 kilometres from Boulder. This would give her far greater opportunities to study classical music. Privately the examiner thought it was high time Eileen left this rough, tough area if she was to accomplish anything.

Father Edmund Campion, the distinguished historian, recounts how Eileen's examiner talked to Father John T. McMahon ('Father Mac'), the Catholic Diocesan Inspector of Schools. The next time Father Mac visited Boulder, he interviewed Eileen and her parents and arranged for her to board at the wealthy Loreto Convent in Perth. Eileen was allowed reduced fees but additional money had to be found for her music lessons as well as school uniform and sports equipment.

According to Eileen, the warm-hearted miners of Boulder were determined to support Joe Joyce's daughter, who played the piano for their sing-songs in the pub. Over the next few nights gambling parties were held around the town, after which many miners tipped their winnings into the hat to pay Raggedy Eileen's expenses 'in the big city'.

Eileen also claimed that Mrs Swift, a kind elderly widow for whom she used to run errands to earn pennies, died at this time. A black leather handbag was found in Mrs Swift's dresser containing the then considerable sum of fifty pounds, together with a piece of paper bearing the words: *For Eileen Joyce's music.*[13]

The archivist of St Joseph's Primary School and Father Campion both related that a fund was opened in Boulder to which people subscribed their pennies and sixpences to send little Eileen Joyce to Perth, and that the miners *did* pass around the hat in their pubs, so that Eileen would have the necessary money.

Joe Joyce, dressed in a suit and tie for the occasion, accompanied his shy, red-headed daughter on the train to Perth to enrol at the Convent, which stood surrounded by grounds that sloped down to the Swan River. Years later Eileen would tell friends and journalists the untrue story that she was embarrassed when her father told the Mother Superior that he did not know on which day his daughter was born, that she had no birth certificate and that neither he nor his wife could read or write, a statement that doubtless had some truth.

As 'a charity child' the skinny girl from Boulder was teased by her schoolmates. She was no good at sports; as someone who preferred to perform individually she hated all team games. However, the school had a swimming pool and Eileen found that she loved swimming. But the constant teasing and bullying she received made the insecure miner's daughter even more determined to study hard and excel at the piano so that her life would be different to that of her parents.

She was fortunate to have been taken under the wing of Loreto's dedicated and exceptional music teacher, Sister John. Eileen's musical talent was a gift from God, Sister John insisted.

By now Eileen, craving friendship and attention like most deeply insecure children, realised that as soon as she sat down at the piano and played, her classmates and teachers paused to listen to her. Lonely and homesick, Eileen's craving to be the centre of attention would last all her life. Like many sensitive creative artists she was subject to severe mood swings. When she was under stress or frustrated she could explode into rage and then burst into floods of tears. Sister John was the only person she really trusted, her only friend.

At the Loreto Convent Eileen practised for many hours a day. Another of the teacher nuns, Sister John Moore, developed a special relationship with the talented but prickly little girl and helped her to cope with the other girls' teasing. Eileen was small for her age, with a pale complexion and delicate physique, highly sensitive and volatile, an easy target for bullies. Sister John taught her she must not burst into tears or fly into a rage but hold her ground and tell the bullies they would be in trouble if they hurt her. She gave Eileen a sense of self-worth, told her she was special and that God had chosen her to give pleasure through her music. For the rest of her life Eileen mingled her devotion to the piano with her devotion to Roman Catholicism.

At the convent Eileen was exposed to refinements she had never dreamed of in Boulder: meals served by maids; the importance of using the right knife and fork, of speaking 'nicely', of brushing her wild mop of chestnut hair each night. Life became a learning curve, essential for her future success. Among the affluent girls from Perth's leading Catholic families, Eileen felt ashamed of her lack of table manners, her roughened, reddened hands and her freckles. She attempted to remove the freckles on her nose and cheeks with lemon juice, which cracked her delicate skin.[14] (In the film *Wherever She Goes*, the director chose a British actress, Suzanne Perrett, to play the child heroine. A blonde, round-faced little girl, Suzanne's hair is neatly plaited into two neat little pigtails tied with satin ribbons and she speaks with the plummy accents of a posh London suburb – nothing like Eileen's description of herself as possessing a strong Aussie accent.)

Sister John stopped Eileen from using slang picked up in Boulder and taught her to speak clearly and distinctly. She insisted on the importance of good table manners – 'No, Eileen, no elbows on the table.' 'Don't hold your knife like that.' 'Sit up straight, Eileen, ladies don't slouch.' 'Eileen, use your handkerchief, not your sleeve!' Most nuns of that period threatened purgatory and hellfire for children who told fibs; if Eileen received such a message, it does not seem to have got through to her, judging from her later difficulty in distinguishing fact from fiction. Deportment lessons, in which the girls had to walk down a long passage with a book on their heads would enable Eileen to walk gracefully onto concert platforms wearing beautiful evening gowns that swept the floor. The one attribute Eileen *never* lost was her down-to-earth Aussie sense of humour.

It was stressful to adapt to a new way of life. Eileen remained deeply grateful to Sister John, who behaved like the traditional fairy godmother, turning her into a different person to the tousled-haired child who had arrived at the convent with her illiterate father. She also encouraged Eileen to read a great deal in order to learn about other countries and their customs, telling her that one day she would study overseas. She took Eileen to a concert attended by Percy Grainger and persuaded the famous Australian composer to visit the convent to hear Eileen play. This marked another turning point in Eileen's life. Grainger listened intently as she played and then examined Eileen's hands and fingers, 'noting their firmness, the already strongly developed fingertips'.[15] Grainger pronounced Eileen 'the most transcendentally gifted child' he had ever heard. He tried to raise money to send Eileen to America to study but was unsuccessful.[16]

From then on Eileen was determined to become a concert pianist and travel the world. Another famous visitor to the Sisters of Loreto convent was German pianist Wilhelm Backhaus, then in his mid-forties. After hearing Eileen play he commented: 'I have heard no one to equal her in the past twenty years.' He recommended that she should further her studies at the Leipzig Conservatorium of Music. In the period between World War I and World War II, Leipzig was regarded as Europe's premier Conservatorium of Music. Eileen learned that the Conservatorium had been founded by the composer Felix Mendelssohn, and that one of her favourite composers and pianists, the Norwegian Edward Grieg, had attended it.

Alice and Joe Joyce had three other children to support and educate. There were no musical scholarships in those days for talented young Australians. Eileen would need financial assistance for her passage to Europe and expensive board and tuition fees in Leipzig. A series of benefit concerts were held at the Convent and in the homes of various parents of girls attending the school. Eileen's talent for the piano meant that she was now viewed by teachers, parents, and fellow pupils as the mascot of the school rather than as a social outcast. At big houses with smooth green lawns sloping down to the Swan river, afternoon tea and cool drinks were served under colourful umbrellas. Then, wearing a pink tulle party dress made for her by the nuns (pink being her favourite colour in spite of her reddish hair), Eileen would play Beethoven sonatas and romantic works by Schumann and Chopin.

Eileen would claim that once again the warm-hearted gold miners of Boulder passed round the hat in the pub to help her attain her goal. However, a sizeable portion of the money needed to send Eileen to Leipzig was raised from the wealthy city of Kalgoorlie. Kalgoorlie's Catholic churches and their congregations, as well as local dignitaries and their wives, helped the 'Eileen Joyce to Leipzig Fund Committee' raise money. Perth's Battye Library holds the Minute Book of the Committee dated 1926, which would indicate that Eileen, born in 1908, went to Leipzig when she was in her late teens, rather than fourteen, as she later claimed.

Although she rarely mentioned this to the press, Eileen was also helped by the wealthy West Australian Sir Thomas Coombe. He owned a chain of local cinemas and arranged for Eileen to play between films. These performances, besides helping to publicise the Eileen Joyce to Leipzig Fund, gave her valuable experience of playing in public. In the end, just over nine hundred pounds was raised by the Committee's efforts – a relatively large sum in 1928, enough to buy a small house. The money would cover Eileen's fare, board and lodging and her tuition fees, providing she did not live extravagantly. An inexpensive boarding house was found for her by German nuns who were in correspondence with the Mother Superior of the Loreto Convent.

Eileen wore the pink dress given to her by the nuns for her farewell concert, a fund-raising event organised by the Convent. Her mother, unused to cities or public events, came to the concert and Sister John ensured that Alice Joyce was seated in the front row. Making a little speech and dedicating the next piece to her mother, Eileen played Alice's favourite piece, Schumann's Liebesträume No. 3 (rather than the more difficult Liszt piece of the same name) followed by McDowell's *To a Wild Rose*.[17]

After the concert, Eileen was the centre of attention, no longer the miner's daughter who 'didn't fit in' but the talented pianist the whole school was proud to have helped to send overseas to fulfil her potential. That evening Eileen said a sad goodbye to her mother. Alice realised that her daughter had grown away from Boulder: the piano was now her future. Quiet and self-effacing, she had no intention of standing in Eileen's way. Until this moment, Eileen had not understood the effect that living over ten thousand miles away would have on her and her family. Now it dawned on the unsophisticated girl that she would no longer return to Boulder for holidays.

That night, Sister John, worried about her favourite pupil, visited Eileen's bedside. She found her crying, filled with doubts and fears about leaving Australia for an unknown future.

'I don't want to go. Please let me stay here and continue learning the piano with you,' Eileen sobbed.

Sister John reassured her, telling her she had nothing left to teach her about music. She reminded Eileen how lonely she had been when she arrived at Loreto. Now, after only a few years, she had finally made friends among her classmates. Of course she would find new ones in Leipzig.[18]

The next day Eileen embarked on the long sea voyage to London. From there she went by train to Paris and on to Leipzig. In press interviews, Eileen Joyce would describe her arrival in Leipzig as a shy, skinny teenager in a school uniform: 'a homesick waif-and-stray without warm clothes or knickers'.[19]

According to Sister Ann Carter, the current archivist of the Sisters of Loreto Convent, it was unthinkable that the nuns would have sent their most promising pupil to Europe lacking warm winter clothes *or* knickers. In the 1920s, with their extreme prudery, they would have *insisted* that Eileen did not arrive knickerless in Leipzig.[20] One can only imagine that the nuns bought Eileen 'suitable' underwear, probably thick blue serge bloomers so hideous that Eileen, whose love of beautiful clothes would become legendary, threw them overboard in disgust once the ship left Perth.

A study of press cuttings shows Eileen enlisting journalists' sympathies, repeating the story about arriving at Leipzig with no knickers and telling them how surprised the reception party greeting her at Leipzig station was when they saw her red hair and freckles, because they had been led to believe she was a black-skinned Aborigine.[21]

Eileen was grateful that the nuns had taught her a few simple German phrases to prepare her for Leipzig. However, the boarding house the nuns had chosen was inhabited by office workers rather than students, and she felt homesick for the convent and Sister John. At Leipzig, language and cultural barriers effectively isolated her: she found communication difficult with her teachers and her fellow boarders.

Initially her piano lessons did not go well. Her first teacher, Max Pauer, was exacting and highly critical: his students were in awe of him. His command of English was poor and he often reduced girls to tears by yelling at them in German, as he did to Eileen on occasions. Fortunately for Eileen, the following year she was transferred to a more sympathetic piano teacher who spoke fluent English.

Leipzig itself she found an attractive city of gabled houses and narrow cobbled streets. Some 145 kilometres south of Berlin, it lay beside the muddy, winding River Pleisse. Leipzig, like neighbouring Dresden, would be bombed flat during World War II; today, little of the city that Eileen knew remains.

It was considered very important for pupils of the piano to have the desired strong 'piano-hands'. They needed adequate finger pads and strong sinews: much time was spent on exercises developing these sinews and the necessary 'stretch' to play difficult pieces.

Eileen soon found that the German city which had produced Bach, Mendelsohn, Schumann and Wagner was saturated in music. Leipzig was the premier music academy in Europe, with special courses for singers and players of all major instruments.[22] There was a magnificent opera house, and students at the conservatorium could attend concerts by some of the world's leading performers at the city's famous concert hall, the *Gewandhaus*, where they received a discount on tickets. Eileen longed to go to all the concerts, but even though her fees at the conservatorium had been paid in advance, she realised that money remaining in the 'Eileen Joyce to Leipzig Fund' had to last for three years until she would be ready to go to London to make her debut on the concert platform. She was aware that promoting herself as a concert player there would take even *more* money than she had.

In order to compensate for her insecurity, loneliness and language problems Eileen immersed herself in study. She rose at five each morning and practised for at least six hours. She went to bed very early, unless she had a concert to attend. Her moods swung between elation at her teachers' praise and despair at the thought that she would never reach the standards of the pianists she heard perform at the *Gewandhaus*.

As her funds ran lower, Eileen became more and more worried about her future. She moved to an unheated room in a cheaper boarding house where meals were not included. To save money to attend concerts and buy sheet music she ate less and less. Winter brought snow and ice, a novelty to the girl from outback Australia, but the cold sapped her energies. She went for long walks in the woods around the city, marvelling at their beauty under layers of snow.

After practising for long hours at the piano, inflammation of the sciatic nerve running from the lower back to the hips gave her a great deal of pain. Finally one foot became so sore that she was unable to use the pedal. An operation was recommended but Eileen delayed, fearing the cost … until one day she fainted from pain and woke up in hospital.[23] The surgeon's fees swallowed up more of her precious funds and left her depressed. She regained the use of her foot but at times the pain from her sciatic nerve was intense. All she could do was to take a couple of aspirin and continue practicing, until finally she had to give in and lie on her bed, with a pillow under her knees to give her relief.

145

But still Eileen refused to abandon her dream of becoming a famous concert pianist.

By the time she reached her final year at Leipzig, she was still unsure of herself, her abilities and her looks. She had gained valuable concert experience by performing at the bi-weekly concerts held in the concert hall of the conservatorium. This taught her not to fear an audience of gimlet-eyed student critics, watching like hawks for any mistake. Unlike the futue novelist, Ethel Richardson, who had left Australia to study the piano at Leipzig, Eileen soon overcame the traditional beginner's fears of forgetting music she had committed to memory and having hundreds of eyes watching her perform.

But Eileen was haunted by the fear that after so much hard work, she would be unable to gain entrance into London's snobbish musical world. She worried that once the aristocratic ladies who acted as patrons to many young musicians discovered she was working-class and a 'colonial', she would be as despised as she had been in her early days at the Loreto Convent.

For Eileen the piano and music were her entire life, her 'gift from God'. Sister John had repeatedly told Eileen that 'she had been put on this earth to play classical music'. Eileen knew that if she did not succeed as a concert performer, she would have to abandon her dreams, return to Western Australia, face those kind people who had contributed to her tuition and tell them she had failed. She refused to think about returning to Boulder or Perth as a piano teacher.

To a girl of her spirit, defeat was unthinkable. She forced herself to continue practising in spite of the pain she felt. She spent some of her precious money on master classes given by the great pianists Artur Schnabel and Adelina de Lara – the last surviving pupil of pianist Clara Schumann, wife of Robert Schumann, the famous composer whose work Eileen loved. On days when it was difficult to obtain the vital six hours of piano practice, Eileen would rise at dawn to obtain a free piano at the conservatorium.[24] She worked day and night to improve her knowledge of musical theory.

At the Loreto Convent Eileen had been taught romantic pieces by Chopin, Tchaikovsky and Beethoven. At Leipzig great teachers and pianists like Artur Schnabel insisted that each soloist had a musical 'identity'. Under his expert guidance Eileen broadened her repertoire to include melancholy, introverted works by Grieg (a former pupil of the Leipzig Academy), the melodic works of Rachmaninov (then in exile from Lenin's revolution), and what were then regarded as daring and *avante garde* works by Shostakovich, Prokofiev and other contemporary Russian composers. These were relatively daring works for a young woman but Eileen would have a lifelong passion for playing them.

Before her final exams Eileen was tense and nervous, prone to floods of tears at the slightest criticism. However, she passed with top marks. But she was still riddled with self-doubts and insecurities, worried about her finances and her future. At Loreto she had been a child prodigy. In London she would have to compete against the world's best musicians. Would she succeed? She was reassured when one of her examiners, the gruff Professor Schilsky, not known for giving compliments, told her in his thick Polish accent: 'You are ze greatest performer I 'ave met in all my travels. Believe me, Fraulein, you *will* succeed.'

Other teachers at the Leipzig Conservatorium had warned her that in London, centre of the performing world, there were legions of young unemployed classical musicians, all *longing* for a chance to have their talents recognised. What she needed was an agent to find her concert work. However, without bookings, no reputable agent would take her on their books: it seemed a vicious circle.

The American stockmarket crash of September 1929 had heralded the start of what would become known as the Great Depression and a huge downturn in the amount of money in circulation. It was not an easy time to enter the highly competitive world of professional music, especially for a girl from the colonies who lacked a private income.

Eileen described how she was 'adopted' by a childless New Zealand couple who were spending a few years in Europe, Mr and Mrs Andreae. (Presumably they were of Greek extraction, although Eileen does not say so.) She would tell the story of how she met this music-loving couple at one of the weekly concerts held at the conservatorium. Her piano teacher pointed her out to them, saying: 'There's a lonely little Australian girl over there, can't you take *her* to your hearts?'

In *Prelude*, Claire Hoskins Abrahall gives a different version of their meeting, presumably provided by Eileen. In it, she arrives too late to be admitted to a symphony concert at the *Gewandhaus*, and sits forlornly outside the hall, on the verge of tears, having missed a piece by Tchaikovsky she was longing to hear: the great Piano Concerto No. 1. The Andreaes also arrive late for the concert. Mrs Andreae talks to the young student, who looks thin and undernourished, and realises how badly Eileen needs someone to support her and look after her while she struggles to find her way in London and tries to obtain concert bookings. Eileen always insisted that this kind music-loving couple took her under their wing, fed her, paid her accommodation, bought her clothes, gave her an allowance and took her to stay with them in their house in England. She described the kind couple as her 'adopted parents'. Yet she does not seem to have kept up with them in later life – possibly by then the Andreaes had returned to New Zealand. (When Eileen became famous, whenever interviewers asked probing questions about her parents, her first patrons and her period of struggle in London, she would change the subject or storm out of the interview.) She perfected the art of becoming vague and elusive whenever dates or details were required. One cannot help wondering *what* she was attempting to hide.

Before she left Leipzig for London, Eileen's favourite teacher, Herr Teichmüller, gave her a glowing letter of introduction to the British conductor Albert Coates. By the time she arrived in London for her first audition, the skinny freckled little girl with the unruly mop of chestnut hair who had arrived at the Loreto Convent had become a slender, titian-haired beauty.

Billed as 'the barefoot girl from the bush', Eileen Joyce leapt to stardom on the London arts scene long before expatriates like Arthur Boyd, Clive James and Barry Humphries had made Australia appear less of a cultural desert to British eyes. Initially, Eileen's Aussie accent proved a drawback to success with the snobbish patrons of amateur music societies who could give struggling musicians an opportunity to be discovered. Trying to obtain an agent, she was told cruelly that the British would regard her as a 'colonial' and she must not mention that her parents were of Irish stock as this would mean doors would remain closed to her, no matter how good her technique as a pianist.

Eileen was no fool. She had the wit to realise that in such circles it would be professional suicide to reveal that her father was an illiterate

Aussie battler from Southern Ireland. Irish working-class girls were viewed as drunken and feckless, only suitable to be housemaids or laundresses. Having parents with an exotic gypsy flavour was *far* more socially acceptable than having them called 'bog Irish'.

The Andreaes freed Eileen from financial worry and provided her with a safe and stable home, nutritious meals and a Bluthner piano to practise on. Eileen had no need to look for a part-time job.[25] She wrote to London's leading conductors asking for an audition. And she sent a copy of Herr Techmüller's letter to the conductor Alfred Coates.

She waited and waited but heard nothing. Meanwhile the Andreaes had arranged for Eileen to appear at a concert given by the local music society in Norwich, as a try-out. Mrs Andreae hired a dressmaker to make Eileen a long silk dress, the colour of maize, which set off her auburn hair to perfection. Eileen's youth and good looks charmed her audience and the concert was a big success. But Norfolk was only a provincial city. What mattered was professional success in London, centre of the Empire and the performing arts.

Anxious months passed before Alfred Coates' secretary finally replied, suggesting a time and place for her London audition.

Eileen was very nervous at the idea of such an important occasion. Always so clothes-conscious, it seems strange that she told friends and journalists she wore 'a cheap little cotton frock' for her first audition.[26] Unfortunately, Albert Coates began by telling Eileen he had already booked all the performers he needed for that concert season. Seeing the look in her eyes, he added that her references from Leipzig had been so good he would still like to hear her play something.

Eileen sat down at the piano and played. The result was electrifying. Coates was so impressed by Eileen's talent that he promptly recommended her to his colleague, Sir Henry Wood, the famous conductor and founder of London's popular Promenade Concerts.

She was summoned by Sir Henry for the audition that could make or break her career. This time Eileen was even more nervous. She had had her hair styled professionally but claimed she could still only afford a cheap dress (although in other accounts she claimed Mrs Andreae had bought her an expensive dress for that occasion). Fortunately Sir Henry was extremely impressed by her performance and agreed to include her in one of his next Prom concerts.

Rehearsals with the orchestra followed. From the outset there were battles between the fiery sixty-year old conductor and the red-headed performer. Sir Henry wanted his beautiful young female 'discovery' only to play romantic, 'feminine' works.

'Leave "hard" masculine works by Prokofiev to male performers,' Sir Henry commanded. Eileen objected. What she saw as Sir Henry's patronising approach contradicted everything Artur Schnabel had taught her about selecting concert programs to suit her musical personality. She was terrified of falling out with Sir Henry and jeopardising her fledgling career, but she decided Schnabel's advice was so important she must make a stand. She was a serious musician and had no wish to be regarded as some sweet young thing filling in with a few 'feminine' works.

White-faced, with clenched knuckles, she requested an interview with the great Sir Henry and insisted on playing 'difficult masculine' works by her favourite Russian composers as well as the more feminine pieces he wanted her to play. Surprised by the passion in her voice, Sir Henry amazed her by ceding to her request without further discussion.

In 1931 Eileen Joyce finally made her debut at a crowded Promenade Concert, attended by London's leading critics. Walking up the steps and into the Queen's Hall on her way to her changing room, Eileen was extremely nervous, but Sir Henry Wood's handclasp and his kind words of assurance gave her confidence. After changing into her long maize-coloured silk dress, she sat quietly in her dressing-room concentrating on the score she would play from memory as the hall filled up with excited concertgoers.

As she walked onto the platform, she saw the hall packed from floor to ceiling with faces all turned towards her. Below her huge baskets of rainbow-coloured flowers were banked up below the grand piano. Remembering Sister John, Eileen kept her head high. The audience had no idea how nervous she was. She seemed to glide effortlessly across the platform. The light shone down on her auburn hair as she spread her skirts around her, sat down at the black Steinway grand and started to play.

Sir Henry Wood need not have worried that Eileen would not seem 'romantic' enough to please seasoned Prom goers. Her youth and beauty won their hearts. But it was Eileen's superb technique, the passion and the power of her playing that created a sensation amongst audience and music critics alike. Her choice of 'difficult' music won respect for her eclectic selection among serious musicians. Even the hardened London critics sat up and took notice. Here indeed was a discovery. Eileen's beautiful arm movements and her powerful playing coupled with her sensitive interpretation of the music won their approval.

As she finished the last chord there was a long moment of silence.

Then waves of applause echoed round the hall. Hearing the cries of *'Encore, encore!'* she could have wept tears of relief that she had not failed her supporters in Boulder, dear Sister John or kind Mr and Mrs Andreae.

The meteoric rise of the girl from Boulder had begun.

Eileen's concert promoters found her photographs useful in securing publicity for her performances. Her heart-shaped face, deep-set blue eyes, magnolia complexion and striking figure meant that journalists often compared her to the red-headed Irish-born film star, Maureen O'Hara.

An Eileen Joyce tour was booked for various British provincial cities and towns, playing with amateur and professional orchestras. At last Eileen was able to show a reputable agent that she had bookings. For her tour, Eileen fulfilled her long-held dream of buying expensive evening gowns in which to perform. It was the start of her lifelong passion for designer clothes.

Doubtless her agent informed Eileen that the cooperation of the titled lady patrons of various music societies was vital for success at this beginning stage of her career. The legend of Raggedy Eileen the gypsy girl gained wide exposure in press interviews. Society ladies, patrons of concerts in country areas, who would have scorned to hold cocktail parties for a colonial miner's daughter, willingly organised them for Eileen Joyce, the former barefoot gypsy girl.

The tour resulted in several more engagements with the BBC but no offers to make records. However, what Eileen needed at this critical stage in her career were contracts to perform with *leading* conductors. Determined to succeed at all costs, she used part of her fees from the tour to hire a sound studio and record one of her favourite pieces, Liszt's Study in F Minor. She sent off copies of her 'test' record to all the leading conductors of the day and waited with some trepidation for the results.

Offers of concerts flooded in from major orchestras. She was also given a contract to cut two more records from the sound studio where she made her first recording and a contract from the BBC for regular radio performances one evening a week. These dinner-time concerts became very popular. As the public bought her records so the fame and the legend of 'Eileen Joyce, the barefoot girl from the bush' grew. More and more offers of concerts poured in from Britain, Holland and Germany. She was now performing with some of Europe's leading conductors.

Eileen had an astonishingly wide repertoire. It included seventy concertos which she played entirely from memory – a dozen concertos by Mozart, piano works by Beethoven, the dazzling piano concertos of Prokofiev and her favourite, the soaring and emotional Rachmaninov 2, with which she would become identified. Eileen described herself as 'a quick learner'.[27] 'I could learn a concerto in a week, or in a weekend if I had to. Nowadays,' she added, 'most pianists only have a repertoire of seven or eight concertos from memory.'

If she felt the occasion required it, Eileen Joyce had no difficulty in mimicking an 'educated' British accent, remembering Sister John and her insistence on the importance of good diction. Among friends, however, her voice had a distinctive Aussie twang. In fact, Eileen had a decidedly larrikin streak on occasion. She was no snob although she now moved in snobbish circles. She was a feisty young Cinderella, fighting against huge odds to succeed. Eileen achieved her celebrity through hard work, and brilliance of technique against overwhelming odds.

In 1936, with her program notes claiming she was only twenty-four, Eileen made a triumphant return to Australia on an interstate concert tour organised by the ABC. Concerts were sold out as crowds flooded in to hear her, proud that an Aussie battler had become so famous overseas.

Arriving back in Perth to a civic welcome and a warm hug from her mother, it seemed that the only person Eileen could *not* please was her father. At an official reception in Eileen's honour, Joe Joyce, by now almost sixty, had arrived at the reception in a shiny new suit, new and squeaky shoes and a bushman's hat accompanied by Eileen's sister Alice, who sported a new perm specially for the occasion. As a special request, Joe asked Eileen to play the Irish folk song 'Believe me if all those endearing young charms'.

When she told him that she could play over a hundred sonatas and concertos from memory but could not play his favourite tune, her father exploded. 'Then what's the point? All that money spent on foreign schooling's been wasted!'

Eileen, in long gloves and an elegant beaded satin gown designed by Hartnell, looked embarrassed. Hastily she promised to learn the song immediately. Alice soothed Joe down so that her father stayed on for the reception, where he heard various speakers praising Eileen and calling her Western Australia's favourite pianist. Eileen's mother said little, overawed by so many civic dignitaries and their wives, all of whom wanted to meet Eileen.

When the reception was over, Eileen's younger sister took her aside and told her angrily that their mother had been deeply hurt when the neighbours told her that the southern newspapers had carried an interview with Eileen claiming the family had been so poor that she was forced to beg for money to feed herself and her siblings and went to school in ragged clothes. Eileen must have been embarrassed when her younger sister reminded her acidly that their parents had *always* provided them with nourishing meals and even though every drop of water had to be boiled, their mother had spent hours at the washboard scrubbing out the clinging red dust so that they both had clean frocks for school, clean socks and clean hankies.[28]

Fortunately, no hint of these family dissensions reached the ears of journalists. The discovery that Eileen had taken great liberties with the truth could seriously have harmed her in Australia. Eileen compared her beaded Hartnell gown, strappy Bond Street shoes and diamond brooch (a gift from the man she would later marry) with the cheap dress and tawdry fake diamonds of her younger sister. How lucky she had been to escape from Boulder!

Requests followed from Sydney impresarios for a second concert tour of Australia but Eileen insisted she must return to London. No hint of romance was made public: it was presumed she was returning to fulfil concert engagements in Europe.

The real reason for Eileen's speedy return to London was revealed when Cinderella married her Prince Charming, the rich stockbroker Douglas Leigh Barratt. Her only child, John Douglas Barratt (at this juncture in her career a baby she probably did not want to have) was born on the fateful day in September 1939 when war was declared and Britain stood alone against the full force of Germany's army and airforce.

Neville Chamberlain, the appeaser of Hitler, was replaced as Prime Minister by Winston Churchill. A few weeks after the Barratts' marriage Douglas enlisted as an officer in the British Navy. Separation from her husband of only a few months meant constant anxiety for the new bride. Each day telegrams arrived from the War Office informing next of kin that their loved ones had been killed.

During London's terrible blitz by the German Luftwaffe, many thousands of civilians were killed and much of the East End was destroyed. Eileen had played several times before King George VI and Queen Elizabeth at fund-raising concerts. Like them, she refused to run away and hide somewhere safe until the war was over.

One night Buckingham Palace was badly damaged by a bomb. The Queen won the undying love of the East Enders when she announced on her next visit to bombed-out families: 'At last we can look the East End in the face!' It was a tense and hectic time for everyone who remained in London. Sirens sounded their warning as the German planes approached on their nightly raids and searchlights raked the night sky. No one could predict if they would be dead or alive the next day. Some theatres and concerts continued to hold performances, although the wailing of the air-raid sirens would mean that everyone in the audience, as well as the performers, rushed to the nearest tube station to shelter from German bombs.

It was an anxious period for Eileen, a young mother with no family to support her other than her mother-in-law, who had never approved of her son's marriage.[29] Her mother-in-law could not understand that Eileen was totally in love with music, driven to perform and filled with a burning desire to create beautiful sound. Eileen now faced a dilemma every supporting mother will understand: whether to continue working or stay at home with her child in reduced circumstances.

For Eileen the decision was simple. She had to continue performing, so she entrusted her infant son to her mother-in-law and to well-trained nannies. Doubtless she believed this was the best thing she could do under the circumstances. Unfortunately separation at this tender age created a rift between mother and son, exacerbated, according to Eileen, by her Scottish mother-in-law who implied that instead of looking after him, his mother was 'gadding about on concert tours'.[30] Eileen later said that she was working extremely hard at her chosen profession in order to support herself and her son, the wages of a Naval officer not being overly generous. However the separation and what her son probably perceived as rejection, set a pattern for a troubled and stormy relationship which would never be resolved.

One morning, three years after her romantic wedding to Douglas Leigh Barratt, there was a ring on the door of Eileen's small studio apartment. She answered it to find a uniformed telegraph boy. He handed her the yellow envelope containing a telegram. She went inside. The telegram informed her that her husband had been killed in a direct hit on the minesweeper in which he was serving on the run to Murmansk.

She did not weep immediately, numbed by the news, then broke down into torrents of weeping as she saw her husband's portrait, handsome in his naval uniform. The horror of the fatal telegram stayed with her: even in old age Eileen would recount the story of the telegraph boy's arrival again and again to close friends.

Cinderella had lost her Prince Charming but life had to go on. With her son away from the bombing in the care of his grandmother, Eileen was alone in wartime London, a bleak place of ration books, black-outs, clothing coupons, bombed-out homes, with nightly air-raids and people sleeping in the London Underground stations to escape the bombs. Fearlessly Eileen continued doing what she loved most, giving paid concerts as well as charity performances in hospitals and clinics for victims of the London blitz at a time when many believed the Germans might cross the British Channel and invade Britain.

'We shall fight them on the beaches, we shall never surrender,' Winston Churchill thundered on the radio, effectively raising the morale of Britons weakened by bereavement, air-raids and food shortages. It became apparent to the British that this young Aussie performer had grit and determination which no threats of German bombs could daunt. They loved her for it.

Eileen gave a series of concerts which did much to raise the morale of Londoners. Eileen Joyce and Dame Myra Hess were courageous pianists who insisted on giving concerts in central London, no matter how great the danger. Eileen gave a series of concerts with Sir Malcolm

Sargent and the London Philharmonic Orchestra around Britain's worst-hit cities, including Coventry and Southampton.

At one Eileen Joyce concert in London, the concert hall was freezing cold: there was no coal to stoke the boilers for the central heating. To huge applause, Eileen Joyce appeared on the platform in a holly-green silk dress that accentuated her magnolia complexion and titian hair. Later, journalists learned that she wore a double set of woollen underwear underneath the long skirts of her dress and kept a hot water bottle in her lap so that she could warm her chilblained hands.

In spite of the cold her performance was faultless. She lifted the audience's war-dampened spirits with a brilliant performance of Chopin, an affirmation of the spirit of freedom and the triumph of the human spirit. The audience clapped and cheered until their hands were sore and they grew hoarse. Eileen gave encore after encore, ignoring the wailing air-raid sirens outside. Such was the power of her music that no one departed until she had gathered up her music, made a final curtsey to the audience and left the platform.

The strain of performing night after night, coping with continual nagging pain in her lower back and the horrors of the bombing of London in the blitz preyed on Eileen's nerves so much that she turned into a heavy smoker. One day she suffered a third-degree burn to the finger of one hand from a car's cigarette lighter. The doctor bandaged her hand and ordered her to keep her arm in a sling, thinking this measure would prevent her from performing. Being Eileen, she insisted she would not disappoint those who had booked and paid for tickets. She replaced the bandage with a sticking plaster and gave another concert to overwhelming applause.

Eileen Joyce was the consummate professional. More than once she fainted from nervous exhaustion in her dressing-room before a performance but insisted on appearing on the platform. She hated to let her public down. Once she squashed the tip of her finger in a door, but forced herself to give the advertised recital. When she made up her mind to do something, no one and nothing would stop her. Sometimes the pain in her back was so bad that a trained nurse was paid to stand in the wings, in case Eileen collapsed during a concert. One evening the pain was so intense that as she stood up from the piano stool to receive tumultuous applause from 6000 people at London's Royal Albert Hall, she collapsed and had to be helped off the stage. Frequently she gave recitals wearing a full-length plaster cast, which she disguised by wearing an intricately swathed tulle gown.

In the final years of World War II, Eileen Joyce gave a series of concerts with the London Philharmonic in various provincial cities around Britain, which meant hours spent in crowded trains and draughty stations. Crowds would gather at the stage door of the concert hall to see her arrive and depart.

Through good looks, inborn talent and hard work, aided by the haunting legend that she was the barefoot girl from the bush, Eileen Joyce had acquired film-star charisma. Some critics classed her in the same league as Horowitcz and Rachmaninov, which was praise indeed. However, she faced stern criticism from some of the older and more chauvinist critics, who found it hard to reconcile Miss Joyce's glamour with her talent and tried to denigrate her achievements. What they failed to realise was that Eileen Joyce was a true virtuoso, dedicated to her career. It was the most important thing in her life.

Eileen was eclectic in her choice of program, always seeking new works to add to her already large repertoire. She declined to slavishly follow popular taste. She was interested in good music no matter from what source it came. Performing works by Russian composers was not a popular choice in wartime Britain; there were already rumours of Stalin's ill treatment of the Poles. Eileen saw great composers as being above politics. She was one of the first pianists in Britain to champion the preludes, fuges and fantastic dances written by Dmitry Shostakovich.[31]

There were plenty of handsome American officers in wartime London, eager for female company. Eileen was invited to play for an audience of American generals and colonels at the Grosvenor House Hotel, headquarters of the American forces. Here she met the brilliant American dancer Ginger Rogers, in Europe to entertain American troops, who became her friend. It may have been here, too, that she first met Christopher Mann, Ginger Roger's London agent. Like many other men, he was fascinated by Eileen's titian-haired beauty and lively personality.[32]

Eileen was honoured by an invitation to play Chopin before leading members of the Polish Government in exile, lodged in style at London's Ritz Hotel. Such a beautiful, unattached young widow was bound to attract male admirers (another point which aroused the ire of her Scottish mother-in-law). Eileen enjoyed the attention, receiving bouquets of flowers and invitations to parties. However, as a strict Catholic she was not interested in extra-marital relationships with married officers and was wary about marrying again. She was aware that marriage could tie her down and prevent her performing. Nor did she want more children. Music was her life.

It was Christopher Mann who finally won her heart. In 1945, when the war was over, Eileen married him. One of the things that drew them together was the fact that he understood the stressful yet exhilarating world of the performer. In this, as in a host of other ways, he was the ideal partner for Eileen. Christopher was very tall, slim in build, with an engaging smile and enormous charm. He too had been married before. A former journalist turned publicist, he had become London's leading film agent. The Christopher Mann agency represented most of the leading British film directors and producers as well as the British and American stars who appeared in their films. The contracts of directors such as Sir Carol Read, David Lean, the team of Powell and Pressburger, and the populist producer Betty Box made up the bulk of the agency's income. Repeat showings of their best films worldwide would continue to bring in large royalties for years to come.

The late 1940s and 1950s was the great age of British films and Christopher Mann was involved in many of the major British films of that era: *Lawrence of Arabia*, with Peter O'Toole; *Zorba the Greek*, starring Anthony Quinn; Alec Guiness' Oscar-winning *Bridge over the River Kwai* and *Dr Zhivago*, with Julie Christie – films which have enchanted audiences worldwide for decades and still bring in money to the Christopher Mann estate today.[33]

Christopher was well-read and loved classical music. Poised and personable, he was equally at ease in high society and the British and Hollywood film worlds. His agency had offices in Park Lane, and his London apartment overlooked Hyde Park from the top floor of 140 Park Lane, near the Marble Arch. The newlyweds soon acquired Chartwell Farm as a country house near Westerham, in Kent, which they bought from Mary and Christopher Soames, Winston Churchill's daughter and son-in-law. Later they would buy two more farms.

In wartime, when clothing coupons were in force, Eileen repeatedly wore the exquisitely beaded long evening gowns she had purchased from London and Paris couturiers before the war. She was such a perfectionist and so disciplined in her diet that neither years of stodgy wartime food nor the birth of her son had put an ounce of weight on her.

Once the austerity of post-war Britain relaxed, Eileen was again able to buy her long gowns from famous couturiers like Norman Hartnell and Victor Stiebel. She was also loaned dresses by leading couturiers to attend film premières with her husband. She rarely had to wear the same glamorous gown twice.

One night a zip broke during the first half of Eileen's performance and she had to change in the interval. It was an unusually hot night for London. For the second half of the concert she wore an Empire-style gown with a high waist. To go with the dress and help her keep cool, Eileen's dresser swept her shining auburn hair into an elegant chignon, pinning it with a diamond clasp.

The audience, used to the deprivations of wartime, burst out clapping as Eileen reappeared. This was an innovation. Most female musicians performed wearing plain black dresses perhaps adorned by a pearl necklace. Eileen had started a trend. Today's concertgoers regard it as normal for female performers to look as glamorous as possible at concerts, instead of blending in with the black-and-white of the orchestra.

Eileen's striking good looks and beautiful gowns, coupled with her brilliance as a performer, made her even more popular. A change of costumes midway through the concert became her 'trademark'. Eileen now chose each exquisite dress to match the mood of the piece she was playing – flame colour or lilac for Grieg, Liszt or Chopin, dark greens or her favourite magnolia satin for the chords and arpeggios of Beethoven, red for the bolder music of Prokofiev.

Her husband's constant visits to Hollywood brought Eileen into contact with leading film directors and producers as well as actors like her friend Ginger Rogers, Katherine Hepburn and the young French star Brigitte Bardot. One younger performer Christopher Mann helped to make famous was the multi-talented Russian-born actor, linguist and writer Peter Ustinov.[34]

To celebrate her husband's birthday, there were parties where Eileen played. Sometimes Eileen and Christopher played duets together on two grand pianos which stood close together. Once, as a birthday surprise for Christopher, Ginger Rogers dressed up in top hat, white tie and tails and gave a spirited rendering of her famous routines from the film *Top Hat* which she had made with Fred Astaire.

Unlike some classical pianists who enjoyed playing jazz for amusement, Eileen would *never* play anything but classical music, even at a party. At one party a leading film director heard Eileen play her favourite Rachmaninov Concerto No. 2, filled with emotion and huge sweeping chords. As a result, she was contracted to record the music for *The Seventh Veil*, a major British film. In *The Seventh Veil* viewers saw the young blonde actress Ann Todd pretend to play a silent keyboard while off-camera Eileen was performing the great romantic Grieg Piano Concerto, with which her public would always associate her.

This and other well-paid film tracks increased her fame and popularity. Eileen spent a large proportion of these fees on her couturier clothes and travelling expenses. Top performing artistes were not paid nearly as much then as they are now.

The first film for which Eileen Joyce played the sound track was *I Know Where I'm Going,* shot on the Isle of Skye. The haunting and unforgettable Highland ballad of that name forms the theme song. It became world-famous after Eileen played it and her recording of the film score was sold in huge numbers in Britain and America. Eileen now belonged to the film world as well as the concert platform. The girl from Boulder had come a long way.

For her second film Eileen played the Rachmaninov Concerto No. 2. *Brief Encounter,* directed by David Lean, starred Celia Johnson and Trevor Howard as star-crossed lovers gazing soulfully at each other in railway stations, fearful their illicit but innocent affair will be discovered.

In the post-war period, most people owned far fewer recordings than today, but as prosperity increased so did the market for records. Eileen soon discovered there was a huge public, deprived by the war from concertgoing, hungry for new musical experiences. Her recordings did a great deal to popularise classical music among a wider public.

Now that Eileen was financially secure, she was able to be generous with both her time and her money. She befriended Ann Todd, then an unknown actress, and invited her to Chartwell Farm to help her make her silent playing look lifelike.

By now Eileen Joyce had become a household name throughout Britain. Stories appeared in *House and Garden, Vogue, Harpers* and *Woman's Weekly,* describing Miss Joyce's seven grand pianos, her Mayfair apartment, her beautiful country house decorated with antiques and English chintzes, her portraits commissioned from leading artists, her triumphs at the Albert Hall playing before the Queen and the young Princess Elizabeth, and her friendship with the Churchill family.

At the end of World War II, a Socialist government under Clement Attlee replaced Churchill's coalition government. Sir Winston Churchill, the man who had saved Britain in her darkest hour, found himself out of office, with more time to spend at his beloved country home at Chartwell. He would spend hours at the easel in his garden studio, then visit his water garden to feed the rare golden orff (a variety of sea-perch) with biscuits, or perhaps walk down to the lake to watch his black swans. Sometimes, when the mood took him, Sir Winston might continue walking the short distance to Chartwell Farm, where he was welcomed as an old friend, and where he would sit and listen attentively while Eileen practised for her next concert. Both Sir Winston and Lady Churchill enjoyed watching the latest British films that Christopher Mann showed in the private cinema at Chartwell Farm.

Eileen and Christopher would often be invited to a meal at the Churchill home, where they might meet other members of the Churchill family, as well as politicians and diplomats, media barons such as Lord Beaverbrook, and artists and writers. In the evenings the card table was always kept ready in case Winston suggested a hand of bezique, his favourite game, which Christopher Mann also enjoyed. The dining room at Chartwell, with its long Tuscan-style windows, overlooked the magnificent garden, Lady Churchill's pride and joy, which she had designed. Eileen, who had grown up in arid Boulder and then spent years living in a studio apartment in central London, knew little about gardens. Lady Churchill helped her to design a beautiful garden for Chartwell Farm. For the rest of her life Eileen would love green lawns filled with daffodils in spring, massed herbaceous borders and rose beds bordered with lavender.

At Chartwell Farm Christopher Mann employed a manager, Jim Mayne, to run his dairy herd. On Friday nights, home for the weekend, he and Eileen would discuss farm business with him. Saturday and Sundays were spent relaxing and with friends.[35] Eileen loved the peace and beauty of Chartwell Farm. If she had no concerts scheduled she would often stay on, taking a train to London later in the week to have clothes fitted or visit her hairdresser, then lunching with friends in her favourite restaurant on the ground floor of the exclusive department store Fortnum & Mason in Piccadilly.

The lessons in deportment and social etiquette she had learned long ago from Sister John stood her in good stead. Eileen was now a socially adept hostess, a perfectionist in everything she undertook. Her homes were furnished with understated elegance in the English manner. She had acquired the manners of a lady: instead of dirt floors and hessian walls, she was now surrounded by all the trappings of wealth and good taste. However she always remained proud of being an Australian, and she and her husband made no attempt to gloss over her huge struggle to become one of the world's leading virtuosos. The nearby village of Westerham, built around a village green, was famous for its antique shops. Eileen would take house guests from America and Australia to Pitt's Cottage, a combined tea room and antique shop with a picturesque cottage garden. She loved the Kentish countryside in spring when the orchards were filled with pink and white cherry and apple blossoms. Show business friends of the couple often stayed at Chartwell Farm. Once Ginger Rogers arrived bringing some inflatable black swans for their swimming pool – a witty reference to the black swans from Western Australia that swam on the Churchills' lake at Chartwell.

Even in Australia, famous for lopping down its tall poppies, no one seemed to grudge Eileen Joyce her achievements. Everyone, that is, except Eileen's siblings and her father, who were always unhappy at the way she presented her 'deprived' childhood to the press. Eileen remained typically Australian in her belief in a 'fair go' and equality of opportunity, topics on which she was never afraid to speak her mind. She was identified with Australia in the same way as her friend Peter Finch, the Australian actor, even though they both resided in Britain.

Eileen spoke her mind fearlessly on racial questions. In Johannesburg, she aroused the wrath of the South African Government when she announced that besides playing to a white audience on a paid basis, she would perform free of charge to a coloured audience.

It was in 1947 that *Prelude,* the children's book by her friend Lady Claire Hoskins Abrahall which purported to recount Eileen's Australian childhood, was published by Oxford University Press. Complaints were received by the publisher. Eileen was asked to explain. The book was withdrawn from sale. *Prelude* aroused considerable mirth when copies went on sale in Western Australia. The illustrations by fashion designer Anna Zinkheisen, who had never visited Australia, portrayed the miners of Boulder like cowboys in a Wild West film, with white sombreros and fringed leather chaps. Other illustrations showed a long-legged, barefoot Eileen running through the bush with Twink, her kangaroo. The book talked of her walking him on a collar and lead.

Even after the book was withdrawn from sale, in the files of countless newspapers and radio networks the legend of 'Raggedy Eileen' running barefoot around Zeehan and Boulder (which is as flat as a pancake) and playing the mouth organ to miners who gave her pennies to pay for music lessons lived on. To cover herself for writing a children's book which was partly fantasy, partly biography, Lady Abrahall wrote in her Foreword:

> Thanks to Eileen Joyce, I have had the privilege of probing back into her childhood days and all the reactions which went with them. At times, it has been a little difficult for her to remember or re-capture the past. On these occasions I have used an author's licence, and drawn upon my own imagination, even conjuring up a few fictitious characters with which to surround her.[36]

Eileen insisted that the book had been written without her cooperation. Given the high reputation of the publisher and the fact that Eileen remained good friends with Lady Abrahall, this seems hard to believe.[37] Lady Abrahall was part of the British arts establishment, one of those leading patrons who had been important to Eileen at the start of her career. Unfortunately, Lady Abrahall had never visited Australia or contacted Eileen's parents or siblings. To give the author her due, Eileen's contradictions over events in her childhood and her unwillingness to describe them in detail would have posed a nightmare for *any* biographer. *Prelude* mentioned the Andreaes, Eileen's kind and generous patrons and raises a number of questions. Was Andreae their real name? Why did Mr and Mrs Andreae disappear from Eileen's life? Did Mr Andreae resent the money his wife spent on launching Eileen's career or did he become overly fond of Eileen and his wife end their relationship?[37]

The next attempt to relate Eileen's life was a black and white, 16mm film made by London's Faun Films in 1950.[38] Called *Wherever She Goes* (taken from the nursery rhyme '*Ride a cock horse to Banbury Cross/To see a fine lady ride on a white horse/With rings on her fingers/And bells on her toes/She shall have music wherever she goes.* The film enjoyed considerable success. It claimed to be *loosely* adapted from *Prelude.* The miners of Boulder were played by Australians, dark-haired Muriel Steinberg played Eileen's long-suffering mother, and a pretty blonde actress, Suzanne Parrett, played the young Eileen, while Tim Drysdale, son of artist Russell Drysdale, played Eileen's brother John. In the introduction and the final reel Eileen played herself.[39] The film perpetuated the legend of Eileen as a penniless barefoot girl who taught herself to play classical music on a pub piano then went to a Perth convent on money donated by the miners. Boulder is well portrayed but parts of the film are unreal. For example, Eileen calls her parents 'Mummy' and 'Daddy', more like a middle-class English child than the daughter of a Boulder miner, who would surely have called them 'Mum' and 'Dad'.

By now the Raggedy Eileen legend 'owned' the world-famous pianist and she could not escape from it without humiliation. Eileen was very aware of the advantages of good public relations stories like those magazine articles that celebrated the Manns' increasingly glamorous lifestyle and their famous friends in show business and the world of international music.

Decades later, ABC producer Felix Hayman related that when he interviewed Eileen Joyce she was very 'prickly' when her early life was mentioned. She was still playing the *grande dame*, flaring up and terminating any interview she did not like. Eileen defended herself by saying that her refusal to cooperate with the author of *Prelude* had been 'because I didn't want to upset my family'. The problem was that she had *already* upset them.

Married to someone as wealthy as Christopher Mann, Eileen no longer needed to play for money but her passion for performing and her need to be the centre of attention drove her on. Christopher paid for Eileen's son John to attend a private school and tried to provide him with the good things in life. However, they were never close.

Eileen continued to play to increasingly large audiences. Like Nellie Melba and the Australian pianist and composer Margaret Sutherland, Eileen lacked the necessary time to be a devoted mother. During John's infancy she left him in the care of excellent nannies, as most upper-class women in Britain did during this period.[40] Friends recall that as a child and a teenager John Barratt never wanted for material things. But working hard and touring constantly meant that Eileen was frequently short of time to spend with her son, to the detriment of their relationship. Money spent *on* children rarely compensates for lack of time spent *with* them. Eileen was often under stress and her temper (inherited from her father) could flare up and then end in tears. Such behaviour confuses children. Close friends noted that the relationship between Eileen and her growing son was now stormy.[41] Like her husband, Eileen had a stressful but fascinating career. She did love her son in her own way, but like most successful performers hers was a driven personality. Being a concert performer, she often claimed, 'demanded the pianist's life and soul'.

The continual striving after subtle nuances of expression and the sheer physical effort involved were emotionally and physically draining to someone as temperamental as Eileen, who was still battling lower back pain after sitting at the piano for long periods. Sister John had told her that God had created her to make music; for Eileen the creation of good music held a religious intensity.

Now that Eileen was seriously wealthy, in addition to paid concerts, she gave recitals free of charge in aid of her 'pet' charity, a home for lepers run by missionaries at Vellore, India. She also generously donated her time to play in churches and schools to raise money for scholarships to enable deprived children to study music. She played in hospitals for the mentally and physically handicapped and on occasions for prisoners in jail. She played on grand pianos and battered old uprights, in hospices for the dying, in small village halls to raise funds for guide dogs for the blind and for visiting dignitaries at Australia House in London.

As the world's highest paid concert pianist, Eileen had never worked harder. She toured Australia in 1948, performing in Melbourne and in Brisbane's City Hall, where the audience was enthralled by her wonderful rendition of the Rachmaninov No. 2 Concerto. It was the first time they had known a performer change in the interval – this time from a blue gown to another of dashing yellow.[42] She did not visit Boulder on this tour. She and her family moved in such totally different worlds that they had little in common. Her family was now quite well off and did not need her money.

Before her sell-out concert at Sydney's Town Hall, Eileen invited a group of excited schoolgirls to hear her practise. Before she started playing, Eileen came to the front of the platform and spoke to the girls 'very sweetly', telling them of her own difficulties and joys as a performer. One of the girls who heard Eileen play (and immediately decided that she too must become a concert pianist) was Deirdre Prussak, who would become a close friend to Eileen in her final years.[43]

Over the next decade Eileen gave concerts all over Britain, in Holland, Russia, South Africa, South and North America as well as Scandinavia. She spent a great deal of time travelling by train, boat and plane. British critics remarked that no other pianist ever filled the Royal Albert Hall more times than Eileen Joyce.[44]

Eileen remained what she had always been: a demanding perfectionist, hard on herself and dedicated to performing. To live up to her high standards of performance meant weeks of constant practice which resulted in bouts of pain, exhaustion and tears. Yet for all her apparent fragility, Eileen was a woman of inner strength and spirit. She was convinced that 'there must be a great deal of hard and mundane practising to achieve anything.' She also said: 'It can't *all* be joy making music, otherwise the joy would be too overwhelming.'[45]

Her decision to retire came in 1960, caused by exhaustion leading to what is now called 'burn-out'. She had made a gruelling concert tour by train around the Indian continent before flying to Hong Kong, where she survived a particularly hazardous landing. She was hot and exhausted. Crossing Hong Kong harbour by ferry to the concert hall, racked with

Eileen Joyce

stabs of pain from her lower back, she asked herself, 'Why am I doing all this? What a crazy way to live, rushing around the world at this pace. Why don't I give it all up and stay at home with my husband?' It should be borne in mind that Eileen's decision to retire took place before jumbo jets made life slightly easier for international performers as they moved across the world from one concert hall to another.

Accordingly, worn out by decades of international travel, Eileen Joyce announced her retirement that same year. She did this at the end of a concert in Aberdeen, symbolically closing the top of the grand piano. Then she turned to the audience and explained that due to muscular pain in her back and fingers this would be her final public concert.[46]

She had injured the little finger of her right hand, which badly affected her ability to 'stretch' (she used to be able to extend her fingers to cover ten notes). At the time she retired Eileen described herself as being 'an empty shell, depleted physically, spiritually and emotionally. I loved the piano which had brought me exaltation as well as despair.'[47]

So give it all up she did.

As a substitute she took up tapestry and gardening. Finally she was freed from the necessity to practise from six to eight hours almost every day – 'blood, sweat and survival' as she now termed it. After she ceased playing professionally and practising for hours on end, and doubtless had some physiotherapy, the pain in her hands and her lower back gradually lessened until finally she was freed from that as well.

She did not touch a piano again for almost six years. Then, pain-free, she started playing again … and experienced the same sense of magic and awe for music that she had felt as a child sitting beside Sister John. Entirely for her own pleasure and that of her friends, she would play the piano or the harpsichord in the evenings. Eileen was unusual in playing the harpsichord as well as the piano, instruments that require a totally different 'touch'. She performed on her hand-painted harpsichord in concerts at London's Royal Festival Hall.

After six years of silence, the public still loved Eileen Joyce. There were countless demands for her to return to the concert platform. Finally, in 1967 she relented and gave one last charity concert, playing works by her favourite composers to a huge audience. At the end the audience applauded, stamped their feet and cheered. They wanted her back. She enjoyed the experience so much that she did consider returning to the concert platform. But she was now in her late fifties, her back had recovered and she abandoned the idea. Remembering Sister John's words she announced to the press: 'I was put on this planet to play with joy. I did my best.'

Reviewing her final concert, one critic wrote: 'Her old sparkle and crackling vivacity has another dimension, that of an inner radiance.' Eileen herself felt that her interpretation of the works of many composers had acquired more wisdom and understanding. Her long rest from performing had given her time to read and study and this was apparent in her profound interpretation of various works.[48]

In 1971 she was honoured by the award of an Honorary Doctorate of Music from the University of Cambridge. It gave her enormous pleasure to have this very public acceptance from the world of academic music, a compensation for all those years of hard work.

Her husband was also tiring. He had cut down staff numbers and moved his agency to smaller premises. He had been a heavy pipe smoker for many years, and had developed a 'smoker's cough'. Eventually he was diagnosed as having lung cancer.

Aided by professional nurses, Eileen nursed her husband devotedly until his death in December 1979, aged seventy-one.[49] Eileen, now in her late sixties, was deeply distressed by her husband's death and found his funeral very hard to endure. There is nothing harder for the bereaved than walking away from the last resting place of a loved one. Loyal friends rallied round. Gradually Eileen's strength of character came to her rescue and she recovered her equilibrium.

Christopher Mann bequeathed his wife some five million pounds in assets and property, making her an immensely rich woman in her own right.

Eileen was a complex and sometimes insecure person. At times she could display an impractical, almost fey attitude, giving away designer dresses, jewels and gifts of money. Fortunately her affairs were looked after by an excellent accountant. Loneliness meant that she was easy prey for sob stories; she was taken advantage of by one particularly charming young man who obtained a large sum of money from her.

She donated large amounts to her favourite charities and to help aspiring concert performers.[50] Nothing could weaken Eileen's determination to continue helping others to create beautiful music. She learned from her Australian friends, Professor Sir Frank Calloway and his wife Kathleen, who used to visit her regularly, that Perth would soon celebrate its 150th celebrations and that the University of Western Australia was to award her an Honorary Doctorate as Cambridge had done, which delighted Eileen. She would commission another portrait in her academic gown to have in her home.

In June 1981, in her seventies, Eileen returned to Perth to inaugurate a very generous and imaginative scheme designed to benefit music students in Western Australia. She told friends that that her late husband had urged her to make a donation to honour her parents' memory *now*, rather than bequeath money to the University in her will. Possibly Eileen felt remorseful that she had not been closer to her mother and father, and Christopher had realised this. Accordingly she donated $110 000 to cover the cost of the Eileen Joyce studio 'in memory of her parents' and to set up an Eileen Joyce Fund which would pay a graduate of the University to study the piano overseas.

The beautiful music studio dedicated to Eileen Joyce's parents is now part of the University of Western Australia's music department. It stands in the University's landscaped grounds, and its glass walls look out onto gardens thick with tree ferns.

Eileen wanted the Eileen Joyce Studio to be used for the teaching of keyboard music, for master classes similar to those she had attended at Leipzig and to house a range of instruments spanning the history of Western keyboard music. The instruments Eileen donated to the studio that bears her name included an organ, a spinet, her hand-painted harpsichord built for her in 1959 by the famous instrument maker Thomas Goff, and an old-style or *forte* piano. She also gifted the portrait of herself by Augustus John and the bronze bust by Anna Mahler as well as her correspondence (now available to the general public on the University of Western Australia's website).

On this third and final visit 'home' to Western Australia (having made previous ones in 1936 and 1948), Eileen was her usual bubbly delightful self. She visited her former convent school in company with Father McMahon (the priest who organised her scholarship to the Sisters of Loreto Convent), and was delighted to have a chance to see her beloved music teacher, Sister John, now Mother John Moore.

Eileen never forgot these two devoted people, who had done so much to change her life. She was still a devout Catholic and while in Perth she attended Sunday Mass at Father McMahon's church. She did not visit Boulder. Questioned by the press, Eileen (reluctantly) confessed that due to living in totally different worlds, with some ten thousand miles separating them, she had lost touch with her siblings.[51]

In the summer of 1981 she was thrilled to learn she had been awarded the Order of St Michael and St George, bestowed on her by H.M. the Queen. Letters and telegrams of congratulation poured in, including one from the Prime Minister of Australia and another from Sir Charles Court, Premier of Western Australia, who had opened the Eileen Joyce studio at the University. Malcolm Williamson, the Maker of the Queen's Music, was also delighted that she, a fellow Australian, had been honoured in this way. 'Countless congratulations from all musicians and from all true Australians,' he wrote. 'Honours should have been poured on you all your life.'[52]

Eileen also felt honoured when she was appointed a Juror at the Sydney International Piano Festival and Competition. With her usual generosity, she donated £20 000 (a large sum for that period) to help mount the Third International Piano Competition and flew out to Sydney to attend it in 1985. Eileen, who did not look her age, was now nearing eighty but refused to acknowledge the fact.

Deirdre Prussak, a former Australian nurse turned magazine columnist, was sent to interview Eileen by *New Idea* magazine. It had been arranged by the magazine that Deirdre would interview Eileen then take her out to dinner. Georgie, Eileen's female secretary, who had been with her for many years, was unable to accompany her to Sydney on this trip. Upon arriving at the hotel, Deirdre learned that without a secretary or a minder Eileen had forgotten she had agreed to do an interview for *New Idea.*

A confused Eileen opened the door of her suite at the Hilton, saw Deidre, apologised profusely and they sat and talked for an hour. When Eileen learned that Deirdre was not just another journalist in search of sensational details about her childhood and that Deirdre's adoptive mother was the famous opera comedienne Anna Russell, so she knew a great deal about music and musicians, Eileen was delighted. She said that Fate must have sent Deirdre, an entertaining, intelligent and caring young woman, to interview her at a time when she badly needed someone to help her.

Deirdre had seen Eileen practice at the Sydney Town Hall almost forty years ago and felt 'there was something ethereal about Eileen's ability to weave dreams with her music and wrap her audience in magic. I was fortunate that many years later I became her friend. When you have admired someone for so many years it is gratifying to discover that, beside their incredible talent, they are also a truly delightful, gentle and beautiful human being.'

Dinner that night marked the start of a long and enduring friendship between the two women. Eileen, usually so guarded with journalists, opened up and revealed her insecurities about her diminishing memory and the fear she had Alzheimer's disease and asked, 'You will help me, won't you?'

Deirdre's heart went out to this valiant women who had come to Sydney because she believed in the aims of the International Piano Competition but who now had problems with her short-term memory and was worried to go out by herself, fearing that she might forget her handbag or get lost.

Eileen had not been provided with an official minder by the Competition's organisers. Over dinner that night she confided to Deirdre that on the outward journey she had got lost while changing planes at Singapore. She said she did not like to admit her fears to the Piano Festival's organisers and ask for help. For Eileen took her role as a Juror of the piano competition very seriously indeed. 'You feel a sense of responsibility and dedication towards being a Juror. You have to give your whole spirit and attention to each competitor. It takes an enormous amount of concentration to fulfil this commitment,' she said, understanding from her own experience just how hard each competitor had worked to get to this point and how disappointed the losers would be.[53]

Deirdre, a former nurse, had enough experience of elderly people with dementia to realise just how vulnerable Eileen was. She volunteered to be Eileen's chauffeur and guide and described how 'each morning I would go to her hotel to be met with "Thank God, Deirdre, you've come!"'

Deirdre found Eileen unpretentious with a marvellous sense of humour and deeply grateful for driving her around Sydney and inviting her to meals at her Balmain home. She did not realise that by now Eileen was a multi-millionaire. She even asked Eileen if she could afford to stay at the Hilton, then Sydney's most expensive hotel. Deirdre was very surprised to learn that Eileen had been able to write a cheque for many thousands of pounds to the Piano Competition's Organisers.

Eileen still harped on the 'Raggedy Eileen' legend. She repeated to Deirdre the improbable story that she had arrived in Leipzig without warm knickers and the Germans had been expecting a black Aborigine. Tactfully, Deirdre suggested omitting this anecdote, but Eileen could not change and went on radio repeating the story. She was very grateful to Deirdre for all her help in Sydney and invited her to stay with her in England.

By now Eileen was tiring easily and found Chartwell Farm and the and pedigree herd of Jersey cows too much to manage alone. So she had sold her beautiful home and moved a few miles away to Limpsfield, a very pretty village not far from Oxted. White Hart Lodge, her new home in the High Street, was smaller than Chartwell Farm. It had once been part of an old monastery and the entrance hall, complete with oak beams and an inglenook, was large enough to house her precious Steinway grand pianos.[54]

'My new home is very strategically placed', Eileen told her friends with her usual sense of humour, 'opposite a booze shop and just up the road from the crematorium!'[55]

At White Hart Lodge, she no longer had live-in staff as both Peggy and Dorothy, her faithful retainers for so many years, had died. Eileen herself suffered a heart attack caused by the stress of the move to Limpsfield, but devoted friends and her own positive approach to life helped her to recover from this, as well as a subsequent car accident.

Now her memory would fail her more frequently, but she was determined not to give in. With the help of friends she organised musical evenings in her new home. In the huge entrance hall her two Steinway pianos stood back to back, beneath a row of portraits of Eileen by various artists. The area was suitable for private concerts. She featured recitals by young 'finds' whose careers she enjoyed helping to promote, out of her own funds, and with whom she would sometimes play duets.

In 1988, aged eighty (but still refusing to admit to it), her figure trim and taut, her hair tinted to its former auburn and her skin remarkably free of wrinkles, Eileen hoped to be well enough to play in public once again. She was scheduled to appear at a concert at London's Theatre Royal to celebrate Australia's Bicentennial, to be conducted by her old friend, Australian-born Sir Charles Mackerras. Sadly, Eileen had to cancel her performance. The muscular complaint which prevented her from stretching the little finger of her right hand far enough had returned. She had intended to perform music by the Australian composer Percy Grainger, but realised she would be unable to play it well enough. Still the total perfectionist, she declined to appear unless she felt that her performance was up to world standard.

Deirdre Prussak was Eileen's guest at White Hart Lodge in 1987 and again in 1988. Eileen, whose memory had once been so superb, now had great difficulty remembering scores and was forced to play from sheet music. Her moods were sometimes badly affected. Deirdre Prussak recalls: 'There were times when I cried with her because she felt lost and could not understand what was happening to her.'

At other times she was still the old Eileen with her impish sense of humour, laughing and joking away. On good days she enjoyed being driven up to London and lunching at her favourite restaurant.

John Barratt, her son, was now married, and Eileen was thrilled to learn that her daughter-in-law, Rebecca, had given her a grandson – especially one with red hair. Perhaps tactlessly, Eileen told the press that she hoped to send Alexander to Geelong Grammar School when he was old enough. John and Rebecca Barratts' reaction to this idea was not reported. At this stage they still visited her and she sent Deirdre photographs showing Alexander sitting on her lap as she attempted to make his baby fingers play the piano. Other visits were not so happy and ended in rows. Then the visits stopped altogether.

Eileen's longstanding friend Professor Sir Frank Calloway, Head of the University Department of Music, had written from Perth to say that if she decided to donate her papers to the University of Western

Australia, the Agent General for that State would arrange for their shipment to Perth.[56] On 17 October 1988, Eileen replied that she 'had not yet reached a decision about the transfer of this material'.[57] English friends, however, advised her to send off the material and finally she agreed. It was as though she realised that the sands in the hour glass were running out.

Eileen had already made five visits to Australia from London – in 1936, 1948, 1981 and 1985.[58] In 1989, frail but undaunted, she returned to Sydney as a guest of honour to give a brief speech at a concert organised by Mary Valentine, General Manager of the Sydney Symphony Orchestra. The concert was held in the Sydney Town Hall on 10 February.[59]

Frail and forgetful as she now was, nothing could stop Eileen from attending the concert where the young pianist Bernadette Harvey played the Rachmaninov No. 2 Concerto. Actor and writer Nick Enright gave a speech in which he reminded the audience that Dr Joyce had received honorary degrees from the Universities of Cambridge, Melbourne and Western Australia.

Eileen was interviewed by Peter Ross for the ABC *Arts on Sunday* program. Yet again she repeated the old no knickers story and the fact that the Leipzig Conservatorium had been expecting a black girl. 'Just fancy, an Aboriginal,' she said. Suavely, Peter Ross never missed a beat and steered her off on another tack. Strangely, Eileen, still looking a decade younger than her real age, told Peter Ross laughingly, 'I was never a great beauty. I had *far* too many freckles and couldn't get rid of them!'

Deirdre Prussak accompanied Eileen to the concert. Eileen, very much the grande dame, seated on the platform, was interviewed, and then read a brief but inspiring speech. It was her last night of triumph.

By now Deirdre was seriously worried by the deterioration in Eileen's memory and concentration and told her so. Eileen was also very worried and asked Deirdre to accompany her to consult a leading Sydney specialist. After a detailed examination, she was told that there *were* signs of Alzheimer's disease, just as Deirdre had feared.[60]

Eileen returned to White Hart Lodge, where she lived out her last two years helped by kind and caring friends. She had good days and others when she could remember very little and was totally confused.

However, in the good times she gained comfort from listening to music and from her dogs and cats.

Eileen Joyce always confronted life with great courage and generosity. By the time of her death she had given away large sums to various good causes. Her impish sense of humour did not lessen as she aged. On a good day she would even joke about her funeral. 'When I die, Deirdre, I want to be dressed in my red Norman Hartnell and laid out over my Steinway pianos!'

'Surely not the *red* one, Eileen, it won't go with your hair!' Deirdre replied and she and Eileen burst out laughing.

Deirdre worried greatly about her and generously suggested that Eileen come 'home' to live out the rest of her life in her Sydney house, where she would care for her. But the doctor said it was too late for such a move. Eileen's Alzheimer's disease had now deteriorated to the point where the long flight to Australia was impossible. The brilliant musician who had once had such a marvellous memory for complex scores was now confused about dates, times and current events. It was a torment for someone who had possessed such a lively mind as Eileen Joyce.

In March 1991, just as the daffodils were coming into flower on the green lawns of White Hart Lodge, Eileen suffered a bad fall and broke her hip, already seriously weakened by osteoporosis. She was moved to hospital and suffered a fatal attack of pneumonia. When she closed her eyes for the last time, all those who loved her could only feel relief that this period of anguish was over, and remember the beauty and the joy that Eileen's playing had brought them.[61]

Eileen had expressed her desire to be cremated. Her wishes were followed. She was given a memorial service in the local church at which the pianist Philip Fowke, who had performed with Eileen in the past, played some of her best loved music and music critic Bryce Morrison gave an emotive valedictory address.[62]

Eileen's loyal friends were saddened that her relationship with her only son had deteriorated to such a point that neither he nor his wife attended Eileen's funeral or her memorial service. The local Rector expressed the wish they would be reunited in heaven.

Her executors chose a simple granite tombstone engraved with the words: 'In treasured Memory of Dr Eileen Joyce, C.M.G., Concert Pianist, died 25 March 1991.' To the left of her grave is the white marble memorial to the famous conductor Sir Thomas Beecham and to the right the granite slab below which the composer Frederick Delius is buried.

Hundreds of floral tributes were received from many different countries, from musical celebrities and from orchestras Eileen Joyce had played with. The attendance at her memorial service was huge. Ornate wreaths and small posies of flowers from those to whom Eileen's playing had given so much pleasure marked the final chapter in the story of a courageous, talented and dedicated woman. Eileen Joyce, had to struggle to win her honoured place in the world of international music. Her phenomenal technique at the keyboard, her innovative programmes and her huge repertoire made her greatly admired wherever the piano is played.

# CHAPTER SEVEN

Portrait photograph: National Library of Australia, Canberra.

## Edith Dircksey Cowan
### *(1861–1932)*

FIRST AUSTRALIAN WOMAN TO SIT IN A STATE PARLIAMENT

'Who is that woman with the sad face?' asked a teller at my local Commonwealth Bank, as she handed me a fifty dollar note bearing Edith Cowan's portrait. I explained that although many women had fought for the right to vote or even stood for election, Edith Cowan was the first woman in Australia actually to gain a seat in Parliament, where she fought for the rights of women and children, the poor and the disadvantaged.[1]

I wondered to myself why, in view of her importance in the worldwide history of women, Edith Cowan had been virtually ignored for half a century following her death.[2] Fortunately we are now rediscovering her achievements. She is the woman whose story all Australians should know.

Edith Cowan's face does appear sad on our currency, but this is hardly surprising. The sadness stems from a childhood and adolescence scarred by tragedy and a blaze of notoriety. Edith's mother, the beautiful and devout Edith Dircksey Brown (born Wittenoom) was the daughter of a Protestant pastor. She became a governess and married a local hero, a grazier turned explorer. Edith's gentle, intelligent mother died when her daughter was only seven, but her love of learning and her ideals would influence her daughter's future.

Edith's father, Kenneth Brown, soon married again, this time a woman with a strong temper and will of her own. Kenneth Brown was now drinking heavily. Edith's life at home was filled with violent arguments between her father and her stepmother. She was sent away to boarding school when she was only nine.

She returned for school holidays to Glengarry Station, Kenneth Brown's remote cattle property near Geraldton in Western Australia. Edith's father was an aggressive, domineering man who fitted well into a male-dominated pioneer society where masculinity was glorified and married women were expected to provide sex on demand. By law, women were the property of husbands or fathers – a man's authority over his wife and children was absolute. Tolstoy described the position of all married women at that time when Anna Karenina laments, 'I am a married woman, my husband owns me'.[3] The distinguished jurist Sir William Blackstone, on whose codification of laws Australian justice depended, insisted that:

... the very being of legal existence of the woman is suspended during marriage ... incorporated and consolidated into that of the husband under whose wing, protection and cover she performs.

In 1876, the studious Edith turned fifteen. Her fellow boarders at the Misses Cowans' boarding school in Perth were horrified to learn from newspaper reports that Edith's father had shot his second wife during a drunken argument. His trial for murder created more headlines. It was the murder of her stepmother in a bout of drunken rage that opened Edith's eyes to women's lack of power in marriage. Edith had no wish to be the slave of any man and would insist on using the name Dircksey, her mother's middle name, for the rest of her life.

Edith suffered agonies of shyness when she was forced to appear in court to give evidence at the sensational murder trial. After her court appearance she was besieged by journalists demanding answers to the most intimate questions. She shed tears of humiliation and despair in the privacy of her room at school.

Kenneth Brown was found guilty and hanged. His execution brought sensitive, retiring Edith face to face with the realities of death. Unsavoury stories about her father and stepmother were whispered behind her back and some girls in her class were told by their parents to shun her. She was thrown into the adult world prematurely.

Edith buried herself in books. She had no close relatives in whom to confide her inner feelings, and in those days there was no bereavement counselling. She now had no home to go to and spent the holidays at school. She read widely, preferring works about social and political reform to the novels read by her contemporaries.

Edith would have loved to go to university. But in the late 1870s, when she was in her teens, a university education for girls was almost unheard of. Her only choices were to stay on at school as a pupil-teacher or to marry. A suitable marriage for Edith Dircksey Brown, daughter of a murderer, seemed impossible. Perth was a snobbish place where middle-class families all knew each other: Edith was now virtually outside the pale.

However, one eligible and attractive man who visited the school was not discouraged. James Cowan, younger brother of Edith's joint headmistresses, found tall, willowy Edith fascinating; her sweet but sad face had haunted him since the day he first met her. Edith studiously ignored him. It took nearly a year for her to realise that James Cowan was as serious-minded as she was. Cowan was a book-loving lawyer with an interest in social reform. He brought the sad, confused young girl presents of books he thought would interest her. At first she refused them, so he left them with his sisters.

At long last, Edith stopped avoiding her suitor: they began to converse and she realised they had much in common. James Cowan was considerably older than her, and had the wisdom to take their relationship slowly. Their friendship ripened and finally Edith accepted his proposal of marriage. She was only nineteen.

On 12 November 1879, Miss Edith Dircksey Brown married Mr James Cowan in St George's Cathedral. James Cowan was Registrar of the Supreme Court and worked long hours. Before children kept her at home, Edith attended some Court sessions and saw and heard the sad stories of battered wives and abused children. She visited the homes of women whose stories had touched her, trying to help with advice and financial assistance.

But family demands soon took over her days. In eleven years Edith bore four daughters and a son and took a long time to recover from each pregnancy. She was a devoted and proud mother who adored children and gave them all the love she had missed when growing up without a mother herself.[4]

In 1890, James Cowan was appointed Police Magistrate in Perth. Their last child was born the following year. By now, the elder children were growing up and Edith could afford domestic help. She wanted to do something to help the women she had seen appear in the courts, but was held back by her shyness and lack of experience.

Invited to become a founding member of the famous Karrakatta Women's Debating Club in Perth, Edith realised that speaking in public might help overcome the problem of her shyness. She was terrified when she mounted the platform for the first time, confronted by hundreds of women's faces beneath fashionable hats, all staring at her. Her soft voice wavered but she continued talking, telling her audience about the abused children and battered wives she had seen in the Magistrate's Court, and saying how much she wished the laws could be changed so that abused women were no longer slaves and prisoners in their own homes. She talked of the need for women's refuges and for pensions for widows and single mothers. She conquered her reticence about the past and told her audience about her murdered stepmother. Her audience listened, wide-eyed. At the end they applauded. Edith Cowan's career in public speaking had begun.

The Karrakatta Club (named after an affluent Perth suburb) had been formed by and for women from a similar background to herself. They were intelligent but most had acquired accomplishments rather than education and, like Edith Cowan, had left school young, married and raised families. All these women were keen to improve their education: all were determined that women should have the vote.

Edith made friends with strong-minded Bessie Rischbieth and Roberta Jull. She persuaded Rischbieth, wife of a millionaire wool broker, to take on some voluntary social work.

Edith proved herself an excellent and tactful organiser with an ability to handle committees and paperwork. The Karrakatta Club increased in size and importance. Their lectures covered areas such as women's health, women's rights, the arts, and legal reform.

Edith was eventually voted chairman of the Club's Education Section; from there she progressed to chairmanship of the Literary Section, then to chairmanship of the Legal Section, informing women about their lack of legal rights in cases of domestic violence, separation or divorce, when most would forfeit the right to see their children again. She became the Club's Secretary in 1894, Vice-President and then President.[5]

Members of the Karrakatta Club knew that the women's vote was vital to their cause. Between 1910 and 1917, Vida Goldstein stood as a parliamentary candidate, and bravely but unsuccessfully attempted to enter the Victorian parliamentary system. Many women were supportive of Miss Goldstein's bravery in trying to enter the male-dominated world of politics. Australia was then an intensely conservative country, where muscle, machismo and virility were glorified and the 'White Australia' policy prevailed. Women were told they should leave all decision-making to husbands, fathers or brothers. Male perceptions of women as weak and unintelligent proved hard to erode. Although Vida Goldstein was a brilliant public speaker, she never managed to gain a seat in Parliament. The Karrakatta Club members would have had no idea at that time that Edith Cowan would become Australia's first woman Member of Parliament.

Over the years, Edith developed more confidence in her own abilities. She had become involved on a voluntary basis with raising the money to found a District Nursing Society, to provide home nursing for women who could not otherwise afford this. She was also deeply involved with running a convalescent home for children and helping to fund and build the Alexandra Home for Women, a refuge for unmarried mothers with a maternity hospital attached.

The Alexandra Maternity Hospital was unique for its period because it would admit unmarried as well as married mothers. At this time, unmarried mothers, known as 'fallen women', were shunned in public maternity wards and pressured to give up their babies for adoption. Unmarried pregnant women were treated like petty criminals. During the latter stages of their pregnancy they were made to scrub hospital floors and empty garbage bins. No one cared if they lost their children. They were often denied access to anaesthetics, in the belief that a painful birth would prevent them repeating their sins. In order that the mothers should not bond with their newborn babies, they were forbidden to touch, hold or feed them. Adoptive parents were found for as many illegitimate babies as possible. Adoption was not popular and babies who did not find adoptive parents were sent to orphanages or 'domestic training' homes, especially if they were of mixed race. These unfortunate children received only the scantiest of education. Many would be sent out as labourers or domestic servants in their teens, and some were horrendously abused in their workplaces.

Edith became involved in finding suitable adoptive parents, and rescuing battered or neglected children from abusive parents. In the days before State or Commonwealth Governments employed social and welfare workers, Edith's voluntary work took her into some of Perth's worst slum areas, where there was poor sanitation and no hot water on tap. She removed abused babies from horrific 'baby minders' who took care of the children of prostitutes or unwanted children for a fee. She found babies lying on filthy blankets or on the floor, some dying from dysentery, typhoid or other contagious diseases, spread by the lack of sanitary facilities. She walked up tenement stairs lined with urine and faeces. She found babies born deaf and blind to mothers with syphilis.

In many cases, a single cold-water tap on the ground floor was the only supply of water for several families: she soon realised that the majority of Perth and Fremantle's poor and disadvantaged lacked access to hot water. Open drains proliferated and lavatories, where there were any, were small reeking sheds in backyards.

Edith was determined things must change. But what influence did she have as a mere woman when men shaped the laws?

She decided she would have more authority as a paid employee than as a 'lady volunteer' and accepted a post as a 'lady almoner' (as social workers were then called) with the North Fremantle Board of Education. This was a landmark. Edith had broken the rigid middle-class barrier that prevented 'ladies' from working for money. The North Fremantle Board of Education was one of the few public offices to employ middle-class women. Edith Cowan quickly gained a reputation as a tireless and selfless worker who donated her income to help those less fortunate than herself. She was invited to serve with the Children's Protection Society,[6] which campaigned against the employment of child prostitutes in brothels. Child prostitutes, often as young as eight or ten, were eagerly sought after by the brothel madams; their male clients demanded 'virgin' prostitutes because syphilis, the disfiguring and ultimately fatal sexually transmitted disease, was so widespread.

Edith saw things that no 'nice' woman of her era even dreamed existed. They fired her indignation and she was determined to ensure that destitute and abandoned children would not be lured into prostitution or used as sweated labour, working long hours for a pittance at looms or sewing machines under terrible conditions.

To achieve her aims Edith organised public rallies, wrote letters to the press and lobbied politicians. In 1906, her courage and hard work helped in the passing of the first State Children's Act, granting children some measure of protection. But much more needed to be done. Aided by her husband's legal expertise, she and other female colleagues successfully campaigned for the establishment of a special Children's Court.

Through working in the new Children's Court, Edith's friendship with Bessie Rischbieth flourished. Childless Bessie, a decade younger than Edith, was imposing, statuesque, expensively dressed and often domineering. Edith Cowan was petite and invariable polite and tactful, securing decisions on committees through consensus. Bessie had considerable artistic talent, enjoyed the limelight and loved to be surrounded by art and artists. She lived in splendour surrounded by domestic staff in what is now known as Perth's millionaires' row, Peppermint Grove.[7]

In 1915, when many men were away fighting in World War I, Edith Cowan was appointed a justice of the Children's Court. In 1920, she and Bessie Rischbieth were amongst the first women to be appointed Justices of the Peace. Edith, who had constantly urged the appointment of women to such positions, was delighted. Both of these remarkable women shared the same aims – to secure better conditions for children and to raise the status of women, both nationally and internationally.

Edith also worked with Rischbieth and with Roberta Jull on specific projects, such as the setting up of free kindergartens for the children of working-class women, which provided these needy and often hungry children with meals and clothes. Roberta Jull and Edith Cowan had been friends since they had worked together to create the Western Australian National Council of Women in 1912 (Edith was its President from 1913–1921). Among other aims, the Council wanted the age of sexual consent to be raised to eighteen, a measure aimed to prevent child prostitution. This was finally achieved in 1914, ensuring that any man or woman who introduced a girl under the age of eighteen to prostitution could be prosecuted and sentenced to years in gaol.

By now Edith Cowan knew only too well the enormous toll syphilis was exacting on a hypocritical society that refused to talk about this disease – just as terrible in its consequences as AIDS. But 'nice' respectable women simply did not mention such matters. Only in response to even higher rates of infection after the troops returned from serving in France during World War I did most State governments finally introduce controversial Health Acts. For decades, the West Australian Parliament had ignored the problem, hoping it would go away. Urged on by activists like Edith Cowan, a special Act designed to protect women and children from venereal diseases was finally introduced in 1917. The Act made all cases of venereal disease notifiable and prostitutes liable for inspection. Infected prostitutes were subjected to compulsory confinement in Lock Hospitals where they received treatment. Many of the children of prostitutes or returned veterans were born with syphilis. They were either blind or deaf, or both, and after a decade of intense physical suffering, their bones and teeth rotted away, they became incontinent and eventually died insane.

Edith was appalled at the rapidly mounting numbers of women infected by soldier husbands and lovers who had contracted syphilis from French and Egyptian prostitutes during the war. At that time, the only treatment was by injecting the patient with mercury, which caused their hair to fall out, or prescribing an arsenic compound known as Salvarsan, which could only delay the onset of the final and fatal symptoms.[8] But the end was always the same: dementia, paralysis, gangrene and death. Only the work done by Adelaide-born Howard Florey on treatment with granules distilled from the penicillin mould would finally provide a cure for syphilis. But penicillin was not produced commercially until the final years of World War II.

Bessie Rischbieth felt that the West Australian Health Act of 1917 made women victims of the men who had infected them: she spoke out against the Act, insisting it was the men who should be confined to the new Lock Hospitals rather than the women they had infected.

Edith was a realist: she considered the Health Act far from ideal but knew that male politicians, some of whom were clients of Perth's many brothels, would never agree to lock up men. After a long struggle with her conscience, she finally decided to support the Health Act as 'the fairest solution yet offered between men and women' and her supporters followed her lead. The Act split the Women's Movement in Western Australia into two opposing camps. It also affected the long and close friendship between Edith Cowan and Bessie Rischbieth and gave rise to bitter arguments between them. However, in public they were careful to gloss over their differences for the sake of their common aim to improve the lives of all women.

Bessie's husband died in 1925, leaving childless Rischbieth a lonely and wealthy widow. She wished to reform attitudes to sex through Theosophy, which entailed comparative study of world religions, belief in man's innate goodness and reincarnation in future lives. On her travels around India, Rischbieth became almost a 'New Ager', announcing that the world was on the verge of a 'new spiritual order' where woman would 'claim her place in the sun'.[9]

Down-to-earth Edith did not share Rischbieth's beliefs that mysticism, mantras and Theosophy would save the world from sexual abuse and disease. Long ago, Edith had received terrifying insights into the darker corners of the human psyche and had seen with her own eyes dire poverty, alcohol addiction and violence. Like Louisa Lawson, Edith believed firmly in education, so that women could earn their own living. She had carried out voluntary work and fund-raising for decades and knew from bitter experience that the rich did not always like to give to those less fortunate than themselves. She insisted that taxes must be raised so that governments could undertake reforms. She saw no point in Rischbieth and her followers spreading woolly concepts about the innate good in all mankind and begging for a few crumbs from the tables of the rich to give to the poor. Something had to be done by Parliament: voluntary work by dedicated women was not enough. She petitioned her Member of Parliament to support more social reforms, but without success.

Edith's ideas were seen as revolutionary. In the right-wing circles in which Rischbieth moved, including the Women's Service Guild, Edith Cowan was criticised for holding 'dangerous' ideas. But Edith, inspired by Christian ideals, had the courage to act on them. Whenever she received money for paid work she gave it away to poverty-stricken women and children.

Edith considered sex education programmes in schools more important than locking up diseased prostitutes (an approach now taken in AIDS education). She was a woman of vision and commonsense and knew it was impossible to suppress sexual urges, as some idealistic members of Bessie Rischbieth's group in the Women's Services Guild urged. Eventually Edith was criticised so bitterly that she resigned from the Women's Services Guild, to which she had devoted so much time and effort.

Edith now aimed to reduce the spread of syphilis using posters, leaflets and educational programmes, including a specially written play, *Remorse, or the Red Scourge*. This play contained a similar message to Ibsen's *Ghosts*, but lacked Ibsen's dramatic talent. Edith helped to fund performances and supported the play against a storm of opposition from women who felt it 'unladylike', improper and even immoral to discuss contraceptives or sexually transmitted diseases in public.

Edith stood firm against attack: she continued to press for sex education in schools to make teenage girls aware of the fact that syphilis was rampant at all levels in the community. She needed to get her message across to single supporting mothers. She demanded refuges for abused women and children. Entering Parliament now seemed to her a logical step towards changing the laws and public opinion.

Women had won the right to vote in Western Australia in 1899. Edith was used to addressing women's meetings, but the idea of speaking to a hostile audience of jeering men terrified her. The idea of entering Parliament seemed impossible. But how else could things change, she wondered.

In 1921, exactly a year after the ban on women entering the Western Australian Parliament was removed, Edith became one of only two Nationalist candidates endorsed for the seat of West Perth. She found herself on the hustings opposing an experienced Cabinet Minister, Mr T. P. Draper. Her whole campaign seemed absurd. How could she, a mere woman, hope to make political history and win a seat against such opposition in an all-male Parliament?

By this time, Edith Cowan was relatively well-known. The previous year she had been honoured with the Order of the British Empire for her vast amount of voluntary work during World War I.[10] Edith's supporters now realised she must have the backing of the whole Women's Movement, and for this she needed the support of Bessie Rischbieth, who had no political ambitions herself. Fortunately, Bessie realised it was vital for women to have a voice in Parliament if they were to achieve anything: somewhat reluctantly she agreed to support Edith's attempt to win a seat.

Mrs Cowan campaigned on her record of providing unpaid service on twenty-four councils and committees, which impressed many of her women voters. On the other hand, some women voters deemed it 'unfeminine' of Mrs Cowan to stand for election; they believed they should put their efforts into lobbying male Parliamentarians for change rather than voting for a woman. Edith also encountered jeers and hostility from some working-class women when she knocked on their doors in her campaign. They believed that such an educated 'lady' could not possibly understand the problems of the poor.

Undaunted, Edith campaigned on draughty street corners and at meeting after meeting. She told the women in her audiences that she was fighting to improve conditions for all women and asked them to support her by giving her their votes. James Cowan supported his wife loyally by leading the applause at most meetings.

During one doorknock campaign, Edith was accused by the lady of the house of neglecting her children and home. The lady informed her that a friend had told her 'that poor Mr Cowan was so distressed by his wife campaigning that he was dying of a broken heart'! James Cowan took it upon himself to explain to the lady in question that he was *not* dying of a broken heart. Edith's political opponents also spread false rumours that she was neglecting a brood of young children in order to campaign. Whenever possible, her husband defended her against these charges, informing hecklers that their children were grown up and no longer dependant on their mother.

No one expected willowy Edith, inexperienced in state politics, to beat a smooth-talking, highly experienced Cabinet Minister into Parliament. But when the votes were counted, the confident Attorney-General, Mr T. P. Draper (sitting Member for West Perth), was in for a big shock. He discovered that fifty-nine-year-old Edith Dircksey Cowan, whose chances of election he had not taken seriously at all, showed a lead when the first preferences were counted. It came as even more of a shock to Mr Draper when, after counting the third candidate's preferences, Mrs Cowan was found to have a majority of forty-six. The figures showed that 1760 women had voted in her electorate, compared to 1325 men.

Edith Dircksey Cowan was now the first female member to take her seat in any Australian Parliament – and women voters had put her there.

The Nationalist Party were furious with Edith. They had lost a Cabinet Minister and in return they gained nothing but a problem: a woman Member of Parliament.

Inwardly nervous but outwardly composed, Edith took her seat in the House, wearing an elegantly simple black dress. Her maiden speech addressed the concerns of women and the need for social reform. Naturally, there was scant applause from male members of Parliament. Edith Cowan soon found Parliament a complex, arcane organisation with its own rules. The male members made little or no effort to help her with Parliamentary procedures. She found sex discrimination and patriarchal attitudes to women deeply engrained. Some Parliamentarians snubbed her, others tried to humiliate her. One male member even asked the House in her presence (amid roars of mirth from the floor) to specify exactly how much money had been spent on modifying the toilets so that she could use them.

Edith worked hard and used her time in Parliament to promote the cause of women and children. She found that male politicians (who formed a vested interest group) were extremely reluctant to share power with women. This was one reason they had not supported the female vote.

Male members did not wish Edith to bring in any measures that could change the balance of power in favour of women. Most of them supported the doctrine of separate spheres for men and women – men at work earning money and status, wives confined to the home and childcare, left powerless to make decisions and lacking access to paid work.[11]

Edith Cowan entered Parliament with the full support of her husband. But that fact did not stop a male journalist on the *Melbourne Age* writing acidly: 'If holding political office for women becomes the latest fashionable craze ... there would be many dreary, neglected homes through the country, sacrificed on the altar of women's political ambition.'

Her enemies thought the best method of denigrating tall, distinguished-looking Mrs Cowan was to ridicule her. Edith Cowan, Member of Parliament, soon became the target of cartoonists such as Percy Leason of *The Bulletin*. Cartoons pictured her dusting the mace, smacking sleeping Members for not paying attention, sweeping the floor of Parliament House or knitting socks while debate raged around her. Only the cartoon that showed her knitting held a grain of truth. Whenever male members screamed insults, cursed or became particularly obnoxious to each other, Edith Cowan, who hated displays of malice, bad manners and insults, would sit in the House calmly doing her embroidery.

In 1919, American-born Nancy Astor became the very first woman to sit in the British Parliament. But Nancy Astor had one asset Cowan did not. Nancy's husband, Waldorf Astor, was an experienced politician who helped her to understand the arcane language and obscure rites of Parliament which could prevent members having their say.[12]

Edith's debating skills soon became formidable. But she was at her best as a committee worker. She lacked a 'background' in State politics, was not given a paid research assistant, and had to struggle against the introduction of endless amendments and other delaying tactics to prevent her raising important questions about women's rights.

Edith Cowan fought her enemies in the State Parliament who tried to prevent her speaking. She managed to contribute substantially to debates on the Shops and Factories Act, which affected working women, and the State Children's Act. She stood fast and refused to be shouted down by male members during acrimonious discussions on the Nurses Registration Bill and the Industrial Arbitration Bill. At every opportunity, Edith spoke eloquently for equal rights for women, for migrant welfare, for funding of infant centres and for Child Endowment. She also pressed for more sex education in State schools.

Unlike most politicians, Edith resisted the iron control of the whip's office on Members. When she thought it necessary, she voted according to her conscience, even if it meant voting against her own Nationalist Party, something which made her many enemies in Parliament.

Mrs Cowan outraged male members of both sides of the house when she argued that a wife should be legally entitled to a share of her husband's income – at that time a revolutionary concept. She also wanted Child Endowment to be given to unmarried as well as married mothers, something we take for granted today, but at that time a concept many people found totally unacceptable. They wished to make mothering as hard as possible for unmarried 'fallen women'.

One of Edith's most outstanding achievements in Parliament was the passing of The Women's Legal Status Act, a Private Member's Bill, which she introduced in 1923. She found it totally unjust that qualified women who had obtained their degrees were being denied the right to practise their chosen professions. It was entirely due to the work of Edith Cowan that in 1930 the pioneer lawyer Alice Mary Cummins, previously banned from the Bar because she was a woman, was finally permitted entrance.

Mrs Cowan's second successful Private Member's Bill was to ensure that married women could inherit property from children who predeceased them. Before the passing of Edith Cowan's bill, all property in a marriage was automatically bequeathed to the husband, even if he had abandoned his wife years previously and she was destitute.

Edith Dircksey Cowan believed that she was not put into Parliament to court popularity from the other members. She was there to represent women who had voted for her. Her courage and determination to remain true to her beliefs was impressive. She dared to challenge male Parliamentarians who yelled abuse at her or schemed against her.

In the 1924 election campaign, Edith's political enemies, some from her own party, determined to see the back of her. They urged every male voter in her constituency to vote against her and provided free transport to get them to the polls. In addition, Edith found that some of her ideas for social reform had been leaked to her opponents, and the Labor candidate hijacked them. This meant that some people who would have supported her now voted for her opponent. The result was that in the next election she failed to win the seat.

The third time she stood for election her opponents were still up to their dirty tricks. Once more she was defeated at the polls, so she decided to turn her lively mind and organising abilities to fresh fields.

She was one of the first Australian women to gain recognition from international women's movements, travelling overseas in 1903 and 1912.[13] In 1925, in her mid-sixties, Edith Cowan was invited to the United States as one of Australia's delegates to the Seventh International Conference of Women.

Even in her old age, Edith continued to speak at meetings all over Australia arguing the case for equality for wives before the law (at the time custody of children was always awarded to the husband in divorce cases), for the establishment of free kindergartens, for a hygienic water and milk supply. She also supported qualifications for hospital nurses and the banning of unqualified nurses (who were sometimes alcoholics or even part-time prostitutes), and she demanded (in the absence of a widow's pension) a rent allowance for widows and orphans.

Before the advent of pensions for widows, single mothers and the disabled, Edith Cowan supported the causes of the war wounded, those born with disabilities, widows and single mothers – some of whom had been forced into prostitution solely through lack of income and job prospects. A true Christian in the full meaning of the word, Cowan struggled against the dogmas of conservative clergymen as well as the selfishness of the rich and powerful in her quest to improve the lives of the poor and destitute. All her life, Edith Cowan was pragmatic and practical: a 'doer' as well as a talker. She gave away almost every penny she earned to those in need and supported several orphans while they studied at school and technical colleges. She changed lives.

Edith Dircksey Cowan lived to eighty-one, adored by her husband and children as well as her much-loved grandchildren. By now, the long struggle had worn her sad but beautiful face into a sombre mask. Her achievements were immense and should never be forgotten. She initiated a social revolution in her term in Parliament and caused an ultra-conservative, reactionary, male-orientated society to become more responsive to the needs of its women and children.

Finally the long struggle took its toll. Her last whispered words were: 'I'm so tired.'

Hundreds attended at her burial in the Karrakatta cemetery. A plaque on a clock tower in a quiet corner of Perth's Kings Park bears witness to the fact that Edith Dircksey Cowan, politician, devoted wife, mother and grandmother, was truly 'One of Australia's Greatest Women'.

# CHAPTER EIGHT

## Dame Enid Burnell Lyons
### *(1897–1981)*

AUSTRALIA'S FIRST FEMALE FEDERAL CABINET MINISTER

At the 1913 Tasmanian Labor Party rally held on the outskirts of Hobart, Enid Burnell, a petite fifteen-year-old pupil-teacher from Burnie State School, climbed onto the seat of her chair to obtain a better view of Tasmania's craggily handsome Minister for Education.

From the platform draped with the Australian flag, The Hon. Joseph Lyons was propounding what many of his listeners considered as radical ideas about reforming the Tasmanian school system. Joe Lyons was speaking to a poorly educated rural audience where women were deemed inferior to men in everything but the ability to bear and rear children. The Minister was putting forward what were then very advanced ideas. He suggested that women teachers should be paid the same salary as their male counterparts and be allowed to continue teaching after marriage if they wished.

A frisson of horror ran round the hall. 'Wives leaving *home* to work. Whatever next?' muttered elderly men in the audience.

Edith Burnell, an overworked and underpaid pupil-teacher, already knew a little about the Minister's background. Almost twenty years older than herself, Joe Lyons was a bachelor, although it was rumoured a few women had tried to snare him into marriage. A deprived childhood had turned Joe into a fighter for left-wing and humanitarian causes. What Edith Burnell did not know was that Joe Lyons' father, a gambler by nature, had lost his entire savings in an unsuccessful bet on a 'safe' horse to win the Melbourne Cup.[1] The shock of near bankruptcy brought on depression and a nervous breakdown, and his father spent the rest of his life in and out of mental hospitals.

At the age of nine, Joseph Lyons, the brightest boy in his class, was forced to leave school to help support his brothers and sisters – there were no welfare allowances at that time. The only work he could find was as a baker's delivery boy and occasional farm labourer; he had to grow up fast. Then, rescued by two maiden aunts who offered to maintain the family, and having missed a year at school, Joe went back to the classroom. He was determined to make something of himself, get the necessary qualifications to become a teacher in the State system and eventually be able to provide proper family support. His radical views, formed by harsh experience, led him into politics. Ability and charm, together with the Irish gift for public speaking, meant that he rose rapidly through the ranks of the Tasmanian Labor Party to become

Minister for Education, deeply committed to a variety of left-wing causes.

While Joe Lyons endured a poor Catholic childhood, with all that entailed, Enid Burnell had been raised in a slightly more secure working-class home in Smithtown where there was little money but where books and education were greatly valued. Her parents were Methodists, suspicious of anything Catholic, and had strong Labor Party affiliations.

After the speeches ended that night in 1913, tea and biscuits were served by volunteers at the rally. Enid plucked up the courage to approach the Minister and ask his views on improving hours and conditions for pupil-teachers like herself, girls from working-class homes whose families could not afford school fees. It was a method whereby working-class children could receive additional years of education which would help them to become teachers. Pupil-teachers were mainly female, bright and intelligent and were used by the staff to keep order at playtime, fill inkwells and attend to children with reading problems. In return for many hours of unpaid work, if they were lucky they received additional tuition themselves, aspiring one day to be accepted as teachers in their own right.

In spite of the fact the Minister was almost nineteen years older than herself, Enid found him disturbingly attractive in the dimple-chinned devil-may-care way that is so typically Irish. At thirty-four Joe Lyons had a mop of unruly dark hair, a craggy profile, broad shoulders, deep blue eyes and an infectious grin. He had been so busy acting as the head of his family and building a career in politics that he'd lacked the time or the energy to think about marriage. He was wedded to politics … that is, until he met Enid.

As Joseph Lyons answered Enid's probing question, he saw an outstandingly attractive young girl with long golden-brown hair, a delicate heart-shaped face and a smile which revealed perfect teeth and brought dimples to her cheeks. Although many others were waiting to talk to him he stayed chatting to this delightful young girl whose brimming enthusiasm for his plans was so infectious.

Over a cup of tea and a biscuit Enid found her normal shyness had vanished. Reforming the work situation for pupil-teachers was a topic dear to her heart. Joe Lyons expanded under the warmth of her smile and told her of his own early struggles to become a teacher. Enid was enthusiastic about the Minister's plans to abolish school fees and pay female teachers the same wage as their male counterparts. Joe realised that Enid's left-wing convictions were as strong as his own. She, for her part, was flattered that the Minister treated her as an adult rather than some naive teenager.

Meanwhile, a long queue had formed, all waiting to speak to the Minister. The Hon. Joe Lyons' secretary caught his eye and pointed to the queue. The Minister apologised to Miss Enid Burnell. He was sorry but he must end their talk as others were waiting. At this her smile faded. Joe could not bear the thought he would never see her again. Hastily he told Enid he would be delighted to answer the rest of her questions the following day. He suggested a time and place. Her dimples returned, she smiled up at him and agreed.

Their second meeting, away from the staff who normally accompanied the Minister on his speaking tours, was a turning point in both their lives. Joe and Enid felt themselves to be in love and realised that this was something very special indeed for them both.

Enid dared not admit her feelings for the Minister of Education to her parents. She feared their opposition which would be based on the difference between their ages as well as the Roman Catholic–Protestant divide. She remained silent, keeping her secret to herself. The budding romance blossomed in letters which were tender but formal: Joe must have feared the results had they been opened by Enid's parents. Everything seemed against a permanent relationship. At fifteen, Enid was underage and needed her parents' permission to wed. A highly intelligent and hardworking girl, she had just won a scholarship to attend the Hobart Teachers Training College and her parents were determined she should have a career to fall back on for the rest of her life.

To understand the couple's predicament it is important to realise that at that time the Australian Labor Party was riven by religious strife. Irish Catholics could not abide Protestants and vice versa; Methodists had been reared to honour the Bible as the Word of God.

Enid's mother, Eliza Burnell (born Taggart) had emigrated from a depressed tin mining area in Cornwall, a hive of Methodism. She was a devout member of the congregation of her local Methodist chapel as was Enid's father, who worked hard as a leading hand in a Burnie sawmill. Edith's parents were hard-working, decent folk who had been brought up to despise the Irish and distrust everything Catholic as 'Popish nonsense'.

When Enid finally plucked up the courage to tell her parents about her feelings for Joe Lyons, they were so shocked and distressed that they forbade her to see him ever again. Eliza was horrified at the mere thought of her much-loved daughter marrying a 'Mick' (as Catholics were known), even if this particular 'Mick' *was* the Labor Minister of Education. Tears and recriminations followed. Enid's parents stood firm; they loved her and had her best interests at heart.

Undaunted, Joe arranged a secret tryst on deserted Co-ee Beach, where they strolled hand in hand along the sands, kissed and swore to love one another forever and to get married as soon as they could. Mores were strict; the virginity of young girls was jealously guarded. It is most unlikely that they had sex before marriage even though they were both head over heels in love for the first time.

In spite of strong opposition from Enid's parents, who saw the age and religious differences as an insoluble problem, and firmly believed they were doing the right thing, Joe and Enid got engaged once she turned sixteen. Enid's parents made them promise that they would not marry until Enid turned seventeen. Their engagement year was one of constant separation; to Enid it seemed like an eternity, but she and Joe were determined to marry.

Joseph Lyons and Enid Burnell were finally married on 28 April 1915.[2] They had kept their promise and waited until Edith had celebrated her seventeenth birthday.[3]

There was other opposition to their marriage. Joseph Aloysius Lyons had the undying support of the Irish Catholic lobby in the Labor Party. He knew that marriage to a Methodist, however devoted to the Labor cause, could spell political ruin for him, since Irish Catholic influence was predominant in the Labor Party. He was warned of the dangers of marrying Edith Burnell by most of the people around him. The circumstances surrounding their marriage forced Enid to convert to Catholicism, causing great distress to her parents. However, as her Catholicism deepened, she derived great strength from her faith.

Enid had been warned by her mother and her chapel-going friends that marriage to a Catholic meant bearing numerous children. Did she want to spend the rest of her life dragging around a brood of snotty-nosed children and playing second fiddle to an important man, her mother asked. Enid smiled, this was not going to happen to her. Joe was different from other men.

In spite of prophecies of doom from family members on both sides as well as Joe's Labor party colleagues, their marriage surprised everyone by proving to be splendidly happy – a partnership of equals.

They honeymooned at a Sydney hotel where Joe was attending a Premiers' conference. This was Enid's first introduction to the Byzantine complexities, blood feuds and shifting alliances of life in the Labor party.

Enid proved to be an astute judge of character and had an excellent grasp of the main issues facing the Labor Party, as well as an understanding of the feelings of the average working man and woman. And she soon discovered that she had a gift for writing down-to-earth yet emotional speeches. Joe perceived Enid's talents. He too was a good speech writer but was totally overworked. So he encouraged Enid to write some of the speeches which won him acclaim. He was by now firmly convinced that Enid herself could achieve great success in politics. But who would pre-select a *woman* for a Labor party seat? Whenever they were apart Joe wrote Enid moving letters telling her, for example, that 'my faith and confidence in you is supreme. That's one of the reasons why I care so much for you. I not only love you but I *believe* in you too.'

In Tasmania, the couple lived at first in rented accommodation. In 1916, they commissioned a builder for the then princely sum of £375 to build them a simple white weatherboard house, which they named Home Hill, in Devonport. At that time, before the advent of commercial airlines, Tasmania was isolated from the rest of Australia and deficient in many amenities that other Australian cities took for granted. Amazing as it seems for a politician's household, the telephone was only connected to their home in 1938.

Enid soon discovered she was carrying her first child. Lacking a phone, she wrote Joe long letters whenever they were apart. In return, he would reply in even more passionate vein, telling her how much he loved and missed her and how he valued her opinions.

They hated being apart so much that Enid joined Joe on the arduous campaign trail of 1916, travelling around the wilder areas of Tasmania.

At that time it was not thought 'quite nice' for pregnant women to appear in public. However, Enid's trim figure masked her pregnancy until the secret was finally out. Then she returned home to Devonport for the birth of their first child.

Enid may have suffered from rickets, due to vitamin deficiency in her childhood, like many working-class women of that era. The birth of her first child took place at a time when little was known about the complications of pregnancy. It was an agonising birth which left her with a badly damaged pelvis, causing intense pain and difficulties with walking.

Enid finally made her first public speech in 1920 and continued to do so in between bearing and raising twelve children, one of whom died in infancy, causing them both intense distress.

Raising and educating a large family in the days before automatic washing machines meant piles of soiled nappies and children's clothes to wash and iron.[4] 'We never had much money,' Enid revealed many years later in her autobiography. 'At one stage we had six children under six. I'd wash out the back in an enormous copper, meanwhile trying to work out my next speech in my head. No helper, no washing machine, and *what* a wash!'

She herself had been brought up in a small family: now she realised what life was like for so many women raising numerous children without help. This gave her a valuable insight into what life was like for married women and the many war widows – who as yet lacked social security payments. She was determined to do everything in her power to improve the lives of ordinary women.

Even the pain from her damaged pelvis did not daunt Enid, who had conquered her initial shyness about public speaking and soon became a powerful and persuasive speaker. Joe realised that his wife's good looks, astute brain, and exceptionally warm personality made her a valuable ally and a great asset to him. He encouraged Edith to speak at Labor rallies and meetings wherever possible.

This was an era when politicians' wives were expected to kiss babies, wear decorative hats, bake lamingtons and remain silent on public platforms. Enid Lyons broke the mould of the typical politician's wife by doing all of that as well as delivering her own speeches. She was an extremely well-organised person; somehow she managed to combine preparing and delivering electioneering speeches with caring for her children. Her sincerity was obvious; like her husband, Enid had a natural gift for public speaking.

In her memoirs, Enid describes how she juggled her political activities with the needs of her large family. When asked to speak at the opening of a federal election campaign, she felt how unfair it was that she had no one to organise things for her and settle the children down; when her husband was writing a speech she kept all the children quiet to allow him to concentrate. Her heartfelt cry echoes down the ages to all working women with children: 'At five o'clock on the day of the meeting I was totally unprepared ... I sat down at the dining table with pencil and paper to write a speech. I felt tired to death. The baby on my knee was crying with fatigue, the other children were quarrelling noisily. Suddenly I burst into tears. It was not fair. No *man* was expected to endure such things.'

What Enid needed was a secretary or else a housekeeper or nanny to organise the household – but there was no one. She was on her own for much of the time with a huge family and not much money.

With Enid's devoted support Joseph Lyons eventually became Premier of Tasmania. Concerned that his wife should have the chance to fulfil her potential, Joe persuaded her to make her own foray into politics by standing as a candidate in the 1925 Tasmanian elections. This was a revolutionary step for a married woman with young children. Enid was seen by the men in the party as no threat. They were convinced that she had little chance of winning. However, fielding a woman candidate was deemed 'good public relations' for the Labor Party, which campaigned heavily on the fact that they were supportive to women's causes (although, of course, some chauvinistic males devoutly hoped no woman would take a seat in Parliament. Why should such seats be wasted on women, they demanded among themselves.)

While coping with several sick children at home, Enid kept up a rigorous schedule of speaking engagements. A passionate believer in equality and women's' rights, she managed to demolish opponents who accused her of 'doing a man out of a job'. Her appearances on the hustings boosted her confidence in her speaking abilities. It also made her even more aware of the prejudice against women achieving *anything* in a man's world. Interestingly enough, Edith's mother, Eliza Burnell, by now reconciled to her daughter's marriage to a Catholic, also stood as a Labor candidate in this election.

Both women failed to win a seat, Eliza by a large margin, Enid by a mere sixty votes. Losing did not upset Enid unduly: in some ways she was relieved that she was not forced to abandon her young children to spend long days in the State Parliament. Campaigning had taught her one important lesson: whatever working-class men might think of her, working-class women would vote for her in droves. It was the down-to-earth quality of Enid's approach to politics coupled with her fresh, unspoiled beauty and her evident sympathy for others that gave her a huge appeal at the ballot box.

From the first Enid spoke her mind about women's domestic roles, especially in rural Tasmania: she knew how hard farmers' wives worked, on household and farm tasks, rearing calves and lambs, cooking for shearers and harvesters in addition to running their own homes. She astounded a rural meeting, composed mainly of men, by drawing on her own childhood experiences of living without gas, electricity or running water, observing: 'While farm life might be very satisfactory for farmers, it may not be as rewarding for their wives. I can't help myself wondering whenever I meet a farmer's wife, if her kitchen still needs a sink with running water and if she still has to boil the washing over an open fire in a kerosene tin.'[5]

Enid describes in her memoirs how her husband was very unusual in that he helped her with the housework as they lacked servants because money was always short raising a large family: 'Joe was determined that I should not sink into a sea of domesticity. If he wasn't away on business, he would be at home with me. If I was ironing, he would talk or read to me. On Sundays he would cook dinner for the family, while I had some time to myself.'

Joe would shop for school clothes for the children whenever she was sick and was proud of his domestic skills. 'You see I can be quite a good mother, when I have to,' he wrote without embarrassment in a letter to his wife.

During Joseph Lyons' second term as Premier of Tasmania, from 1923–28, he began to realise that more money was needed if he was to reform the education system and he began courting big business and industry to donate funds. In her memoirs, Enid describes how 'Joe mellowed with the years'. They no longer subscribed to the trade union journal *The Australian Worker* because they both found it 'too bitter in its denunciations, far too intolerant and too biased'.

The fiery left-wing couple were both softening their views as they grew older. Now Tasmania began to seem like a very small pond indeed. With Edith's blessing, Joe switched to Federal politics. Elected Federal member for Wilmot in 1929, he joined the Scullin Labor Government as Postmaster General and Minister for Works and Railways, and from August 1930 was Acting Treasurer – not an easy position to hold at this juncture. The country was soon in a ferment due to the American stockmarket crash of October 1929, which led to the start of the Great Depression. Thousands of men were thrown out of work and the Labor Party was divided against itself on many important financial issues. Joe's alarm at the Labor Party's unconventional financial policies was shared by a group of fellow conservatives.

Like most Australians of their era, both Joe and Enid were imbued with respect for conventional economics. They favoured following the ultra-cautious advice of the economists Giblin, Copland and Melville. This trio, like many foreign economists, believed that inflation and the soaring deficit would bring economic and political chaos. Joe soon fell out with his own party over how to manage the worsening financial situation caused by the New York stockmarket crash – which, somewhat like Australia in the 1990s and Paul Keating's 'recession we had to have', caused soaring rates of unemployment and a galloping financial deficit, breeding lack of confidence internationally. Joe and Enid believed that Australia should pay its way out of recession – Joe insisted all financial commitments should be honoured. They agreed with the economists that depression could be cured by tightening the belt, balancing the budget and reducing Government spending. There were fiery caucus meetings with those in the Labor Party who wanted to increase the deficit, create thousands of new jobs and *spend* their way out of trouble.

As Acting Treasurer, Joe Lyons defied them, demanding both a reduction of Government spending and a reduction in the salaries of leading public servants. He won on the last issue but the larger conflicts of economic policy remained unresolved.[6] By now the stock market had totally collapsed in Britain and Australia, financiers were jumping out of windows, men were laid off in droves. There was a world trade slump and scant prospects of the situation improving.

Despite the famous 'Don't do it Joe, don't do it,' plea of a Labor colleague, after considerable soul-searching Joe Lyons resigned from his Cabinet post in January 1931, and finally left the Labor Party for whom he had worked so hard. He had Enid's unwavering support. In May that year he became leader of the newly formed United Australia Party. The new party was vigorously supported by press baron Keith Murdoch, who felt Joe Lyons was the man to solve the economic crisis; he sensed his ability to unite different groups and opposing factions, a skill which Enid also possessed.

In a snap election in December 1931, as things were going from bad to worse, 'Honest' Joe Lyons, as the papers styled him, became Prime Minister of Australia with an absolute majority, just nine months after he had left the Labor Party. By now the 'golden couple' of Labor politics had acquired some very powerful political enemies. Joe Lyons would need all his skills as a consensual politician to manage a difficult cabinet and the worsening economy of the Depression.

On 6 January 1932, Joseph Aloysius Lyons was sworn in as Prime Minister of Australia in Canberra. Honours never went to Joe's head and that night he found the time to write to Edith, who had stayed at home to nurse a sick child. 'Whatever honours or distinctions come are *ours* not mine ... it is grand to know that our love for each other is still our most cherished possession ... It has been a great day for me, but I would be happier on Home Hill with you and all the children.'

Joe and Enid moved into The Lodge with their younger children; Enid had to divide her time between Canberra and Tasmania where the older children were at school. She found coping with lengthy separations from her husband and older children stressful and longed for the time when they could all be together once more. The Lyons' still cherished their ideal marriage. After the birth of their twelfth and last child, Joe wrote to Enid: 'Remember that the chap who came to you at Co-ee Beach because he loved you. He still loves you more than ever tonight.'

Few people expected Joe Lyons would last more than one term as Prime Minister. However, supported by excellent speeches written by Enid, and using her suggestion to contact the nation by speaking more frequently on the radio, Joe won three successive elections. At the time, this was a record unmatched by any other Australian Prime Minister.

Prime Minister 'Honest' Joe Lyons remained in power from 1932–39, a very difficult time in Australian politics. He implemented the 'equality of sacrifice' plan to combat the Depression, consolidated an alliance with the Country Party, cracked down on Communism, and, faced by the threat of another world war, remained fiercely anti-conscription.

Despite her large family and the loss of a stillborn child, which depressed her considerably, Enid travelled all over Australia for official speaking engagements during those Depression years.

A young Liberal politician named Robert Menzies actually suggested that she should not be making speeches but instead stay at home in the kitchen. Edith ignored his patronising advice but never forgave Menzies and blamed her husband's subsequent heart problems on him. Curiously enough, her anger did not extend to Dame Pattie Menzies, whom she both respected and liked.

As the Prime Minister's wife, Enid aimed to win support from women Australia-wide and was frequently invited to address women's associations and conferences, both religious and secular. Women's organisations such as the Victorian Women Citizen's Movement and the Sydney Feminists Club sought her as an ally in various causes because she was known to be deeply committed to 'women's rights'.

When Enid Lyons accompanied her husband to England in 1934–5 they attended a large number of official functions at which her intelligence and grace won approval even among the snobbish British, who tended to sneer at Australian accents. Wearing a borrowed ballgown, Enid looked magnificent at an official reception hosted by King George V at Windsor Castle. She remained engagingly fresh and unspoiled by all the pomp and ceremony that surrounded them as representatives of the Australian people. She described how, at times, she felt a sense of unreality – as though she was in a dream. She and Joe were an ordinary Australian couple from working-class backgrounds, being entertained by leading politicians and by royalty.

As Catholics, they had always dreamed of an audience with the Pope. Their wish was granted. They travelled to Italy and visited the

Vatican before sailing to America to stay at the White House with President Roosevelt and his wife. There they had the chance to see first-hand how Americans were dealing with the Depression before returning home to Australia.

In 1937, they sailed to Britain for a second visit, to represent Australia at the coronation of King George VI. Once again, Enid's unspoiled nature and dignity in her official role aroused favourable comment. She found time to speak at a number of feminist rallies and Catholic meetings in Britain. And this time Enid was put up for an honour of her own. Returning home via a brief visit to Venice, which she loved, Edith received a telegram advising her she had been made a Dame Grand Cross of the Order of the British Empire, an honour she would cherish for the rest of her life.

Serious problems awaited the Lyons on their return home. Long hours of argument and invective in Parliament and in Cabinet meetings, and disloyalty from party members were extremely stressful for them both. There was also the looming menace of war in Europe as Hitler revealed his ambition to gobble up the smaller nations of Europe. Australia, as a Commonwealth member, was pledged to support Britain if war broke out.

Enid, worried about her husband's health, urged him to visit the doctor, something he was reluctant to do. Eventually, he did and was diagnosed with high blood pressure. No drug treatments to combat high blood pressure or cholesterol were available at that time; as Prime Minister, charged with a heavy workload, he was advised either to slow down or resign.

Each time Joe Lyons attempted to resign, however, colleagues pressured him to stay in order to give the appearance of party unity. Enid was extremely worried about him but did not like to interfere. Both Enid and Joe placed their own happiness second to the good of the party. Joe's blood pressure went up rather than down with the long hours and the tension. He continued to reassure Enid that once the next crisis was over he would resign ... but always another one arose.

The result was that Prime Minister Joseph Lyons suffered a massive heart attack while travelling to Sydney in April 1939, just as the situation concerning Hitler and Poland was worsening. Joe was rushed to hospital but died a few days later.

The obituaries praised Joseph Lyons for his honesty, saying that he believed in politics as a vehicle for creating a better world for all Australians. At the same time they noted that he had made many enemies in his career, including the formidable Robert Menzies. Many of his colleagues felt guilty that they had persuaded him to stay on rather than resign as Enid had wanted.

For Enid it was a terrible time. At the age of forty-one, she found herself a sole supporting mother with a huge family to educate, no private income or savings of her own and at times suffering severe pain from her damaged pelvis. Joe's will revealed just how little money or investments he had. There were no large superannuation payments for politicians then, as there are today, and scant financial provision for Parliamentarians' widows and children. In addition, Enid had the constant feeling that she should have overridden the wishes of her husband's colleagues and insisted he resign.

The United Party Government tabled a bill proposing an annuity for Enid and her children. This modest provision evoked outrage among many Labor members who felt Joe had betrayed them by joining the Liberals. There were angry speeches in the house, reported in the press and over the radio. Enid received carping critical letters and hate mail, even death threats, all of which greatly upset her. She was unable to sleep and scarcely ate. She lost weight dramatically and became clinically depressed, an illness now treatable with Prozac or other anti-depressants but at that time not properly understood. She was told to 'snap out of it', that things would get better – but clinical depression does not respond to such injunctions. Enid's worries about finance and her children increased and her grief and despair worsened.

She soldiered on, sometimes in severe pain, becoming more and more depressed. Finally she collapsed, overwhelmed by exhaustion, grief, and guilt that she had not defied her husband's colleagues and insisted Joe resign from politics sooner. Taking her doctor's advice she retired completely from public life and devoted herself to her twelve children.

Slowly, over a period of time, her strong and stable personality reasserted itself as she came to terms with her grief and guilt. She eased her grief by making notes for a book about her years in politics and discovered that writing was cathartic and writing about their lives lessened the pain of Joe's death and that she had a real talent for it.

World War II was still raging in the Pacific and in Europe and North Africa where Australians were fighting. Many men were away in the armed forces. Women were needed to take their place. In 1943, when the Tasmanian Federal seat of Braddon (not her husband's old seat of Wilmot) became vacant, one of Enid's daughters persuaded her to contest it for the United Australia Party.

Ironically, although women had achieved the right to vote and Australian women had been granted the right to sit in Federal Parliament in 1902 – even before women in Britain had the vote – twenty years later they *still* experienced huge difficulties gaining pre-selection rights. As yet, no Australian woman had been elected to Federal Parliament, ensuring woman had little influence on Federal politics. In a male-dominated world many of them were still told by their husbands exactly how they should vote.[7] Men of both parties refused to admit women through the pre-selection process. This scandalous state of affairs would continue for the next forty years – and continues today in certain electorates.

Enid campaigned vigorously, determined to win, buoyed up by Joe's vision of her as someone ideally suited to politics. Her seat was by no means a safe one, and only after the distribution of preferences from four other candidates was she finally declared the winner. On 21 August 1943, Enid was doing some ironing at home when she heard over the radio the announcement that history had been made: Dame Enid Lyons had become the first women elected to the Federal House of Representatives.

The United Australia Party, then led by Sir Robert Menzies, was now in Opposition; as Enid took her place in Parliament, the entire country waited to see how a woman would perform in Federal Parliament. Enid did not disappoint the country, winning support from the press and the general public. She used her maiden speech to make the point that women entering Parliament had to 'attack the same problems and ... shoulder the same burdens' as men because 'every subject from high finance to international relations, from social security to the winning of the war, touches closely on the home and the family.'

In politics, Enid Lyons was motivated by a firm belief in the right of women to a place in government. She saw her role in Government as a nurturing one and enjoyed fostering talents in others. She was known by male parliamentarians as 'The Mother of the Parliament' a sobriquet with more patronising overtones than 'The Father of the Parliament', traditionally bestowed on the longest-serving male MP. She had to grin and bear the title in public but among close friends she used to joke about it.[8]

In spite of all her commitments, Enid Lyons remained a devoted mother, who had to work hard to provide for her numerous brood, all growing up and needing education. She was always a loyal friend and colleague but a great hater of those she felt responsible for her husband's premature death, including Sir Robert Menzies, whom she regarded as 'the enemy within the gates'. She felt that he had unjustly attacked her husband in a speech he made in 1938, for which she never forgave him.

Five years later, by which time the UAP or United Australia Party had become the Liberal Party, Sir Earle Page, the leader of the Country Party, who had been Deputy Prime Minister in the Bruce-Page coalition, suggested to Dame Enid Lyons a way of bringing Menzies down. Page insisted the Country Party would follow Enid if she broke away from Menzies and the UAP and formed a separate party.

Enid was cautious and inquired from the politicians how she would fare as Leader of the Opposition in place of Menzies. They told her: 'You wouldn't have to do a thing. We (the men) would do all the work. You would only be a *figurehead*'. Not surprisingly, even though it would have defeated Robert Menzies, she indignantly rejected what she now realised was a patronising offer. Dame Enid Lyons was her own person and would not be a puppet leader for anyone.

In certain respects, Enid bore a resemblance to Elizabeth Bowes-Lyon, the Queen Mother. Both women were greatly loved by the general public for their charm, radiant smiles, innate dignity and naturalness. Like the Queen Mother, Enid Lyons derived evident enjoyment from meeting and talking with people from all walks of life. But while the Queen Mother rarely spoke in public, Enid Lyons delivered her speeches with great feeling. She is supposed to have been the first Australian politician who could move her fellow politicians to tears.[9] She dressed simply but with good taste in her younger days, choosing striking but tasteful colours; Billy Hughes described her on the historic day when she nervously walked into Parliament for the first time as 'a bird of Paradise among carrion crows'.

Even a woman as hard-working and well-organised as Enid Lyons found it hard to cope with all the commuting by boat and slow train between home and family in Tasmania and her busy parliamentary office in Canberra. She was still battling constant pain; the fact that this was due to a fractured pelvis was not discovered for some years. She also suffered from an undiagnosed thyroid deficiency which caused her to tire easily.

Wartime civilian rail services were infrequent. Returning to Tasmania by ferry and train took two days from Canberra and was dangerous: during the overnight trip across the Bass Strait, her ship had to pass through mined waters.

Although she asked for no special favours, Prime Minister John Curtin granted her permission to travel by air whenever possible. This gave her additional time to spend with her children, which she greatly valued. However, juggling work and home duties, organising her large family, coping with their childhood illnesses and medical problems, liaising with their teachers, keeping herself well-dressed (photographers delighted in taking pictures whenever she appeared), fulfilling social duties in her constituency, without the support of a husband, were extremely tiring. Her heart-felt cry touches a nerve in women today: 'I would sometimes look at the men about me and envy them for having wives. Were there any of those politicians, I would ask myself, who even washed their own socks?'

During her first term of office as Member for Braddon, Edith Lyons made her Parliamentary speeches before hostile male chauvinists who chattered and joked while she spoke seriously on the need for extended social services, including maternity care for women in the city and in the outback, for increased child endowment, widows' pensions and more government housing for those in need. She spoke with first-hand knowledge about the difficulties which war-induced inflation and shortages of essential foods and clothing posed for the nation's wives and mothers. She retained her concern for the poor and underprivileged and, as a devout Catholic, opposed divorce and abortion.

Dame Enid Lyons continued to enchant the public and win elections. She easily trebled her majority in the post-war 1946 election and quadrupled it in 1949. Turning her attention towards consumerism, she saw beneath the hype that accompanied salesmanship and realised how easily women were being manipulated by advertising to enrich manufacturing firms. She observed: 'The trouble is that we live in a commercial world geared to keeping women appearing trivial and light-minded. They are made to feel that they must do what they're told by men and that they haven't got minds of their own.'

In a Parliamentary chamber known for male histrionics and searing insults, Enid Lyons was always firm but courteous. Rather than ranting like some of her male colleagues, she managed, by explaining the matter under discussion in a pleasant way, to persuade people to do things for her. She upheld the need for ante-natal care, sought to raise widows' pensions and always tried to eliminate discrimination against women at work.

She spent years lobbying for the rights of Australian women to retain both their nationality and citizenship when they married foreigners, and this legislation was finally passed in 1948. She also secured Government endowment for *all* children. (Previously the first-born child was omitted and child endowment granted only for second and subsequent children.) She joined with other MPs to secure the free distribution of certain life-saving drugs to those most in need.

At first, Dame Enid could not afford a secretary and had to write all her correspondence by hand. Eventually she managed to secure the services of a secretary but could not afford a live-in housekeeper. Sometimes she was so busy she had to dictate letters to her secretary while preparing a family meal.

She spoke out on sex discrimination when she discovered that Government plans for re-employment, demobilisation and training allowances for returned servicemen would be far higher than for returned servicewomen. 'Is the cost of living any lower for a woman?' she pointedly demanded of her male colleagues in Parliament. During her second term of office she used the same argument over equal pay for women. Her opponents found it difficult to answer her logic – a quality they had previously believed was rarely found in a woman. They were forced to respect her.

Dame Enid Lyons' second term in parliament with the Liberal Party – as the United Australia Party was now known – was marred by an undiagnosed thyroid deficiency which caused a painful goitre in her throat. She struggled on, but a few weeks before the 1949 election she was admitted to hospital. She made a dramatic pre-election appearance with her slender throat swathed in bandages. She could only whisper her speeches, yet by now she was so well loved by voters of both sexes that she quadrupled her majority.

In the new Liberal-Country Party ministry, Prime Minister Menzies appointed her Vice-President of the Executive Council. Enid Lyons entered the pages of history once more as the first Australian woman to break into the all-male world of a Federal Cabinet. Unfortunately, her thyroid deficiency now made concentration difficult; she tired easily and began to believe she was doing Australian women a grave disservice by remaining in office. She felt she could no longer lobby effectively for them.

Enid Lyons retired from Parliament in 1951, due to illness. Even her bitterest opponents had to admit she had been a charismatic leader who had accomplished a great deal. She had been an exceptional minister, always loyal to her staff and mindful of their problems. Without exception, her staff members were devoted to her and very sad to see her go.

Eventually advances in medicine resolved the thyroid problem and finally Enid's fractured pelvis was diagnosed and repaired by means of a number of complex operations. For the rest of her life, Dame Enid remained involved with family and women's issues. In 1951 she chaired the Jubilee Women's Convention. She was also a member of the Australian Broadcasting Commission from 1951 to 1962.

Other honours followed. She became an Honorary Fellow of the College of Nursing, Vice-President of the Elizabethan National Theatre, which was responsible for bringing many important actors to prominence, and held high office in the National Trust of Australia.

From 1951–54 she contributed to an influential newspaper and found she enjoyed writing so much that she produced three books of memoirs. In the first, *And So We Take Comfort*, published in 1965, she related the story of her remarkable marriage, describing it as one in which 'two people who loved each other ... set out on the great adventure together when she was only seventeen and he was twice that age ... They laughed and knew sorrow and great happiness and it all happened in twenty-four years.'

*The Old Haggis* (1970) was her second book. The title was based on a family joke. Once, when Dame Enid recounted how she had been given a salute by a group of Highland pipers, one of her many grandchildren quipped: 'And I bet the crowd probably said "Here comes the auld haggis!"' Her third volume of memoirs, *Among the Carrion Crows,* appeared in 1972 and concentrated on her experiences in Federal Parliament.[10]

Her final book, *Once on a Windy Hill,* was all about her beloved family home at Devonport, which had been enlarged over the years as her family grew. At the age of seventy-five she created a small fishpond complete with water supply and drainage outlet at Home Hill, her Devonport house, emphasising that she had done it all 'with my own two hands and a bucket'. She wrote: 'As you grow old, you become conscious that happiness is something you create for yourself. *Creating* something gives a real sense of achievement.'

In 1971, when her son Kevin finally retired from the position of Deputy Premier of Tasmania, she observed wisely: 'Politics is a nerve-wracking business. If you want life without anxiety, keep out of it.'

Dame Enid still played the organ each week at Our Lady of Lourdes Church. She also continued, when asked, to make speeches to women's groups, at which she insisted:

Women have special attributes, special insights of immense value. Of course, they also have special problems too. But these problems must be solved in *partnership* with men if women are to fulfil their public and private roles. I don't think that we should lose those attributes and priorities that are natural to us as women ... We shouldn't imitate men, the world's far too male already. Nor should we lose our sense of humour. I say to girls – don't abandon marriage. For women the sexual revolution can mean a loss of human dignity. A lot of people have a false idea of freedom. Even in a society of three you can't be free to do exactly as you like. Life has ... taught me that real freedom lies in the control of self.

In 1980, Dame Enid was delighted to be awarded the highest grade of the Order of Australia, a magnificent gold sunburst on a blue-and-gold ribbon. She died the following year, on 2 September 1981.

Apart from all the honours heaped upon her, Enid Lyons founded a dynasty of over one hundred children, grandchildren, great-grandchildren, nieces, nephews and grand-nieces. However, contrary to expectations, she did not leave the family home to any of them but to 'the people of Tasmania'. Her will contained the wish that Home Hill would be kept 'as a place for the public to visit and enjoy'.

Throughout her long and productive life, Enid Lyons had always believed that 'we owe the public something. Many things that have occurred in my life would never have happened if the public had not had confidence in my husband and myself.'

The women of Australia owe her a great debt.

# CHAPTER NINE

### Ethel Florence Lindesay
### (Henry Handel) Richardson
*(1870–1946)*

AUSTRALIA'S FIRST INTERNATIONALLY ACCLAIMED WRITER

As a medical student at the University of Edinburgh, Walter Richardson must have been aware of the dangers of catching syphilis. Did he catch this then fatal disease from one of the many prostitutes that haunted Edinburgh's Grassmarket and the courtyards of the High Street, or years later in the gold-rush town of Ballarat? Syphilis takes four to five decades to develop into what was then known as 'grand paralysis of the insane'. Decades later, Walter's eldest daughter, Ethel, would write three novels about the life of a fictitious doctor who marries for love, achieves great wealth in Australia's mining boom but is finally overcome by madness and mania as he realises he will die of syphilis.[1]

In real life, Walter Richardson also made his fortune in Australia in the goldrush. After qualifying from Edinburgh Medical School, he was engaged for a very low salary (as there was then an oversupply of medical graduates) in a practice near London. A disagreement with the local Board of Guardians (Medical Board) made Walter restless, as did the premature death of his younger brother, so he decided to emigrate.

The discovery of gold in New South Wales and Victoria in the 1850s meant that many gentlemen of good education sailed for Australia to try their luck at the diggings. When the son of the doctor for whom Walter Richardson worked announced that he was off to look for gold in Australia, Walter decided to join him.

He arrived in Melbourne in June 1852, and set off for the goldfields at Ballarat, the sort of gentleman digger complete with top hat, gold fob watch and waistcoat observed by the goldfields artist S. T. Gill. Walter soon found the physical effort of digging, cradling and panning dirt unpleasant and had no success at it. He was proud, lonely and withdrawn, unable to fit into the rough and tumble of life on the goldfields. Looking around him and seeing everyone in the mining settlement of Ballarat busy making money out of the miners, he started a general store in a timber shed to the south of the tented shanty town. He realised that if the gold rush continued Ballarat would soon become a thriving city. The crudity of the miners and the way they drank away their money appalled him. He made few friends but was kind-hearted enough to gave credit to miner's families down on their luck. Richardson's General Store had many debtors and Dr Richardson felt homesick.

On trips to Geelong to buy more supplies for the store, Dr Richardson stayed at Bradshaw's Family Hotel. There he met Mary Bailey, an ambitious eighteen-year-old English girl from Leicestershire, employed by the Bradshaws to look after their young children, and do housework and other odd jobs. Mary, who came from solid yeoman stock, had left school at fourteen; she was impressed that a doctor in his thirties should take an interest in her. She was a handsome, dark-eyed girl. Walter, lonely for female company and convinced that he could educate her and make her into a suitable wife, proposed marriage. Doubtless he believed that having treated with mercury the small chancre that denoted syphilis, he was cured of the disease. Sadly, this was not the case.

Walter Richardson and pretty little Mary Bailey were married in Geelong in August 1855, then lived in Ballarat over his general store. The following year, the store was flooded. Since he was making little money, Walter prudently obtained a licence to practise medicine in the colony of Victoria.[2] He was saddened to discover that sturdy, practical Mary completely lacked his own lifelong love of literature. Physically in love with his hardworking young wife, he was disappointed they had so few interests in common. Dr Richardson set up his shingle as a general practitioner, and channelled much of his energy into helping to found Ballarat's first hospital. But he was both too outspoken and too erudite to be successful in a country that worshipped mateship and money. At this point, like so many others at this time, he and his wife discovered a common interest in spiritualism.

Like the general store, the medical practice had bad debts from the families of failed miners. Despite their hard work he never made much money. However, in the booming economy of the gold rush, Walter bought a bunch of mining shares on the advice of a barrister friend. These soared in price when gold was found: suddenly the Richardsons found that they had become very rich indeed.

They moved to Melbourne, which was prospering in the mining boom. They made several visits to England, but Irish-born Walter Richardson now felt himself to be an outsider there as well. Undecided whether to remain in Australia or return to Britain permanently, the Richardson's rented a house in Melbourne's Fitzroy.

After fifteen years trying to conceive and several miscarriages (possibly due to Walter's latent syphilis), the Richardsons, who had despaired of having a child, were delighted by the birth of a daughter, born on 3 January 1870. They called her Ethel Florence, names she would come to hate; she preferred to be known as 'Ettie'.

By the time Ettie could walk, Dr Walter was in his late forties, worn out by years of hard work. His wife had aged well: she was a tall, strikingly handsome woman, with dark glossy hair, an ivory-white skin and black eyes.[3] Mary fell pregnant again and the Richardsons moved to a larger rented house in Chapel Street, St Kilda. Keen to keep their money in their very profitable shares, they did not buy a house. They named their second daughter Ada Lillian – she was known as Lil. Sunny, blonde and cuddly, everything dark-haired moody Ettie was not, Lil became Mary's favourite.

Now that mining shares had made him rich, Dr Richardson retired from general practice and devoted himself to his young daughters' upbringing and his study of spiritualism. He was a kind, affectionate father. Ettie was his delight, his 'heart's darling'. He taught her to read at an early age and was delighted by her progress.

When out riding one day, Dr Richardson suffered what he believed to be a fit and fell off his horse. He told Mary of his hidden fear of insanity, which she refused to believe. However, he did not reveal his other secret fear, that he still had syphilis. Mary nursed her husband devotedly, but as Ettie would write in *The Fortunes of Richard Mahony*, whose central character is based partly on her father, 'things would never be quite the same again.'[4] Dr Richardson developed *tic douleureuse*, a facial twitch that embarrassed his patients and Ettie, a symptom that can be associated with tertiary syphilis.

Ettie was intelligent, quick-tempered and ultra-sensitive. When she turned four, her father took his family to Britain so that his children could meet their English and Irish relatives. Like so many migrants, Dr Richardson was caught between cultures, unable to feel truly at home anywhere – not in Ireland nor in England or Australia.

He was in denial over the warning signs of the disease he dreaded and planned a romantic holiday with his wife, touring Italy, France and Switzerland in grand style. They left Ettie and Lil in the care of a devoutly Protestant cousin who lived in Cork, whose husband was

Registrar of the Court of Probate. Ettie, used to her parents' sceptical attitude towards organised religion, was dismayed by her church-going Bible-thumping cousins.

The Richardson's 'second honeymoon' became a nightmare when Walter read in a newspaper that shares in the New North Clunes Mining Company, in which most of his money was invested, had crashed. Suddenly he was worth very little. They had been spending a great deal in Britain and he feared his finances were now in very poor shape indeed.

Dr Richardson traveled overland to Bombay and from there took the first available ship back to Australia. Meanwhile, Mary returned to Ireland, collected Ettie and Lil, and the three of them sailed back to Australia aboard the *Sobraon*. In Melbourne, Dr Richardson came out of retirement, put up his brass plate again and tried desperately to persuade former colleagues to send him patients. He was worried that his family did not own a house, and somehow managed to purchase a block of land at Burwood Road, Hawthorn, then an outlying district of Melbourne. There, on money borrowed from the bank, he built a five-bedroomed mansion with wide balconies and a playroom so that 'the children can have a decent home to grow up in'. In later life, Ethel remembered the Hawthorn house as having 'huge empty rooms'. The reason for this was that before visiting Britain, her parents had sold off most of their furniture (but not Walter's precious collection of books), planning to buy handsome antiques overseas.

However, they still had a piano. By this time, Ettie's musical talent has shown itself; she loved playing the piano.[5]

Re-establishing himself in practice in his fifties proved harder than Dr Walter Richardson had imagined. By now, his undiagnosed illness was making him ill-tempered and eccentric, which offended his patients. Hawthorn was isolated, 'full of new roads, running nowhere', Ettie noted. The few patients Walter did have complained that he was behaving very strangely. At this point, he became obsessed about the large port-wine birthmark that extended from shoulder to wrist on one of Ettie's arms. Possibly, he feared it was a sign of syphilis, which it was not. He photographed the birthmark and then made an unsuccessful attempt to remove it surgically. This made Ettie feel that her birthmark was something to be ashamed of.[6] The birthmark embarrassed Ettie more and more as she grew older, especially in summer when everyone wore sleeveless dresses. She felt ugly (later she described herself as 'a thin lanky child adorned with a crop of black curls'), and suffered agonies of jealousy of her younger sister, pretty, sweet-tempered Lil.

Dr Richardson continued to buy books, something that his wife bitterly resented, she said she needed the money to run the household. Economy became the chief topic of their arguments. Apart from her piano playing, the only bright spots in Ethel's young life were the evenings when her father was well enough to read to her. Later she remembered him as: 'a thin, stooped figure coming up the path, carrying a big carpet-bag full of books, which was plainly too heavy for him. Such a sight would bring me running downstairs, for there was usually something for me in the bag, some child's story suited to my age which he had gone to the trouble of picking out for me.'[7]

The Hawthorn practice made no money; Dr Richardson had strong competition from a younger doctor who was more popular with the patients. When Ettie was six and Lil five, the family moved again, this time to the isolated mining town of Chiltern, where the local doctor was retiring from practice and there was talk of a mining boom. Valiantly, Dr Richardson attempted to run a surgery from their new home, Lake View, but patients were scarce. Now Walter Richardson began to behave even more eccentrically. He tired easily and worried about his large bank loan. Ettie heard her parents arguing bitterly. Failing finances meant there were no more presents of books from her father. Instead, she made up stories to tell to Lil – an excellent start for a future novelist.

Years later, when Ethel Richardson was living in England, she described Chiltern: 'There for the first time I saw wattles in bloom. It was an unforgettable sight. To this day I have only to catch a whiff of mimosa in a dingy London street, and I am once more a small girl, sitting on a fallen tree under the bluest of skies, with all around me these golden, almost stupefyingly-sweet masses of blooms.'[8]

The Richardsons' debts were helped by rent from a tenant Mary had installed in the Hawthorn house, which proved to be unsaleable at anything near the cost of building it. Mary engaged a governess for the two girls, not wanting them to attend the local State school and mix with what she called 'rough children'.

Summer at Chiltern was blisteringly hot. Mary took the two girls to the beach in Melbourne and they stay with friends at Queenscliff. Alone in Chiltern, terrified that the symptoms of tertiary syphilis were setting in, but unable to share his fear with his wife, Dr Richardson suffered an attack of aphasia, reeling like a drunken man and unable to talk, he wrote to his wife and finished by saying, 'I hope you will come home soon before I go *quite* mad.'

To Mary he blamed his symptoms on a severe attack of sunstroke suffered years ago. By now the Chiltern practice was very low on patients. Walter's physical and mental health was deteriorating so badly that he could no longer run it single-handed. Sturdy Mary had to cope with her husband's mental decay and try and do her best for the children.

In 1877, when Ettie was seven, her father applied for what he thought would be a relatively easy Government job. He was appointed as quarantine officer at Queenscliff, a small harbour situated on Port Phillip Bay. His strength was failing, he had rheumatic stiffness and swelling in one knee and found climbing the long ladders up to the sailing ships to check on the crews and passengers extremely tiring.

As the fatal disease progressed, he started to suffer from memory loss and delusions, and people laughed at him in the street, which was agonising for Ettie and Lil. At eight years old, the sensitive Ettie was called to fetch her father home from the main street when he forgot where he was. She saw that people were laughing at her father. She became rebellious and petulant. Lil, on the other hand, was timid and clung to her mother. Ettie's mother realised she had to find a job or they would be forced to live on charity.

Finally, Dr Richardson collapsed completely and was sent to a private asylum, where his condition deteriorated to such a point that he was committed to the Yarra Bend Asylum. Here doctors made the diagnosis of general paralysis and insanity. (At this stage it is a conjecture; not until 1913 would two doctors establish definitively that general paralysis of the insane is caused by syphilis acquired decades previously.)

It was generally rumoured that Dr Richardson was dying of syphilis and the shame would haunt Ettie for the rest of her life. As was customary with a dying patient, Mary Richardson's husband was released into her care in February 1879. For the next seven months Mary bravely nursed her paralysed husband until gangrene set in and he died a harrowing death on 1 August that year. Nine-year-old Ethel saw it all but she blocked those memories in an attempt to forget. Decades later, under the influence of Freudian theory, she would recall her memories of her father when she was creating a major work of fiction set in Australia during the gold rush, *The Fortunes of Richard Mahony*. But all she remembered about her father's funeral was how she and her sister were made to wear scratchy black crepe dresses. She would close her famous trilogy with an account of the burial of the fictitious Dr Mahony, writing how 'the rich and kindly earth of his adopted country absorbed his perishable body.'

Dr Walter Richardson's widow had little schooling, no training and now possessed only a tiny income. How would she manage to feed, clothe and educate her daughters? There was no social security, no Government support systems for widows and children. The only paid job she could apply for was that of a housekeeper, which could mean it would be difficult to keep the girls with her.

Thanks to the kindness of a family friend, the Post-Master General of Victoria, Mary secured a job as postmistress at the remote village of Koroit in the Western Districts of Victoria. It came with a two-bedroom primitive stone cottage where she had to manage the post-office in her own sitting room. The house and the job spelt salvation. Mary could keep her daughters, rather than farming them out to relatives. But Ettie and Lil were no longer the doctor's adored daughters, wearing white muslin dresses, black stockings and boater hats: they were 'those poor girls whose father died of syphilis.'

Mary was given some training for post office duties, holding her head high that she now had to work for a living at a time when middle-class ladies did not work outside the home except in dire need.

It was still impossible to sell the Hawthorn house – due to the general economic downturn, so Mary continued to rent it, saving the income for Ettie and Lil's school fees. Mary found her highly-strung, temperamental elder daughter difficult to manage but recognised her musical talent and high intelligence. Ettie withdrew into herself, making up stories and telling them to Lil or reciting them out loud.

Indoors, she fought with her strong-minded mother but, at other times, she tried to protect both her and Lil against the savage gossip that surrounded them. Ettie admired her mother for her strength and determination but found her difficult to live with. Years later she would recognise her mother's strength and write: 'Undaunted, Mary Richardson, who had previously lived the cloistered life of a Victorian lady, trudged daily to the local Post Office for instruction in telegraphy and account-keeping. Bravely she faced the loss of caste that must inevitably follow in a community where a woman who worked for her living was considered definitely outside the pale.'[9]

By now most of their possessions had been auctioned off. Little remained of their former prosperity.[10]

Mary was good at her job, and was soon promoted to run a much larger post office at Maldon. Ettie described Maldon as:

a lovely spot. Trees abounded. The main street was lined with great gums and almost every house had a garden. Blue ranges banked the horizon and to the rear of the little town rose its own hill, old boulder strewn Mount Tarrangower, an hour's climb up a trickling gully. Round our back veranda hung a muscatel-vine, in season so laden with grapes that neither we nor our friends could cope with them and they ultimately went into the pig tub … Vegetables were supplied by Chinamen, who trotted from door to door with their hanging baskets … The result of Mother being away at work was that I ran wild, letting out all the rowdy, tomboy leanings till then held in leash.[11]

She continued to make up stories and write them down. Without her mother to supervise her, she read everything she could get her hands on, not all of it appropriate for her age.

By working hard and saving money, Mary managed to send clever Ettie, now thirteen, to Melbourne's Presbyterian Ladies' College, which had an excellent academic record and was attended by girls from leading professional and pastoral families in Victoria. The education Ettie received was based on the curriculum offered in boys' private schools, something very unusual at that time. The staff encouraged the girls to attend university and take up careers at a time when most girls' schools were only interested in teaching ladylike accomplishments such as drawing, French, music and deportment.

Ethel Richardson arrived at the Presbyterian Ladies' College in 1883. Her father's illness had made her a precocious, moody teenager. She was argumentative, believing she had musical talent, and her mother had told her she was sure to top her class. However, she was sensitive about her appearance and her hand-me-down clothes, and underneath her pushy exterior, Ettie was ashamed of her clumsy feet and port-wine birthmark, which she tried to hide by wearing long sleeves. She was deeply convinced that Lil was pretty and she was ugly. This was far from the truth. Ettie was described by one of her classmates as 'a dark, distinguished looking girl with a peculiarly high and rounded forehead and most intelligent eyes. She had a grave almost melancholy expression and a somewhat cynical way of talking.' Receiving nothing but 'snubs and sneers I came in for a very bad time,' Ethel described how she was deeply wounded by the reaction of her classmates, she became a good student in every subject except mathematics, geometry and algebra, which totally defeated her. She managed to survive the teasing she received due to her sharp tongue by burying herself in her books and spending hours practising the piano. Her only friend was a much older girl, beautiful Connie Cochran.

The college had been established to educate the daughters of Presbyterian clergy, and the students had to learn chapters of the Old Testament by heart. Ethel always maintained that the sonorous cadences of the King James Version of the Bible formed her prose style. Surprisingly enough, her teachers did not spot her remarkable talent for creative writing. Instead, the school's Principal advised Mary that Ettie should take up a musical career. As a widow left to fend for her family as best she could, Mary Richardson was determined the same would not happen to her girls. They would have brilliant careers.

Decades later, in 1910, Ethel published an ironic novel, *The Getting of Wisdom*, based on her time at the college. The novel tells the story of tall, dark, ungainly Laura Rowbotham (aka Ettie) and the turmoil of her adolescence. Laura is teased by the other girls and tries to enhance her standing by inventing a romance with the handsome married curate, Mr Shepherd. After spending a short holiday at the curate's home Laura discovers that he is odiously bad-tempered and treats his wife appallingly. Laura's lies about her 'romance' are exposed by a girl who loathes her. She is ostracised by her classmates but is saved by the friendship of an older girl, Evelyn Soultar (aka Connie Cochran.) Ettie's relationship with Evelyn becomes a passionate one, undetected by the teachers who allow them to share a room. Finally Evelyn leaves school for her 'coming out' season in Melbourne, from which Laura's poverty excludes her. Laura's pride is such that she cannot bear to be dropped; so it is she who abandons Evelyn rather than the other way round. A girl, rather than Mr Shepherd, is the *real* subject of Laura's infatuation.

In real life, Connie Cochran, like Evelyn in *The Getting of Wisdom*, was everything Ethel was not, beautiful, rich, sophisticated and about to have a coming out season in Melbourne. In her memoirs, Richardson described her passion for the older girl:

> who stirred me to my depths, rousing feelings I hadn't known I possessed and leaving behind a heartache as cruel as the new and bitter realisation that to live meant to change'. She also expressed her surprise that they were allowed to share a room 'when it must have been clear to the blindest where I was heading. Some may see in my infatuation merely an overflow of feelings that had been denied a normal outlet. But the attraction this girl had for me then was so strong that few others have surpassed it. The affinity was mutual and hard to understand for Connie was eighteen and fully grown up while I was still skinny and half-grown. It was Connie's last year at school and she went to considerable lengths to keep things going. But I felt myself an interloper in her family circle, a sort of pariah among her new and stylish friends, I, poor and unsuitably dressed and always on the watch for slights and patronage ... And so we gradually drifted apart.[12]

In *The Getting of Wisdom*, the failed relationship with Evelyn convinces the lonely Laura of the eternal 'fleetingness of things'. She left school with the 'uncomfortable sense of being a square peg which fitted into none of the round holes of her world'.

Some sixty years after the book's publication, an Australian film based on the novel aroused worldwide interest in its author. In the final scene in Bruce Beresford's film, Laura, having come to terms with losing Evelyn and about to leave school, celebrates her freedom from the restrictions of boarding school by running at top speed down an avenue of trees until she is lost to sight.

Ethel Richardson published all her novels under the pen-name 'Henry Handel Richardson' (Handel being a family name on her father's side). When *The Getting of Wisdom* appeared in 1910, British reviewers couldn't imagine why 'Mr Handel Richardson' should wish to turn 'his' attention to a story about a bullied girl attending a boarding-school in Melbourne. They claimed the title was misleading and that 'this novel tells us *nothing* at all about education'. One reviewer remarked that the book was 'far too concerned with the sexual obsessions of a group of nasty minded schoolgirls' and was nothing like the usual stories of girls at boarding school.

What Ettie enjoyed most about the storm aroused by the publication of *The Getting of Wisdom* was the fact that not one of her critics guessed the book was by a woman. Not all the critics were unfavourable. Gerald Gould, in the London *Observer* of 20 April 1924, described *The Getting of Wisdom* as 'the best of contemporary school stories' and urged his readers to buy a copy.

In real life, unlike the fictitious Laura Ramsbotham, Ettie did well at PLC. She was a champion tennis player, won a scholarship for her piano playing and prizes in French and History.[13] However, she was led by her teachers to believe that music was her forte.

Before coming infatuated with Connie she had a teenage crush on the handsome vicar of Maldon, and (like Laura's 'romance' with Mr Shepherd) Ettie made up stories about an imaginary affair with him. These gained her some prestige among the girls, but were finally perceived as lies. Ettie was ostracised, sent to Coventry, and scarcely anyone would speak to her for the rest of that term. Telling stories was all part of her creative talent.

Towards the end of her life, after it was revealed that 'Henry Handel' was a woman, readers wanted to know *why* she had called herself by a man's name to write a book about schoolgirls in a lesbian relationship. The answer was that she wanted to be seen as a serious writer at a time when it was believed that women could only write sentimental trash. Ethel Richardson published under the name Henry Handel Richardson for the same reason Charlotte Brontë called herself Currer Bell in order to write about a love affair between a governess and a married man, the central theme of *Jane Eyre*. The same criteria applied to painting as writing. Women were only good for painting flowers and children, 'high' art was reserved for men. Doctors like Henry Maudsley, founder of the London psychiatric hospital that bears his name, claimed that 'men's bodies are bigger than women's so their brains must be bigger', explaining that women should not study hard or it might affect their menstrual periods, making them infertile. An absurd theory, but at the time, people believed it.

Ethel Richardson could never be accused of writing romantic trash. Her style was powerful and polished and her novels compared by literary critics to those of Flaubert or Dostoyevsky. Her books dealt with what were at that time regarded as 'shocking' topics such as homosexuality, lesbianism, suicide and syphilis, which were deemed highly unsuitable for the delicate ears of ladies. The horrific circumstances of her father's madness and death, and the permanent sense of insecurity it inflicted on Ethel Richardson, would affect all her relationships and permeate her writing, which was often concerned with the darker side of human nature.

Another topic Ettie wrote about from bitter experience was jealousy, eating away from within. Clever little Ettie had been her father's favourite, the daughter who shared his love of books. After his death she had to share a bedroom with Lil, the pretty little girl with the sunny nature whom her mother obviously preferred. Ethel's intense jealousy of Lil, bottled up for decades, made her even more insecure about her looks, her future and her chances of marriage. Relations between the three females during school holidays often reached boiling point.

In 1887, her final year at school, Ethel turned seventeen. By now her mother had been promoted to postmistress in the Melbourne suburb of Richmond, so now both Ettie and Lil attended the college as day girls. Lil was also musically talented and played the violin.

After leaving school Ettie spent a few months teaching music at a small private school in Toorak, a job she hated. She spent her afternoons alone at home. She read Tom Paine's *Rights of Man*, the novels of Walter Scott and the poetry of Tennyson. She also wrote gloomy entries in her diary and surreptitiously pored over her father's papers, which must have been a revelation to her, since he often expressed sexual desire for her mother with extreme frankness. Reading this material marked the end of innocence. Ethel was fascinated by sex and these letters and diaries would furnish her with material for her three novels about the fictitious Richard Mahony.

In 1888 Mary Richardson resigned from the postal service. At last she had been able to obtain an excellent price for their huge Hawthorn house, which they had despaired of selling and called 'the white elephant'. Mary's aim was to 'finish off' her girls in Europe using the money from the sale of the house to support them. She was anxious that no one should know she had been a humble postmistress, and determined that her teenage daughters should be seen as clever, accomplished and eligible: once they had carved out careers, she hoped they would make 'good' marriages.

Aboard the ship taking them to Britain, Ettie was mortified that all the eligible men were attracted to pretty Lil rather than herself. Only one elderly Australian showed any interest in her but she was not interested in him.

They visited English relatives, who insisted on taking the girls 'to every museum in London', believing them to be 'raw colonials'. In reality, the excellent education received at the Presbyterian Ladies' College meant that Ettie and Lil were far better educated and more cultured than their English relatives. After spending some time in Britain, which Ettie found dismal and dirty, the three Richardson women went by boat and train to Leipzig, the pleasant university town in eastern Germany. Here, in April 1889, both Ethel and Lillian enrolled at the famous Royal Conservatorium. Ethel was to study the piano while her younger sister studied the violin. They were soon immersed in the musical and social life of the town and Ettie described her three years there as 'the happiest I had yet known'. Leipzig, then the most highly regarded centre of musical studies in Europe, was saturated in music. Young composers like Richard Strauss and Gustav Mahler came there to conduct their first symphonies at the local concert hall. The two high-spirited Australian girls had the time of their lives, attending lectures, concerts, the opera and the theatre. Weekends were devoted to tennis, swimming and walks in the woods surrounding the city. Ettie was filling out and becoming far more attractive, while beautiful Lil shrugged off her shyness and became something of a flirt. Unlike her older sister, she was not seriously interested in a musical career. Ettie was not good at dealing with young men; she tended to be competitive and aggressive, which put them off. Jealously she watched as men swarmed around Lil.

Ethel worked hard at the Conservatorium but feared her slender fingers were not strong enough for a performance playing. Uneasy about her future she was flattered to receive two proposals, unfortunately from men she found unattractive. Meanwhile, at several parties she had observed a tall quiet Scot, George Robertson, who had what she described as 'a gentle face and keen blue eyes hidden behind spectacles'. The penniless Glaswegian post-graduate was three years older than Ettie. After gaining his degree in science, as his parents wished, George had come to Leipzig to study German language and literature – to the concern of his father, a lecturer at the Glasgow Church of Scotland Training College, who was convinced that his son's best hope of a good academic job lay in science.

George invited Ettie to accompany him to the autumn cycle of Wagner's operas, the highlight of the opera season in Leipzig. Ettie found the life of a student in Leipzig liberating and intellectually stimulating. With Robertson's help she discovered the richness of German literature and learned German to please him. With his help she was able to read the works of Sigmund Freud, which at that time were scarcely known outside Germany. They shared a passion for writing. Her developing friendship with George gave her self-confidence: now men were eager to dance with her at student parties.

She and George begin a clandestine romance within that free-living student community and their relationship deepened. But Mary, Ettie's mother, soon discovered where her elder daughter's interest lay. Appraised that the Robertson family had little money, she did *not* view George Robertson's interest in Ethel with favour and remained blind to any sort of prospects his academic studies might bring. Meanwhile, flirtatious Lillian's heart remained untouched.

Mary Richardson had no doubt that her elder daughter had the makings of a professional concert pianist. Initially, Ettie yearned to pursue a musical career and became deeply interested in great musicians such as the composer Edward Grieg, who she saw perform at Leipzig's concert hall, the *Gewandhaus*. She was heartened by the news that fellow Australian Nellie Melba (Nellie Armstrong) had enjoyed a huge triumph singing at the Paris Opera and longed to emulate her.

However, she was receiving warning signs that although her 'stretch' was good, her lean long fingers were deficient in staying power. She spent hours practising, but completely lost confidence in her ability after a disasterous student concert. Finally she admitted to her mother that she couldn't bear the thought of hundreds of pairs of eyes staring at her as she performed in public. After all these years of study, she realised that she was temperamentally unsuited to the concert platform. But she had absolutely no intention of becoming a music teacher. Instead, she would marry George Robertson. Her mother was disappointed and angry, as were some of Ettie's teachers. Tantrums and recriminations ensued.

Ettie was no longer the 'musical genius' and far more distressed by her failure than she admitted in her memoirs, *Myself When Young*, written at the end of her life. In reality, she was distraught. Her father had failed and so had she. Her only consolation was that George adored her. By now she had turned into a handsome young woman, whose heavily lidded sensual eyes and Roman nose give her a patrician appearance. She realised that she was now attractive, to women as well as men. Mat Main, an admiring young Scottish girl who had shared the Richardsons' rented apartment on Leipzig's Mozartstrasse developed a hopeless crush on Ettie and even threatened suicide when she learned of her engagement to George, which was formally announced in 1891.

Miss Ethel Richardson graduated from the Conservatorium with honours in all branches of her subject. At her *Hauptprüfung* on 25 March the following year, she received 'great and well-deserved applause' for her performance of the first movement of Beethoven's piano concerto in C major. Yet in *Myself When Young*, her (sometimes unreliable) memoirs, she says she did not complete her course at Leipzig. Ettie was always prone to lies and silences when recounting her past.

George Robertson did not want to tell his parents about their engagement; having switched from a career in science to studying German (which at that time had few career prospects) he knew they would fear for his financial future and try to talk him out of marrying Ettie. So while the Richardsons returned to England, George had to remain in Leipzig to complete his thesis, hoping he would be able to find a lecturing position in the German department of a British university after he had a postgraduate degree.

Meanwhile, the Richardsons drifted around Britain staying with friends, then rented rooms in Cambridge, where once again Ettie had to share a room with Lil, who was recovering from an unhappy affair in Leipzig. Lil had lost her virginity (a huge step in those days and enough to render a girl unmarriageable in certain cases) to a German who now refused to marry her. Both sisters were lonely, and miserable and felt cold uncomfortable and alien in England.

However, Ettie cheered up after discovering a capacity to write articles, and found a good market for her writing in English magazines. Her first published work was a short story, 'Christmas in Australia'. Away from her fiancé, she was tortured by jealousy and desperately worried that his parents would talk him out of the marriage. She saw herself and George as twin souls and was longing to be involved with him in literary work; she felt this was the one hold she had over him which other girls could not share. So she undertook a paid translation of Jens Peter Jacobsen's influential bestselling novel *Niels Lyhne*, lent to her by George. By now, the Richardsons were living with Australian friends in London. George arrived from Germany to carry out research work in the British Museum Reading Room. He was beginning to realise he would not be able to get a post in the German department of any British university, since they only employed German-born lecturers. He helped Ettie with her translation, and their work on this awakened in her a passion for writing. (Her translation, *Siren Voices*, was eventually published in 1896.)

George went home to Scotland, hoping to find work there. Ettie's insecurities that the marriage would never take place due to pressure from his parents caused her real anguish and jealousy. Without a job, George could not set a marriage date, and Ettie was very aware that her mother did not want them to marry either. She alternated between delight when she sold an article and floods of tears whenever she did not receive a letter from George. She said she hated London and wanted to return to Germany after her marriage.

Although Mary Richardson had desperately wanted her daughters to have careers before they married, Ettie's tantrums and scenes wore her down and eventually she offered Ettie a sum of money to pay for a quiet wedding and support her and George for the first year of their marriage. Ettie was now twenty-five; in that era of young brides, she was in danger of being regarded as being 'on the shelf'. This explains why Mary gave in to her wishes; it also explains Ettie's fear that George might find a younger, prettier girl – a fear that was lifelong.

As George had predicted, his parents were furious that all their financial sacrifice had been in vain and that their clever son could not get a job in a Department of German Language and Literature. They blamed him for not continuing with science and were scathing about his proposed marriage. Ettie swore over and over again she could not live or write without him: she urged that they should use the money from her mother for a quiet wedding and 'at least enjoy some years of happiness before they were old'. George was flattered by her need for him. He, too, was feeling lost and insecure. Finally, they were married at the Church of St John the Baptist, Clontarf, Dublin (her father's birthplace) on 30 December 1895.

Close family friends hosted a champagne breakfast for the wedding reception but there were thirteen places laid at the wedding feast, a bad omen it is said, but their marriage confounded the dismal predictions by proving a remarkably happy and productive relationship. They received over 200 wedding presents from friends and relatives, some of which were cheques to help support them until George found a university job.

They honeymooned along the Rhine and spent time in Munich, where George at last obtained work in the university there. Mary and Lil joined them there, until the married couple moved to Strasbourg (then in Germany) for the next seven years. George had secured a lectureship there. They both loved living amid the German/French ambience of this university city. With the appearance of Dr George Robertson's monumental *History of German Literature*, his career as a scholar of considerable repute was established. Ethel was overjoyed that after all her mother's gloomy predictions, her adored husband was now widely respected in the academic world. Their love, based on mutual respect and intellectual companionship, endured. It seemed that neither Ettie nor Lil wanted children when they married, doubtless because they feared passing on their father's dreaded affliction. One has only to read Ibsen's *Ghosts* to realise that before Alexander Fleming and Howard Florey discovered penicillin, syphilis, the 'Red Plague' and its inheritance by children who risked being born deaf, blind and crippled was one of the preoccupations of the era.

Mary continued to write to Ettie each week – homely letters giving household hints and recipes which fell on deaf ears. Ettie *hated* housework and hired a housekeeper.

She was earning money from her translation of Björnson's *The Fisher Lass* and a published article on Jacobsen, *A Danish Poet* – both works aided by her husband. When he suggested that she should write a novel dealing with their student days in Leipzig, Ethel immediately started plotting the storyline and creating characters based partly on students and musicians they had known. She would write during the morning, take walks or play tennis in the afternoon, and after dinner George would read what she had written and make suggestions for cuts or alterations. It was the bond that held them together. 'My twin soul', she called him, 'my rock.'

In the autumn of 1896, a telegram arrived from Lil in Munch with the news that Mary was ill 'with an inflammation'. It was followed by a second telegram saying that Lil was also ill and Ettie must come. Ethel could not believe that her mother, the mainstay of all their lives for so long, could be seriously ill. She took the train for Munich and learned that the doctors thought Mary had an internal blockage in her intestines. They gave her an enema which made Mary writhe and scream with pain. Her condition did not improve but Ettie went back home to Strasbourg, then returned with George. Lil blamed her sister for leaving her to deal with their mother alone. It now appeared that the doctors suspected Mary had cancer of the stomach or the bowel. Her condition worsened; her lips, covered in sores, were bluish-black, her eyes sunk deep into their sockets. It was clear she had not long to live.

Ettie ventured to say, 'Don't worry about us, mother.'

'You're all right, dear,' Mary replied. 'You have George to take care of you. It's Lil I worry about.' These were her final words before she cried out, 'Hold me up, hold me up,' and died.

Later, they learned that Mary died of undiagnosed appendicitis followed by peritonitis. Both her daughters were distraught. Ettie was consumed by remorse that she had not showed more love for her mother while she was alive. Lil still blamed Ettie for leaving her mother and going back to Munich. They quarrelled and all their old bitterness re-emerged.

In an attempt to resolve her feelings of grief and the anger she felt against the doctors she felt should have saved Mary, Ettie wrote an account of her mother's death. She was run-down and emotionally at a low ebb. As a result, she suffered a severe attack of bronchitis; for the rest of her life she would suffer from a 'weak throat' and severe attacks of bronchitis each winter.

In 1903, Dr Robertson accepted the first chair of German and Scandinavian studies at the University of London and proceeded to set these subjects on a firm foundation in Britain. The honours bestowed on him by the German, Swedish and Norwegian governments were well deserved. Ethel, the professor's wife and aspiring author, basked in reflected glory. However, she did not enjoy living in London, where she felt patronised as an 'uncultured colonial'. She thought of herself as Australian and European but not British. The Robertsons' German housekeeper had accompanied them to London and Ethel was able to devote her mornings to writing her first novel. During the university vacations the Robertsons took walking tours in the Rhineland or went skiing in Austria, visiting the opera and concerts, staying with friends or in small *gasthauses*, leading a very European and cultured lifestyle.

In London they lived in a narrow, five storey house in Regents Park Road, a pleasant tree-lined street close to the park. What Ettie most enjoyed were the evenings she and George spent together at home, reading and discussing books. In her emotional dependence on her bookish husband there are echoes of Ettie's relationship with her bookish father. She wanted her husband's academic career to prosper and conquered her usual feelings of shyness at meeting new people to entertain his colleagues at dinner parties. However, she always refused to discuss the novel she was writing with anyone but George. She was working hard at what turned out to be an extraordinarily powerful first novel. Begun in Strasbourg in 1897, *Maurice Guest* was the result of prodigious research, meticulous writing and rigorous re-drafting. 'Henry' was both disciplined and imaginative. She required a tray of freshly sharpened pencils to be lying on her desk when she began work punctually at 9.30 each morning. Nobody was allowed to enter her study once she had started to work. If anything was required she would summon her German secretary and housekeeper, Irene Stumpp, or a maid on the house telephone.

In 1908, five years after their move to London, *Maurice Guest* by 'Henry Handel' Richardson was published by Heinemann. The publishers had accepted *Maurice Guest* and its 'daring' passages dealing with homosexuality and explicit sexual references because Ethel's editor believed that this was a major work of literature.

*Maurice Guest* is about a talented young English music student in turn-of-the-century Leipzig who abandons his musical studies at the Conservatorium for the sake of Louise Dupleyer, an amoral Australian woman. She is having an affair with a leading conductor famous for his womanising (partly based on the famous composer Richard Strauss), and at the same time she consoles her vanity by sleeping with the naive and inexperienced music student, Maurice Guest. She does not feel any love for him. Maurice, an extremely talented musician, has problems defining his sexuality. He experiences the same intense stage fright at performing in front of hundreds of people that Ethel suffered. Deeply in love with Louise (his first affair), he is tortured by feelings of jealousy and self-doubt – as Ettie had been. But for the probably bisexual Maurice there is no happy ending. He puts an end to his financial problems and his doubts about his sexuality by committing suicide. It is a very psychological novel, an extraordinary first novel for anyone at that time, let alone a woman.

To Ethel's extreme dismay, the critics hated the topics treated in *Maurice Guest*. 'An intolerably long book about people not in the least worth writing about,' pronounced the *Sheffield Independent*, a provincial and very conservative paper, 'when the person who gives the title to the tale commits suicide, the reader feels relieved.' Another critic called the book's candid story about love, lust and student life in Leipzig 'morbid, verbose and erotic'. It seemed the British had problems dealing with the world of music students living the Bohemian life, as sexually liberated as the artists of Montmartre.

Ethel's editor had led her to believe that her work was modern, psycho-analytical, in the spirit of the times, and would be acclaimed for its lack of hypocrisy, its characterisation, for revealing how a group of students and aspiring musicians really behaved. Now, to her horror, 'Henry' became the subject of attack over a book which was not seen as great literature but as morally degrading, an outrage against decency. All her old insecurities surfaced. Was she always to be the outsider, mocked and humiliated, just as she had been at school? Ethel claimed that reading the reviews left her speechless, unable to communicate even with her domestic staff, physically nauseated by mortification every time she thought about the critics' acid comments, yet unable to retaliate. No criticism would ever wound her again like those first reviews. Childless by choice, Ethel regarded her books as her progeny, and suffered deeply when critics attacked them.

What the critics were not prepared for was the wildly promiscuous life of most of Richardson's young musicians. Men and women competed for the affections of the same lover. One character was definitely bisexual, conducting affairs with partners of different sexes at the same time. At that time, same-sex relationships were taboo, unmentionable in polite society. Before the theories of Sigmund Freud were bandied about by the chattering classes and emulated by a host of psychologists and counsellors, homosexuality and lesbianism were regarded as unmentionable in novels. Although the upper classes indulged in countless affairs after marriage, both heterosexual and homosexual, and country house parties consisted of endless bed-hopping around stately homes, the status quo of marriage contracts, based on property and possession, was maintained. The horrific fate of Oscar Wilde, who had died only eight years previously, gaoled then exiled to France for love of Lord Alfred Douglas as well as mindless couplings with guardsmen, was at the back of everyone's mind. Homosexuality was still a prosecutable offence. *Maurice Guest* was condemned for its 'lack of moral tone'. 'The book will have little general reader appeal,' critics predicted correctly. Some copies were withdrawn and a second, expurgated edition was published; by now the publishers were scared they could be prosecuted for immorality for the homosexuality revealed in Ethel's novel. Many bookshops flatly refused to stock it.

A German translation was published in 1912, also heavily cut and it was highly praised. Edited American and Danish editions followed. In the end the second English edition of *Maurice Guest* was reprinted seven times. Those broad-minded and well-travelled people who *did* buy 'Henry's' book and enjoyed it appreciated the deeper understanding she gave them of men, women, human sexuality and human frailties. She wrote perceptively about jealousy, a subject she understood very well. Fellow writers like Hugh Walpole and Somerset

Maugham praised Henry Handel Richardson's first novel and became her friends. But for Ethel, the damage had been done. She had always been reserved when meeting people for the first time, especially those with whom she felt she had little in common. Some people thought her proud but it was insecurity and shyness, rather than pride. Now, bitterly hurt by the critics and averse to discussing the reviews or the topics she had chosen to write about, she became a virtual recluse, even though the true identity of 'Henry Handel Richardson' was still not revealed. Now she allowed very few visitors to the tall, silent house. George Robertson, who had always urged his wife to 'aim high' in her writing, shared her dismay – but although he had advised her over the years it was taking shape, it was not his book: he was one step removed from the anguish the author endured.

The Robertsons' move to London suited George better than his wife. The onset of World War I distressed both of them greatly as they had many German friends in universities and musical circles there. Lillian, too, was living in Germany, having married Dr Otto Neustatter, a Munich eye specialist. The marriage was initially a happy one and eventually Lillian's only son, Walter Lindesay Neustatter was sent to school in Britain, where he lived with the Robertsons and was like a surrogate son to them. The war caused divided loyalties for Ethel's nephew, who would remain in Britain and study to become a psychiatrist, influenced by his aunt and uncle's fascination with the writings and research of Sigmund Freud.

The war changed pretty effervescent Lillian. Her loyalties, too, were divided but her Australian background won. She left her husband, came to live in London with Ettie and George and her son Walter. After a period of loneliness, she met a charismatic young teacher and writer named Stuart Neill, and after the war she helped him to set up a school in Austria with progressive ideas on education and the teaching of music. Lil was still married to her very Germanic husband, whom she now found safe and dull, and started an affair with Neill. She and her husband and Neill spent a great deal of time together. Eventually this strange *ménage à trois* broke up, and Lil and Neill then opened a similar school in England to the one they had run in Austria, backed by Dr Neustatter's money. An amicable divorce was arranged: Lil married Stuart Neill and devoted the rest of her life to running Summerhill School.

Besides his lecturing workload, Professor Robertson conducted intensive research and undertook extra work to maintain the large house and staff at Regent's Park Road. He and Ettie spent long vacations walking, bicycling or skiing in Germany, Austria and Scandinavia. At home, Ettie continued to compose songs in English and German and to play the piano for her husband's pleasure but writing and involving her husband in critiquing and editing her work became the focus of her life ... perhaps a substitute for the children she felt she could not have.

No man could have done more than Professor Robertson to ensure that his wife was free to devote herself to her writing. He was in a good position to advise her. By now, his knowledge of literature, music and the arts was immense; in Ethel's novels there are distinct traces of his literary criticism: for example, his knowledge of Freud's research, which Ethel shared, and of the works of Wagner (on whom he lectured). 'Henry' as he affectionately called his wife, sometimes in jest, sometimes in tenderness, learned from her hardworking academic husband the habits of prolonged work and the dedication required to research and write her books. He always found time to discuss her work with her. She wrote in longhand for a few hours each day and employed a typist. Then, very conscious of maintaining her svelte figure, she kept to her regime of walking in Regent's Park, playing tennis and swimming. She was a member of the London Society for Psychical Research, the London Spiritualist Alliance and the International Society for Psychical Research, consciously or unconsciously echoing her father's interests.

Ethel's childhood had been spent moving from one home to another. She craved stability, security and her husband's undivided attention. She was jealous of his female students, hated change and insisted they should remain in the house at Regents Park Road that had become her refuge and her work place. They lived there for the next thirty years. By now 'Henry Handel Richardson' was making a name for himself. 'Henry' had no intention of changing her name and her image, especially not to the name Ethel, which she had always hated. She said that the idea people would call her Ethel Richardson, the *lady* novelist, 'made her flesh creep'. She wanted to be known as a *literary* writer on contemporary themes.[14]

Used to the wide open spaces of country Victoria and the woods surrounding Leipzig, Ethel Robertson never felt entirely at ease in London and often felt homesick for Australia, the country she had left as an adolescent. In 1912, the Robertsons visited Australia to allow Ethel to research her next book, a fictionalised account of the life of her father in Australia during the gold rush. Young children are rarely concerned with their parents' lives and Ettie, while her father was alive, had never asked questions about his past.

Ethel was now forty-two, an age when most people attempt to make sense of their own lives. She became fascinated by the history of her own family and by the huge social changes brought by the gold rushes in Australia. This, she realised, was a great turning point, the period that changed Australia from a penal settlement into a thriving rough-and-tumble male-dominated society linked by the concept of mateship, where Jack was as good as his master and the theory of the 'fair go' for all was born.

The trip was a success and as her research continued, she realised that she now had enough material for three separate books. They would take her almost twenty years to complete. Her parents' story had sparked a deep creative well-spring within her and turned her into a fine writer, although not always a *truthful* one.

Now, decades after her father's death, she unleashed, from the hidden depths of her consciousness, the details of her father's madness and horrific death. *The Fortunes of Richard Mahony* was the first novel in the trilogy; the three books are now called *Australia Felix*. Together, they tell the story of a doctor who dies of syphilis. *The Fortunes of Richard Mahony,* published in 1917, brought the Victorian diggings to life as no other contemporary novel had succeeded in doing.

In it, Ettie managed to communicate her father's passion for finding gold (a passion, shared by so many, which resembled a craving for heroin), as well as his eventual disillusionment. She wrote perceptively on this topic, describing how: 'A passion for gold awoke in them an almost sensual craving to touch and possess. The glitter of a few specks at the bottom of a pan or cradle came to mean more than home or wife or child ...' and how:

This dream ... of vast wealth ... had decoyed the strange motley crowd in which peers and churchmen rubbed shoulders with the scum of Norfolk

Island, to exile in this outlandish region. The intention of all had been to snatch a golden fortune from the earth; and then hey presto back to the Old World again ... But many became prisoners to the soil. The fabulous riches amounted to a few thousand pounds: what folly to depart with so little, when mother earth still teemed. Those who drew blanks laboured all day for a navvy's wage. Others broken in health, could only turn to an easier handiwork.

She wrote about people who became addicted to digging for gold, describing how: 'Those, who, as soon as fortune smiled on them dropped their tools and ran to squander the work of months in a wild debauch before returning, tail down to prove their luck anew.'

Writing as 'Henry Handel Richardson', Ettie was able to define the Australian experience. She saw how Australians worshipped Lady Luck. She described how those new Australians who succeeded were not viewed in the same way as their American counterparts, as being talented or hard working. Luck – in property speculation, the stockmarket, the race track, in a game of two-up – became part of the Australian ethos. Luck is the reason for Australia's fabled egalitarianism.

In describing the role played by luck and gambling in the Australian psyche, 'Henry Handel' had just written an important passage in Australian literature.

World War I was still in progress when *The Fortunes of Richard Mahony* was published. London was in the midst of Zeppelin raids and bombs and the horror of young Britons and Australians dying in the trenches of France. During wartime, paper was rationed and the book did not have huge sales. Few copies were shipped to Australia.

Nor did her second novel, *The Way Home* (1925), achieve much success. Some critics and fellow authors in Australia considered the chapters that dealt with Richard Mahony's return to England the most revealing expose of English snobbery and social attitudes they had ever read. When the time came for the third novel of the trilogy, *Ultima Thule*, to be sent off to the printers, Heinemann baulked at the prospect of having another novel about syphilis by Henry Handel Richardson left unsold on their shelves. Only the direct intervention of Professor Robertson, and his undertaking to guarantee the publishers against loss and to cover the cost of printing, saved the day for 'Henry' Handel Richardson's latest novel.

Review copies of *Ultima Thule* were sent out late in 1929. Two agonising weeks went by, during which the author and her husband anxiously awaited the final verdict on a work which had been nearly two decades in the making. Finally, the influential critic Gerald Gould wrote in the *Sunday Observer*: 'The book is a masterpiece, a work of genius worthy to rank with the greatest and saddest masterpieces of our day.' Reflecting the feelings of hundreds of thousands of readers in England, Australia and America, the eminent music critic Ernest Newman described how the illness and final break-up of Richard Mahony had moved him 'as much as any passage in Beethoven'. Reading the review one can imagine that, after the mauling she received from previous critics, Ettie would have wept with sheer relief.

To the surprise of the publishers *Ultima Thule* sold well. The monumental tragedy of the author's theme was recognised. The book was quickly reprinted by Heinemann in Britain and by Norton in America. There were several European language translations. Heinemann hastily bought back all rights from Dr Robertson. Today the *Australia Felix* trilogy has become an Australian classic, taught in university literary courses and helped to literary prominence in Australia by the writer and critic Nettie Palmer.

*Australia Felix* describes the great upswing in nineteenth-century Western capitalism fuelled by Australia's gold discoveries as well as the sense of cultural alienation and isolation experienced by British migrants in a land ten thousand miles away from Britain. She saw Australia as a land where different social values prevailed due to the harshness of life and the cult of mateship.

The three books deal with issues which were to define the direction of white Australian society from the 1850s onwards, set within the framework of a troubled marriage and an inevitable and horrific death from syphilis – an illustration of what Tolstoy called 'the universal human vulnerability to pain and loss'.

Richardson's three Dr Mahony works are powerfully written, haunted by images of guilt, separation, alienation and death. English novelist Somerset Maugham greatly admired the Richard Mahony trilogy and described it as similar in its imagery and layers of meaning to Dostoyevsky's *Crime and Punishment*.[15] The sins of the fathers visited on their children is a theme common to both authors.

The Richard Mahony trilogy has also been described as 'one of the great inexorable books of the world'. Dostoyevsky's medically qualified father had been brutally murdered by serfs at his country home in revenge for his treatment of them, a tragedy that haunted the Russian author in the same way that the harrowing death of Dr Walter Richardson haunted his daughter.

What Dostoyevsky, Zola, Flaubert, Balzac, Dickens and other great writers, including Henry Handel Richardson, realised in their writing is the infinite complexity of human nature rather than the black-and-white version portrayed in much popular fiction and films. They see no good or bad characters but realise men and women may commit heinous crimes and yet be brave, generous and loving towards their fellow beings. There are no villains or heroes here, only complex people coping with problems that face *all* humanity. This is where Ettie's talent as a novelist lies – 'character drawing' she called it.

Heinemann had published John Galsworthy's hugely successful *The Forsythe Saga*. They realised that in Richardson's trilogy they had a family saga with bestseller potential, as well as a literary success. By now, British newspapers were clamouring to know the identity of the author. Journalists eventually ferreted out the truth. The writer, it transpired, was a *woman, and* one born in Australia.

Interviews were scheduled but Ethel declined to speak to journalists. The professor's wife continued to hold herself aloof from London society and would not sign books or speak at literary lunches. When a brash journalist almost cornered her on one occasion in a department store, she took refuge from him by hiding in the ladies' lavatory for so long that he left. It made a good story.

The vulnerable insecure schoolgirl had not changed very much. She still disliked talking about her work and did not make friends easily. Her second live-in secretary, Olga Roncoroni, and her nephew Walter were her closest companions apart from her adored husband. She received The Australian Literature Society's gold medal for *Ultima Thule* as the best novel of 1929, and now that the trilogy was completed, her husband and other literary figures gave her hope of being nominated for a Nobel Prize for Literature. Then, without warning, her husband became ill and grew steadily worse.

In 1933, the sudden death of Prof Robertson from cancer was a huge shock to his wife and an irreparable loss. Writing had been her hobby, her career, her passion and had left her little time to cultivate many other interests or intimate friends. Ethel remained in the Regents Park Road house with Olga for a year after her husband's death, then they both moved to the south coast. But Ethel never became reconciled to living in England.

When she was sixty-four, Ethel's book, *The End of Childhood*, a collection of short stories about young Cuffy Mahony, son of Dr Mahony, was published. It was 1934 – a year after her husband's death.

Richardson and Roncoroni loved visiting the cinema. Ethel belonged to a private film club which enabled her to see films proscribed in England, which then had very tight censorship – as did Australia. She had contacts in Germany and Paris, and in what was a very restrictive era, they supplied her with banned novels, including works by D. H. Lawrence.

Ethel's letters and diary entries for this period show that she suffered a long period of depression after her husband's death. Her letters mention neuralgia, sciatica and influenza. She wrote how 'a weariness of things in general ... sometimes takes possession of me' but 'it goes hand in hand with a vigorous hold on existence and with the unyielding toughness of the born fighter'.

She was helped in her fight against a reactive depression, sparked by her husband's death, by Olga Roncoroni. Olga had battled to overcome severe panic attacks – she was agoraphobic, a neurotic condition defined as a morbid fear of entering public spaces. The sufferer only feels safe at home and becomes progressively less able to venture outside. In the 1920s and 1930s, little was known about this condition. Olga, whose parents were friends of Lillian and her second husband, had been encouraged to seek treatment by the Robertsons, whom she met in 1921, when they were staying with Lil and Stuart Neill at their home in Lyme Regis.

Appraised of her difficulties, the Robertsons had invited Olga to stay with them in London so that she could seek psychiatric treatment. She had consulted a psychiatrist who had helped her, and she had also been helped by her friendship with Lil and her son Dr Walter Neustatter, who was staying with the Richardsons while doing his postgraduate training in psychiatry. Eventually, Olga had recovered sufficiently to continue her teaching of Dalcroze Eurythmics at a London school. The Richardsons liked her and found her vivacious, intelligent and very European in her approach to life, as well as an accomplished pianist. And so she remained at Regents Park Road, and in time became invaluable to Ethel as a secretary. Olga's sense of fun appealed to Ethel's lighter side and they became good friends, so Olga agreed to a death-bed request by George Robertson 'to look after Henry' when he had gone.

Much speculation has surrounded Ettie and Olga's friendship, often erroneously based on the premise that Ettie's literary interest in homosexual relationships meant she had a lesbian relationship with Roncoroni after her husband's death. There is no concrete evidence to support this view. Handel Richardson's greatest novels *Maurice Guest* and *The Fortunes of Richard Mahony* deal with heterosexual as well as homosexual relationships. While it is not possible to deny that Olga and Ettie were more than good friends, when Ettie was widowed, she had spent almost forty years in a loving relationship with her husband with no more than the usual conflicts of a married couple. She was devastated by his death, and her constant wish to get in touch with him through the spirit world does not suggest someone in a lesbian relationship.

Ettie now took up her father's interests in spiritualism and the paranormal. Her sessions at the ouija board and attendance at séances were a desperate attempt to get in touch with her husband 'on the other side of death' and re-establish what she insisted was 'a permanent marriage', claiming that their souls were 'twinned for eternity'. She 'discussed' her writing with her husband in expensive séances with various mediums, who claimed they were in touch with him in the spirit world. The grieving widow told her dead husband about problems with her latest book, even played the piano to him and continued the co-dependent relationship which had lasted nearly forty years. She even read him part of her unfinished novel *Nicky and Sanny*.

This novel was supposed to be based on Lil's first marriage to a German doctor. Notes by the author indicate that its plot hinged on a marriage breakdown. It seems logical to assume that, like almost everything she wrote, *Nicky and Sanny* was based on something she had seen unfold, a contemporary middle-class drama. It would seem that Ettie, for so long jealous of Lil's hold of her mother's affections, had avenged the wounds of their past in *Nicky and Sanny*. She described in detail Lil's marriage breakdown, based on intimate details she knew about Lil's engagement and marriage to Dr Otto Neustatter, their initial happiness and growing prosperity, and their divided loyalties as tension mounted in the 1930s between Germany and Britain. As war seemed inevitable and the forces of the Third Reich increased in power, venting their hatred of the Jews, Lil realised it would be impossible for her to remain in Hitler's orbit, even though she had helped to establish a school in a beautiful part of Austria. She attempted to resolve an impossible love triangle with an Englishman who shared her views on education. She had genuinely loved her husband when she married him but experienced distaste for sex with him after she became involved with her new lover. The novel detailed the death of love in a marriage that convention ordained must survive for the sake of the child, and the eventual divorce and re-marriage of the female protagonist to a more compatible man.

Doubtless Lillian and her son, Dr Walter Lindesay Neustatter, had every reason for wishing this novel would never be published. (It has been assumed that this was the reason that Olga Roncoroni, possibly at the request of Dr Walter Neustatter – Lil's psychiatrist son, who had done so much to help combat her panic attacks and agoraphobia – destroyed the manuscript after Ettie's death.[16])

In 1934, Ethel and Olga moved to Fairlight, near Hastings on the Kentish coast. Ettie bought a large touring car, an old Armstrong-Siddeley. In it they visited Austria and Germany, Ettie happy as ever to be in the mountains and lakes she loved. But all too soon came the long hot September of 1939 when Hitler invaded Poland and the wireless message was relayed over the BBC that Britain was at war with Germany. Like Virginia Woolf, Ettie was extremely depressed to think that war with Germany was about to erupt once again. This, together with George's death, depressed her spirits and badly affected the quality of her writing.

Now, when she was sixty-nine, Ethel's final published novel, *The Young Cosima*, appeared. Unfortunately, it fell far below the standard of the Richard Mahony trilogy. It deals with the tortured relationships between Cosima von Bulow, Wagner, her father Lizt and her husband the conductor Hans von Bulow. The novel provided an opportunity for Richardson to re-examine the themes of genius, passion and intimacy and the universal human vulnerability to pain and loss.

Ettie and Olga remained at Hastings all through heavy bombing raids by the German airforce on south-eastern England, where in 1940–41 German planes would off-load any remaining bombs after they had devastated London. The dreaded 'doodlebugs', the V2 rockets which menaced southern England in 1944, were another hazard. 'The one that would kill you and destroy your home,' Richardson dryly observed, 'was the one you did not hear.' Her complex personality remained surprising resilient. She was as sharp-eyed, shrewd and caustic as ever.

At the age of seventy-four, frail, grey-haired and in poor health, especially in winter when her bronchitis caused problems, Ettie insisted on keeping a log of all flying-bomb attacks that occurred in the Hastings area. The house was often shaken by the bombs, which gave her severe migraines. There was rationing for food and clothing, and a lack of new books or concerts. Surprisingly, Ettie claimed that she found the war 'intensely interesting. It's *far* more relaxing than writing books,' she claimed wryly. Because of the bombs, she abandoned work on the new novel but she managed to write part of her memoirs, *Myself When Young*.

In her memoirs *Myself When Young,* Ethel claims that she was refused entry to the Presbyterian Ladies' College when she made this trip to Australia in 1912, but this claim is now known to be grossly exaggerated. As a pupil she had often *felt* rejected – by Connie, by other students and by her teachers, and this probably coloured her feelings towards returning to her old school and scenes of her childhood.

Her unreliable memoirs were completed by Olga after her death and published by Heinemann in 1948. They are very important in understanding the way she used her own life and her family history to create fiction.

'Henry' died of cancer at Hastings on 20 March 1946, a year after peace with Germany was declared. Olga's own health was failing; the eighteen months she spent caring for her friend and employer, who by now could afford to pay very little for her care, was a heroic gesture. Ettie was cremated at a dismal funeral service held in chilly wintry

London: her ashes were scattered out to sea along with those of her husband as she had requested.[17]

In 1957, the Robertson house in Regents Park Road acquired a blue memorial plaque to 'Henry Handel Richardson, novelist', but the building was later demolished. The Victorian Fellowship of Australian Writers saved Ethel's Australian birthplace from demolition and the Victorian National Trust restored the former Richardson home, Lake View, at Chiltern.[18] Among the relics on view there is Richardson's ouija-board. Three portraits of her by the Melbourne-born artist Rupert Bunny are in the National Library of Australia. Portraits and photographs usually show her in profile; they all reveal a strong nature and a handsome young woman.[18]

Ethel Richardson's Richard Mahony trilogy (later republished as *Australia Felix*) suffered from the long intervals between the publication of its volumes. World War I badly affected sales of the first volume, *The Fortunes of Richard Mahony,* published in 1917. All three volumes were published in one large edition in 1930. Ethel signed a contract for a film during World War II but the film's production was halted due to lack of funds and never recommenced. The trilogy was translated into Danish, reprinted in 1931, 1934, 1937 and 1939. In 1941 it had an American edition with an introduction by the eminent writer Sinclair Lewis, and an Australian edition by Heinemann in 1947. (Even in 1977, when London's feminist Virago Press republished *The Getting of Wisdom,* several British literary journals still referred to the author as '*Mr* Richardson'.)

Henry Handel Richardson is surely Australia's most significant woman author of the early twentieth century. Because Miles Franklin funded a well-known and sometimes controversial literary prize, she is often considered more important – we hear her name more often. But Miles Franklin, after the initial success of the ironic *My Brilliant Career* and her prize-winning account of pioneering on the Monaro, *All That Swagger,* wrote little else of significance.

Some Australian critics have sought to downplay Handel Richardson's significance as a great Australian writer on the grounds that 'she spent so much of her life overseas'. Yet art critics happily call long-term expatriates Arthur Boyd, Sydney Nolan and Geoffrey Smart 'great Australian creative artists' and the novelist Christina Stead, who left Sydney in 1928, married an American and *never* returned to live in Australia is always viewed as an Australian writer.

Henry Handel Richardson's place in Australian literature remains a very important one.[19] She wrote *major* novels about big issues and created unforgettable characters that haunt the mind. In Britain, she is viewed as an Australian author, a foreigner living in London and writing in English, as Joseph Conrad did. This has militated against Henry Handel Richardson in the British literary stakes. As Henry Handel Richardson she made little effort to become part of British literary life. Although she enjoyed close friendships with H. G. Wells and several other notable British authors.

In 1932, at the height of her fame, Henry Handel Richardson was finally nominated for a Nobel Prize for Literature, one of the first women to be so honoured. However, the prize went to a male author. 'Australia's greatest female novelist,' as her obituary called her, died at the age of seventy-six over ten thousand miles away from the Australian bush she had loved. Her reputation as an author lives on.

# CHAPTER TEN

## Sister Elizabeth Kenny
### *(1880–1952)*
### WHO GAVE HOPE TO POLIO VICTIMS

Elizabeth Kenny was born in Warialda, New South Wales, in 1880. Her father was a farmer who, when necessary, practised as an untrained bush vet. Later the family moved to Nobby, on Queensland's Darling Downs. As a young girl Kenny had dreamed of becoming a doctor, but such chances were denied to women. She had been taught bush nursing techniques and a knowledge of human musculature by Dr Aeneas McDonnell, a Toowoomba general practitioner who admired her bravery when he had to set her broken arm. He had taken her on as his assistant.

For a nurse to practise at that period, formal nursing qualifications were not mandatory. Initially, Elizabeth Kenny never registered as a nurse and her subsequent problems with the medical profession stemmed from this.[1]

In her youth, Elizabeth Kenny may well have suffered the pangs of unrequited love but she never recorded her feelings. She loved children and adopted a young girl named Mary Stewart at a time when adoption was not the popular option it is today. She did this so that Mary could take her place and fulfil her responsibility of caring for her widowed mother when she went to America. Elizabeth Kenny never married. Her work was her passion and would always come first.

At Federation, the Darling Downs was desperately short of hospital facilities and to reach Brisbane meant a long journey by horse-drawn ambulance. In 1913, at the age of thirty-three, Nurse Kenny set up her own tiny hospital on the Darling Downs, at Clifton. That year she was called out to treat a two-year-old girl, Amy McNeil. The child was suffering from a mysterious fever, previously unknown to Nurse Kenny who telegraphed her former mentor, Dr McDonnell. He replied that the child must be suffering from infantile paralysis, a relatively unknown illness which was rapidly becoming a scourge for children in the southern states of Australia and proving difficult to treat. This was the first mention Elizabeth Kenny had heard of infantile paralysis – or polio, as it would soon be called, by which time the disease would have reached epidemic proportions.

A few years earlier, Elizabeth's own young brother had suffered from a mysterious attack of paralysis and she had alleviated his pain and restored movement to his limbs by soaking strips of blanket in hot water and applying them as poultices. She did the same for Amy, after which she was able to move the girl's rigid limbs and alleviate the child's pain.

Amy's father was a stockman and the family lived in a bark hut with dirt floor. They were far too poor to pay Nurse Kenny, but money was never her principal interest. In her teens she had dreamed of being a medical missionary and her overriding aim was to cure her patients, regardless of whether they could pay or not.

Kenny's success with little Amy (as well as her own brother) led to her formulation of a radical new treatment for polio. Her remedial treatment was contrary to the instructions of many doctors, who refused to let their patients move their limbs and kept them with their arms and legs in splints.

Sister Kenny treated her patients by immersing the stiffened limbs in hot baths, and giving them hot packs and intensive massage. The prevailing medical theory held that patients' limbs should be kept immobilised to avoid further damage to their muscles. Kenny insisted that her patients discard the splints and braces prescribed by their doctors as soon as possible and strengthen their muscles by moving around and exercising.

In 1915, Elizabeth Kenny joined the Australian Army Nursing Service and made twelve sea voyages between Britain and Australia with returning wounded. During World War I, nearly 3000 Australian nurses volunteered to serve in areas ranging from the British Isles to France, Italy, Egypt, Palestine, the Persian Gulf, Burma, India, the Balkans, Vladivostok and Abyssinia. Many, like Nurse Kenny, served with great dedication aboard hospital ships. On board the cramped, overcrowded hospital ships, Kenny observed that those wounded men who were encouraged to get up and move around stood a far better chance of regaining the use of their limbs than those who remained bedridden. She was in advance of her time in understanding the psychological effects of encouraging patients to move their limbs.

After the war, Sister Kenny, who had adopted the title of Sister in view of her seniority rather than by examination, returned to the Darling Downs. Now she gave her polio patients remedial exercises to perform as well as hydrotherapy treatment, and stressed the psychological importance of instilling in her young patients the idea that their condition was curable.

Sister Kenny was strong-minded, authoritative and commanding, attributes which would have been highly admired had she been male and medically qualified; but in a nursing sister (even one running a large clinic), they were deemed by doctors to be assertive and unfeminine. Nurses were meant to be in awe of doctors, not to contradict their advice when they recommended immobilisation or surgical operations for polio patients. She made powerful enemies by airing her opinions. Soon Sister Kenny's methods and philosophies and her suitability to be treating patients at all were seriously challenged by medical authorities. Her big mistake was that initially, Sister Kenny implied that she was able to *cure* polio. This caused many doctors to view her with grave suspicion. Her later experience taught her that she was able only to *alleviate* the symptoms of the disease.

Terrifying epidemics of polio occurred all round Australia during the long hot summers of 1931–32 and 1937–38. At that time, there was no vaccine against polio.

Queensland farmers christened it 'cow disease' because they believed that it had been started overseas in cattle and could spread from humans into their herds. Everywhere she went in the bush, Sister Kenny encountered hysteria and fear of the dreaded disease. Many quaint bush remedies were recommended to halt its progress, none of which worked. These included painting fences with creosote 'to kill the germs', hanging camphor blocks around children's necks and sending them to school with sulphur in their socks.

Sister Kenny now had some measure of financial independence, receiving a small pension for war service and having made money from inventing what became known as the 'Sylvia stretcher' – a cushioned stretcher which became popular for transporting patients over bumpy unmade roads in the outback.

After years of crusading for children to throw away their splints and braces and refusing to let them lie in the wards with their limbs immobilised in metal cages, in 1934 Sister Kenny set up a small polio treatment clinic in Townsville.[2] Parents turned to her in desperation. They brought their paralysed or semi-paralysed children to her clinics rather than going to doctors. Naturally, the doctors were not amused. They claimed that when they sent Sister Kenny patients for exercise and hot baths, she would brush them aside and take over the case completely.

Over the next four years, Sister Kenny received assistance from the Queensland Government to set up small rehabilitation clinics in other towns, including one in the grounds of what is now the Royal Brisbane Hospital.

In 1937, Sister Kenny aroused even more wrath from leading members of the medical profession when her book *Infantile Paralysis and Cerebral Diplegia* was published in Sydney. In it she deplored the prevailing medical treatments for the effects of polio. She claimed that muscles atrophied in splints or cages and bones were drained of vital calcium, leaving the patients deformed and pain-ridden. She described their muscles as being 'in spasm'.

Some doctors called her 'an untrained charlatan', ignoring the fact that paralysed children treated by the Kenny method were no longer bedridden but walking to school. One of the patients she helped was a boy named Johannes Bjelke-Peterson, who would become Premier of Queensland. Dr Aubrey Pye, the Medical Superintendent of the Brisbane Hospital, had no choice but to recognise her success.[3] But other doctors made certain that nurses trained by Kenny, working in the small clinic in the grounds of the Brisbane Hospital, were not allowed to mix with regular hospital nurses or wear the same uniform, claiming she lacked sufficient knowledge of physiology.

Sister Kenny claimed that she was denied valuable hospital space and given only long-term cases, patients already deformed through months of 'orthodox' immobilisation. Kenny's enemies were powerful members of the Queensland medical establishment. In 1935, doctors and administrators insisted on a Royal Commission headed by the eminent medico Sir Raphael Cilento to investigate Sister Kenny's 'radical' treatment and its outcome and to oversee a full report.

While the judge and medical specialists on the panel of the Royal Commission were preparing their report, Sister Kenny went to Britain, where a polio epidemic had broken out. She found herself treated with far more respect by the medical profession there than in Queensland: a Kenny Polio Treatment Clinic was opened in Carshalton, Surrey. On her return from the United Kingdom, she was invited to Melbourne by the Victorian State Government. The rapid spread of polio terrified them and they also considered trying the Kenny method.

The day after Sister Kenny arrived in Melbourne, the Royal Commission released its long-awaited report. She was horrified to find that the report damned her treatment methods in favour of hospital treatment by immobilisation.[4] Ironically, some of the doctors who condemned the Kenny method would quietly adopt some of its techniques when, years later, they discovered that total immobilisation in splints had failed with many patients.

Despite the Royal Commission's findings, Sister Kenny continued to receive support from the general public, many of whom saw her as an angel of mercy and a victim of medical conservatism. Kenny continued her work; she remained as dedicated as ever. Sometimes, after working all day, she would keep watch by the bed of a sick child through the night until, at dawn, totally exhausted, she fell asleep.

When Annette Kellerman, the champion swimmer and Hollywood film star, returned to Australia, the land of her birth, she heard about the polio epidemic and saw the fear it inspired in parents living in the bush and small towns. Sister Kenny's clinics were often featured in the press, and many journalists who had seen paralysed children walk again supported her.[5]

Nearly thirty years after Sister Kenny's first success, Annette Kellerman visited several Kenny Clinics and offered her services for voluntary work with the young patients. The children were delighted to meet her. Endorsement by Annette Kellerman, a star of the sports world in a nation that was sport mad, did no harm to Sister Kenny, either.

Bruised by the harsh verdict of the Royal Commission, Sister Kenny had toyed with the idea of going to the United States with its willingness to embrace new ideas. A few Australian doctors did support her, and in 1940, six Brisbane doctors signed a letter on behalf of Sister Kenny to the prestigious Mayo Clinic in Rochester, Minnesota. The Queensland Government offered to pay Sister Kenny's fares to the United States and she was also supported by Annette Kellerman, who was well-known to Americans for promoting exercise as the way to health. A polio epidemic had erupted in Minnesota, which prompted the American authorities to give Sister Kenny a teaching position at the University of Minneapolis Medical School and beds for her patients in the University teaching hospital.

In 1942, the Elizabeth Kenny Institute opened in Minneapolis to give therapists a thorough training. The National Polio Foundation of America gave her an allowance, and a Minneapolis club voted her $416 a month for life, so that she now felt financially secure. She gave up her Australian war pension and bought a house in Minneapolis, donating all gifts she received to the Kenny Foundation. In 1952, during another epidemic of polio in America, a Gallup Poll found that she was even more popular than Eleanor Roosevelt.

After this, Sister Kenny's methods were widely accepted: she became famous beyond her dreams, additional Kenny Clinics were opened and she received honorary degrees from Rutgers University, as well as the Universities of New York and New Jersey.

Like Annette Kellerman, Elizabeth Kenny was idolised and feted in the United States. The film *Sister Kenny*, starring Rosalind Russell, was released in 1946. Billed as 'the life of the woman who brought hope to the hopeless', it was based on her autobiography, *And They Shall Walk*, written in collaboration with Martha Otenso three years previously. The film was a success: Sister Kenny became a household name across America. She was invited to the White House and presented to President Franklin Delano Roosevelt, himself a victim of polio. The American public adored her. With her striking appearance and commanding and charasmatic presence, she was in huge demand as a public speaker. Kenny, with her bluntness of speech, could still arouse controversy. The medical profession argued over her concept that the disabilities in poliomyelitis are caused by the virus invading peripheral nervous tissues, rather than the central nervous system – the accepted medical opinion.[6] But to the mass of people the doctors' arguments seemed irrelevant. In their eyes, Sister Kenny was simply the woman who saved children from the terrible after-effects of infantile paralysis. They flocked to her treatment clinics and her public lectures.

Kenny declined to relinquish her Australian citizenship. She received many offers to lecture around the world, and to enable her to travel freely throughout the United States, Congress passed a special Act which enabled her to come and go in America as she pleased without having to obtain a passport or visa.

Towards the end of her life, Elizabeth Kenny discovered that one of her feet was dragging and she could not prevent her hands shaking slightly. A motor neurone disease was diagnosed for which there was no cure. She yearned to see the mauve plumes of the jacarandas once again in springtime in Queensland, and to be cared for by Mary McCracken (née Stewart), the girl she had adopted way back in 1926. Mary had looked after Kenny's widowed mother, and after Mrs Kenny's death had run one of Queensland's Kenny Clinics before she married. In an interview in 1996, Mary McCracken said that Sister Kenny showed the same devotion to her patients as Mother Theresa and Albert Schweitzer.[7] Mary welcomed her back home.

But now the Queensland nursing sister, who had cured so many others that she was known as 'the lady with the blessed hands', was suffering from Parkinson's Disease. Gradually this independent woman became totally dependent.

Sister Kenny died in November 1952, at the age of seventy-two. Friends who were with her in her last hours reported that just before she died she prayed that a vaccine might be found to abolish infantile paralysis forever.[8] She was buried at Nobby, on the Darling Downs.

Soon after, an American doctor named Jonas Salk produced the answer to Sister Kenny's prayer: the Salk vaccine against polio.[9] Within two decades, thanks to the Salk vaccine (which would eventually be replaced by another preventative which could be hidden in a sugar lump), poliomyelitis virtually disappeared in the developed world. The Sister Kenny Institute in Minneapolis still exists, but has been changed into a rehabilitation centre for victims of spinal cord injuries.

Today, Sister Kenny remains a legendary figure, especially in Queensland where so many people still have relatives who were treated by her.

# CHAPTER ELEVEN

## Sister Lillie Goodisson
*(1860–1947)*
PIONEER OF FAMILY PLANNING CLINICS IN AUSTRALIA

*I am convinced that our lives are not in vain. We, and other women like us, have been forces of change. We can depart the world in the belief that we leave it in a better condition than when we first encountered it.*[1] – Dr Aletta Jacobs, pioneer of the use of the 'Dutch cap' pessary, which Sister Lillie Goodisson imported and sold in her Sydney family planning clinics.

Lillie Goodisson is very important in the history of family planning in Australia. Her invaluable work in promoting birth control contributed to the acceptance of today's contraceptive techniques. Sex education and condoms have, in the age of AIDS and the sexually transmitted and often lethal disease, Hepatitis B, saved the lives of many girls and young women. Today, with relatively reliable contraceptives available, the average age for a white Australian woman bearing her first child is around twenty-eight.[2] Better nutrition and sanitation, better obstetric care and new forms of contraception have extended women's lives.

At the time of Federation, women married young and died relatively young. They were taught by Church and State that women's role was to have sex with their husbands on demand, 'be fruitful and multiply', preferably raising as many sons as possible.[3] While the rich wanted sons to inherit, the cry of poor working class mothers of families, on learning they were pregnant yet again was heartfelt. 'Oh no! Not another mouth to feed and another bottom to wipe!' Yet in the Federation era, when no Government support was given to the poor, providing such women with contraceptive advice or contraceptives was punishable by imprisonment.

Lillie Goodisson became a campaigner for birth control (then known as family planning) because she had nursed many women dying from botched backyard abortions. Condoms had been available for centuries, firstly made for the rich out of silk and then out of vulcanised rubber or fish skins. However, most husbands refused to wear them, believing that they ruined the pleasure of sex and should only be used with prostitutes to prevent catching venereal disease, rather than with their 'innocent' wives. There was also an old wives' tale that using a condom could make the wearer epileptic: even men as intelligent at the philosopher Bertrand Russell were told this by their fathers as children.

Lillie's greatest challenge was providing women with reliable information about contraception when this was a punishable offence. Most working-class women bore their first child in their late teens or early twenties, raised a family of at least eight or nine children, were considered old at forty and faced death in their fifties. Many women still died in childbirth due to unsanitary conditions.[4]

In hypocritical and censorious colonial Australia, the sale of contraceptives was illegal in most States. No respectable woman was supposed to know much about family planning. Condoms were only for protection from venereal disease; used only by prostitutes. Many married women wished to limit their families, but Church and State frowned on doctors or nurses giving out sample contraceptives or advice on their use. Anyone who sold them privately or in pharmacies risked prosecution.

In the Federation era and after, childbirth was hazardous, even for the rich. Mid-life crises and divorce were rare amongst married men: deaths in childbirth meant many were widowers and married again.

Single mothers were seen everywhere. Some 'fell' pregnant because they had received no family planning advice but were regarded as little better than common criminals and shunned. Male employers abused their positions, taking sexual liberties with hired help without their wives knowledge, believing that lowly paid maids or washerwomen had no rights. Once the servant's pregnancy became apparent, the husband would disclaim any responsibility, or else insist the girl had 'led him on'. The unfortunate girl (often Irish or a mixed-race Aborigine and barely literate) would be thrown on the streets without a character reference to find *no one* would employ a single mother. Most working-class families rejected daughters who fell pregnant. Many of these young women were left to take their pathetic little bundle onto the streets and beg for a living or became prostitutes.

Church and State treated single mothers as 'fallen women'. In the Lying-In-Hospitals for unmarried mothers, or in segregated wards in general hospitals, single women were made to give birth with a cloth over their faces, or else held down by nurses so they never saw their newborn babies and could not bond with them. Adoption was the recommended course of action for single mothers.

Governments in Britain, Australia and America did nothing to help working-class mothers limit their families because they needed cheap labour. Australia was extremely exploitative in this respect. As a developing nation fearful of a takeover from its Asian neighbours ('the Yellow Peril'), cheap unskilled male labour was required to build the Lucky Country.

State Governments (and after Federation, Australia's Federal Government) wanted uneducated youths for Army service in case of war. So the authorities issued colourful posters urging all patriotic women to become mothers 'for the good of Australia'. 'Australia *needs* populating by white people' was the catch-cry of men in power. To encourage this, in the 1920s a Commonwealth Grant, roughly equal to one week's basic wage, was paid to every new mother. This baby bonus was not specifically intended to help poorer women but to encourage procreation of the white races in Australia.

Just after Federation, the average family size in New South Wales was nine children. In spite of the 'baby bonus' or motherhood grant, Australia's birth rate began to fall. As the birth rate fell, fewer women died in childbirth. While Government spokesmen *still* urged women to have *more* children as their patriotic duty.

Before the advent of family planning clinics, many working-class women, debilitated by annual childbirth and rearing children, lost all interest in sex after a few years, causing problems in many marriages – hardly surprising when the end result was yet another mouth to feed on very little money. A hidden army of prostitutes and child prostitutes helped to sate the sexual appetites of married men. Lack of contraceptives, together with male disinterest in using them, fearing condoms hindered pleasure, caused millions of women of all social classes to die in childbirth, as women activists like Rose Scott and Miles Franklin recorded.

Medical authorities did not help, especially if they were Catholic. In 1907, in his presidential address to the Medical Society of Victoria, Dr Michael O'Sullivan thundered that:

> when a wife defiles the marriage bed with the devices and equipment of the brothel [condoms] and interferes with nature's mandate [sex on demand by husband] by cold-blooded preventatives and safeguards [pessaries]; when she consults her almanac and refuses to admit the

approaches of her husband except at stated times ... can it be otherwise that estrangements and suspicions of wifely faithfulness should occur? Many husbands will ... be tempted to seek elsewhere those pleasures denied them at home. Such are Nature's reprisals.[5]

Dr O'Sullivan referred to 'the devices of the brothel' as he did not wish the dreaded word 'condom' to appear in print. Lillie Goodisson and a handful of other significant women defied male-dominated authorities, demanding reasonably reliable methods of contraception. There was much trial and error, but in the end contraceptive advice became freely available to married women and finally to everyone.

The fact that by the end of the twentieth century, most Australian women were limiting their families with the cooperation of their partners, shows how important was Lillie Goodisson's battle with the authorities for family planning advice.

Today women live longer. Crones in black have disappeared; women no longer automatically put on dark colours on reaching forty. In fact, by the time they reach forty-five, many have launched off into starting a business or have gone to university as mature-age students, where they often perform exceptionally well. Healthy women who reach the age of fifty can expect to see their eightieth birthdays. For most Australian women, fifty is not what forty used to be, due to fewer pregnancies and better obstetric care.

Before contraceptives were widely available, popular (but usually unsuccessful) ways of procuring an abortion consisted of drinking gin in a hot bath or throwing oneself down the stairs in a desperate attempt to detach the foetus from the lining of the womb. The latter was also a face-saving measure: the woman concerned could tell her neighbours she had slipped and suffered a 'miscarriage'. Many women died from illicit back street procedures in unsanitary conditions, using unsterilised knitting needles. Australian city women could buy a bottle of Widow Welch's pills. These could only be sold in pharmacies to women who claimed they needed them to 'regulate menstruation'.

Working-class wives were often more prudish about sex than their middle-class contemporaries. Sex was something few people talked about, mostly performed with the light turned off. Women would sometimes ask male doctors what they could do to prevent having another baby. They received unsympathetic replies, such as: 'Get your husband to sleep out on the veranda' or 'Lock the bedroom door till you want another baby'. Women doctors, horrified by the misery of worn-out or battered wives, were often pioneers of sex education, especially in the new all-women's hospitals which opened in Sydney and Melbourne. By the time of Federation, women's 'temperance' leagues were formed to guard women against alcoholic husbands, syphilis and other venereal diseases. However, the societies issued their message in such guarded language that it was often hard for unmarried girls to understand exactly what the pamphlets or speeches were driving at.

Lillie Goodisson was born in Britain, on the Welsh coast, where her Methodist father was a doctor. Urged on by her father, Lillie trained as a nurse but would have preferred to have studied medicine.[6]

At the age of nineteen, she stopped her nursing studies in order to marry a Welsh doctor named David Evans. In search of a better life for their as yet unborn children, the newlyweds migrated to New Zealand, where they worked long hours establishing a general practice in which Lillie was the practice nurse. There and in Britain, Lillie had seen young women made old before their time from bearing enormous families in stark poverty. Like Margaret Sanger, the pioneer of birth control in America, Lillie had nursed many women dying in childbirth or who, destroyed by numerous and unwanted pregnancies, had been desperate enough to resort to the services of backyard abortionists and had paid for this with their lives.

Eventually, Dr and Mrs Evans moved to Melbourne. When the children were old enough, in 1897, just before Federation, Lillie set up a small private hospital in St Kilda where she acted as matron.

Dr David Evans died in 1903. Widowed, and with her son and daughter married, aged forty-three but still full of energy, Sister Lillie Evans sold her share in the St Kilda hospital and emigrated to Western Australia. Here she met and fell in love with an Australian businessman named Albert Goodisson, whom she married the following year. From their pleasant Geraldton home, Lillie continued her crusade for married women to be able to control their own fertility. Providing birth control for unmarried women at this period could have put Lillie in prison but she did what she could to provide information to women in need.[7]

It is interesting that Britain's pioneer of birth control, Marie Stopes, had a dark secret in her first marriage which inspired her to help other women and so did Sister Lillie Goodisson. Lillie's dark secret was syphilis.

Decades before Lillie married Albert Goodisson, a man in his sixties, he had unprotected sex, caught syphilis and like Ethel Richardson's father and countless other men of the period, now the symptoms of tertiary syphilis, the nervous symptoms and strange behavioural patterns, manifested themselves. He knew what the end would be, and the scandal that would be attached to his family, so he went overseas to die in a mental asylum without telling his wife. Lillie only discovered too late the cause of his illness, as syphilis was a topic no one wanted to mention. The shock turned her into a campaigner for preventative measures like condoms.

As a result of her husband's tragic death, Lillie had become preoccupied with the prevention of sexually transmitted disease, a topic then banned from polite conversation.

Emotionally and financially drained by her husband's illness and death, and fearing the syphilis might have infected her, Lillie borrowed money from Belle, one of the famous Goldstein sisters, returned to Melbourne and set up a small medical lending library to alert women to the horrors of syphilis and other venereal diseases. At this time, penicillin, which would eventually provide a remedy against syphilis, would not be discovered for another twenty years or so. Lillie's lending library shocked some people and failed to make money, ensuring she had to cut her losses and close it.

Lillie corresponded with Britain's Marie Stopes, who had a first class degree in science. Marie had married a botanist named Reginald Gates, who was impotent and unable to consummate their marriage. At that time, sex was never discussed and there were no marriage guidance clinics. Marie struggled to understand what was happening in her marriage, which eventually broke down, and later she would write a book of advice for women called *Married Life*, copies of which reached Australia.

Marie married again, this time a wealthy man willing to support her crusade to help women everywhere. Humphrey Verdon Roe's fortune helped his wife set up marriage guidance clinics which she felt necessary after receiving pathetic and harrowing letters from women denied access to birth control, such as this one, which Marie ensured received wide publicity:

> I have had 7 children, lost my eldest girl with consumption about three months ago and have six children living. My youngest eleven months. Three of them are consumptive. My husband is only a laburer (sic) and has been out of work 4 years. I don't want any more children and it seems how[ever] careful I try I seem to fall wrong. I am three days past my time and feel worried because I am 43 in October. Of course it might be the change but I want to be on the safe side. I thought I would write and ask you [for information] ... It is a shame that pore [sic] people should be dragged down with families, fed up with life [and] keep having children. I hope you will oblige me by writing return of post. Yours sinculy [sic].

In 1926, Lillie moved interstate to join the daughter of her first marriage, now married herself and living in Sydney. In that city, five years after her friend, Marie Stopes, founded the first birth-control clinic in Britain, and ten years after Sister Margaret Sanger opened America's first birth control clinic for poor women in Brooklyn, Sister Lillie Goodisson founded her Society in New South Wales to promote sex education, give clear and accurate information on birth control, limit mentally defective girls being drafted into prostitution, and in doing so attempted to limit the spread of venereal disease which was then widely prevalent in Australia. While some of Lillie's ideas are considered extreme in the light of our knowledge today, as a dedicated nurse she was motivated to do *something*, knowing that sufferers often unwittingly passed on syphilis to their wives, who could die from it, and to unborn children, who would be born blind and deaf or crippled as a result of the disease.

In 1933, Sister Lillie Goodisson's Family Planning Association established Sydney's first birth control clinic, selling condoms and fitting contraceptive devices (probably the Graffenberg Ring and Dr Rutgers' diaphragm imported respectively from Germany and Holland) to married women unable to give 'a decent upbringing, proper food, clothing and education to their children'. She also tried to prevent women and girls from undergoing illegal and life-threatening abortions, and wherever possible arranged private adoptions for their children.

As well as the unpopular condoms made of thick vulcanised rubber, the clinic sold thinner ones made from fish skin, sold under the 'Fiskin' brand label. Fish skins may not have been ideal but at least they were an improvement on the dried sheep's intestines, always readily available in the bush, which had served as condoms, usually tied on by a ribbon.

Sister Goodisson's Family Planning Society did valuable work, selling subsidised contraceptives to whoever wanted them. In the Great Depression of the 1930s, when so many working men and their families were thrown out of work onto the streets, Lillie was a tireless worker. She campaigned for contraceptive devices to be available and for measures to prevent the spread of venereal disease until she was in her eighties. When she started giving women advice, charging a small fee to help run the clinics, there was *no other* source of free birth-control. The clinics were visited by desperate women (some of whom had played Russian roulette with the 'rhythm method' of contraception and lost), and who were prepared to risk their lives to abort children whose birth might kill them or drag them into destitution. At that time a husband had the legal and moral right to force his wife into having sex, even if he was drunk, violent or suffering from venereal disease.

In Sister Goodisson's clinics, she trained her all-female staff to give advice to women whose children had been born mentally defective through inherited syphilis. She fought against the 'double standard', whereby well-off men infected by syphilis visited prostitutes but the authorities only treated the female prostitutes who they accused of spreading the disease, ignoring the fact that legions of infected Australian soldiers had returned from Egypt and France after World War I. The only known treatment for syphilis then was by repeated application to the vagina or penis of an ointment containing mercury, which, in fact, did not halt the progress of this lethal disease and could cause women to develop kidney disease. Sister Lillie Goodisson donated money to various hospitals to help find a cure for syphilis, but no progress would be made until it was discovered during World War II that penicillin, developed by Alexander Fleming and Australian born Howard Florey, cured the disease. Thanks to Fleming and Florey and Howard Florey's wife (Dr Ethel Hayter Reed, a graduate of Adelaide

University in 1924), who supervised her husband's clinical trials of penicillin at Oxford that resulted in it going on the market but never received any recognition for her work, penicillin became widely available after 1945. And so, finally, the scourge of syphilis was ended.

It is an interesting fact that 'men fight: women cooperate'. Lillie Goodisson was fortunate to have received remarkable cooperation from strong-minded women who set up birth control clinics overseas. From Dr Aletta Jacobs and Marie Stopes she received the latest information on contraception like cervical or Dutch caps and Graffenberg and Mensinga rings. However, her Sydney clinics did not dare to provide contraceptive advice for unmarried women or, in that restrictive period, the Federal Government would have closed them down. The Australian clinics imported the Mensinga Ring, invented in 1882 by Dr Wilhelm Mensinga which, like the Graffenberg Ring, was a precursor of the IUD or inter-uterine device. Both these devices prevented pregnancy by inhibiting sperm attaching to the walls of the uterus.

The fact that we have birth control clinics today, as well as sex education classes in many schools, is due to the pioneering work done by remarkable Australian women like Lillie Goodisson and grocery store owner Brettena Smyth (who in the nineteenth century sold contraceptives to bush women from the back of a grocery cart). Lillie Goodisson was supported by Dr Aletta Jacobs in Holland, Marie Stopes in Britain and American-born Sister Margaret Sanger, who was imprisoned *seven* times for providing contraceptive advice.

Due to the dedication of these women, we rarely see tired, careworn, pregnant mothers, looking ten to fifteen years older than their age. Most women today look ten or more years younger than women looked at the time of Federation and few women die in childbirth, the part Government, part privately funded Family Planning Association of Australia now has branches Australia-wide and provides aid to women in many developing countries.

# CHAPTER TWELVE

## Ella Simon
### *(1902–1981)*
AUSTRALIA'S FIRST ABORIGINAL JUSTICE OF THE PEACE
### *and*
## Kundaibark
### *(dates unknown)*
HEALER OF THE BIRIPI PEOPLE

Ella was born in a tent on the outskirts of Taree and, like so many part-Aboriginal children, her birth was never registered; her father was anxious to keep it a secret. Her mother (whose name, like that of her father, Ella never revealed in her memoirs) was a 'fringe-dweller' with no money and no home. Ella's mother was a pale-skinned Aborigine who worked for a white family in Wingham. She had been 'taken advantage' of by her white employer, an important man in Wingham's ultra-conservative community. After Ella was born, her mother survived on part-time domestic work, but lived in fear that either the police or welfare authorities would be alerted and remove or 'steal' her daughter. Whenever the police inspected the fringe-dwellers' camp, she would black Ella's face to make her look darker, since the police were instructed to remove pale-skinned children either for adoption or to orphanages. In 1902, the New South Wales Aboriginal Protection Board had been given the power to remove mixed-race children if they thought the child was suffering neglect. It was a Catch–22 situation for Aboriginal fringe-dwellers. Their camp had no sanitation or piped water, so 'neglect' could easily be defined as the absence of the everyday amenities white people took for granted.[1]

Ella's father was fond of her mother, but already had a wife and five legitimate children. Ella's mother had worked for him and his wife as a resident domestic. Ella had been conceived after a party at which Ella's mother was employed to serve her father's guests.

Shortly after Ella's birth, her mother returned to work as a domestic servant for another white family. She loved the baby and managed to keep Ella with her for some time – this was difficult as unmarried domestics, black or white, were not usually allowed to bring babies with them. Although she was unaware of it, Ella's mother was suffering from tuberculosis, which would eventually kill her. The disease was endemic in poor living conditions, and the pittance she was paid meant she would have been unable to afford specialist treatment in any case. She then married a young Aboriginal man, but he was unable to care for a young child and an ailing wife and Ella's health suffered.

As a result, around the time of Ella's second birthday, she was sent to live with her maternal grandparents on the Purfleet Aboriginal Mission just outside Taree.[2] Ella's grandparents had been relocated to Purfleet in 1902, the year when it was set up. As members of a Protestant church, for a small sum they were able to purchase a block of land and build their own little wooden house. At that time, jobs on the land had been plentiful and the mission self-supporting. Ella's grandfather was a fine man, a pure-blood Aborigine who had always worked as a stockman on a neighbouring property. But during the Depression years of the 1930s and the rural poverty that resulted, he lost his job due to the Unions objections to the employment of low-paid blacks over unskilled whites. Suddenly, in late middle age, he was denied work.

The little girl was too young to understand what was happening to her; for many years Ella believed that her grandmother was her real mother. She had no idea that scarcely a year after she went to live on Purfleet Mission, her mother was dead of tuberculosis. Her father's family refused to take her in due to her illegitimacy and her coffee-coloured skin.

Unlike many white men who fathered a child by an Aboriginal or part-Aboriginal woman, Ella's father showed remorse for his actions. He visited Ella at her grandmother's home during her childhood, although initially Ella was not told their visitor was her birth-father. He ensured that she was provided with clothes and shoes, but her education at the mission school was very limited. The rest of his family (who were prominent figures in New South Wales) would have nothing to do with Ella and considered her existence an embarrassment.

Ella did not discover the truth about her mother's death and her own parentage until she turned twelve. Her maternal grandparents had always cared for her as though she was their own child. So she was shocked to learn that the couple she believed were her parents were, in fact, her grandparents, that her real father was the white man she was sometimes taken to visit, and that her mother had died of tuberculosis. Ella described her sense of loss and anger:

> The bottom fell out of my world as I sat listening to Kundaibark, my grandmother. Looking back on it I think it's the greatest mistake to wait until an adopted child is set in her ways before telling her the truth. When someone tells you that they are not your real mother or he's not your real father, suddenly you are tormented about who you really are and what you are. You just don't know what to think. Then a kind of rebellion starts to creep into your heart and slowly you begin to lose your love for the person who reared you. Oh it's still there of course

but you have this nagging thought, 'Well you're not my mother, you have no right to say this or that to me.'

Ella was probably better off with her grandparents than living in a tent on waste ground with an ailing mother, but no adopted child is willing to believe this. Adopted children, learning of 'missing' parents, spend nights sobbing into their pillow for what might have been, instead of taking advantage of the love that is offered to them.

Fortunately for Ella, her grandmother, Kundaibark, was a remarkable woman and a traditional healer. Kundaibark had also had a disturbed childhood. Her mother (Ella's great-grandmother) was a full-blood Aborigine of the Biripi people, who lived a nomadic life. While Ella's mother had been seduced by a man she knew, Kundaibark's mother had been raped by a white stranger. She had died giving birth to Kundaibark while going walkabout. At that time, full-blood nomadic Aborigines regarded half-caste children as bringing bad luck and some abandoned their mixed-race babies. In Kundaibark's case the Biripi did not want to take a mixed-race baby with a pale skin along with them on their travels. She would hinder their progress and there was no one who could feed her. So, according to nomadic custom, they moved on, leaving the baby under a tree to die. Fortunately, little Kundaibark was found by a passing stockman, taken to the nearest homestead and bottle-fed by the station owner's wife. Kundaibark lived in the household and became the family domestic.

No one bothered to teach Kundaibark to read and write. But she showed a talent for nursing the sick, and being quick and intelligent she learned a great deal about white medicine by nursing sick stockmen and the children of the station owner.

Her own people may have abandoned her, but Kundaibark yearned to return to them. In her twenties, she returned to the Biripi and set herself to learn all she could about Aboriginal lore. She married a Biripi man, Ella's grandfather. He was a devout Christian, whose father had been a Scots engineer working on the railways.

On the mission at Purfleet, Kundaibark combined her experience of white man's medicine with her knowledge of healing plants gained from the Aborigines. She nursed Aborigines who were sick and dying and acted as a midwife. Kundaibark believed colour was only skin-deep, that it was a person's character that mattered, not the colour of their skin.

Ella was far paler than most of the children on Purfleet Aboriginal Mission. (She was termed 'light-skinned' on her Mission papers.) In the Mission School, the darker-skinned children refused to play with her because of her light colour. Kundaibark brought up Ella not to have a chip on her shoulder about life and to forgive others. She taught Ella to assert her dignity as a human being and gave her a sense of mission to help her fellow Aborigines achieve citizenship and a better life. She taught Ella a great deal, including the bush remedies she knew; she also passed on to Ella a sense of duty, that she should help Aboriginal people even though some of them might reject her, believing her pale skin brought bad luck. Kundaibark had no sense of racial prejudice or inferiority. She reared Ella to believe that *all* people were equal in the eyes of God and to be proud of her heritage rather than ashamed of it.

Ella needed this reassurance. For much of her life she would battle prejudice against the colour of her skin from white people as well as from Aborigines, who resented both her pale skin and her European features. Refusing to say she was of mixed race, Ella described herself as a 'light-caste Aboriginal'. She loathed the fact that white people called the Purfleet Settlement 'the blacks' camp'. She was proud that her grandparents had bought the land on which their house was built rather than having it given to them. She hated to think that white people looked down on her.

The knowledge that her mother was dead and that the two people she had believed to be her parents were really her grandparents strengthened Ella's resolve to achieve something more with her life than her mother had been able to achieve. She dreamed of a life as a trained nurse.

At the Mission School, the children jeered at her for trying so hard and told her she should be at the school in Taree for white children. She learned only the rudiments of reading and writing. The tuition and equipment provided was dismal and the Aborigines on the Mission lacked the knowledge or the will to demand better schooling for their children. Ella left school in sixth grade aged twelve, still unable to write well, although she was highly intelligent and had an extremely retentive memory. At Purfleet she cared for family members who were having babies and performed a variety of resident domestic jobs. She still dreamed of becoming a trained nurse, but her difficulty in reading and writing ruled out nursing, at that time the province of white middle-class girls.

Discipline was strictly enforced on missions. It was impossible to leave without a certificate from the manager. On the other hand, there was always the danger Ella might be removed from her grandparents' care by the police and placed in the dreaded Cootamundra Domestic Training Home.

On the mission the traditional Aboriginal way of life was banned. Corroborees were forbidden and the Aborigines were punished if they swore, gambled or drank. Any mail they might receive from distant relatives (usually written for the senders by well-meaning Europeans) was censored.

In 1915, the Aboriginal Protection Act was amended to give the Protection Board the power to remove any child at all without parental consent. Aboriginal children of mixed blood with fair skins were the most likely to be 'stolen' by police and sent to be 'educated' in schools or in white homes. Officially, these children were removed from their mothers to give them 'better chances' in life. For intelligent and sensitive girls like Ella there was scant education and only one kind of employment – as a domestic. When Ella turned twelve her grandmother became too ill to keep her and she was sent to live with a maternal uncle. She travelled by train, then by horse-drawn milk van, the only vehicle that went up into the mountains behind Gloucester, where her uncle lived.

Ella's uncle was poor and his home overcrowded. She was sent to work at Coneac Station, on the understanding she would be trained for a lifetime of domestic service. At the age of twelve, Ella found herself overworked and unloved, virtually an unpaid slave to a white family where the mother was ill and she was left to do most of the work. She had to round up the cows, milk them, feed the animals and do the housework. When the white or Aboriginal station hands got drunk and, as she described it, 'talked stupidly' there was no one to defend her. Ella was a well-developed and attractive girl but sexually innocent and with a strong sense of Christian ethics given her by Kundaibark. The situation at Coneac Station worried Ella.

She wrote to her aunt describing how she had to bar and bolt her room each night and how the men were harassing her at work. Her maternal uncle sent a horse for her and she managed to leave the property, but there was still not enough room for her at her uncle's. She returned to Purfleet Mission, but found the former kindly missionary gone, replaced by an autocratic, overbearing manager, who insisted she go to Sydney to work as a domestic.

Ella's first employers in the city were not very kind to her, but she was smart and hardworking and managed to find herself a different post. Ella found some white employers kind, others not. Using the small portion of her salary she was allowed to keep for herself (the rest being held in trust for her by the Protection Board), Ella wrote away to Britain for books on nursing. She worked from early morning until eight o'clock each night, struggling with the nursing books, determined to improve herself.

Ella's birth-father kept in touch with her and came to visit her in Sydney when he visited his legitimate children, who, of course, never wanted to acknowledge Ella and never had anything to do with her.

By 1928, when she was twenty-five, Ella was working as a resident maid in Mosman for a white family who were reasonably kind to her. However, at that time, life for all resident domestic staff, white or Aboriginal, involved long hours, backbreaking work and little regular time off. The hours of work were not regulated by Unions. Uniforms with starched collars and cuffs needed frequent ironing – as did other garments in the weekly wash. Vacuum cleaners and refrigerators were in their infancy, housework and food preparation consumed enormous amounts of time and effort.

Ella befriended another fair-skinned part-Aboriginal girl named Margaret, a fringe-dweller like herself who had been torn away from her mother. Margaret had suffered the fate Ella's mother and grandparents feared might happen to her. Margaret and her sister had been snatched by the police as she left school one day and bundled into a waiting car. Her mother had arrived on the scene just as this was happening; in the confusion Margaret feared that the police might shoot her mother, so she had gone willingly. In the end, it turned out that what the child had seen hanging from the white policeman's belt was not a gun but a bag containing handcuffs. Margaret, sent to the Cootamundra Domestic Training Home, felt isolated and depressed. She had never received any tuition in reading and writing. All she had been taught was to sew, sweep and clean. None of the girls at the home had ever seen a proper stove, yet they were expected to cook European recipes. If they made a mistake in the kitchen, using unfamiliar pots and pans and ingredients, their white teacher slapped their faces.

At thirteen, Margaret had been sent to work with a white family who were to pay her board and wages of one shilling and sixpence a week. But her employers had not paid her for five years, and fed her very poorly. The girl had no one to complain to, and, as she could neither read nor write, she had scant redress. Her employer appears to have been mentally disturbed. The woman had three children and must have been suffering from some phobia about cleanliness. If she found a dirty nappy she would rub Margaret's face in it. Margaret's life (and Ella's at this time) consisted of dusting, polishing, sweeping and scrubbing. Coals had to be carted up to bedrooms in buckets in the days before central heating.

Ella, older and stronger in character than Margaret, was outraged at the treatment her friend received and her employer's cruelty. She took up Margaret's cause with the Aboriginal Protection Board, but got nowhere, so she found Margaret a new job with friends of her own employer, at twenty-five shillings a week. The wage was duly paid.

This is how Ella's career as activist for the rights of Aborigines began. An Irish friend told her:

> Ella, you're a fighter. You'll always be noticed because of the colour of your skin, and you'll always feel you have to do things better than everyone else because of it.

When her beloved grandmother Kundaibark became ill, Ella returned to the Purfleet Aboriginal Mission – now designated an Aboriginal Reserve – to nurse her. Kundaibark, a committed Christian, had been nurse and midwife to her people. Although she had no formal training, she had acquired a fair amount of nursing skill which she passed on to Ella. While nursing her grandmother (and taking her place as bush nurse to the Aboriginal community), Ella met Joe Simon, a full-blooded Aboriginal who fell deeply in love with her. She refused to marry him while her grandmother needed constant nursing.

In spite of her fair skin and European features, Ella always felt she belonged among the Aboriginal people. Her grandmother had instilled in her from childhood the maxim: 'It's character that matters: not skin colour.' Now, having been to the city, acquired some self-confidence and more knowledge, Ella was determined to stand up for Aboriginal rights against the authoritarian Scottish-born manager who now ran the former mission. She was determined that with her city experience and her verbal skills, she would speak out for those who could not defend their own interests.

The manager took an instant dislike to Ella. He insisted on his right to enter houses as he wished and to send away any Aborigines who stood up for themselves. They were branded as troublemakers. One of Ella's uncles protested about the 'stolen children' who were brought to Purfleet and warned the manager that if he laid a finger on any of his children he would knock him down. Ella's uncle was ordered to leave the mission immediately. His children were to be sent to a reformatory. Ella raised an outcry to prevent her uncle and his family from having to leave their home. But the manager had by now marked Ella down as a troublemaker.

One day, the manager came barging into Kundaibark's tiny shack without knocking. Ella, standing behind the door, busy turning her grandmother in bed, was nearly knocked over. Tired and stressed, she lost her temper and told off the manager in no uncertain terms. He threatened to expel her. Fortunately, he was replaced before he could carry out his threat and Ella was allowed to stay with her grandmother on the condition she apologised ... in writing. Ella, who could scarcely read, was embarrassed by her poor skills at writing. She had to ask someone else to write the letter of apology to the new manager for her. She vowed that one day she would learn to write properly.

When Kundaibark died, Ella was free to marry Joe Simon. They stayed on at Purfleet Reserve, where she continued to nurse the sick and act as midwife to the community.

During the Great Depression of the 1930s, life was hard for all Australians, black and white. As more and more Aborigines lost their jobs they flooded into the Reserve. In 1939, when war was declared, Joe tried to enlist in the Army along with some of his Aboriginal friends. But he was rejected on medical grounds: the doctors discovered he had a weak heart.

Joe and Ella were employed by a farmer at Avoca who had been given a contract by the Australian Army to provide one of their camps with vegetables. Growing and picking the vegetables and digging up potatoes was hard, backbreaking work and had to be done in all weathers. To spare her husband, Ella would work all day in the fields with him, then cook dinner for the farmer and his family, and rise at 4 am each morning to pack vegetables ready for the Army truck that called to take them to the base.

In 1945, the Army camp was disbanded and Joe and Ella returned to their home at Purfleet Reserve with their child. This child seems to have died soon afterwards, but Ella does not give any further information, in accordance with Aboriginal tradition whereby a dead person is never named. After their return to Purfleet, Ella entered into a struggle with the manager for better facilities for her people. She wanted the women to have proper stoves in their houses (at Purfleet the women still cooked in camp ovens on open fires in the backyard) and for the manager to hand over to mothers their unpaid instalments of the recently awarded Government benefit known as 'child endowment'.[3]

The manager, a mean and bitter Scot, ignored Ella's claims and hung onto her own child endowment for nearly six months. One day, determined not to be swindled out of money that was rightfully hers, she took a bus into town, went to an electrical store and ordered a cooking stove. Inwardly trembling at her daring, she calmly told the white store owner to send the stove out to her house and the account to the Purfleet manager as 'he has my child endowment and should pay out of that'. By using her head and a degree of daring for those times, Ella got her 'proper stove' and helped others to do the same.[4]

At this time, Ella's birth-father was living with her. His wife was dead and his own family had rejected him. He was very sick and Ella had taken pity on him. The manager told her that even if he was her father, no white man could stay on an Aboriginal Mission – this was despite the fact that Ella owned the land and house, which her grandparents had bequeathed to her.

In vain, Ella pleaded that her father had no one else to care for him. The manager was adamant. Ella was forced to put her father into a poorly managed all-white nursing home, where he died. Having neglected him shamefully while he was ill, his legitimate children refused point-blank to allow Ella to attend her father's funeral. She tried to overcome the considerable pain and resentment this caused her by determining to educate herself better. She and Joe were members of the Presbyterian Church. Helped by her local church, Ella taught herself to speak in public and borrowed books to fill the gaps in her inadequate education.

Ella was horrified to find that in order to leave the Reserve, she, an Australian, needed a piece of paper which would act as:

> a passport in my own land. I had to have it to go to any place from which an Aboriginal was banned, to take government jobs and to leave the reserve. I could never work this out, in spite of my fight for rights. I had to have this piece of paper like a passport, to give me rights in my own land, to be a citizen of Australia – my own country. That manager told my uncle that the Aboriginal was really nobody – not a human being in the land which should have been his own by right of birth. I was born here, I am in my own right an Australian. But I had to fill in a form to get this passport to become a citizen.[5]

Joe and Ella moved away to the Gulargambone Reserve, where Ella helped the inhabitants to obtain a community hall, where young people were able to learn to read and write. She dreamed that one day Aboriginal and mixed races would be shown a better life than the one forced on them by the white authorities. On reserves they were denied the right to open a bank account, or to go into town, even for medical reasons, without permission.

Ella Simon showed herself a natural leader. She was occasionally reviled by both sides for the colour of her skin, but continued in her efforts to help Aboriginal people help themselves. She did not wish to retreat to the past but to build a bridge to the future by obtaining citizenship, with its responsibilities and privileges.

In 1957, in her mid-fifties, Ella was finally granted a Certificate of Exemption from the degrading restrictions under which Aboriginal people were forced to live. She was allowed to open a bank account and to leave the Reserve when she wanted to. She moved back to Purfleet.

Ella dreamed that one day 'her' people would achieve financial independence through their own efforts and gain proper medical facilities. She was angry that the manager kept their old age pension money and refused to give it to them so they could improve their situation. She lobbied visitors to the Reserve, asking for better conditions and a chance for the women to use their skills to earn money.

In 1960, Ella was permitted to form a Purfleet branch of the Country Women's Association and was elected its first President. With a little capital provided by the Association she encouraged the women to continue traditional Aboriginal crafts and organised a committee to open The Gillawarra Gift Shop, selling Aboriginal artefacts. (Gillawarra was the name of the old bora ground, a few miles from Purfleet.)

Through further support from the Country Women's Association, she was able to arrange for electricity to be installed on the Reserve. Profits from the gift shop paid for electric stoves for all the houses. It was a great step forward. Ella was now the spokesperson for the women on the Reserve. She fiercely resisted the demands the white inspector put over them by the 'Protector of Aborigines' (Mr Donaldson) that light-skinned children be sent away. Donaldson painted rosy pictures to these light-skinned children of the delights awaiting them at the Cootamundra Domestic Training Home. Their eyes were opened when one little girl called Daisy believed him and let herself be sent away to be 'trained' at the Cootamundra Home. Daisy caught a chill and without proper care died there of pneumonia. After that women fought to stop their children being taken away from them, sometimes with success. But more often than not the children were removed.

Tourist buses started to call at Purfleet to buy the Aboriginal artefacts produced there. Ella did the shop's accounts and oversaw the staff. Her own baby had died – she had no other children herself, but cared for the children of others. She was a surrogate mother to many of the children on the Reserve, determined that they should have better opportunities than she had been offered.

Ella had very little money but was always neatly dressed, even if her clothes were hand-me-downs from white people. She spoke with fluency and passion. It was the way she put her people's cause to the women of the CWA that gained their help in improving conditions for women on the Reserve. This, together with her striking looks and warm personality, drew people to the cause.

None of the Purfleet children had ever seen the sea. Using money earned by the gift shop, Ella and a local schoolteacher started a scheme whereby Aboriginal children could spend holidays with white or Aboriginal families in Newcastle and go to the beach. She made sure the children had swimming costumes and shoes for their holidays, paying for them out of shop funds. There was no doctor on the Reserve, so when the children needed in-patient treatment she accompanied them down to a hospital in Newcastle or Sydney. When roused, Ella could be a tiger, but as a nurse she was gentle and caring, much loved by everyone at Purfleet Mission.

In 1962, Ella was appointed Australia's first Aboriginal Justice of the Peace, so that she could help to fill in and witness documents for those who could not read and write. In her efforts to improve life on the Reserve she concentrated on issues such as poor Aboriginal health and the lack of any medical facilities. These included pregnancy and ante-natal care; high rates of diabetes in adults; blindness in Aboriginal children caused by trachoma; and the segregation of whites and Aborigines in hospitals. Other issues which concerned her were the banning of Aborigines from public places; the meagre 'rations' of tea, sugar, tobacco and bread paid in lieu of wages by the Aboriginal Protection Board; and Aborigines' right to sit where they wanted to in the local cinema, where they were still discriminated against as 'fringe-dwellers from the Blacks' camp'.

Ella was viewed as an 'uppity' troublemaker by the manager. When her husband died, she was evicted from her home, even though she owned the land on which her grandparents' house had been built. According to the manager, Ella's home was now under the control of the Housing Commission, and since the house was sub-standard according to their regulations, it was condemned and she had to leave. He was obviously settling old scores and did not offer Ella, now elderly, any alternative housing.

After a period of great anxiety when it appeared that she would be homeless, and as a result of efforts on her behalf by various concerned friends, Ella was eventually given a Housing Commission home at nearby Gillawarra. She continued to nurse old people and work at the gift shop for another year. But she resigned from the gift shop committee when the Black Panther Movement demanded a share of the store's profits to further their own aims. Ella felt saddened that the women who worked in the store on a voluntary basis were being forced to hand over money intended to help their own children.

Ella's health was now poor; she was too frail to carry on fighting. She had blazed a trail through a maze of prejudice and fear. In her final year, she dictated her memoirs to a typist for publication.[6] By then things had changed on the former Purfleet Mission. Ella commented:

> I read all the criticism about money given to Aborigines but I am writing down what happened during my lifetime. I know there are selfish people abusing the privileges my generation had to fight for but that's not because they are Aborigines. That's because they are *people*.

Ella believed that one of the distinguishing characteristics of human beings of all races is that:

> Some grow up to be greedy, grasping and anti-social while others don't. Some, because of trauma suffered in childhood, never sort out their problems and may have to turn to professional counsellors, to religion or drugs in attempts to sort out their problems.

A third group, in spite of suffering deprivation and abuse as children, have a strong sense of identity and a belief system implanted into them. Adversity and suffering strengthens them. They turn bad experiences outwards instead of inwards and convert their anger into determination to help others in similar or worse situations rather than into anti-social behaviour or drug taking. So it was with Ella Simon. 'Skin colour doesn't matter', she always said. 'In the end it's *character* that's important'.

Ella Simon died just before she reached her eightieth birthday. She was cremated and in accordance with her wishes, her ashes were scattered over the graves of Kundaibark and her husband. She had gone home to her people.

# CHAPTER THIRTEEN

## Florence Mary Taylor
### *(1879–1969)*
#### AUSTRALIA'S FIRST FEMALE ARCHITECT

At the age of forty-one, thirteen years after she had gained her degree in architecture at the University of Sydney, Florence Taylor, rejected by male members of her profession, managed to gain professional accreditation. After years spent trying to gain admission, in 1920 she was finally admitted as an Associate (rather than a full member) of the New South Wales Institute of Architects.

Until 1923, there was no Board of Architects in New South Wales to register members of the profession.[1] Before this, when Florence was seeking admission as a member, the male-dominated Institute of Architects determined who gained professional accreditation and won architectural awards. They organised dinners and presentations and acted as the 'boy's club' of the profession of architecture.

In hindsight and in our less prejudiced age, it seems incredible that the Institute of Architects were able to reject the membership application of a truly exceptional woman like Florence Taylor. Not only was Florence a talented architect, she was also a fully qualified structural and civil engineer. But in spite of her excellent results on her architecture course at the University of New South Wales, Florence was discriminated against by the professional body which should have welcomed her with open arms. For years she was able to work only as a designer rather than a fully fledged architect.

In addition to her other skills, Florence Taylor had a flair for publishing, was a good editor and technical journalist and a talented print-maker. She also made the first glider flight recorded in Australia by a woman. Despite this impressive range of achievements, she received little recognition during the early years of her professional life. It is only today that we can see her as a catalyst in the lengthy and tortured process by which Australian women fought long and hard to gain recognition in their chosen professions.

How did Florence manage to become an architect in the early years of this century? It was a male chauvinistic era. Most clients for important buildings believed any architect worth their salt must wear a small pointed beard and sport a bow tie. Florence followed a long and rocky road to gain accreditation and acclaim.

Florence Mary Parsons was born in England on 29 December 1879 at Bedminster near Bristol. She was the eldest of four clever and attractive daughters of John Parsons, a public servant.[2]

In 1888[3] John Parsons, who suffered from a weak chest, emigrated to Australia in search of a warmer climate. He also believed he could give his daughters a better future in a new and developing country.

The Parsons family settled in Sydney. John Parsons was employed as a draftsman-clerk in the sewerage construction branch of the Parramatta Council, and with a regular income was able to educate Florence, the eldest and cleverest of his daughters, at private school. Florence attended the Presbyterian Ladies' College, Croydon. At an early age she excelled at mathematics and was soon able to help her father with complex engineering calculations.

At first, life in the Antipodes went well for the Parsons. But disaster struck the family when John Parsons died prematurely in 1899, before he had time to accumulate any significant assets. His widow received only a minute sum in compensation and the whole family faced considerable hardship. Australia was just emerging from the depression of the 1890s. There was no social security net to fall back on: a widows' pension was not regarded as a right of all women at this period. Mrs Taylor inherited the family home in Sydney, but with younger siblings to feed, clothe and educate, it was necessary for Florence to leave school and go to work in an office to earn money.

Florence was only nineteen[4] when her father died and had to take on responsibility for supporting her mother and younger sisters. This could have been the death of her ambitions. Like so many young women of her period, Florence could have remained a typist or telephonist, condemned with the rest of her family to a life of genteel poverty.

However, Florence's ambitions remained. She found herself a job as a clerk with her father's friend F. E. Stowe, head of a combined architectural and engineering firm in Parramatta. At that time, construction disciplines were not as specialised as today; frequently the functions of architect and engineer would be combined in one office.

Highly intelligent and creative, Florence soon found menial tasks and clerical work boring. She decided to become an architectural draftsperson instead. As a woman of great spirit and purpose, she did something totally unusual for her period and enrolled herself for evening classes in architecture at the Sydney Technical College. She was the *only* woman studying building construction, quantity surveying and architectural drafting and found herself marooned in the midst of two-hundred male students. She worked extremely hard and often topped the class.

Now in her early twenties, Florence was a tall, willowy, strikingly attractive young women. In addition to her architectural studies and her long working days, she managed to attend lectures at the School of Engineering at the University of Sydney as well. Here she was one of the first female students; engineering was also viewed as a tough, 'masculine' profession. But with her family responsibilities, work and study, Florence had attempted to achieve far too much for anyone, male or female. She studied hard in what little free time was available but failed her first year examinations in all architectural subjects.

This setback did not deter Florence. She was determined to repeat the year and set herself the goal of being in the top ten in her class, which she accomplished. At the same time, she was serving her practical apprenticeship (or articles) with the Sydney architect Edmund Skelton Garton. The work she was given in Garton's' office was anything but creative. She toiled over the tedious task of technical specification writing, while her male colleagues received all the more stimulating tasks, such as preparing sketches, designs and working drawings.

Florence was always the first to arrive at Garton's office, often as early as 7.30 am. She would work very hard in an attempt to finish her specification writing by lunchtime, hoping she would be given drafting or design work in the afternoon. But however hard she worked, she only received more and more specifications to write. The men continued to receive all the design work. Referring to her time in Garton's employ Florence would describe how, 'The (specifications) seemed to be never ending. I thought I would never get around to designing homes and other buildings though I used to get in at 7.30 am every day in a desire to overcome my work load.'

Frustrated creativity prompted Florence to apply for another job as soon as she had completed her articles. She succeeded in getting a job as chief draftsperson in the prestigious office of John Burcham Clamp, the Diocesan architect. Unlike her previous employer, Clamp recognised Florence's professional competence and dedication – she was allowed to design and was put in charge of the plans for some very expensive homes on Sydney's North Shore, which she did very well. But the name on the designs was always that of John Burcham Clamp, rather than her own.

But Florence's sense of purpose was strong. She *would* become a qualified architect. Finally, after eight years arduous study, combined with practical experience in two architects' offices, in 1907, Florence completed her architectural course. She had already qualified as a structural and a civil engineer: it was unheard of at that time that a mere woman could achieve so much.

Immediately after Florence qualified as an architect, John Clamp nominated her for associate membership of the New South Wales Institute of Architects so that she could receive official recognition by that august professional body. Clamp gave Florence an excellent reference. He praised her architectural skills and excellent design sense. All to no avail. As a woman, her nomination to join the Institute of Architects was rejected by the powerful men on the Committee. Clamp was furious when he heard the Committee's decision and demanded, 'Why did they reject her? On what grounds? She can design an entire home while an ordinary draftsman is still sharpening his pencil.'

Florence Parson's male colleagues did not recognise her abilities and made it plain they did not want her to join them. But like other professional pioneer women, Flos Greig, Joan Rosanove and Dr Constance Stone, Florence refused to give up the right to practice the profession she loved and had been trained for.

However, she had to wait another thirteen years before her professional governing body, the Institute of Architects, finally admitted her as the first qualified female architect in New South Wales. In the meantime, the long years of rejection by the Institute did not deter Florence. Working as a draftsperson in John Clamp's office she had designed a large number of private homes in Mosman, Neutral Bay and Darling Point – for which, of course, she could not command an architect's salary.

While Florence was studying engineering she fell in love with one of her lecturers. George Augustine Taylor was as multi-talented, resourceful and adventurous as Florence. He did not feel threatened by her brilliance but admired her work.

George Taylor was an engineer by profession as well as a skilful cartoonist, working in black-and-white as a freelancer for the *Bulletin* and *Punch*. His friends were artistic and literary and he was a council member of the Royal Art Society of New South Wales. By the time he met Florence he had also become interested in the technology of wireless and telephony; he carried out much pioneering work in these fields, particularly for military purposes.

On 3 April 1907, Miss Florence Parsons married Mr George Taylor at St Stephen's Presbyterian Church, Sydney. It was a love match, and husband and wife shared many interests and ambitions.

Shortly after their marriage, George became interested in aviation and learned to fly gliders. He became so fascinated by aeronautics that he established his own factory where he manufactured gliders and light aircraft. In 1909, he promoted the Aerial League of Australia and expressed his view to the Government that it was important to establish an air force. Urged on by her husband, Florence conquered an initial fear of heights and gained a pilot's licence. In 1909, she made the first glider flight ever attempted by a woman. There was enormous public interest when she took off in her glider from the Narrabeen sand hills near Sydney and she was cheered by all the onlookers. Flying and the romance of the air became a passion with both of them.

Florence and her husband went into business together and formed their own 'Building Publishing Company'. They published major technical and professional journals such as *The Australian Engineer*, *Building, The Commonwealth Home* and the *Radio Journal of Australia*. In these building and engineering publications they promoted the interests of architects, engineers and builders and made the Australian Government and the public more aware of the merit of professionalism in construction activities.

As a feature writer and as the editor of a diverse range of journals, all published by their own company, Florence campaigned for urban planning, improved construction methods and superior material application. The Taylors advocated modernism in architecture and town planning. One outstanding example of their joint achievements was to organise a petition, in which support from architects and engineers was enlisted for the acceptance of Walter Burley Griffin's revolutionary designs for the new national capital, Canberra.

Their publications became well-known in the fields of construction and technique. However, it took considerable time before Florence's journalistic input became as highly respected as that of her husband.

In 1913, the Taylors founded the Town Planning Association of New South Wales. The following year they travelled abroad and spent some time in America. They greatly admired Theodore Roosevelt's progressive outlook, in particular his involvement with the finalisation of the Panama Canal project.[5]

Florence and George Taylor's marriage was a happy one in every respect. They spent many exciting and productive years together, both as business partners and as professional colleagues. George was a devoted husband and an exceptional man, having succeeded in many differing fields, in spite of the fact that he was an epileptic. Florence had to learn to manage his condition and prise open his teeth to free his airways when he succumbed to an epileptic fit. Perhaps the fear that epilepsy was congenital (although now it is believed not to be) was the reason the Taylors never had children, but concentrated on their careers.

Then, after twenty-one years of happy marriage, disaster struck. George died in their Sydney home on 20 January 1928. He had an epileptic fit while taking a bath alone in their house, slumped into the bath water and drowned. Florence found his corpse when she returned home. She was devastated and grief-ridden.

Florence was determined she would never marry again. She carried on their joint publishing business and took full responsibility for managing it. But she had to reduce her workload and cease publishing eight out of their eleven periodicals. She carried on producing the most successful of their journals, *Building* (later *Building, Lighting and Engineering*) and *The Australian Engineer*.

Florence was a fighter. She submerged her grief and loss in a surge of creativity, threw herself into a host of professional activities and produced several town planning schemes and civil engineering projects. The time she had to spend on running the commercial side of their publishing firm made it necessary for her to employ draftsmen to draw up the detail work for the vast engineering projects she designed.

Her biggest challenges were traffic subways for Sydney and an express route from the centre of the city to its eastern suburbs. She also had the foresight to realise that Sydney Airport would eventually become overcrowded and that the city would need a second airport, so she designed one to be based out at Newport, to the north of Sydney.

In spite of Florence's technical aspirations and skills, she remained extremely feminine, and always dressed in the height of fashion. In Australian's male-dominated society it must have been most disconcerting for men that a highly feminine woman like Florence Taylor achieved so much. In descriptions of the period, she appears as a walking contradiction: an extremely attractive and feminine woman, who was highly competent in 'masculine' disciplines. To male colleagues and critics she was often perceived as a threat. Some saw her as far too forceful in personality; other male critics hinted that she must be eccentric in wanting to enter a male world rather than staying home and baking cakes. Art historian John Berger has argued the case that:[6]

> men look, women appear – men are socialised to be active and women to be passive models. If this is so, what happens when women begin to 'look' as well as to 'appear'? How should women manage the complexities of 'appearing' when undertaking an active role in public life?

Florence Taylor addressed this tension by ... accentuating her femininity. She loudly proclaimed her conviction that 'every woman should be able to stand shoulder to shoulder with the men folk without losing the characteristics of her sex.'[7]

Florence's strategy was to wear expensive clothes, French perfume, long kid gloves and carry lace-frilled parasols.[8] In the Federation era, women dressed to kill. She sported sweeping skirts, piled-up hair under eye-catching hats in the style of *My Fair Lady*. Defiantly she continued wearing flowing skirts and the ultra feminine look, even when 'flappers' bobbed their hair and shortened their skirts in the jazz-mad Roaring Twenties, by which time she was in her forties.

Contemporary journalists swallowed the bait she offered them and gave her all the publicity she needed. But instead of reporting her achievements alongside her outstanding good looks, they described how:

> despite these exacting occupations, Mrs Taylor's gracious personality is the very essence of femininity.[8] Despite her achievements in male strongholds Mrs Taylor is essentially feminine. She has a weakness for outsize hats with ostrich feathers.[9]

These statements about 'gracious personality and hats with ostrich feathers' create an impression that Florence Taylor's claim to fame was not her architectural and town planning design skills, nor in the influence of her articles advocating better town planning and airport facilities for Sydney, but rather in her skill of presenting herself as a beautiful lady in a large and extravagantly feathered hat. This misleading description led some men in power to refer cynically to Florence Taylor as 'The Great Lady of Sydney Town'.

Today, some women in male-dominated professions react to criticism by taking on men on their own ground, deepening their voices and power-dressing. Florence did the opposite. One wonders whether, by wearing the outrageous fashions of an upper-class woman of the Edwardian era, she actually diminished her reputation as an architect, engineer and town planner.

Would Florence have been taken more seriously as a professional woman if she had dressed more like a man? Probably not. Australia was then so male dominated that in the first half the twentieth century Australian women were generally not taken seriously, *whatever* they were wearing. Those were the days when a woman's place was firmly in the home. Most men regarded women as inferior in brainpower, at the mercy of their 'frail' physiques and 'feminine' whims.

Fortunately for Florence Taylor, she lived long enough to experience a marked change in men's attitudes towards women in business and professions. She was a perfectionist, never satisfied with local knowledge, particularly in respect to town planning and engineering. Consequently, she travelled to Europe and America to broaden her own vision. In America, which was more in love with the new and with success than Australia (where 'tall poppies' in every sphere were constantly denigrated and women seen as totally inferior to men), Florence fascinated all those she met with her knowledge, her design skills and the charm of her personality. She expressed delight with the labour-saving designs of American homes, their excellent plumbing, and the open and easier way of life for women. In return, her hosts gave her a detailed run-down of plans and schemes just completed or on the drawing-board. She proved herself an excellent Ambassador for Australia – and, just as important, she and her revolutionary ideas *were* taken seriously by her fellow American professionals. The American architects and town planners were most impressed by the breadth of Mrs Taylor's knowledge on many aspects of architecture and planning, and by the range of technical publications produced by her company.

Enriched with a host of new and progressive ideas, she returned home. Full of enthusiasm for the approach to town planning in Europe and America, she conveyed her newly acquired knowledge through her articles and speeches to members of various professional bodies, trying to convince her largely sceptical and predominantly male colleagues that Australia was lagging behind America in the fields of town and regional planning.

In spite of her outrageous way of dressing, the technical professions eventually started to take Florence Taylor more seriously. Gradually, her progressive ideas began to take hold. Even the die-hard prejudices of some of her male colleagues slowly mellowed as she grew older. And the journals she continued to publish after her husband's death had now become highly respected among the engineering and building industries.

In middle age, Florence sponsored and gave financial support to several design awards, some of which were named in her honour. The most important award was that given under the auspices of the Australian Institute of Metals, duly named the Florence M. Taylor Medal.

In 1939, Florence was honoured by King George VI with an OBE (Order of the British Empire). Much later, when she was in her eighties, she was awarded a CBE (Commander of the British Empire), a clear indication that, finally, her enormous competence and dedication were fully appreciated.

Florence's wide interests kept her in close contact with a large number of friends and colleagues. In her later years, she was associated or involved with an astonishing number of organisations, clubs and societies, many of them almost exclusively male. She had become an Honorary member of the Australian Institute of Builders and of the Engineering Society of New South Wales, a Life Member of the Master Builders' Federation of Australia and of the Master Builders' Association of New South Wales (whose Award of Honour she received in 1952); a Life Member of the Town Planning Association of

New South Wales; a Member of the Society of Women Writers; a Member of the Arts Club; a Member of the International Society of Australia; a Member of the Royal Aero Club of New South Wales, and of the prestigious British Royal Society of Arts – an honour granted to few Australian men, let alone women.

All her life she spoke out for women to be taken seriously in whatever field they entered. She also voiced an unpopular opinion at that time, namely that marriage could, and often did, confine women and limit their talents and potential. She dared to speak about the sadness of 'the empty nest syndrome'. She was one of the first to voice an opinion that in their later years, when children had left home, married women with no work experience or qualifications to fall back on often become deeply depressed. (Now we know that many of the symptoms attributed to the physical side of menopause are psychological, caused by this 'empty nest syndrome'.) When Florence was in her mid seventies she stated her credo that:

> For a woman to marry, to get trapped in the small confines of her home and never be articulate, is a disgrace. There is not enough mental occupation in home duties only and women never get the chance to shoulder life's full responsibilities.[10]

Despite all Florence Taylor's achievements, even in later life she could not avoid the fact that there was often more interest in her appearance than in her remarkable record of activities. A journalist writing in the *Daily Telegraph*, on 30 December 1959, observed:

> It would be hard to find anyone more feminine than Mrs Florence Taylor. And almost impossible to find any woman with less feminine interests. When I dropped in to see Mrs Florence Taylor on her 80th birthday yesterday, I was struck by her beautiful perfume, her frivolous hat, her soft feminine dress. But immediately she began talking about tunnels, bridges, high density buildings and car parks.

It is interesting that the anonymous reporter (male or female?), did not bother to write down one single word Florence uttered about urban planning, architectural design and the problems confronting the built environment of Sydney. Florence Taylor's brilliant ideas and sophisticated concepts – including her important plans for a second airport for Sydney, which would have saved airlines from the long delays entering and leaving that city which have plagued them for years – must have been beyond the comprehension of the reporter, who confined themselves to superficial comments on Florence's femininity.

In 1961, Florence's health started to deteriorate. Now in her eighties, she finally retired from her wide variety of occupations and spent her final years living with her younger sister Annis Parsons, who nursed her until her death.

Florence Taylor died in Sydney on 13 February 1969. Like her brilliant husband, she was cremated in the Anglican Church. It is interesting to observe that the enquiring and analytical minds of George and Florence Taylor made them change their religious faith, in George's case more than once.

The achievements of this remarkable woman are commemorated in the annual Florence Taylor Award for outstanding services to engineering, currently administered each year by the Australian Society of Mechanical Engineers.

# CHAPTER FOURTEEN

Photograph reproduced courtesy of the Hon. Peg Lusink.

## Joan Mavis Rosanove (Lazarus)
### *(1896–1974)*
WHO FOUGHT FOR THE RIGHT TO PRACTISE LAW
ON EQUAL TERMS WITH MALE COLLEAGUES

Joan Rosanove, a woman who battled prejudice against women in the legal profession all her life, commented wryly:

> To be a [female] lawyer you must have the stamina of an ox and a hide like a rhinoceros. And when they kick you in the teeth you must look as if you hadn't noticed.

Charismatic Joan Rosanove, daughter of a Jewish barrister, was more than a match for most men. She endured discrimination because she was a woman in an almost exclusively male profession and because she was Jewish (by race rather than religion). In Melbourne's clubbish Anglo-Saxon Protestant legal circles, the old boy network operated strongly to keep out women and foreigners. Most of Joan's legal colleagues had bonded together as boys. They had played cricket and rugger against each other at Victoria's exclusive private schools. They did not welcome outsiders into their club. In spite of her remarkable talents in the courtroom, it would take over a quarter of a century for Joan Lazarus' intelligence, tenacity and superb cross-examining skills to receive their due recognition.

Joan was born into the law. Her father, Mark Lazarus, was unusual in working as an amalgam, operating both as a solicitor and a barrister, with offices in Ballarat and Melbourne, Joan's mother, born Ruby Braham, came from another leading legal family, who were part-Jewish and part-Irish. Joan's parents enjoyed a happy and stable marriage with seven lively, attractive and intelligent children. Two of their sons entered the law in addition to Joan. She was the second daughter in this large and multi-talented family.

Joan and her sister inherited their mother Ruby's sparkling dark eyes and long dark lashes. As a plump, dimple-cheeked teenager, Joan feared she was destined to play second fiddle to her elder sister Vida, whose slender figure had a devastating effect on the local youth.[1] While Vida flirted with the boys, Joan Mavis, with her dark unruly curls, had to push her younger siblings around the streets of Ballarat in a pram.

Joan and Vida attended Loreto Convent before changing to Clarendon College.[2] Bob Menzies, who attended a neighbouring school, recalled Joan as the more intelligent of the two sisters.

In those days, wives of successful middle-class men like Mark Lazarus were not expected to do housework. They were expected to employ maids, run the household and bring up children. An endless succession of Irish girls lived in as domestic staff, washed, cleaned, cared for the younger children and did most of the cooking. Joan recalled that most of them were called either 'Bridie' or 'Cissy'.

At the time when the majority of the middle-class girls were taught accomplishments and prepared for marriage rather than educated for jobs or careers, both the Lazarus girls were encouraged to study hard by their father. They showed scant interest in learning about household management, although Joan did learn the rudiments of cooking from her mother, who was far more interested in dressing beautifully and attending the races than in being a housewife.

At the age of fifteen, Joan was allowed to accompany her father to the prestigious Selborne Chambers, where Melbourne's leading barristers had their chambers, and to sit in the courtroom. Joan was fascinated by the drama of the law courts: she vowed that one day she would become a barrister with rooms in Selborne Chambers.

On leaving school, she became articled to her father as a law clerk and worked in his Melbourne office. However, her mother felt that Joan was too young to live away from home. So every morning Joan would rise at 5 am, cycle to Ballarat Station, catch the 6.45 train to Melbourne and work in her father's office, as well as studying compulsory law subjects at Melbourne University. Then she would return home to Ballarat by the 8 pm train, eat the dinner cooked for her by one or other of the servants and work on her law assignments. So much hard work in pursuit of her ambition meant little time for socialising.

Cycling to the station slimmed Joan down until she became just as attractive as her mother and sister.

Joan's closest friend at University was a pharmacy student, Annie Cunningham, who was of Scottish Protestant extraction. Annie was invited to tea at Queen's College by a male student with Scottish connections. He had a close friend who was a medical student, so Annie took Joan along with her. Both girls were charmed by the lively, amusing auburn-haired medic, Emmanuel (Mannie) Rosanove. Mannie's father was a Russian-born Jew, an agricultural expert from Broken Hill, who had worked in Palestine before migrating to Australia. Annie found Mannie extremely attractive and amusing: she went out with him a few times while Joan went out with their host, the Scottish student.

Annie, a practical Scot, soon realised that a prolonged relationship with Jewish-born Mannie was bound to bring serious problems. One day they were discussing the subject when Joan, who had also taken a strong liking to Mannie, observed, 'Annie, you have a Jew while I have a Scot. What about a swap?'

So Joan and Mannie started to go out together. Their only means of transport was Mannie's ancient and unreliable motorbike with sidecar, which he expected Joan to get out and push, whenever it broke down. Joan's old friend from Ballarat days, Bob Menzies (the future Prime Minister of Australia), was also studying law at Melbourne University and often helped the pair of them push-start Mannie's motorbike when it broke down on campus.

At the time when Joan started working as an articled clerk in her father's office, only a handful of outstanding women worked in the law. Although Melbourne University's Law School had been operating since 1857, for its first forty years women were denied admittance. The argument men in power used to prevent the admission of women to law school was the hoary old fable that, as their brains were small, studying would have a bad effect on female health and render them sterile – although for some reason this did not happen to men who studied hard! The authorities also claimed that women would not have the necessary toughness to deal with the horrifying details of sexual depravity and domestic violence encountered in legal practice. Joan would prove these arguments wrong on all counts.

In Joan Rosanove's day, there was male prejudice against women lawyers in every State in Australia. When they were employed by the Government, women lawyers had to fight for the right to be paid the same as their male colleagues.

In 1917, when Joan Lazarus (as she then was) gained her LL.B, most of the male students had been called away to fight in World War I.[3] Possibly Melbourne University authorities were embarrassed at the high proportion of women graduating in law. The ceremony that marked their admission to the bar was delayed for two years until June 1919, so that male students could finish their degrees and make the ceremony seem more 'serious' and less female.

Reporting Joan's entry to the law, the newspapers placed her name at the bottom of the list and ignored her when trying to spot which students would become barristers and judges. Only the *Jewish Herald* commented favourably on Joan's achievements, describing how 'Miss Lazarus was the first Jewess in Australia to be admitted to the law'.

The fact that Joan was Jewish as well as female intensified discrimination against her from Melbourne's Anglo-Saxon Protestant legal fraternity. This tightly bonded clique with their antipathy to Jews and women lawyers would ensure that in later years Joan Rosanove's many applications to take silk or become a QC were passed over in favour of less qualified candidates – who were, of course, both male and Protestant.

Ironically, neither Joan nor her husband-to-be actually practised the Jewish faith: both the Rosanove and Lazarus families saw themselves as Australians first and foremost. But multi-culturalism had not been invented, Australia was still a racist society and unsympathetic to women.

Mr Ah Ket, a Chinese barrister trying vainly to practise in Melbourne, once told Joan: 'You and I have chosen the wrong profession and will never satisfy our ambitions. Neither of us will ever be made a judge: you because you are a woman, I because I am Chinese.' He recommended that they both return to University and study medicine, because he felt there was less discrimination against doctors from 'ethnic' backgrounds than in the legal profession. The idea of going back to University and studying medicine held little appeal for Joan. The law was in her blood. She was determined to succeed in court, a side of the law that attracted her dramatic temperament and vivid personality. The histrionic side of her character, which stemmed from her mother and her Jewish heritage, might have enabled Joan to become a successful actress. Certainly her acting abilities stood her in good stead in a career in which many theatrical techniques are employed by barristers.

Fortunately, Joan was blessed with a strong constitution, which meant she could stand for long hours in court without tiring. Her deep contralto voice never became shrill when addressing the court; this and her personal charisma would prove an asset with juries, confronted (as Joan described in an interview with *Table Talk*) 'with the spectacle of a comely woman locked in seemingly unequal combat with a man'.[4]

In July 1919, Mark Lazarus instructed his daughter in her first brief. It was nearly a disaster: the prejudiced judge was loath to listen to her evidence. However, Joan held her ground and won her case. Under the laws of the State of Victoria, lawyers were admitted to practice both as barristers and as solicitors and could appear in both roles, although most chose one or other branch of the profession. Young lawyers who did both, the 'amalgams', gained excellent experience in both office and court work.

From the outset Joan encountered strong prejudice from certain judges. Anti-feminine prejudice in court was especially marked in one case, tried by Mr Justice McArthur. Joan was defending Alfred Thomas Ozanne, Labor MP for Corio, who had sued the *Geelong Advertiser* for slander. Mark Lazarus had accepted the case but then discovered he was defending in the Ballarat court. So Joan, still relatively inexperienced and only in her early twenties, had to defend Ozanne in the Supreme Court of Victoria against an experienced barrister twice her age, and cross-examine Billy Hughes, then Prime Minister of Australia.[5]

Hughes was an experienced politician, practised at techniques to fend off awkward questions. He *was* somewhat deaf and played on this, taking care to shield himself from Joan Lazarus's piercing questions behind his hearing aid. As the trial wore on the politician's deafness became progressively worse, allowing him sufficient time to formulate suitably evasive answers. However loud Joan bellowed, Billy Hughes pretended he could not hear her – until he had played for time to consider his reply. Of course the anti-feminist Mr Justice McArthur did nothing to help Joan. The Ozanne case dragged on for months before Billy Hughes' delaying tactics won the day. Joan and her father suffered a humiliating defeat.

But Joan was a fighter. Defeat made her even more determined to succeed. She became smarter, worked harder and won most of her cases in Ballarat and Melbourne. She was astute enough to realise that to succeed as a woman in a man's world she must capitalise on every advantage that offered. She emphasised her femininity, dressing fashionably, wearing very high heels to make her petite slim figure appear taller and hence more imposing. Fortunately for Joan, she had an outstanding personality: her husky contralto voice, combined with a rapier-like wit, made her a charismatic figure and a formidable opponent in the courts. She had a fund of witty stories for every occasion; hard-bitten Melbourne courtroom journalists loved writing about her because she was so entertaining and never patronising towards them, unlike some of her male colleagues.

When the proposed marriage of Joan Lazarus to Dr Emmanuel Rosanove was announced one journalist commented:

> All kinds of cases are absorbed by her brief bag, and among these, divorce cases are most prominent. If Miss Lazarus shrinks from marriage – she is yet almost too young to give the matter serious thought – it will be because of a prejudicial idea born of an extensive experience in the courts, that marriage is a failure; the number of [divorce] cases she has handled tend to prove that it is so.

Although Joan must have realised it would not be easy to combine the joint role of barrister and wife to a young doctor with a busy practice, Mannie Rosanove was the man she wanted. And when Joan wanted something, she usually got it.

On 2 September 1920, Miss Joan Lazarus and Dr Emmanuel Rosanove were married by Rabbi Lenzer. This ceremony probably took place out of deference to Mannie's parents, who were more orthodox than Ruby and Mark Lazarus. The bride and groom, both highly intelligent and hardworking, were obviously well-suited. Mark Lazarus could not help feeling slightly antagonistic to his new son-in-law for taking his much loved daughter away from the Ballarat courtroom, where she was now making a name for herself, to a sleepy, isolated country town like Tocumwal, on the Murray River. Mark Lazarus was also worried because he knew Mannie had spent all his savings to buy into a general practice – as was usual in the days before a national health service was introduced.

After a brief honeymoon the new bride found herself in a small wooden house in the centre of Tocumwal. She was no longer a barrister but the wife and unpaid secretary to a country GP. Their little wooden house was extremely primitive, a far cry from her parents' home in Ballarat. Like most bush homes at that period, it had an outside water lavatory complete with gigantic huntsmen spiders and no piped hot water – only a cold tap set in the kitchen wall, connected to an outside water tank. The kitchen had a temperamental wood-burning stove that demanded patience and cookery skills, which Joan did not possess.

Housekeeping in the bush was not Joan's strong point: her husband soon observed 'as a housewife Joan is a marvellous lawyer'. She had done a crash course in cooking and picked up hints from her mother and the maids, but although Joan was a devoted wife to Mannie, she never took much interest in the details of cooking or housework. In this small New South Wales country town, where the train only ran three times a week, uneducated country girls flatly refused to work at Dr Rosanove's combined house and surgery because they feared they might catch some fatal disease there. The few girls that did apply for jobs were either mentally retarded or too fond of the bottle and provided Joan and Mannie with scorched shirts and culinary disasters.

Adapting to the role of wife of a country GP in a pioneering society, where women were seen as inferior to men, was not easy for a city lawyer. To add to their problems, Joan's first child was stillborn. This was her first serious setback: like women today who experience cot death through no fault of their own, she had to work through a period of intense grief and guilt.

Their second child, Rose Margaret (Peg), was born at Tocumwal in 1922. Mannie's medical practice proved a tiring one. He was constantly on call with little free time and had to make home visits to remote areas in emergencies. In the 1920s, Tocumwal was too small to warrant a commercial pharmacy so Mannie had to spend long hours making up his own prescriptions. Joan missed the drama and excitement of the courtroom and found no friends to share her interests.

When the visiting GP from neighbouring Cobram told them with pride, 'I've been here for thirty-four years tomorrow', Joan and Mannie looked at each other, each thinking that it was high time to move on. So Mannie put the practice on the market and sold it within a month.

Much to Joan's delight, they moved back to Melbourne.[6] In the northern suburb of Westgarth, Dr Emmanuel Rosanove took out a huge overdraft to buy a combined practice and home only a few minutes by train from the city, so that his young wife could continue with her profession. She was longing to return to legal practice, and she was fortunate that Mannie was an exceptionally understanding husband. In those days, it was considered positively shameful that a professional man would even consider allowing his wife to go out to work. But instead of demanding Joan turn into the 'Angel of the Home', unlike most men of this period, her husband had the wisdom and maturity to encourage her to employ a nanny for her child and return to practising law. This would not prove easy, because by now the legal profession was overcrowded with male lawyers back in practice after fighting in World War I.

On 2 September 1923, the Melbourne *Herald* found it important enough to record that Mrs Rosanove had signed the Roll of Counsel of the Victorian Bar, undertaking that henceforth she would work only as a barrister.

An interview with an admiring journalist for *Table Talk* recorded that the attractive Mrs Rosanove was the first woman in Victoria to work solely as a barrister when she was still only in her mid-twenties. But male solicitors flatly refused to send her work. They rationalised their prejudices by claiming clients did not want 'women to defend them'.

As Joan could not get chambers in the traditional barristers' building, Selborne Chambers, Mannie had to rent a tiny backroom office for her in a dilapidated building in Chancery Lane, where cockroaches lurked in the cracks and rats gnawed Joan's legal books during the night. In between running her house at Westgarth and organising a stream of changing domestic staff to look after the house, and nannies to take charge of Peg, Joan sat alone in her tiny office and waited for briefs. She waited in vain: the only briefs she did receive came from her father's office. And when she did go into court, she experienced discrimination from patriarchal judges like the distinguished Mr Justice à Beckett Weigall, who would either yawn or look bored when Joan was called upon to plead.

This particular judge absolutely loathed the idea of women 'invading law'. He preferred to concentrate on a fly on the wall rather than watch a mere woman perform in court. Joan had no option but to grit her teeth and bear it. Her briefs were few but she made the most of them. Her rare but striking court appearances and her examining skills invariably attracted newspaper publicity.

In 1925, Joan decided to leave the bar and had her name removed from the Roll of Counsel. Her abrupt departure was sparked by a traumatic incident in which a Jewish legal colleague named Philip Jacobs, on the point of departing to spend a year in England, offered Joan the temporary use of his room in exclusive Selborne Chambers 'to get the fellows used to having a woman there'. Immediately after they heard of Phil Jacobs' offer, the male inmates of Selborne Chambers called a protest meeting. They were *outraged* at the thought of a woman's presence amongst them. Phil Jacobs was informed by the directors of Selborne Chambers (Joan Rosanove's fellow barristers) that if he allowed Mrs Rosanove to use his room, they would have no option but to cancel his lease.

Had Joan Rosanove considered using Philip Jacobs' room as a brothel rather than to practise law, her legal 'colleagues' could not have been more outraged by her proposed presence. This hurtful and public rejection by her colleagues was one of the most humiliating moments in Joan Rosanove's entire career, the 'kick in the teeth' that she would never appear to have noticed. But now, after so many 'kicks in the teeth', Joan felt it was pointless trying to continue practicing solely as a barrister. She realised she would never receive briefs from solicitors, however good she was in court, if her own professional colleagues would not support her.

Determined to prove herself, she decided to put up her brass plate at home and work from a joint suite of consulting rooms there. She would return to being an 'amalgam' – practising as a solicitor and also appearing in court on occasions as a barrister. She would limit herself to those areas of the law she knew best, criminal and divorce law.

In view of the overwhelming male prejudice which had been displayed against her, this decision proved a wise one. Over the next twenty-two years Joan Rosanove became incredibly successful, handling thousands of cases and earning a very good income. She specialised in defending women and twice appeared for females accused of murder, one of whom was a backyard abortionist. She did not succeed in getting them acquitted, but in both cases the women were found guilty of the lesser charges of manslaughter.

She went to the trouble of designing her own version of the legal costume. Under her barrister's robe Joan added a distinctively feminine touch, a *broderie anglaise* frill around the starched linen collar, from which hung two white bands. In court her beautiful dark intelligent eyes and her dazzling smile were seen to their best advantage set off by her white legal wig.

During working hours, the Rosanoves Westgarth home was filled with Mannie's patients and Joan's clients. 'Crocks and crooks', as she and Mannie joked in private, were their speciality. Like John Mortimer's fictitious barrister Rumpole with his terrible Timpson family, one curiously inefficient family of burglars now formed the foundation of Joan Rosanove's criminal practice. She soon discovered that getting members of this feckless family off their charges of burglary was a thankless task: no sooner was one free than another family member would be arrested. The parents were always desperately keen for their offspring to be out of gaol by Christmas. It took Joan some time to realise that this Antipodean Timpson family's wish for a Christmas reunion was not so they could sing carols together, but because the Christmas holidays (when wealthy Melbournians were away at the beach) were much the best time to do a spot of housebreaking.

Joan's burglar-clients combined to protect her home. As long as Joan Rosanove defended criminals, the Rosanove residence was never burgled; but when her divorce cases became so numerous that she had to give up criminal work, their 'magic' immunity from burglary ceased.

Eventually Joan's dual life as wife and barrister became so hectic that she found it difficult to find the time to buy clothes. That is, until the Melbourne *Truth*, which specialised in sensational court cases, reporting her spirited performance in the lower court (where legal gowns and wigs were not worn), commented that Joan Rosanove was a 'haphazard dresser'. From then on, Joan determined to spend on designer clothes, shoes and expensive model hats. She paid a small fortune for one particularly flattering red hat, which became her trade mark in the lower court. Joan Rosanove always maintained that women in the law should be allowed to tax-deduct money spent on good, well-cut clothes, as these formed part of their stock in trade along with their armoury of legal books.

In private life, Joan's good manners remained unchanged. But once she entered the higher courtroom in her white wig and black gown she took on a different persona: she could become as tenacious, tough and inquisitorial as her male colleagues. At the peak of her legal career, Joan Rosanove was handling one-eighth of Victoria's divorce list.[7] By the end of the 1930s, she had become well-known for fighting for women's interests in breach of promise or divorce cases, where the law was often stacked against them. To gain a divorce, women needed to prove cruelty or adultery on *various* occasions by the husband. Faced with an attractive woman in a wig with a charming smile and dimpled cheeks, powerful and wealthy men defending themselves against charges brought by their wives often became tongue-tied, or trapped themselves into admissions they had no wish to reveal. Joan Rosanove's verbal skills became a legend in the divorce courts, along with her flair for discovering exactly what assets the husband possessed that had not been declared to the court.

Through Joan's burning desire to see that women were not taken advantage of, many men found themselves paying far more in alimony or property settlements than they had envisaged.

At this period, most legal firms looked on divorce cases as being an unsavoury branch of the law. Many male barristers flatly refused to touch divorce and advised their clients to take their business elsewhere. Such an attitude was extremely distressing to women undergoing the harrowing process of separation and divorce. Divorce was a procedure that carried strong undertones of disapproval in the rigid paternalistic society of Australia before World War II.

In contrast to the prevailing attitudes of lawyers, whenever women lacking in self-confidence and distressed by the thought of a court appearance arrived in Joan Rosanove's office, they were greeted with kindness and understanding. But Joan had a totally different way of dealing with arrogant Toorak ladies who looked down their noses at her and announced, 'My normal solicitors are Messrs X and X. But they say they don't deal with *dirty* matters like divorce, so I've *had* to come to *you*'.

Joan found the perfect way to deal with this. She would smile sweetly at the arrogant lady and touch the bell concealed under her desk for her assistant, the faithful Miss Caffrey, to enter. Then she would turn to her and say, 'Miss Caffrey, this lady's usual solicitors are Messrs X and X. But she tells us they don't do *dirty* work; so she has had to come to us to get her a divorce'. Miss Caffrey would give an understanding nod, return to her desk and add twenty guineas to that particular client's account as an 'annoyance' fee.

In 1932, Joan was in her late thirties and her daughter, Peg, was ten. Joan, who had felt she was too old to have another child, became pregnant again. She solved the problem of whether or not to go to work during her pregnancy by planning an extended trip overseas with her husband and daughter, determined not to let her male colleagues have the pleasure of sniggering over her increasing girth in the communal robing room. She planned to have her baby in London. Mannie had been talking about studying overseas for a post-graduate qualification in dermatology, having been appointed as a part-time clinical assistant in dermatology at the Alfred Hospital. She decided they would combine both aims. Naturally the press were not told the real reason for their departure.

Joan asked their old university friend, Bob Menzies, for an official letter of introduction which would open doors for them in London and America. A locum was engaged for Mannie's practice and Joan's father agreed to take care of her legal clients. On 26 July 1932, the Rosanoves boarded the *SS Mariposa*, to find their cabin brimming with red roses and *bon voyage* telegrams from friends and relatives.

The Rosanoves left the ship at San Francisco and travelled by train to Seattle, then on to Vancouver and over the Rockies by Canadian Pacific. They ended their spectacular train journey in New York, then crossed the Atlantic to England. They rented an apartment in London's elegant Buckingham Gate, and found a leading Harley Street obstetrician for Joan. Mannie attended post-graduate lectures at London teaching hospitals, and Peg was sent to a private school in Knightsbridge, while Joan went sightseeing. On 28 November 1932, Judith Anne Rosanove was born in a nursing home in Devonshire Place. Shortly after the birth, Mannie left for Edinburgh to be examined for Membership of the Royal College of Physicians. He passed with flying colours.

Joan met three English female barristers who told her that nearly one hundred women were now practising as barristers in Britain. She attended meetings of the Fabian Women's Group discussing Britain's economic crisis where the Depression was causing severe social problems for women and families. Joan, an excellent public speaker, talked to various women's organisations, giving them an Australian point of view on women's rights and conditions of work.

In February 1933, Mannie and Joan took the boat train to Vienna to attend lectures by leading Viennese skin specialists. The Rosanoves had intended to travel on to Berlin, where friends had offered them the loan of their apartment, but Jewish friends warned them not to go. Hitler's Brownshirts were persecuting Jews, confiscating their assets, beating them up in the streets. The first pitiful flood of Jewish refugees was escaping, others were 'disappearing'. It was too dangerous. So on 7 April 1933, Dr and Mrs Rosanove, an English-trained Norland nanny in her brown uniform and their two little girls embarked for Australia on the *Cathay*.

Back in Melbourne, the press described how Mrs Rosanove, the famous barrister, arrived with her six-months old baby in her arms. They said Joan was 'the latest word in smartness – hair immaculately waved and crowned by a tiny hat in the latest style'.

After an absence of ten months, Joan was pleased to return to the courtroom. Mannie sold the Westgarth general practice and took rooms in Collins Street where he put up his brass plate as a dermatologist. Eventually they built themselves another home, a large two-storey house just off Orrong Road.

Joan never refused an invitation to speak out against injustice to women and those from a non-English speaking background. And she was haunted by what she had heard about the persecution of Jews in Europe. On behalf of a committee of left-wing writers and artists, she was asked by the author Katharine Susannah Prichard to handle a clear case of government injustice to a Jewish Czech journalist named Egon Kisch. Katharine Prichard, pale, composed and elegant, visited Joan and handed over money she and other supporters had organised to pay for Kisch's defence at a public rally.

Kisch, who had been living in Germany, had been due to address a series of left-wing meetings about the dangers of Hitler's Germany, where he would plead for world peace. But the Australian Government had become alarmed when King Alexander of Serbia was shot down by a Czech gunman. This led to a series of raids on Czech Socialists and the result was that the Australian Government panicked and decided to ban Kisch from entering Australia.

Although Egon Kisch had a British visa, on arrival at Fremantle he had been denied entry to Australia on the grounds that he was actively involved in Communist propaganda, and his passport was seized. In Parliament, Menzies issued the unfortunate statement: 'Kisch shall *not* set foot on Australian soil.' Joan was placed in a position of divided loyalties between her support of Kisch as a fellow Jew and her friendship with her old university chum Robert Menzies. She could have backed out at this stage. But having recently returned from Europe, she knew that Kisch could face a firing squad if he were shipped back to Nazi Germany, where he had already spent a terrible period in a concentration camp.

Joan decided her sympathies *had* to lie with Kisch. She had prepared hundreds of cases for her father in attempts to rescue hapless Chinese immigrants who, along with their families, were forbidden to enter Australia by Customs officials acting under the 'White Australia Policy' and detained on board ship. She decided to obtain a writ of *habeas corpus* and demand that the ship's master should produce Kisch in court, where the matter could be argued on legal grounds.

As the *Strathaird*, with Kisch aboard, approached Port Melbourne, Joan was taken out to it by launch. She boarded the ship and demanded that Captain Carter release Kisch, who, she told him firmly, was being detained illegally. She was allowed to meet Kisch, a small, dark-haired man with a moustache, who seemed stunned by the furore that his speaking tour had aroused in Australia. The Captain refused to allow Joan to take Kisch back with her to Melbourne.

The following morning, Joan, along with Kisch's friend Mrs Aarons and a justice of the peace, returned to the ship, now moored against the dock. The affidavit from Mrs Aarons was signed and sealed but once again they had to leave the ship without Kisch. There was no High Court judge available. Joan went into the Practice Court and demanded that Captain Carter show due cause why a writ of *habeas corpus* should not be issued to produce Kisch in court, as he already had a valid entry visa. The writ was issued. The faithful Miss Caffrey sped down to the ship and served it on the Captain. But the Commonwealth Government countered this action by seeking an adjournment, pleading through their solicitor that instructions from Canberra were on their way.

On her return to the courtroom Joan was besieged by journalists and photographers. But now top legal names had been brought in against her. The legal expert acting for the Commonwealth Government insisted that Kisch, as an alien, had no right to claim admittance to Australia. To Joan's despair, and that of the committee who had retained her, the court's decision was telephoned to the ship, the gangway was drawn up and the *Strathaird* made ready to depart. The waiting crowd saw the desperate Kisch, terrified of being sent back, appear on deck, climb over the rails and jump six metres down onto the wharf below. He landed badly, his leg crumpled under him, and remained motionless. (Later it was discovered he had broken his leg in two places.) The waiting police pounced on the unfortunate Kisch, dragged him screaming with pain up the gangplank and back on board. Those watching felt it was like some terrible scene in a South American dictatorship. All over Australia people of conscience were appalled.

Joan maintained that the police had seized Kisch unlawfully, as by jumping he had actually 'landed' on Victorian soil complete with a valid visa. Her father urged Joan to try to board the ship and accompany Kisch to Sydney. Although she always had at least two domestic staff at home, she did not wish to spend months away from her husband. She feared the case would drag on for months or years. She believed it was better for the extreme left-wing Sydney barrister Christian Jollie-Smith to take over, as she was a close friend of Katherine Susanah Prichard.

Time proved her decision the right one: the legal battle to free Kisch took a long time. Kisch was arrested by New South Wales police, given the infamous dictation test in Gaelic, a language which he had no chance of understanding, and sentenced to six months hard labour as an illegal immigrant. An appeal was made to the High Court and Kisch, now the subject of front-page headlines, was freed. Joan and Mannie followed the case with horror. It was a low point in Australian history.

Joan's starring role in the Kisch affair, and the fact Jollie-Smith had taken over the case, meant that a file was opened on her as a 'suspected person' by the consular authorities. An additional entry was added to her file, claiming that Mrs Rosanove had 'revolutionary tendencies', having chaired an anti-war meeting addressed by Jessie Street, whose father was a member of the squattocracy.

Twenty years later, when applying for a visa to visit America, Joan was shown her top-secret dossier, which contained the text of an anti-war speech by Jessie Street given at the meeting Joan had chaired. It looked as though the authorities would deny her an American visa. Quick-witted as ever, Joan pointed at her elegant hat and fur coat and demanded: 'Do I *look* like a revolutionary? I have defended many criminals, but that doesn't mean I *believe* in crime.' She was granted her American visa – but only after she had filled out a statutory declaration that she was not, and had never been, a Communist.

What was 'revolutionary' about Joan was that in the 1930s, when society decreed that wives of professional men who could afford to support them should not work, she insisted on continuing her career. She wrote:

I look on life primarily as a barrister for that is my chosen career ... I think that every women, married or otherwise, is better with a career. A career, in my eyes, offers an outlet for the enthusiasm and abounding energy of every intelligent woman ... [Her] children are better off, for they learn to be self-reliant and in addition, probably see more of their mothers than those children whose mother [has] so much time on her hands that she is at the beck and call of every bridge-playing and golfing friend. The mother who is engaged in carving out a career for herself tends to give up more of her spare time to her children than would otherwise be the case. Also, I think the woman who is actively engaged in the work of the world keeps young in mind as well as appearance. And both of these things are desirable in her children's eyes.

The statement that a woman has no business taking up a career because her husband is able to support her is utterly ridiculous. We would not dream of saying that a man who is married to a rich woman, however great her riches, was justified in not working. It is my opinion that a woman should enter the field of work on an even footing with men. Her fees should be the same as a man's, not only because her work is equally good, but because she must on no account undercut the work of her masculine rival, who may be the sole supporter of his family.

But even then, success is not allowed to be hers – it is said of her 'she has a brain like a man', although I can never see why it is not considered the hallmark of success to have a brain like a *woman*! To have a career, and at the same time to be a wife and mother requires a cast-iron constitution, an equable temperament and a sense of humour ... Married life is the most difficult thing in the world as I find out in the course of my work. ... Marriage is a partnership, which to be successful ... calls for the deepest commitment on both sides ... and for wisdom, tact and understanding – and once again it is invariably up to the woman to provide them![8]

So that Joan and Mannie could sometimes forget the stress and pressure of work, they bought a block of land close to the beach on the Mornington Peninsula and hired architect Roy Grounds to design them a family weekend retreat. Their main home was called 'Medlore', a clever word play on their joint professions, so they named their beach house 'Little Medlore'.

In addition to her heavy workload, Joan found time to give lectures to women's groups about much needed reforms to the divorce laws, which she believed utterly disadvantaged women. She also campaigned for uniform divorce laws in each State and believed women should be allowed to serve on juries – from which, at that time, they were barred.

Joan's quick mind would often enable her to win a case by turning unexpected evidence to her client's advantage, no matter how unpromising it seemed. One of her clients, a woman suing for divorce on the grounds of her husband's cruelty, explained to the Court how he had thrashed her with a whip. The husband's barrister brought in the whip in question as an exhibit, saying it was only a riding crop, not a stockwhip. Joan remembered her childhood, when she had attended race meetings with her parents. When it was her turn to address the Court she picked up the riding crop.

'My client *never* implied she had been thrashed with a stockwhip', she declared, and went on to tell the Court how riding crops were used by jockeys for the express purpose of thrashing their horses past the winning post. She held the whip in her hand as she spoke and 'absent-mindedly' cracked it a few times against the mahogany bar table, smiling pleasantly at the judge as she did so.

The judge got the message and Joan's client got her divorce, on most favourable terms.

In 1940, the Rosanoves were delighted when Peg married a fourth-year medical student, Graeme Larkins. The couple had two sons; now in her mid-forties, Joan became a grandmother.

During World War II, Joan practised from rooms in Chancery House and during the war, because many male barristers were away in the armed forces, her legal practice became busier than ever. The presence of American troops in Australia and the prolonged absence of many husbands led to an increasing number of marriage breakdowns.

After the war, Joan and Mannie took another overseas trip to Britain and Europe, and returned to Melbourne in 1949, just before their old friend Bob Menzies became Prime Minister.

Joan Rosanove was admitted to the bar in New South Wales shortly after resigning from the Roll of Counsel of the Victorian Bar. Thereafter, she practised exclusively as a barrister. But she still had her teenage dreams of practising from Selborne Chambers, still Melbourne's most exclusive address for barristers. After her previous humiliating rejection over twenty years earlier, for her Selborne Chambers became more than just an address on a letterhead: it represented acceptance as an equal by her male colleagues. She could easily have rented rooms in Equity Chambers, where she had many friends; but she had decided that if she was not accepted by her male colleagues in Selborne Chambers, she would work nowhere else.

While she waited for rooms to fall vacant, Joan ran her legal practice from the Supreme Court Library.[9] However, a hint reached her on the legal grapevine that seeing clients in there was frowned upon by the upper echelons of the legal fraternity. Joan thought laterally and came up with a novel idea on how to achieve her ambition to enter Selborne Chambers – by working as 'reader' or pupil to a male barrister, which meant she would have to share his rooms. She believed once she was in chambers she could win the barristers over to accepting her. Edward Ellis, a barrister younger than herself both in years and practice, was greatly tickled by the idea that the famous Joan Rosanove would work as his 'reader'. Although, in theory, Ellis was meant to be instructing her in the practice of law, everyone in legal circles knew this was only a device to get Rosanove into Selborne Chambers. At this stage in her career, there were no objections to her presence. In jubilation she had her dingy room repainted in brilliant Matisse-like colours, which made some of the more crusty old barristers complain that it looked more like a boudoir than legal chambers.

It had taken Joan Rosanove twenty-five years to climb the glass ladder but her persistence had paid off. She had defied prejudice and achieved her long-held ambition to work from Selborne Chambers.

Joan was above all a practical person, and she always gave her clients excellent advice on their courtroom appearances, something many barristers did not bother to do.

'If you *look* good, you'll *feel* good', she advised women clients, especially those receiving legal aid. Joan knew only too well that the poor and needy rarely received sympathy in court.

Remembering how Billy Hughes had taken advantage of her inexperience by fiddling with his hearing aid, Joan acquired a long black-and-ivory cigarette holder, which she used as a theatrical prop. During the 1940s and 1950s, no one was aware of the dangers of smoking; everyone smoked, from film stars to factory workers.

At a Vice-Regal levée in the Queen's Hall of the Victorian Parliament House, yet another public humiliation lay in store for her. An open invitation, requesting barristers to attend the levée, appeared on the notice board at Selborne Chambers. Joan had been appearing in a suburban court; returning to the city, she changed into her black silk legal gown and black high-heeled shoes. An exception to attend an all-male Vice-Regal function had been made for a Victorian woman MP, Fanny Brownbill, and Joan assumed that this would apply to her as well.

But no. She found that the Victorian establishment was as hidebound as ever. As she waited alongside her male colleagues to be presented to Governor Sir Dallas Brooks, a uniformed Parliament House attendant approached and whispered a firm request for her to leave. Joan allowed herself to be led away through the dingy back corridors and shown out like a tradesman. This time, she was more amused than annoyed. However, the whole affair made her even more determined to continue fighting against male discrimination.

In 1951, Joan Rosanove addressed a meeting of the Legal Women's Association, urging women's organisations and women lawyers to work for more rational divorce laws which would benefit women rather than men. Women had few rights over property when they divorced and stood to lose a great deal. The law was also most unjust when dealing with adultery. A woman could be divorced if found guilty of *one* single act of adultery. But a woman wishing to divorce her husband for adultery had to prove it had taken place *repeatedly*, or else produce firm evidence of adultery coupled with several acts of cruelty. She had to obtain evidence from a detective who would stand up in court and say he had seen the husband in bed with another woman. Obtaining this evidence was often expensive and difficult.

Joan was outraged by the hypocrisy of this double standard by which men and women were judged. She wrote: 'I feel ashamed that in spite of all my attempts I have never been able to alter the provision that a woman may not sue for divorce after producing proof of one act of adultery.'

In 1954, she compiled an exhaustive survey of the current divorce laws in the various States of the Commonwealth together with her proposed changes. Her report was published in the *Australian Law Journal* later that year. She found curious anomalies in the attitude of each State towards the grounds for divorce for women petitioners. In Queensland, habitual drunkenness did not qualify a woman to seek a divorce. Laws governing divorce for bigamy, sodomy and bestiality varied in each State. However, in male-dominated Australia little notice was taken of Joan's proposed reforms.

Not until five years after her review was published did the Commonwealth Attorney-General, Sir Garfield Barwick, introduce a Matrimonial Causes Bill in Parliament, embodying many of the reforms which Joan Rosanove had recommended. It was not until 1975, the year following Joan's death, that the Family Law Act was passed by the Commonwealth Government, abolishing 'fault' in marriage from the Statute book and making family law uniform throughout the Commonwealth.

In 1954, Joan decided to make a valiant attempt to become Australia's first-ever female Queen's Counsel. Male barristers who had entered the profession years after her had taken silk and then been appointed judges. Why should promotion be denied her just because she was a woman?

Joan was now so successful she could afford to take a drop in income if male solicitors would not give her the more expensive briefs normally handled by QCs. When Chief Justice Sir Edmond Herring summoned her to his Chambers to discuss her application for silk, he was amazed to learn just how much Mrs Rosanove was earning from legal practice.

The reply from the Chief Justice's office, when it finally came, was humiliating. Yet another 'kick in the teeth' for Joan Rosanove:

> I have very reluctantly come to the conclusion that it would be wrong for me to grant your application. I am very sorry to have to disappoint you but personal considerations cannot be allowed to weigh with me in the exercise of such an important function as the granting of silk.

The Chief Justice's decision was certainly a blow to Joan Rosanove's self-esteem. But once again she followed her own maxim: 'when kicked look as if you had not noticed'. She gained additional strength from the fact that her Jewish ancestors had fought for centuries against prejudice and never given up.

Resolutely, she continued to apply to take silk and become a QC whenever a male barrister years junior to her sent her a notice informing her that he had applied. But Joan was continually passed over in favour of more junior male applicants and eventually, at the request of her daughter Peg, who thought it was undignified to continue trying in the face of such prejudice, Joan Rosanove closed her 'Queen's Counsel Application' file.

The general opinion was that Joan Rosanove had been shabbily treated: dozens of her colleagues and even some judges sympathised with her. Premier John Cain (Senior) enquired why she had been passed over and was informed Mrs Rosanove's practice was 'too specialised', but everyone knew that other highly specialised barristers had been granted silk. Joan's rejection become something of a *cause célèbre* when the famous poet and feminist Mary Gilmore (*q.v.*) wrote to the United Association of Women in Sydney requesting *their* support to nominate Joan Rosanove as a judge or Queen's Counsel. Mary Gilmore's submission pointed out that Joan Rosanove had a 'long stable and notable career in Law. She is of suitable age and her citizenship [possibly a veiled reference to Joan's Jewish background] is impeachable. As a barrister she stands high. I do not know of any other woman whose standing in the Courts is higher.'

In 1962, Joan and her husband were on a working holiday in San Francisco when Peg sent them a cable informing them that the

Adelaide 'establishment' barrister and solicitor Roma Mitchell (*q.v.*) had just been appointed Australia's first female Queen's Counsel. Joan was naturally disappointed she had been pipped to the post by a woman younger than herself and less senior in law (Roma Mitchell had been admitted to the Bar in 1936, seventeen years after Joan Rosanove). Hiding her hurt Joan quipped that 'she couldn't have heard the news in a nicer place'.

Joan knew full well that Roma Mitchell also specialised in matrimonial and divorce law.[10] She was deeply hurt, although she admired Roma Mitchell for her philanthropic activities and as Governor of South Australia.

In 1964, the Chief Justice of Victoria retired. The following year, on 16 November, Attorney General Arthur Rylah announced the appointment of eight new Queen's Counsels. Among them was the valiant, determined, dedicated Joan Rosanove, undisputed leader of the Victorian Bar in matrimonial and divorce law. Mrs Joan Rosanove, QC: her appointment had taken her eleven years from her initial application.

Getting your wish sometimes has hidden drawbacks. Queen's Counsels command higher fees and are usually only briefed for more important cases. As a QC, Joan Rosanove's actual workload was no lighter. Although she now had fewer cases, the work that did come her way was even more complex and demanding than previously. As Victoria's only female QC, Joan was now a highly public figure in the media. She could not afford to make any mistakes. Because men had the money and the power, her clients, formerly 60% women and 40% men, now became 75% men and only 25% women. Slowly her practice was reduced. As her fees were now higher, many of her clients preferred to employ a man rather than a woman, however brilliant that woman might be.

In 1959, the close-knit Rosanove family suffered a bitter blow when Peg's husband, brilliant Dr Graeme Larkins, died of a brain haemorrhage at the age of thirty-nine. Showing the same courage as her mother, Peg Larkins enrolled at Melbourne University and became a first-year law student while her son was in second year.

Peg would subsequently remarry a Dutch-born lawyer, Theodore Lusink. In 1966, Joan Rosanove QC moved the admission of her daughter Peg Lusink to practise law, her junior in support being Joan's grandson, John Larkins. Peg Lusink went on to have a highly successful career in law and became a distinguished judge in the Family Court and Adjunct Professor of Law at Bond University.

As Joan and Mannie aged, they finally moved to a new home they had built behind their Frankston beach house. On 2 June 1969, Joan celebrated fifty years in the legal profession. Eventually they both retired. Joan, ever the skilled negotiator, reached a peaceable accord with her husband that many married women would envy: Dr Mannie Rosanove, the perfect husband, took over much of the cooking as well as the work of running the household, smiling and saying gently that he was better at housekeeping than his adored wife.

In 1970, when Victoria's first female QC was in her seventies, a female journalist queried why brilliant Joan Rosanove had never received the award of DBE. It is significant that through her long and successful career, Joan Rosanove never received any royal or Commonwealth award, nor any lucrative appointment to a Royal Commission or any Government QANGO – these being reserved for her male colleagues.

In April 1974, Joan was admitted to the local hospital, ostensibly for rest and relaxation. She was now seventy-eight. But Peg Lusink felt instinctively that something was very wrong with her mother. She took the afternoon off work and she and her husband collected her father from his home and they drove to the hospital. They found Joan in the sunroom. Peg described her mother 'surrounded by four or five obviously enchanted old boys'. Not wanting to alarm her mother, Peg pretended they were only there because her husband had business in the area. Joan accepted that, then berated her husband gently for bringing her the wrong shade of nail varnish. Even in hospital she insisted on looking as immaculate as ever. Mannie promised to bring her the right shade when he came back that evening.

As they were about to leave, Peg Lusink, who describes herself as 'not into fortune-telling, crystals or beads' had a terrible sense of foreboding that she might not see her mother again. She had already kissed her mother goodbye. Now she recrossed the hospital's polished floor and kissed her again.

Joan looked surprised. 'What's that for?' she asked.

Not wanting to sound alarmist, Peg replied: 'Oh well, you're not such a bad old girl! And if I can still entrance the old boys when I'm your age, I'll think I'm doing all right too.'

Joan, with her usual sense of humour, burst out laughing, and on that happy note Mannie and the Lusinks departed.

About 5.30 that afternoon, Peg Lusink entered her Melbourne apartment and found her husband on the phone to Mannie.

'Oh no, Poppa!' he exclaimed.

Peg's heart missed a beat. Her immediate response was: 'Mum's dead.'

'My God, Peg, how *did* you know?' her husband cried out.[11]

The remarkable Joan Rosanove died as she had lived, with style and panache. She had suffered a fatal heart attack while talking animatedly to an admiring audience, her hair immaculate as ever and her face beautifully made up – but with her nails unpolished.[12]

In 1999, a block of barristers' chambers with the name: 'Joan Rosanove Chambers' engraved about its door in large letters opened in Melbourne's Londsdale Street. This granite-faced building was named in honour of the formidable woman barrister who, seventy-five years earlier, was banned from Melbourne's all-male Selbourne Chambers. From the grave, Joan Rosanove QC had won her last battle.

# CHAPTER FIFTEEN

## Roma Flinders Mitchell
### *(1913–2000)*
### THE LAWYER WHO BLAZED A TRAIL FOR AUSTRALIAN WOMEN
### AND WOMEN INTERNATIONALLY

Over 2000 people attended the state funeral and requiem mass for Dame Roma, which took place on a warm March day in Adelaide's Cathedral of St Francis Xavier. Among the mourners were the Governor-General, Sir William Deane, the governors of most States, politicians and people from all walks of life, representing the many charities and arts organisations with which Dame Roma had been involved. So many people wished to pay their final respects to a woman who had been deeply loved as well as honoured, that crowds of mourners spilled out of the cathedral porch and onto the pavement.

Inside the cathedral, roses and wreaths of late summer flowers sent by relatives, friends and organisations covered the coffin and decorated the cathedral. Eulogies spoken by the Governor-General and the Premier of South Australia were personal and deeply moving. Both men acknowledged Dame Roma's many outstanding achievements. These included her appointment as the first female Queen's Counsel in 1962; three years later her appointment as the first female Supreme Court Judge; then as the first female Vice-Chancellor of the University of Adelaide in 1983 (and the first woman in the British Commonwealth to hold such an appointment). She was also the first Chairman of the Australian Human Rights Commission and its representative at the United Nations. From 1991–1996 Dame Roma became the first female Governor of South Australia, the first woman governor to be appointed in Australia.

Roma Mitchell's achievements were all the more remarkable because her rise to prominence took place in a conservative and male-dominated era at a period when women found it hard to gain positions of trust in high places. Roma Mitchell, 'the quiet achiever', was no red radical and initially described herself as 'a conservative sort of feminist'. In later life she frequently expressed the belief that all public appointments should be made on competence and merit rather than quotas. By the 1990s, when I talked to her about the outstanding Australian women whose lives and achievements I had chosen to relate, she acknowledged that she had changed with changing times. She preferred to work from the inside at changing public opinion rather than by confrontation, which she felt solved very little. She would answer traditionalists by saying gently but firmly: 'Yes, I used to think like that but now I've moved on.'

Dame Roma was not born into a background of power and prestige, she achieved them by her own efforts but remained unchanged by them. A deeply religious woman from her youth, she had a delightful sense of humour and scant use for pomp and ceremony. As Governor of South Australia she insisted on walking from Government House in North Terrace to the cathedral in Victoria Square for morning Mass, greeting fellow Australians on her walk. Some of the staff at Government House were amazed when each week the Governor of South Australia would put on a battered pair of sneakers and walk to the local shopping mall to make her own purchases; she felt that it was important she should keep in touch with the concerns of ordinary people, and this was one of her ways of doing so.

Roma Mitchell's childhood in Adelaide, city of churches, was far from affluent. She was born the year before the outbreak of World War I, the second daughter of Harold and Maude Mitchell, a couple who had already lost another daughter.[1] Her father was a lawyer who went away to fight in the trenches in France. When Roma turned four her mother received the dreaded telegram containing the news that her husband had been killed in action.

Finances were strained. Maude Mitchell had not been trained for any profession and was unable to earn enough to support her daughters, Ruth and Roma, in the way she and her husband had planned. Maude now realised very forcibly that tertiary education was vital for her clever daughters if they were to achieve good careers, and she encouraged them to study and read in their free time. Roma Mitchell always said how close she had been to her mother.

> Being a widow wasn't easy in those days. The fact that my mother was not trained for any occupation other than home duties was one of the things that influenced her and she was determined that her daughters would have a career that they could follow. For as long as I remember I wanted to be a lawyer and I don't quite know why.[2]

Since her father had been a lawyer, possibly the law was in Roma Mitchell's blood: it would certainly become her passion. The Mitchell girls lived very modestly; their mother made all their clothes, struggling to keep up appearances on very little money. Through her mother's economies and self-denial it was possible for Roma to attend

St Aloysius College in Adelaide. She showed great aptitude and determination from an early age, but described herself as a small skinny girl, poor at sport. She was unsure about her appearance, regarding herself as 'no great beauty'. A keen and conscientious student, she liked French and debating best and eventually became dux of the school. She told me: 'I was always willing at school to push *for* things that I thought were right and to push *against* anything that I thought was an injustice. I was regarded as the spokesperson for our entire class.'

She won the coveted David Murray scholarship to study law at the University of Adelaide and soon proved herself as a hardworking and brilliant student. Roma, still extremely slim, was energetic and highly disciplined in everything she undertook. However, friends told her mother that it was a waste of money for her to study at university. 'A woman can't get anywhere,' they said.

Adelaide was still in the grip of the Great Depression and Dame Roma described how:

> on the way to uni, I would pass Kintore Avenue where men were lined up waiting to get their ration cards. I was horrified to learn that was *all* they got, a ration card which they could exchange for certain groceries ... I felt that justice demanded that we shouldn't have another Depression. It strongly influenced me to study law because I thought that through it people could be helped.[3]

Just as she was about to finish her degree she read a Department of Foreign Affairs notice calling for graduate employees; it did not specify gender. Although Roma Mitchell hoped to become a lawyer, it was doubly hard during those Depression years for a woman to be accepted into law. Even though Roma had graduated as the outstanding student of her year, she was not at all confident that a law firm would accept her. So she applied to the Department of Foreign Affairs. She was in fact relieved when they replied saying they only wanted *men* with good law degrees. 'I don't think I would have been a very diplomatic diplomat,' she said in later years.[4]

Women in the late nineteenth and early twentieth centuries had great trouble getting *access* to study law, by the time Roma Mitchell left university, they had considerable trouble gaining *employment* in the law. However, as a young graduate Roma Mitchell was fortunate. In 1934, at the age of twenty-one, she was appointed managing clerk in an Adelaide city practice. Only ten law graduates succeeded in finding legal employment that year: nine men ... and Roma.

One of only a handful of female lawyers practising in South Australia in the 1930s and paid far less than her male counterparts, Roma Mitchell worked very hard and took on cases which male lawyers did not want, such as domestic problems involving drunken or violent husbands and divorce. (Her work, in fact, echoed exactly that of Joan Rosanove in Melbourne.) Barristers and judges were always male, middle-class and usually Anglican. Clever, hardworking Roma Mitchell's ambition was to become a barrister; in this restrictive period for women, she did not look further – the mere idea of a woman becoming a judge would have seemed ridiculous at that time.

In 1934, at the tender age of twenty-one, Roma Mitchell achieved her wish. She was admitted to the Bar and for the next twenty-eight years she worked as a barrister representing clients in the courts. It was a tough job demanding long hours and complete commitment. She said:

> You need a fair amount of courage. It's a fearsome thing at first to fight for people in front of a judge and jury. You have to have a certain amount of determination and a certain amount of persistence. ... Even the attire was difficult for a woman. In summertime in non-air-conditioned Courts I didn't like wearing stiff collars and thick jackets. The men were accustomed to wearing dark suits: I was accustomed to wearing sleeveless dresses. When it became very hot the judge would suggest we might like to remove our wigs ... I was always hoping he might say 'Let's remove our stiff collars' but he never did![5]

Her work was noticed and brought her promotion – eventually she became a partner in the city law firm she had joined. This was most unusual at that period, when the law was considered a male club and law courts 'unfeminine' places. Specialising in matrimonial causes, Roma also lectured on law at the University of Adelaide, her *alma mater*. During her last year in practice as an Adelaide lawyer, Roma Mitchell was chosen as the Australian representative at a United Nations seminar on the Status of Women in Family Law.

That same year she became the first woman in Australia to be appointed a Queen's Counsel. This (as well as her subsequent appointment as a judge later) sent shock waves through the legal system; for her part, Roma Mitchell was in turn extremely shocked by such a reaction. Working long hours she became a noted advocate, continuing to specialise – again like Joan Rosanove in Melbourne – in matrimonial law and the breakdown of marriage. She said:

> I was very gratified when I became a QC because that was really the recognition within the legal profession of achievement as a barrister. I was the first woman in Australia to do this and I really did take pleasure in it.[6]

As a QC, Roma Mitchell supported the efforts of the League of Women Voters to change South Australian legislation so that women could sit on juries and the arguments she put to Premier Tom Playford proved successful. She also advocated equal pay for equal work. She said:

> In my experience, the law client doesn't care two hoots about the sex of the Counsel. What he or she wants is somebody to win the case. But briefs to barristers come from the solicitors, most of whom are men. I have seen far too many women solicitors who give good service to legal practices working as managed clerks or as employed solicitors – but when it comes to promotion they are passed over for young men ... And it's not for lack of qualifications. I think these days women have got to have a certain amount of gumption and get out and make their own legal firms.[7]

In 1965, just before she was due to assume office as President of the South Australian Law Society, Don Dunstan, then Attorney-General in South Australia's newly elected Labor Government, recommended to Premier Frank Walsh that Roma Mitchell be appointed a judge of the Supreme Court in that State. This meant that she became the first woman ever to be appointed to an Australian superior court. She said of Don Dunstan, 'I doubt if anyone else in this day and age would have pushed so hard for a woman in this job.'

Even though it was a huge honour to be chosen as Australia's first woman judge, she could not help feeling some regret. She had greatly enjoyed being a barrister – the work, the courtroom, the arguments. In fact she was quite sad to be leaving the Bar.

'A WOMAN JUDGE!' exclaimed the newspaper feature writers, while some of her fellow judges wondered what the world was coming to as they passed around the port in their exclusively male clubs.

Roma Mitchell's own reaction was characteristic:

I was surprised when I was asked to accept the appointment of Supreme Court Judge, because once again there had never been a woman on the bench in an Australian court nor in England at that stage. As far as being a woman is concerned, I am hopeful that, in my lifetime, appointments such as this one will not excite comment.

Ironically, when she retired from the Bench in 1983, eighteen years later, she was *still* the only woman judge of a superior court in Australia. When she was first appointed there were endless legal wrangles over how she should be addressed. Roma Mitchell settled the matter by firmly refusing to be called Mrs Justice, Ms Justice or even Miss Justice. She wished to be addressed as Justice Mitchell, pure and simple, an appellation which blazed a trail for female judges in other countries. As a judge she was outstanding and a pivotal member of two of the landmark State Supreme Courts in Australia's legal history, the Bray Court and the King Court.

On her appointment to the Supreme Court Bench in 1965, Justice Mitchell observed:

Women should be able to take whatever place they are fitted to take in the professions. I do not mean that a woman should ever be appointed to any significant office merely because she is a woman. But women's intellectual and other attainments should be recognised objectively. I am sure that they are being more widely appreciated nearly everywhere in today's world.[8]

Sir William Deane related an incident which reveals Dame Roma's sense of humour. During an interview in her early years at the Supreme Court, a journalist interviewing her inquired brashly: 'You are not married?'

'I am not,' she replied.

'And do you drive a motor car?'

'I do not.'

Undeterred by her terse replies, the journalist pressed on. 'The Chief Justice, Dr Bray, is also unmarried. Is there any chance you might get together?'

Keeping a straight face Dame Roma replied, 'No, that would be no good at all. He doesn't drive a car *either*.'

In 1975, after three years as Chair of a South Australian Committee of Inquiry into Criminal Law, Justice Mitchell was selected to deliver the prestigious Boyer Lectures, broadcast by the ABC. She chose as her title 'The Web of the Criminal Law', and her lectures are considered by lawyers to have been among the most insightful analyses of criminal law and its problems in Australia ever made. She rarely gave press interviews and was scathing about magistrates and judges 'who went out of their way to attract the attention of the press'.

Busy as she was, she still found time to do things for other people and think about them. As an instance, she wrote me a letter of congratulation when I was awarded a Winston Churchill Fellowship to study Italian Renaissance Art in Florence, a topic dear to her heart as she had personally funded the Churchill Fellowship in the area of the arts. The Winston Churchill Memorial Trust was founded in 1965, the year in which Sir Winston died, 'to reward proven achievement with further opportunity in the pursuit of excellence for the enrichment of Australian society'. Over the years, Churchill Fellowships have enabled many hundreds of Australians to enlarge their field of practice through travel and study overseas. Roma Mitchell became a member of the South Australian Regional Committee in 1965, then became its Chair. Subsequently, she was appointed Chair and then Federal President of the Churchill Memorial Trust, and finally its Patron.

Elvie Munday, the Trust's Executive Officer, and a good friend of Dame Roma, told me that:

Dame Roma had a wonderful way of combining her judicial role with warm personal relationships. She had a great sense of humour coupled with an extreme sense of fair play. The Trust gained much from her wise counsel over the years and she has left a void which I do not think will be filled in my lifetime.

Roma Mitchell held strong views on issues such as the need for changed attitudes towards working wives, refresher courses for women graduates wanting to return to work after raising children, the need for housework to be shared by married couples and a unified retirement age for men and women. In 1994, at a Women's Week meeting organised by the Trades and Labour Council, she said: 'As women's roles in the work force increase in number and in variety, their influence in the unions should also increase.'

Dame Roma was a staunch advocate of equality, justice and human rights. Here is her advice to women:

> If you have a particular ambition, follow it. Don't be put off by thinking it's too difficult. You just *have* to go on trying at the thing you think you do best.[8]

Between 1981–86 she became the first Chair of the Human Rights Commission, whose establishment in Australia she had lobbied for over a long period. She believed the Commission had to be controversial in order to be effective and she never shied away from tough topics. She used her influence to advance the human rights of disadvantaged Australians in every field, particularly indigenous Australians. She created something of a furore when she announced that boys in kindergarten and early primary school should be taught to play with dolls. (JUDGE URGES BOYS TO PLAY WITH DOLLS! the newspaper announced.)

In 1983, her seventieth birthday brought with it retirement from the Bench ... and a new beginning. Later that year she was appointed Chancellor of the University of Adelaide, the first woman to be honoured in this way. As Chancellor (from 1983–90), she was always very keen to see more women appointed to university teaching positions and to the boards of public companies. She said:

> Women should not be forced to achieve. Why should we? But we cannot afford to be complacent. I think that, on the whole, there is still a problem of prejudice. There is still a problem of power ... I think we have still got a lot to achieve.

Dame Roma always claimed that she had so many interests and friends that she never felt lonely. Why did she never marry? Was the fact that she did not have a husband and children one of the reasons that she was able to achieve so much? She always resolutely refused to discuss her private life, claiming that it was entirely her business. However, those close to her claimed she was very sensitive about a love affair when she was very young with someone she felt she could never marry. In an interview with feminist author Susan Mitchell for her book *The Matriarchs*, Dame Roma denied that she had fallen in love with a man who died in World War II, and abruptly changed the subject. In subsequent interviews with other journalists she refused to mention the topic again.[9] If journalists asked too many personal questions she would clam up. 'I'm of that generation that keeps oneself to oneself,' she would say.

It is possible that the young Roma Mitchell fell in love with a married lawyer or barrister, and her strong religious feeling would not permit the relationship to develop. It does appear that there was someone in her life, years ago, but she steadfastly refused to mention his name. Ruth, Dame Roma's elder sister, was her closest confidante. It is likely Ruth would have known who the man was, but she is no longer alive, so her sister's secret died with her. All this is speculation, but perhaps it makes Roma Mitchell seem more human to realise that such an outstanding woman may have suffered the pangs of love like the rest of us.

Dame Roma often said that the Women's Movement had brought great changes into Australian life, and that what had been very rare when she was young, that a woman could have a career and be a wife and mother, was now possible for most women. She emphasised the progress that had been made, especially in a restrictive area like legal practice, saying that this had benefited women as a whole.

Like Joan Rosanove, Roma Mitchell experienced discrimination during her long legal career, but she dealt with it in a different way. She was less confrontational than Rosanove and lacked the vibrant sex appeal of her Melbourne counterpart. Roma Mitchell never thought of using her femininity in court, as Rosanove did to such devastating effect. She disapproved of such gambits. When I interviewed Dame Roma, she told me firmly: 'I think it's fatal to ask for concessions for being a woman. Never ask or give quarter. *Never* play the sex game at work. It can rebound on you.'

On a lighter note, Dame Roma also suffered from that hairy old excuse proffered to so many professional women during the early years of this century: 'We'd like to give you the job, my dear, but unfortunately we don't have any lavatories for women.'

When Roma Mitchell started practising at the bar there *were* no lavatories for lady barristers, so she was forced to use the public lavatories, risking a confrontation with a jury member or a dissatisfied spectator from the public gallery. By the time she was Acting Chief Justice she had become much more confident about women's rights issues; she issued instructions for a latch to be put on the door and used the barristers' lavatory, regardless of what anyone thought.

In addition to Dame Roma's interest in the Winston Churchill Memorial Trust, she was an excellent Vice-President of ADFAS, the Australian Decorative and Fine Arts Society, an organisation staffed by devoted volunteers which has over thirty branches in Australian cities and country towns. ADFAS is the offshoot of the huge British organisation NADFAS with its huge pool of specialised lecturers, who make lecture tours of Australia. ADFAS has brought to Australia a deeper knowledge of all the arts, and in addition the different branches sponsor art prizes and restoration work in churches, museums and galleries, and Dame Roma was a member of the Adelaide branch for many years and attended their lectures.

After being sent by ADFAS to Longreach during a severe drought to give a slide talk about the Australian artist Conrad Martens, I told Dame Roma how much it meant to women in remote country areas to have a chance to extend their knowledge. I added that I felt very humble when some of them told me they had driven for several hours to reach my lecture – and had to drive back that same night. Country members told me about the horrors of drought, including plagues of mice that invaded their homes, and said how pleasant it was to have another topic of conversation. I was finding it hard to continue writing books and lecturing but Dame Roma urged me to continue with art lectures, and gave me the quotes I have used in this short account of her story but politely and firmly refused to reveal any more of her private life. She said that she had grown up at a time when it was considered bad form to explore one's feelings about family and relationships in public and I respect her wishes.

What I most admired about Dame Roma was the fact that, even though she was an incredibly busy person she would become deeply involved whenever she acted as patron to a worthy cause. After retiring from the bench she *personally* delivered meals on wheels to elderly pensioners. As Governor of South Australia from 1991–1996 she always showed a deep interest in the disadvantaged and the homeless and did what she could to help. She was also very much involved in creating opportunities for young people. She travelled around the State attending functions and talking to people at all levels. Roma Mitchell and Leneen Ford (also a lawyer), who was appointed Governor of Queensland in the 1990s, have been two of our most loved and admired State Governors. Leneen Ford, another outstanding woman, as a gesture towards gender equality, appointed a woman as her equerry.

People loved Dame Roma's warmth, her friendliness, her generosity, her courage and her spirit of adventure – on one occasion, she climbed the highest peaks in Irian Jaya. She loved life ... good food, good wine, music, drama, art. She was a true Christian, staunch in the Roman Catholic faith yet ecumenical.

In 1992, Dame Roma was appointed a Companion in the Order of Australia, the highest honour possible, and received the Order's beautiful sunburst medal on its blue and gold ribbon, which she wore with pride on official occasions.

Friends were always hugely important to her. She had the gift of friendship and made close friends in different walks of life. She listed her recreations as cooking, going to the beach, the opera, the theatre, and art and music. She believed firmly in appointment on merit, regardless of gender. By the mid 1980s, men and women had begun to graduate from Australian law schools in equal numbers, yet it is interesting to note that at the time of her death few other women had been appointed as senior counsels or to judicial posts.[10]

Dame Roma was also National President of the Sue Ryder-Cheshire Foundation which, apart from other worthy causes, carries out enormously important work among disadvantaged children. In her will, Dame Roma bequeathed money to the Foundation, as well as to the Winston Churchill Memorial Trust and two other charities. Other influential appointments were those of Chair of the Ministerial Board on Ageing in South Australia, and Patron of Disabled People

International, of the Overseas Aid Bureau, and the Diabetic Association of South Australia. It is a measure of Dame Roma's popularity in the community that every time I have talked about writing this short account of her life, people from all works of life have told me: 'I admired Dame Roma so much, I'm glad you are writing her story.'

Women's causes were always dear to Dame Roma's generous heart. In 1994, she helped launch a tapestry which contained a portrait of herself for the South Australian Women's Suffrage centenary, and remarked:

> I have often been requested to speak at meetings in favour of the proposition that women should receive equal pay for equal work. In theory this was achieved. But in practice, there is still leeway to be made up ... in affording women equal opportunities for promotion and having regard to the fact that women who are mothers ... may necessarily have to put 'on hold' their professional advancement while their children are young.

In June 1999, Governor General Sir William Deane unveiled a life-size bronze statue of Dame Roma 'as a permanent tribute to her lifetime achievement in South Australia'. The statue stands in Prince Henry Gardens, in front of Government House on North Terrace. Aware of her own mortality but, as yet, unaware that she had a fatal bone cancer, Dame Roma donated her papers and correspondence to Adelaide's Mortlock Library, requesting some restrictions over her private correspondence.

In 1999, Dame Roma, the quiet and discreet achiever, was made a Commander of the French Legion d'Honneur. In the week before she died she was invested as a Commander of the Victorian Order, an honour conferred on her by H.M. Queen Elizabeth II. She was to have received this award personally from the Queen on her visit to Canberra in the year 2000. Hearing that Dame Roma was not expected to live very long, Governor-General Sir William Deane cancelled other appointments to visit Dame Roma in hospital and made the award at her bedside shortly before she died.

Not only was Dame Roma greatly admired by men and women in high places but she was held in great affection by ordinary folk throughout the country. In her funeral oration Sir William Deane said:

For my part, I venture to suggest that there has been no better-loved Vice-regal representative in the whole of this land. Her death is an occasion of deep sadness ... but also an occasion for celebration ... A life of wonderful achievements, including an incomparable number of nationally significant firsts, a life which blazed a trail for all Australian women, in law, in government, in academic life, in public and philanthropic service. A life which is truly an inspiration for all Australians.'[11]

# ENDNOTES

## Chapter 1

1. At the time of writing, Sydney's only remaining all-female swimming baths are still at Coogee.
2. Anon, 'Fanny, World Beater', *Sydney Morning Herald*, 29 July 1992.
3. Anon, 'Nude Men and Clothed Women Swam in the Old Domain', *Sydney Morning Herald,* 3 December 1966.
4. See Chapter 7 on Louisa Lawson and her struggles with Rose Scott.
5. Fanny's friends, swimmers Peter Murphy and F.C. Lane, had learned the stroke from a visiting seaman, John William Trudgen, who had in turn learned it from South American Indians on a visit to the estuary of the Rio de la Plata in 1904. See also entry under 'trudgen' in the *Shorter Oxford English Dictionary*, Oxford University Press, Oxford, 1973.
6. Hartung, Greg, 'The Kellerman Legend': obituary of Annette Kellerman in *The Australian*, 7 November 1975. See also entry on Annette Kellerman in *The Australian Encyclopedia*, Vol VI, Grolier Society of Australia, 1977
7. A copy of Annette Kellerman's *Fairy Tales of the South Seas* is in Sydney with other Kellerman memorabilia in the Performing Arts Collection at the Sydney Opera House Museum.
8. New South Wales Ladies' Amateur Swimming Association *Annual Reports*, 1904–11
9. Gordon, Harry, 'The First Heroes', article in *Time* magazine, July 1992.
10. Stell, Marion K., *Half the Race. A History of Australian Women in Sport.* Harper Collins, Sydney, 1991.
11. King, Helen, ed. Radi, Heather, *200 Australian Women*. Women's Redress Press, Sydney, 1988. See also King, Helen, entry in *The Australian Dictionary of Biography*, Vol 8, *op. cit.*
12. Cited by George Blaikie in 'Great Women of History' in the *Australian Women's Weekly*, 3 November 1982. Unsourced quote.
13. Phillips, Dennis H., *Australian Women at the Olympic Games*. Kangaroo Press, Sydney, 1992.
14. *Op. cit.*

## Chapter 2

1. Gilmore, *Mary, Old Days, Old Ways,* Angus & Robertson, Sydney, 1986.
2. The story of this sudden proposal is credited in several sources to family legend. True or not, it illustrates that Louisa knew very little of her husband's mania for gold before she married him.
3. Details of Henry Lawson's birth are from accounts related by Louisa's daughter, Gertrude, who grew up hearing her mother's reminiscences about this event.
4. Henry Lawson's story *A Child in the Dark* was written to revenge himself on his mother. It presents a portrait of a kind, caring father and a mother 'bad in the head' and 'with nerves', quarrelling with the father in a rundown household without light or running water, unable to cook or clean or do anything except read and write poetry, and neglecting her three (rather than four) children. In his desire for revenge, Henry overplays his theme. Women who are deeply depressed are unable to concentrate, and reading or writing poetry would be impossible.
5. Sheep's intestines were sometimes used for condoms in the bush, but were generally regarded as devices a man would use with a prostitute but not with his wife. See also chapter on Sister Lillie Goodisson.
6. See Matthews, Brian, *Louisa*, McPhee Gribble, Sydney, 1987, for a moving and well-written but fictionalised account of this distressing period of Louisa Lawson's life, also *Louisa Lawson, Collected Poems with Critical Commentaries*, University of New England Centre for Australian Literary Studies, Armidale, 1996.

7   The destructive relationship between Henry Lawson and his mother is covered in some detail in Lorna Ollif's biography *Louisa Lawson*. Rigby, Sydney, 1978, and in Brian Matthew's *Louisa, op. cit.*

8   Matthews, Brian, entry on Henry Lawson, *The Australian Dictionary of Biography*, Vol. 10.,Melbourne University Press, Melbourne, 1986.

9   Radi, Heather, entry on Louisa Lawson, *The Australian Dictionary of Biography. Op cit.*

10  *Ibid.*

11  Lawson, Olive, Ed, *The First Voice of Australian Feminism*: *excerpts from Louisa Lawson's 'The Dawn'*, Simon and Schuster, Sydney, 1989.

12  *The Dawn* was not Australia's first magazine for women, but it was the first to be published entirely by women, with the occasional help from Henry Lawson.

13  Adelaide, Debra, *A Bright and Fiery Troop*, Penguin Books, Melbourne, 1987.

14  *The Dawn*, issue dated October 1889, informs readers that the paper employs ten women.

15  The author was shown an issue of *The Dawn* in which the paper was still white and corners had been rounded off to prevent 'dog-earing'.

16  The first subscription list for *The Dawn* is held in the Lothian Collection of Lawson Papers, La Trobe Library, The State Library of Victoria. It is cited in full in Lawson, Olive, Ed., *The First Voice of Australian Feminism*, *op. cit.*

17  *Ibid.*

18  *The Dawn*, January 1889.

19  Lawson, Olive, Ed., *The First Voice of Australian Feminism*, *Op cit.*

20  *Ibid.*

21  Wilde, Professor W.H., *Courage a' Grace: A Biography of Dame Mary Gilmore*, Melbourne University Press, 1988 gives an excellent account of Mary and Will Gilmore at Cosme and of her relationship with Henry Lawson.

22  *Ibid.* Professor Wilde's biography contains Mary's account of her courtship by Henry Lawson, describes her possessive feelings towards him and the decline and breakdown of his marriage to Bertha. See also important sources in Mary Gilmore's letters. Parts of an autobiographical account, *Henry Lawson and I,* appear as footnotes in Wilde, W. H. and Moore, T. Inglis, Eds, *Letters of Mary Gilmore*, Melbourne University Press, Melbourne 1980, in *Mary Gilmore: A Tribute*, Australasian Book Society, 1965, and in Professor Colin Roderick's biography of Henry Lawson.

23  De Vries-Evans, Susanna, *Historic Sydney.*, Pandanus Press, Brisbane, 2000.

24  Matthews, Brian, *Louisa, op. cit.* Thanks to psychiatrists Dr Marian Tyrer and Dr Lilian Cameron for discussions about the mental states of Louisa Lawson and her son Charles.

25  Lawson, Louisa, *Dert and Do*, published Sydney, 1904, followed in 1905 by *The Lonely Crossing*, a collection of her poems.

26  Matthews, Brian, entry on Henry Lawson, *The Australian Dictionary of Biography, Vol. 10, op. cit.*

27  Louisa Lawson Papers, Mitchell Library, State Library of New South Wales.

28  Matthews, Brian, *Louisa, op. cit.*

29  Eyewitness accounts by Gladesville mental patients reveal how bad conditions were. Little was done in Australia for many years to improve conditions for psychiatric patients in State mental institutions.

# Chapter 3

1   De Vries, Susanna, *Strength of Spirit: Australian Women of Achievement*, Pandanus Press, Brisbane 1997, contains the story of Martha's mother, Ann Caldwell.

2   Gunn, Mrs Aeneas, author of *We of the Never Never*, first published 1907 in London, reprinted Angus & Robertson, Sydney, various editions.

3   Under the Selection Acts, which sought to break up very large land holdings of squatters, free selectors were able to buy a 'selection' on a mortgage.

4   Martha says that Dave 'claimed my hand'.

5   Livingstone Gully was named after a tree on the property on which Surveyor-General Thomas Livingstone Mitchell had carved his name when surveying there. A century and a half later, members of the Cox family still live on Livingstone Gully, and run the historic property.

6 'Dummying' meant land-rich squatters rorting a system designed to help working-class selectors. Using the names of poorer relatives or paid agents, squatters would buy land on a cheap mortgage reserved for selectors, thereby deceiving the Lands Department. To 'peacock' or pick the eyes out of the best land, was the practice whereby squatters (sometimes under false names) bought the good blocks around waterholes and creeks, leaving nothing but marginal areas for selectors. When drought occurred and selectors' sheep and cattle died the squatters would simply buy out the selectors at rock-bottom prices. 'Pre-empting' was the practice whereby selectors took up good land on payment of a deposit before it was subdivided ( a 'pre-emptive' lease). David and Martha Cox lost their land after it was formally subdivided and gazetted for agistment (to feed cattle travelling through the outback). Sometimes a corrupt Lands Department official would be bribed to do this. Later the land could be rezoned for selection and a neighbouring squatter could purchase it.

7 Information about the effects of scurvy kindly supplied by Emeritus Professor John Tyrer, formerly of the School of Medicine, University of Queensland, who in his early years in the medical school treated several bushwomen suffering from this terrible disease, caused by lack of vitamin C derived from fresh vegetables and fruits. Today, as a result of improved diet and the use of refrigeration in the bush, scurvy has all but disappeared.

8 The son of the Inspector of Stock on Brunet Downs, Australia's second largest cattle station, stated that it was generally the half-caste girls, despised by their full-blood husbands, who were pimped out to white men. See also *Coonardoo* a novel by Katharine Susannah Prichard in which her female progagonist, Coonardoo, dies of syphilis.

9 Martha would have known little about scurvy. Not until 1928 was lack of vitamin C isolated by Waugh and King as the cause of scurvy (although as early as 1753, ship's surgeon James Lind wrote a treatise naming the disease and advocating the preventive role of oranges, lemons and limes in diet). After receiving adequate ascorbic acid, the body usually restores fairly quickly. His words were heeded by Cook and other mariners who took limes and lemons on their voyages. Tragically for those in the bush, Lind failed to connect scurvy with the dietary absence of leaf vegetables. Australian farmers often abandoned their vegetable gardens in times of drought and used all available water for drinking, and for cattle and sheep.

10 Mrs Davidson's diet of raw vegetables was the right treatment for scurvy. Bush diets normally consisted of mutton, well-cooked vegetables and potatoes. Salads were not eaten as no one knew the importance of vitamins, and it was thought that raw foods were too tough on the digestion.

11 The John Oxley Library, State Library of Queensland, has no separate entry for Caldwell and it has not been possible to trace the exact site where the property was located near Charleville.

12 A double-seated buggy is a vehicle for two people, drawn by one or two horses.

13 Martha uses 'milepeg' rather than the English 'milestone': milepegs were used by surveyors to establish boundaries.

14 The year was 1887 when Priscilla married.

# Chapter 4

1 Bourdillon, Hilary, *Women As Healers*. Cambridge University Press, Cambridge 1988.
2 Neve, M. Hutton, *This Mad Folly – The History of Australia's Pioneer Women Doctors*, Library of Australian History Sydney, 1980.
3 Forster, Margaret, *Significant Sisters*. Penguin, London, 1986.
4 Kerr, Charles, entry in The *Australian Encyclopaedia*, Vol. 6, Grolier Society of Australia, Sydney, 1983. Gandevia, B, Hostler, A and Simpson, S., *An Annotated Bibliography of the History of Medicine in Australia*. Royal Australasian College of Physicians, Sydney, 1984 and Gandevia, Bryan, *Tears Often Shed – A History of Childbirth in Australia*. Pergamon Press, Sydney, 1978.
5 Neve, M. Hutton in *This Mad Folly see footnote 2*. cites the first medical students in Melbourne as Lilian Alexander, Elizabeth and Annie O'Hara, Helen Sexton, Clara Stone, Grace Vale and Margaret Whyte. *Op. cit.*
6 Neve, M Hutton, *Op. cit.*

[7] Bennion, Elizabeth, *Antique Medical Instruments*. University of California Press, Berkeley, 1979.

[8] Frances, Raelene and Scales, Bruce, *Women at Work in Australia. From the Gold Rush to World War II*. Cambridge University Press, London, 1993.

[9] Kerr, Charles, entry in *The Australian Encyclopedia,* Vol. 6, *op. cit.*

[10] Frances, Raelene and Scales, Bruce, *Women at Work in Australia. From the Gold Rush to World War II. Op. cit.*

[11] In the early 1960s Dr Marion Tyrer won the Dagmar Berne Medal but was not told the sad story of Dagmar's brief career. Interview with Dr Tyrer, 1998.

[12] Neve, M Hutton, '*This* Mad Folly' – The *History of Australia's Pioneer Women Doctors, op. cit.*

[13] Information supplied to M Hutton Neve by Dagmar Berne's sister, Eugenie Berne, later Mrs E N Buswell.

[14] Cited in Neve, M Hutton, '*This Mad Folly'-The History of Australia's Pioneer Women Doctors. Op. cit.*

[15] *The Parkes Examiner*, 27 August 1900 recorded Dr Dagmar Berne's death, stating: 'The deceased lady had long suffered from chest afflictions'.

[16] Russell, Penny, entries on Dr Constance Stone, Dr Clara Stone and Dr Mary Page Stone in *The Australian Dictionary of Biography*, Vol. 12 Melbourne. University Press, Melbourne, 1990, also in Neve, M Hutton, '*This Mad Folly'-The History of Australia's Pioneer Women Doctors, op. cit.*

# Chapter 5

[1] Manson, Cecil and Cecilia, *Dr Agnes Bennett,* Michael Joseph, London, 1969, pp 22–25.

[2] Entry on Dr Agnes Bennett by Ann Curthoys in *Australian Dictionary of Biography, Vol 7,* Melbourne University Press, 1989. See also Manson, Cecil and Cecilia, *Dr Agnes Bennett, op. cit.* and Agnes Bennett papers, National Library of New Zealand.

[3] Dr Elsie Dalyell, *Magazine of Women's' College* [Sydney], November 1915, pp 10–13 and November 1920, pp 37–41.

[4] De Vries, Susanna, *Blue Ribbons, Bitter Bread: The Life of Joice NanKivell Loch, Australia's Most Decorated Woman.* Hale & Iremonger, Sydney, 2000. This biography covers her childhood in Queensland and Gippsland, her time in Ireland during the Troubles, her period as an aid worker on the Polish-Russian border, 1921–22, her time in Greece before World War II, her spectacular escape from Rumania after the Nazis entered Bucharest in Operation Pied Piper, when she and her husband were jointly responsible for saving over 2,000 Polish and Jewish people from death camps, escorting them via Constantinople to Palestine. The biography also covers the Lochs' return to post-war Greece.

[5] Byzantine symbols, depicted in manuscripts held in the monastic libraries of Mount Athos, were used by Joice Loch as design motives for the Pirgos Rugs.

[6] Australian Nancy Wake, code-named 'The White Mouse', in World War II, worked with the Resistance in France, helping British airmen to escape from the Germans. Her heroism was honoured by the British with a George Cross. Like Joice, Nancy Wake has never received any official recognition in Australia.

# Chapter 6

[1] Eileen commissioned portraits from Doris Zinkheisen, Anna Zinkheisen, Augustus John (then London's most expensive portraitist), John Bratby and a host of minor artists as well as a superb bronze bust from Anna Mahler, daughter of composer Gustav Mahler, which were gifted to the University of Western Australia.

[2] From Abrahall, C.H., (Lady Claire Hoskins Abrahall. *Prelude*, Oxford University Press, London, 1947, pp 1–48.

[3] *Ibid*, pp 66–67.

# Endnotes

4  Eileen's time at Kununoppin is recorded in Abrahall, C.H., *Prelude, op. cit.* She also described her experiences at the bush school to English journalists, often giving the impression to them that she was talking about St Joseph's Primary School at Boulder. This may account for some of the confusions surrounding stories about her childhood.

5  Blainey, Geoffrey. *The Golden Mile – the Story of Kalgoorlie and Boulder,* Sydney (n.d.) and Casey, Gavin and Mayman, T., *The Mile that Midas Touched*, Sydney, 1968.

6  Eileen's younger sisters, the late Mrs Norma McNabb and Mrs McPherson.

7  Telephone interview, Deirdre Prussack, 18 July 2000.

8  Conversations with the archivists of St Joseph's Convent, Boulder and Loreto Convent, Perth, reveal that the class records for the period of Eileen's attendance no longer exist to verify her accounts.

9  Felix Hayman told me that when he presented an 'Eileen Joyce week' for the ABC, listeners from Boulder phoned in saying some of Eileen's stories were inaccurate.

10 This may or many not be true but appears as a scene in the 1950 film *Wherever She Goes.*

11 During his ABC 'Eileen Joyce week', producer Felix Hayman received a call from an elderly Boulder resident informing him that Eileen Joyce had been allowed to practise at Nicholson's piano store. Thanks to musical historian Cyrus Metier-Homji (Ph.D.), confirmed by local by local historian Miss R. Eriksson, for information that Joe Joyce owned a buther's shop in Boulder.

12 Telephone interviews by the author with Felix Hayman, ABC music producer, 15 May 2000, and with Mrs Deirdre Prussak, 18 July 2000, in which Mrs Prussak recalled that Eileen asked her to invite her younger sister, Mrs Norma McNabb to lunch when Eileen's friend was visiting Perth. Mrs Prussak observed at first hand the huge chasm which separated the Joyce sisters, one accustomed to an international lifestyle, the other having led a sheltered life in Boulder.

13 Abrahall,C.H., *Prelude, op. cit.,* pp 103, 115.

14 Eileen Joyce to Deirdre Prussak, interview with the author.

15 Abrahall, C.H., *Prelude, op. cit.,* p 143.

16 Father Edmund Campion wrote an article about Eileen Joyce titled '*A Most Transcendental gift',* published in the May/June 1998 issue of *Madonna,* citing Sister John and Sister Veronica's involvement with Eileen's career as well as that of the nuns of her primary school in Boulder. Both convents confirm this.

17 Details of the pieces from Abrahall, C.H., *Prelude, op. cit., p. 177–8.*

18 *Ibid.*

19 Eileen Joyce obituary, *Sydney Morning Herald,* 9 April1991.

20 Telephone interview, Sister Ann Carter, Archivist, Loreto Convent, Perth, 4 July 2000.

21 Cited by Ava Hubble in the *Sydney Morning Herald,* 9 April 1991, following the death of Eileen Joyce on 25 March 1991.

22 Leipzig and its Conservatorium are described in H. H. Richardson's novel *Maurice Guest,* published London, 1908 and in her autobiography *Myself when Young,* London, 1948.

23 Abrahall, C.J., *op. cit.,* pp 208–9 and repeated by Eileen Joyce at various press interviews.

24 Eileen Joyce, interview with Peter Ross, ABC 'Arts on Sunday' Program, 1988.

25 Abrahall, C.H., *Prelude,* Oxford University Press, London, 1948, p 230.

26 Eileen to Mrs Deirdre Prussak.

27 Cited by John Coomber, London correspondent of the *Melbourne Age* in an interview with Eileen Joyce, 12 May 1985.

28 Story from the late Mrs Norma McNabb, Eileen Joyce's sister, as told to Deidre Prussak and related to the author on 16 July 2000.

29 Eileen to Mrs Deirdre Prussak in her later years. Author interview, Deirdre Prussak, 16 July 2000.

30 As told by Eileen Joyce to Deirdre Prussak, her close friend in the final years of her life.

31 Mathias, Paul, Essay in program for the opening of the Eileen Joyce Studio at the University of Western Australia, 1981.

32 Eileen's son, who bore her considerable ill-will, told Richard Davies that Eileen and Christopher were never married but no concrete evidence for this has yet emerged.

33 Details provided by George Cole, former accountant to the Manns, in interview.

[34] Telephone interview dated 28 July 2000 with George Cole, who worked as accountant for the Christopher Mann agency.

[35] Information about Christopher Mann from George Cole, the Manns' accountant in London.

[36] Introduction. Abrahall, C.H., *Prelude,* Oxford University Press, London, 1947. pp. 7.

[37] Barbara Ker Wilson, editor, worked for Oxford University Press two years after the publication of *Prelude,* by then withdrawn from sale, remembers complaints about the book. Somehow Eileen managed to salvage her friendship with Lady Abrahall and they were on good terms in the 1980s when Deirdre Prussak stayed with Eileen. Interview, Deirdre Prussak, July 2000.

[38] Details provided by Barbara Ker Wilson.

[39] *Ibid.* Parrett was blonde, unlike red-haired Eileen.

[40] Margaret Sutherland's life is in De Vries, Susanna, *Strength of Purpose – Australian Women of Achievement,* HarperCollins, Sydney, 1998, pp 199–208.

[41] Author Richard Davies has written a comprehensive biography of Eileen Joyce's musical career, to be published by the University of Western Australia Press. In a telephone interview, July 2000, he told me he had talked to John Barratt, Eileen's son, who explained that his mother could on occasions be very difficult. Deirdre Prussak and Eileen's Joyce's executor and close friend, Zovita Moon, were distressed that neither her son or his wife attended Eileen's funeral or her memorial service and saw little or nothing of Eileen during her last tragic dementia-ridden years. Mrs Moon related that Eileen planned to cut her son and his family out of her will but finally agreed that her grandson Alexander should inherit White Hart Lodge and its contents.

[42] Account given to the author by Susan Stratigos, who attended the concert in Brisbane's City Hall as a child.

[43] Interview, Deirdre Prussak, July 2000.

[44] Mathias, Paul. Essay in the official program for the Opening of the Eileen Joyce studio at the University of Western Australia. 28 June 1981. Many thanks to Emeritus Professor Sir Frank Callaway, CMG, OBE for drawing my attention to this program and for help with details about Eileen Joyce's career.

[45] Eileen Joyce to Deirdre Prussak, 1984.

[46] Eileen Joyce, obituary, *Sydney Morning Herald,* 9 April 1991.

[47] *Ibid.*

[48] Cited by Father Edmund Campion in *Madonna,* May/June 1998.

[49] Date taken from Christopher Mann's obituary, held in the State Library of Queensland, Arts Library.

[50] Deidre Prussak, telephone interview, 27 July 2000.

[51] Eileen Joyce, obituary, *Sydney Morning Herald, op. cit.*

[52] Quoted in a London interview between Eileen Joyce and Margaret Jones in the *Melbourne Age,* 26 June 1981, of 26.6.81, when Eileen was about to visit Australia.

[53] Not all the jurors have been as committed as Eileen Joyce. In the Sydney 2000 Piano Competition a Russian juror was accused of falling asleep and snoring during the competition.

[54] White Hart Lodge was built on the site of a former monastery, destroyed in the time of Henry VIII. A small part of the monastery was incorporated into the modern house.

[55] John Coomber, London correspondent of the *Melbourne Age,* article dated 12 September 1985.

[56] Letter from Emeritus Professor Sir Frank Calloway, C.M.G., G.B.E., dated 22 September 1988.

[57] Reply by letter from Eileen. Collection of Deirdre Prussak.

[58] For dates see entry under Eileen Joyce in the *Monash Biographical Dictionary of 20th century Australians,* National Centre for Australian Studies, Monash University, Melbourne, 1994.

[59] An acquired 'English' accent, unlike Eileen's normal 'Aussie' accent was noticeable in the series of recorded interviews which she broadcast over the ABC in January 1995. Eileen Joyce had to modulate her voice when making her debut in pre-war Britain at a time when a strong Australian accent was definitely a hindrance in obtaining an *entrée* into artistic and social circles in London.

[60] Deirdre Prussak, telephone interview with the author 20 July 2000.

[61] From a memorial article written by Deirdre Prussak.

[62] A letter dated 24 April 1991 to Deirdre Prussak from Eileen's close friend, Zovita Moon records Mrs Moon's distress that Eileen's son refused to attend her memorial service and the Rector's pious wish that she and her son would eventually be reconciled in heaven.

# Endnotes

## Chapter 7

1. The banknote featuring Edith Cowan's portrait was first issued in September 1995.
2. In 1990 the Edith Cowan University, Western Australia, was named in her honour.
3. Tolstoy, L., *Anna Karenina*, Moscow, 1877. In his novel Tolstoy questions the institution of marriage when his heroine observes that her husband 'owns' her. She is explaining to her lover why she cannot leave her husband – she would be unable to keep her little son, as her husband legally owns the child. Divorce or legal separation would ensure that she was barred from ever seeing him again.
4. Cowan, Peter, *A Unique Position*, University of Western Australia Press, Perth, 1979. A good but discreet biography by Edith Cowan's grandson.
5. Jull, R., *Papers and History of the Karrakatta Club 1894–1954*, privately published, and Lees, Kirsten, *Votes for Women – the Australian Story*, Allen & Unwin, 1995.
6. Children's Protection Society, Annual Reports, 1909–32. Copies in the Battye Library, Perth.
7. *The Dawn*, Bessie Rischbieth's Perth-based paper, had no connection with Louisa Lawson's women's journal of the same name, produced in Sydney.
8. This was the treatment given to artist Paul Gauguin in the French hospital in Tahiti. Gauguin was one of the very few sufferers who described his treatment for syphilis.
9. Hunt, L., ed., *Western Portraits*, cited in entry on Bessie Rischbieth in Steadman, Margaret, ed. Radi, Heather, *200 Australian Women*, Women's Redress Press, Sydney, 1988.
10. *Ibid.*
11. Haines, Janine, *Suffrage to Sufferance: 100 Years of Women in Politics*, Allen & Unwin, Sydney, 1992.
12. Nancy, Lady Astor, was elected to the British Parliament as MP for Portsmouth. Her husband, the sitting member, was unable to take his seat because he had inherited his father's title of Viscount, so his wife stood as candidate in his electorate and won by an overwhelming majority.
13. Lees, Kirsten, *Votes for Women – the Australian Story, op. cit.*

## Chapter 8

1. Hart, P.R. and Lloyd, C.J., entry on Joseph Lyons, *Australian Dictionary of Biography*, Vol 10, Melbourne University Press, Melbourne, 1986. It seems significant that no entry was made for his wife.
2. Anne Sells, entry on Enid Lyons in *200 Australian Women*, (ed. H. Radi), Women's Redress Press, Sydney 1988.
3. Hart and Lloyd, *op. cit.*, cite Enid's age as 18, while Anne Sells, in *200 Australian Women, op. cit.*, p. 203, gives Enid's age as 17.
4. Interview with Dame Enid Lyons, *Australian Women's Weekly*, 6 July 1977.
5. In 1973, on the occasion of the publication of Enid Lyons' book *Among the Carrion Crows*, Rigby, Adelaide, she talked freely to correspondent Suzanne Baker in an interview published in the *Sydney Morning Herald*, 15 April 1977.
6. Hart, P.R. and Lloyd, C.J., *op. cit.*
7. Edith Cowan had been elected to the West Australian Parliament in 1921 and Millicent Preston Stanley to the NSW Parliament in 1925, Irene Longman to the Queensland Parliament in 1929 and Millie Peacock to the Victorian Parliament in 1933. In 1943 when Edith Lyons was elected both Tasmania and South Australia still had to elect a woman MP.
8. Haines, Janine, *Suffrage to Sufferance,* Allen and Unwin, Sydney, 1992.
9. Sells, Anne, *200 Australian Women, op. cit.*
10. A list of Enid Lyons' books and her honours and political and other appointments appears under her name in *The Monash Biographical Dictionary of 29th Century Australia*, Reed Books, Melbourne 1994 and in the *Australian Dictionary of Biography*, Vol 10. Her full biography written by Kate White, *A Political Love Story: Joe and Enid Lyons*, published 1987, is out of print at the time of writing.

# Chapter 9

[1] The outward signs of tertiary syphilis varied from patient to patient. Ethel Richardson described her father as suffering from premature aging, delusions, memory loss, partial and then complete paralysis. The artist Edouard Manet had a paralysis of the lower limbs which started with an ulcerated leg, Paul Gauguin's paralysis started with an ulcerated ankle. The composer Robert Schumann suffered from terrifying visions which led to madness, paralysis and death.

[2] Richardson Papers, Australian National Library: Dr Richardson's Commonplace Book.

[3] Henry Handel Richardson, *Myself When Young*, Heinemann, London, 1948, p. 4.

[4] *The Fortunes of Richard Mahony*, the first volume of Henry Handel Richardson's trilogy *Australia Felix*, partly based on her father's life and part of his character 'on my own', she said.

[5] Richardson, Henry Handel, *Myself When Young, op. cit.*

[6] Clarke, Axel, *Henry Handel Richardson. Fiction in the Making*, Simon & Schuster, Sydney, [n.d.]. Clarke mentions Dr Richardson's attempted surgical removal of the port-wine birthmark, a disfigurement which badly affected Ethel's self-confidence.

[7] *Ibid*, p. 16.

[8] *Ibid*, p. 20.

[9] *Ibid*, p. 25.

[10] *Ibid*, p. 25.

[11] *Ibid*, pp. 37–8.

[12] *Ibid*, pp. 71–2, recounts the love story of Evelyn (Connie) and Laura (Ethel).

[13] *Ibid*, p. 147.

[14] Ethel Carrick Fox, wife of Australian artist Emanuel Phillips Fox, also loathed the name Ethel and flatly refused to use it, signing her paintings 'Carrick Fox' instead.

[15] Maugham, Somerset, *Great Novelists and their Novels*, John Winston, New York, 1948.

[16] For a discussion about Roncoroni's role in Ettie's life see McLeod, Karen, *Henry Handel Richardson, a critical study*, Cambridge University Press, Cambridge, 1985. MacLeod met Roncoroni and recorded her agoraphobia.

[17] Olga Roncoroni completed the unfinished memoir, *Myself When Young*, published posthumously in London by Heinemann in 1948 with a chapter by Professor Robertson.

[18] Olga Ronconi, Preface to *Myself When Young, op. cit.*

[19] For a discussion of Ethel Richardson's place in literature, see the following: Wilde, W., Hooton, J. and Andrews, B.,*The Oxford Companion to Australian Literature*, Oxford University Press, Melbourne, 1985, pp 584–87; Kramer, Leonie, *Henry Handel Richardson, Some of her Sources*, M.U.P. Melbourne, 1954; Clarke, Axel, *Henry Handel Richardson, Fiction in the Making*, *op. cit.*; and McLeod, Karen, *Henry Handel Richardson: A Critical Study*, *op. cit.* A most perceptive essay on Richardson by Dorothy Green is contained in *Women In Victoria – 150 Years*, edited by Marilyn Lake and Farley Kelly, *Penguin Books*, Melbourne, 1985.

# Chapter 10

[1] Elizabeth Kenny was not the only unqualified nurse who continued to use the title 'Sister' after the war, a title many felt she had justly earned.

[2] Kenny Treatment Clinics were formed at George Street, Brisbane, the Royal Brisbane Hospital (where Ward 7 was converted into a Kenny Clinic for Children), Cairns, Rockhampton and Townsville. Sister Kenny's most famous patient was a young farm boy of Danish extraction who was greatly helped by her methods. He grew up to become Queensland's controversial Premier, Joh Bjelke-Petersen. For a medically based but objective account of Kenny's achievements in Queensland, see Tyrer, Prof. John H., *History of the Royal Brisbane Hospital*, Boolarong Publications/Royal Brisbane Hospital, Brisbane, 1993. Other writings on Sister Kenny are *The True Book About Sister Kenny*, Shakespeare Head Press, London, 1965 and Levine, Herbert, *Sister Kenny: A Story of a Great Lady*, Christopher Publishing, Boston, 1954. A short account of her life with excellent reference sources is Barren, J. and Hacker, D., *Women in History: Places of Purpose*, Queensland Women's Historical Association, Brisbane, 1994. See also Patrick, Dr Ross, entry in *The Australian Dictionary of Biography*, Vol 12. Melbourne University Press, Melbourne, 1990.

# Endnotes

3   See Spearitt, Peter and Gammage, B. (ed.), *Australians: A Historical Library*, Fairfax, Syme, Weldon, Sydney, 1987, for a discussion of polio epidemics in all Australian States. In 1937 Kenny published her own book, *Infantile Paralysis and Cerebral Diplegia*.

4   Blaikie, George, information from interviews with patients treated by the Kenny method, published in 'Women of History', *Australian Women's Weekly*, November 1984.

5   During the 1930s a letter published in the Brisbane *Courier Mail* related how, among polio sufferers, the writer had seen 'cases of paralysis that would make one's heart ache'. He commented: 'Good luck, Sister Kenny, you alone can save these children'.

6   Patrick, Dr Ross, entry on Elizabeth Kenny in *The Australian Dictionary of Biography*, Vol 12, *op. cit.*

7   Mrs Mary McCracken: interview with Stephen Lamble, *Brisbane Sunday Mail*, 24 December 1995. Mrs McCracken revealed how her natural mother, the victim of a family break-up, had placed an advertisement in the paper for someone to adopt her nine-year-old daughter. Sister Kenny, who was too old to adopt legally, falsified her age to do this. Mrs McCracken cared for Kenny's widowed mother until she died in 1937. She then worked in Kenny's clinics and was present at Elizabeth Kenny's death. She claimed that Sister Kenny was the equal of Florence Nightingale but said that when she died, not one Australian University would accept custodianship of Kenny's many awards, including Florence Nightingale's Bible, given to her by an old soldier. These items were donated to the United Nations Organisation. Additional Kenny papers are in the Fryer Library, The University of Queensland, and with the Countrywomen's Association, Nobby, Darling Downs, Queensland.

8   Blaikie, George, interview, *op. cit.*

9   Production of the anti-polio vaccine developed by Dr J. Salk began in Australia in July 1955. In the following years children all over Australia were vaccinated and the battle against polio was gradually won with this and the Sabin. vaccine. In 1964 Tasmania was the first state to immunise children using live Sabin vaccine given to children on a sugar lump. For further information on polio in Australia, see Camm, J.C.R. and McQuilton, J. (ed.), *Australians. A Historical Atlas*. Fairfax, Sydney & Weldon, Sydney, 1987.

# Chapter 11

1   Dr Aletta Jacobs, writing in 1828 to fellow suffragette, American-born Carrie Chapman Catt.

2   Brindle, David, 'Baby Boom for Women over Forty', *The Guardian*, 20 March 1995. Australian Bureau of Statistics, Canberra. Census figures, 1996.

3   Interestingly enough, in the year 2000 a leading Sydney IVF clinic, where gender selection is carried out, claims that more women are now asking for girls than boys. See also *Parenting Girls*, Pandanus Press, 1999 by Dr Janet Irwin, Susanna de Vries and Susanne Stratigos Wilson.

4   Sheehy, Gail, *New Passages*, Harper Collins, London and Sydney, 1996.

5   *Inter-colonial Medical Journal of Australia*, 20 February 1907.

6   Foley, Meredith, entry on Lillie Goodisson, *The Australian Dictionary of Biography*, Vol 9, Melbourne University Press, Melbourne, 1983.

7   During the 1960s the author lived in Spain, where all contraceptives were banned. Female friends implored her to bring a supply from Britain – an offence which carried a heavy fine. In 1971 she worked for a time in a birth control clinic run by the Newcastle Health Authority, Northumberland, England in a working-class dockside and factory area with high unemployment. The clinic was set up to monitor patients with large families who were on control trials to compare the efficacy of contraceptive pills and IUDs. Both gave rise to problems, but the majority of patients found them better than the alternative, having another child.

# Chapter 12

1   When Ella was born the Aboriginal Protection Board under their chairman (who happened also to be Inspector of Police) had the right to remove paler-skinned Aborigines (if they were deemed 'neglected') from their mothers. In 1910 the Aboriginal Protection Act changed. Proof

of 'neglect' was no longer required before removing any Aboriginal child to a Mission or a Training School. All that was required was for the child's surroundings to be deemed 'unsuitable' to white eyes. The children were forcibly removed by police from their mothers or as they left school and taken to two Training Institutions – Cootamundra for girls and Kinchela for boys. They were worked extremely hard, denied affection and received no instruction in reading or writing.

2   Purfleet Mission, outside Taree, was founded in 1902, (the year of Ella's birth) on twelve acres of land later designated a Government Reserve. The United Aborigines Mission in Sydney, a strictly inter-denominational organisation, sent a Missionary to run Purfleet. The Aborigines on the Mission worked as a cooperative and built their own houses, a church, a school (unfortunately with an indifferent teacher) and a Mission House. Work was plentiful in country areas at that time; male Aborigines worked as stockmen and station hands for less than award wages. Jealousy of white Union members ensured many lost their jobs and the Great Depression of the 1930s completed the process. By 1932 so many Aborigines were on welfare that the Aborigines Protection Board changed the set up at Purfleet. The kindly missionary was removed and a stern Manager appointed. So many adult Aborigines and 'stolen' children were being sent to Purfleet that the land was increased to fifty-one acres. Reserves like Burnt Bridge, Bellbrook, near Kempsey, Stony Gully and Woodenbong were all created at this time. The morale of the Aborigines reached a low ebb as a result of being denied work and land and because of their new regimentation. In 1978, information on poor conditions at Purfleet provided by Professor A. P. Elkin of the University of Sydney (who was a friend of Ella Simon) did a great deal to help Aboriginal people raising white consciousness of the wrongs done to them.

3   By now the Aboriginal Protection Board had been renamed the Aboriginal Welfare Board. In the 1940s the Government closed segregated schools and placed Aboriginal education under the control of the Education Department. The white Manager had the right to issue certificates or 'identity cards' to Aborigines like Ella, granting them freedom of movement and access to places such as hotels, from which they had been banned. Aboriginal children were now sent to Homes as wards of the State.

4   For a fuller description of the background to Aboriginal Missions and the assimilation problem, see the entry under 'Aborigines – The Early Missions and the Big Reserves' in *The Australian Encyclopaedia,* Vol. 1, pp 205–212, Grolier Society, 1983.

5   Ella Simon, foreword to *Through My Eyes,* Rigby, Adelaide, 1978.

6   Ella's life story in *Through My Eyes, op. cit.* She dedicated her autobiography to 'my grandmother, who taught me about being both Aboriginal and Christian and who cared for all people. And to my father for his honesty with the people he knew he had wronged'.

# Chapter 13

1   Information kindly provided by the Board of Architects, Sydney, in September 1996. The NSW Board was set up by Act of Parliament in 1923 to regulate the profession.

2   *The Australian Dictionary of Biography,* Vol. 12, Melbourne University Press, Melbourne, 1990, gives John Parsons as starting working life as a labourer.

3   *The Australian Dictionary of Biography,* Vol. 12, *op. cit.,* gives the year of Florence Parsons' emigration to Australia as 1884, while her entry in King, Helen, ed. Radi, Heather, *200 Australian Women,* Women's Redress Press, Sydney, 1988, quotes the date of arrival as 1888, which seems more likely.

4   According to Bronwyn Hanna's entry on Florence Taylor in the *Dictionary of Women Artists,* Sydney, 1995, Florence became an orphan at the age of nineteen, which may imply that her mother had died before her father, leaving her to support her three younger sisters.

5   Although no itinerary remains of the Taylors' journey, they probably visited the Panama Canal, which was opened for shipping in 1914.

6   Berger, John, art critic, in *Ways of Seeing,* Penguin Books, London, 1972.

7   Hanna, Bronwyn, extract from article 'Hats' in the *Architecture Bulletin,* October 1994 (referring to *Women's Weekly,* 8 July 1933).

8   Article on Florence Taylor, *Women's Weekly*, 8 July 1933.
9   Unreferenced newspaper article from Florence Taylor's Papers in the Mitchell Library, State Library of New South Wales, cited by Bronwyn Hanna in her article 'Hats', *op. cit.*
10  King, Helen, ed. Radi, Heather, *200 Australian Women*, Women's Redress Press, Sydney, 1988.

# Chapter 14

1   Carter, Isabel, *Woman in a Wig. Joan Rosanove*, QC, Lansdowne Press Melbourne, 1970
2   *Table Talk*, Melbourne, 28 November 1929.
3   Nairn, Bede and Serle, Geoffrey, *The Australian Dictionary of Biography*, Vol. 9, *op. cit.* Also Campbell, R. J., *A History of the Melbourne Law School 1857–1973*, Melbourne University Press, Melbourne, 1973.
4   Interview with Joan Rosanove (Lazarus) in *Table Talk*, 28 November 1929.
5   A full account of Joan Lazarus's role in the celebrated Ozanne libel case provided by lawyer Arthur Dean. See Dean, Arthur, *A Multitude of Counsellors*, Cheshire, Melbourne, 1968.
6   Carter, Isabel, *Woman in a Wig. Joan Rosanove*, QC, *op. cit.*
7   *Ibid.*
8   Joan Rosanove's article *My Outlook on Life*, dated 1936, from the *Melbourne Herald* is cited by Isabel Carter in *Woman in a Wig. Joan Rosanove, QC, op. cit.* However, the date and month of the article are not given.
9   Carter, Isabel, *Woman in a Wig. Joan Rosanove, QC, op. cit.*
10  Mitchell, Susan, *The Matriarchs*, Penguin Books, Melbourne, 1987; Paine, Jonathan, *Taken on Oath: A Generation of Lawyers*, Federation Press, Sydney, 1992.
11  Joan Rosanove's obituary in the Melbourne *Sun* is dated 10 April 1974. I am indebted for the story of Joan Rosanove to her daughter, Judge Peg Lusink, who also checked my manuscript for errors and kindly gave permission to reproduce photographs of her mother.
12  The remarkable Dr Mannie Rosanove finally remarried at the age of eighty and died ten years later.

# Chapter 15

1   Dame Roma Mitchell at the 1984 Woman of the Year Luncheon.
2   Dame Roma Mitchell in a speech to the Women of the Year Luncheon, Canberra, 1984.
3   Dame Roma Mitchell to the author. Telephone interview, 1997.
4   *Ibid.*
5   *Ibid.*
6   *Ibid.*
7   *Ibid.*
8   *Ibid.*
9   Mitchell, Susan, *The Matriarchs*, p 29, Penguin Books, Melbourne, 1987.
10  An important article on this topic by barrister and anti-discrimination commissioner, Jocelyn Scutt, 'No merit to endemic sexism in the legal system' was published in *The Australian*, 19 July 2000.
11  Extract from Sir William Deane's address quoted in the May 2000 newsletter of the Churchill Fellowship Association of Queensland.

# INDEX

Index